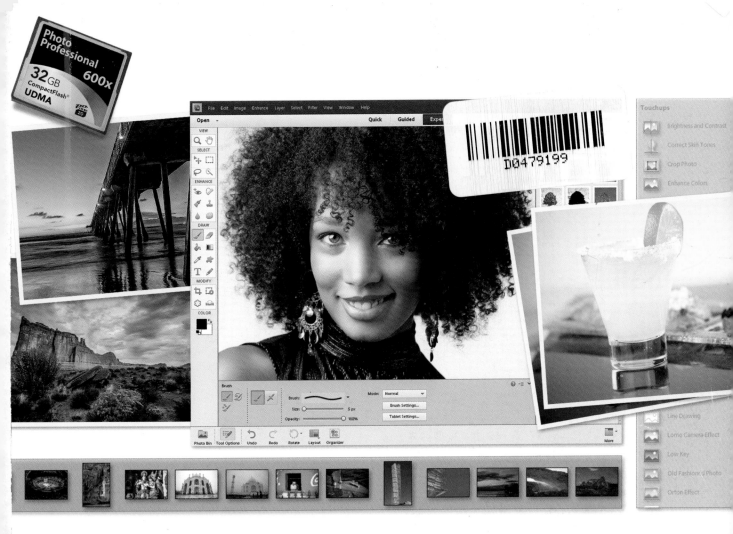

the photoshop® elements 11 book

for digital photographers

Scott Kelby and Matt Kloskowski

The Photoshop Elements 11 Book for Digital Photographers **Team**

CREATIVE DIRECTOR
Felix Nelson

TECHNICAL EDITORS
Kim Doty
Cindy Snyder

PRODUCTION MANAGER
Dave Damstra

ART DIRECTOR
Jessica Maldonado

COVER PHOTOS BY
Scott Kelby
Matt Kloskowski

Published by
New Riders

©2013 by Scott Kelby

Composed in Avenir, Myriad Pro, and Helvetica by Kelby Media Group, Inc.

Trademarks
All terms mentioned in this book that are known to be trademarks or service marks have been appropriately capitalized. New Riders cannot attest to the accuracy of this information. Use of a term in the book should not be regarded as affecting the validity of any trademark or service mark.

Photoshop Elements is a registered trademark of Adobe Systems, Inc.
Windows is a registered trademark of Microsoft Corporation.
Macintosh is a registered trademark of Apple Inc.

Warning and Disclaimer
This book is designed to provide information about Photoshop Elements for digital photographers. Every effort has been made to make this book as complete and as accurate as possible, but no warranty of fitness is implied.

The information is provided on an as-is basis. The authors and New Riders shall have neither the liability nor responsibility to any person or entity with respect to any loss or damages arising from the information contained in this book or from the use of the discs, electronic files, or programs that may accompany it.

THIS PRODUCT IS NOT ENDORSED OR SPONSORED BY ADOBE SYSTEMS INCORPORATED, PUBLISHER OF ADOBE PHOTOSHOP ELEMENTS 11

ISBN 13: 978-0-321-88483-1
ISBN 10:   0-321-88483-3

9 8 7 6 5 4 3 2

http://kelbytraining.com
www.newriders.com

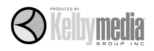

PRODUCED BY
Kelbymedia
GROUP INC

To Julie Stephenson, whose hard work,
dedication, absolute commitment to quality,
and warm smile are an inspiration to us all each day.
—SCOTT

To my youngest son Justin,
for always making me smile.
I love you buddy!
—MATT

ACKNOWLEDGMENTS (SCOTT)

In every book I've ever written, I always thank my amazing wife Kalebra first, because I couldn't do any of this without her. In fact, I couldn't do *anything* without her. She's just an incredible woman, an inspiration to me every day, and the only thing more beautiful than how she looks on the outside is what's inside. As anyone who knows me knows, I am the luckiest guy in the world to have made her my wife 23 years ago this year. Thank you, my love, for saying "Yes."

I want to thank my wonderful son Jordan, and the most adorable little girl in the world, my daughter Kira, for putting a smile on my face and a song in my heart, each and every day. Thanks to my big brother Jeff for continuing to be the type of guy I'll always look up to.

I owe a special gratitude to my good friend Matt Kloskowski. I'm truly honored to have shared these pages with you, and I can't thank you enough for working so hard to once again make this the best edition of the book yet. As a company, we're very lucky to have you on our team, and personally, I'm even luckier to count you among my best friends.

My heartfelt thanks go to the entire team at Kelby Media Group, who every day redefine what teamwork and dedication are all about. In particular, I want to thank my friend and Creative Director Felix Nelson, and my incredibly awesome in-house Editor Kim Doty and way cool Tech Editor Cindy Snyder, for testing everything, and not letting me get away with anything. And to Jessica Maldonado, the duchess of book design, for making everything look really cool.

Thanks to my best buddy Dave Moser, whose tireless dedication to creating a quality product makes every project we do better than the last. Thanks to my friend and partner Jean A. Kendra for everything she does. A special thanks to my Executive Assistant Susan Hageanon for all her hard work and dedication, and for handling so many things so well that I have time to write books.

Thanks to my Publisher Nancy Aldrich-Ruenzel, my Editor Ted "Teditor" Waitt, marketing madman Scott Cowlin, Sara Jane Todd, and the incredibly dedicated team at Peachpit Press. It's an honor to work with people who just want to make great books.

I want to thank all the photographers and Photoshop experts who've taught me so much over the years, including Jim DiVitale and Kevin Ames (who helped me develop the ideas for the first edition of this book), Joe McNally, Jack Davis, Deke McClelland, Ben Willmore, Julieanne Kost, Moose Peterson, Vincent Versace, Doug Gornick, Bill Fortney, Manual Obordo, Dan Margulis, Helene Glassman, Eddie Tapp, David Ziser, Peter Bauer, Joe Glyda, Russell Preston Brown, Bert Monroy, and Calvin Hollywood.

Thanks to my friends at Adobe Systems: Sharon Doherty, Mark Dahm, Bryan O'Neil Hughes, John Nack, Mala Sharma, Terry White, Julieanne Kost, Tom Hogarty, Scott Morris, Russell Preston Brown, and the amazing engineering team at Adobe (I don't know how you all do it). Gone but not forgotten: Cari Gushiken, Barbara Rice, Jill Nakashima, Rye Livingston, Addy Roff, Bryan Lamkin, Jennifer Stern, Deb Whitman, Kevin Connor, John Loiacono, and Karen Gauthier.

Thanks to my mentors whose wisdom and whip-cracking have helped me immeasurably, including John Graden, Jack Lee, Dave Gales, Judy Farmer, and Douglas Poole.

Most importantly, I want to thank God, and His Son Jesus Christ, for leading me to the woman of my dreams, for blessing us with such a wonderful son and an amazing daughter, for allowing me to make a living doing something I truly love, for always being there when I need Him, for blessing me with a wonderful, fulfilling, and happy life, and such a warm, loving family to share it with.

ACKNOWLEDGMENTS (MATT)

Of course, there are many people behind the scenes that helped make this book happen. One of my favorite parts of writing a book is that I get to thank them publicly in front of all the people who read it. So here goes:

To my wife, Diana: You've been my best friend for 13 years, and I've had the time of my life with you as we enjoy watching our family grow. No matter what the day brings, you always have a smile on your face when I come home. I could never thank you enough for juggling our lives, being such a great mom to our kids, and for being the best wife a guy could ever want.

To my oldest son, Ryan: Your inquisitive personality amazes me and I love sitting down with you for "cuddle" time at night. And even though you always grenade launcher yourself to a win, I enjoy our quality Xbox 360 time. By the way, you're grounded from playing until I get better!

To my youngest son, Justin: I have no doubt that you'll be the class clown one day. No matter what I have on my mind, you always find a way to make me smile. Plus, there's nothing like hearing your nine-year-old shout, "Say hello to my little friend!" as an RPG comes flying at you in a video game.

To my family (Mom and Dad, Ed, Kerry, Kristine, and Scott): Thanks for giving me such a great start in life and always encouraging me to go for what I want.

To Scott Kelby: Having my name on a cover with yours is an honor, but becoming such good friends has truly been a privilege and the ride of my life. I've never met anyone as eager to share their ideas and encourage success in their friends as you are. You've become the greatest mentor and source of inspiration that I've met. More importantly, though, you've become one heck of a good friend. Thanks man!

To the designer that made this book look so awesome: Jessica Maldonado. Thank you, Jess!

To my two favorite editors in the world: Cindy Snyder and Kim Doty. You guys do so much work on your end, so I can continue writing and working on all the techniques (which is really the fun stuff) on my end. I can't tell you how much I appreciate the help you guys give me and the effort you put into making me look good.

To Dave Moser, my boss and my buddy: Your militaristic, yet insightful, comments throughout the day help motivate me and sometimes just make me laugh (a little of both helps a lot). Thanks for continuing to push me to be better each day.

To Corey Barker, Rafael (RC) Concepcion, and Pete Collins: Thanks for the ideas you guys generate and the friends you've become. You guys rock!

To Bob Gager (Elements Product Manager) and Sharon Doherty at Adobe: Thanks for taking the time to go over this new version of Elements (with a fine-toothed comb) with me. It helped more than you know to see your perspective and how you and your team are constantly pushing Elements to be better each year.

To all my friends at Peachpit Press: Ted Waitt, Scott Cowlin, Gary Prince, and Sara Jane Todd. It's because you guys are so good at what you do that I'm able to continue doing what I love to do.

To you, the readers: Without you, well…there would be no book. Thanks for your constant support in emails, phone calls, and introductions when I'm out on the road teaching. You guys make it all worth it.

OTHER BOOKS BY **SCOTT KELBY**

The Adobe Photoshop Lightroom 4 Book for Digital Photographers

Scott Kelby's 7-Point System For Adobe Photoshop CS3

The Digital Photography Book, parts 1, 2, 3 & 4

Photo Recipes Live: Behind the Scenes: Your Guide to Today's Most Popular Lighting Techniques, parts 1 & 2

Professional Portrait Retouching Techniques for Photographers Using Photoshop

The Adobe Photoshop CS6 Book for Digital Photographers

The Photoshop Channels Book

Photoshop Down & Dirty Tricks

The iPhone Book

Mac OS X Leopard Killer Tips

Getting Started with Your Mac and Mac OS X Tiger

OTHER BOOKS BY **MATT KLOSKOWSKI**

Photoshop Compositing Secrets: Unlocking the Key to Perfect Selections & Amazing Photoshop Effects for Totally Realistic Composites

Layers: The Complete Guide to Photoshop's Most Powerful Feature

The Photoshop Elements 5 Restoration & Retouching Book

Photoshop CS2 Speed Clinic

The Windows Vista Book

Illustrator CS2 Killer Tips

ABOUT THE AUTHOR

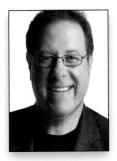

Scott Kelby

Scott is Editor, Publisher, and co-founder of *Photoshop User* magazine, Executive Editor and Publisher of *Light It* (the how-to magazine for studio lighting and off-camera flash), and is host of *The Grid*, the weekly live videocast talk show for photographers, as well as co-host of the top-rated weekly videocast series, *Photoshop User TV*.

Scott is President and co-founder of the National Association of Photoshop Professionals (NAPP), the trade association for Adobe® Photoshop® users, and he's President of the software training, education, and publishing firm Kelby Media Group.

Scott is a photographer, designer, and an award-winning author of more than 50 books, including *The Digital Photography Book*, parts 1, 2, 3 & 4, *The Adobe Photoshop Lightroom 4 Book for Digital Photographers*, *The Photoshop Channels Book*, *Scott Kelby's 7-Point System for Adobe Photoshop CS3*, and *The Adobe Photoshop CS6 Book for Digital Photographers*.

For the past two years, Scott has been honored with the distinction of being the world's #1 best-selling author of photography books. His book, *The Digital Photography Book*, vol. 1, is now the best-selling book on digital photography in history.

His books have been translated into dozens of different languages, including Chinese, Russian, Spanish, Korean, Polish, Taiwanese, French, German, Italian, Japanese, Dutch, Swedish, Turkish, and Portuguese, among others, and he is a recipient of the prestigious ASP International Award, presented annually by the American Society of Photographers for "…contributions in a special or significant way to the ideals of Professional Photography as an art and a science."

Scott is Training Director for the Adobe Photoshop Seminar Tour and Conference Technical Chair for the Photoshop World Conference & Expo. He's featured in a series of Adobe Photoshop online training courses and DVDs and has been training Adobe Photoshop users since 1993.

For more information on Scott, visit him at:

His daily blog: **http://scottkelby.com**
Google+: **Scottgplus.com**
Twitter: **http://twitter.com@scottkelby**
Facebook: **www.facebook.com/skelby**

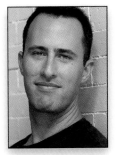

Matt Kloskowski

Matt is a best-selling author and full-time Photoshop guy for the National Association of Photoshop Professionals (NAPP). His books, videos, and classes have simplified the way thousands of people work on digital photos and images. Matt teaches Photoshop and digital photography techniques to thousands of people around the world each year. He co-hosts the top-rated videocast *Photoshop User TV*, as well as *The Grid*, a live talk show videocast about photography and other industry-related topics. He also hosts the *Adobe Photoshop Lightroom Killer Tips* podcast and blog (http://lightroomkillertips.com), which provides tips and techniques for using Lightroom. You can find Matt's DVDs and online training courses at http://kelbytraining.com, and a large library of his weekly videos and written articles in *Photoshop User* magazine and on its website at www.photoshopuser.com.

You can find out more about him on his blog, The Ski Report, at: **http://www.mattk.com**.

CONTENTS

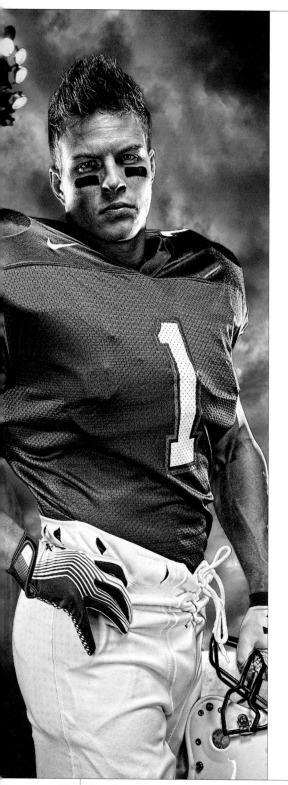

CONTENTS

CHAPTER 3	**97**

Scream of the Crop
How to Resize and Crop Photos

CHAPTER 4	**131**

edIT
Using Quick, Guided, and Expert Editing

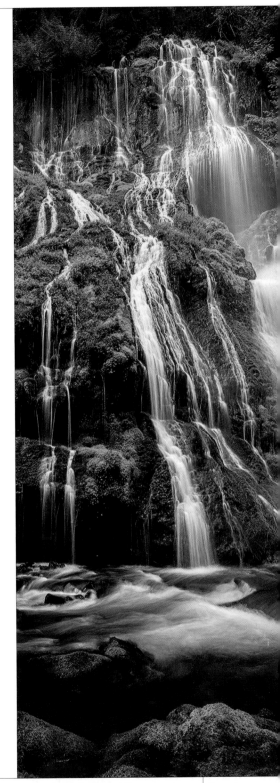

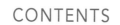

CONTENTS

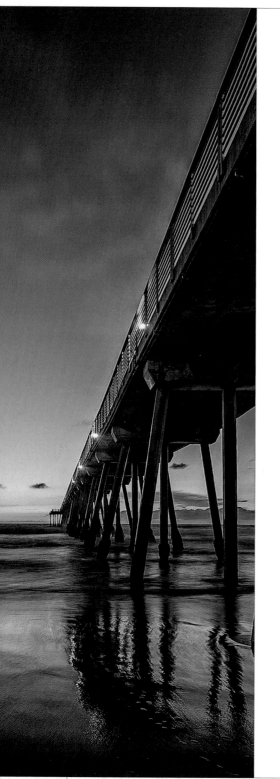

CONTENTS

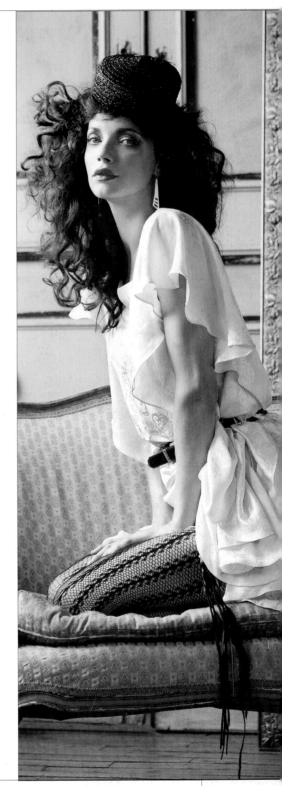

CONTENTS

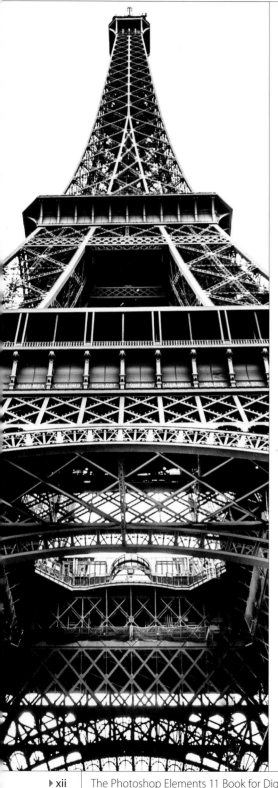

CHAPTER 11	373

Sharpen Your Teeth
Sharpening Techniques

CHAPTER 12	397

Fine Print
Printing, Color Management, and My Elements 11 Workflow

INDEX	426

It's really important to us that you get a lot out of reading this book, and one way we can help is to get you to read these nine quick things about the book that you'll wish later you knew now. For example, it's here that we tell you about where to download something important, and if you skip over this, eventually you'll send an email asking where it is, but by then you'll be really aggravated, and well… it's gonna get ugly. We can skip all that (and more), if you take two minutes now to read these nine quick things. We promise to make it worth your while.

Nine Things You'll Wish You Had Known Before Reading This Book

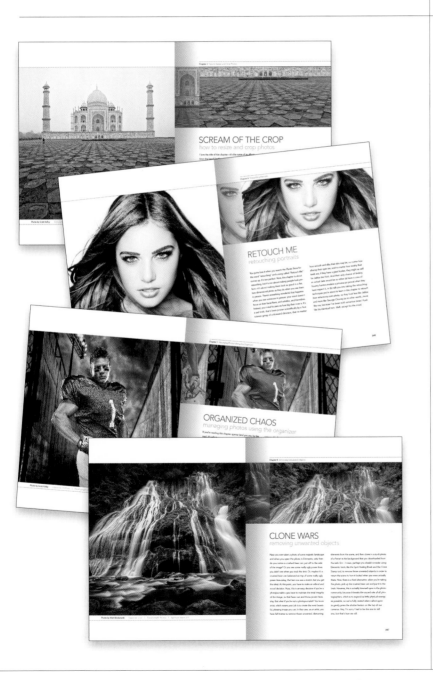

(1) You don't have to read this book in order.

You can treat this as a "jump-in-any-where" book, because we didn't write it as a "build-on-what-you-learned-in-Chapter-1" type of book. For example, if you just bought this book, and you want to learn how to whiten someone's teeth for a portrait you're retouching, you can just turn to Chapter 8, find that technique, and you'll be able to follow along and do it immediately, because we walk you through each step. So, if you're a more advanced Elements user, don't let it throw you that we say stuff like "Go under the Image menu, under Adjust Color, and choose Levels," rather than just saying "Open Levels." We did that so everybody could follow along no matter where they are in the Elements experience.

(2) Not everything about Elements is in this book.

We tried not to make this an encyclo-pedia of Elements features. So, we did not include tutorials on every feature in Elements. Instead, it's more like a recipe book—you can flip through it and pick out the things that you want to do to your photos and follow the steps to get there. Basically, we just focused on the most important, most asked-about, and most useful things for digital photog-raphers. In short—it's the funk and not the junk.

(Continued)

(3) Practice along with the same photos we used here in the book.

As you're going through the book, and you come to a technique like "Fixing Shots with a Dull Gray Sky," you might not have gray sky image hanging around. We made most of the images used in the techniques available for you to download, so you can follow along with them. You can find them at **http://kelbytraining .com/books/elements11** (see, this is one of those things I was talking about that you'd miss if you skipped this and went right to Chapter 1).

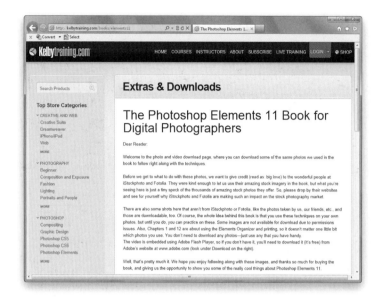

(4) The intro pages at the beginning of each chapter are not what they seem.

The chapter introductions are designed to give you a quick mental break between chapters, and honestly, they have little to do with what's in the chapter. In fact, they have little to do with anything, but writing these quirky chapter intros has become kind of a tradition of Scott's (he does this in all his books), so if you're one of those really "serious" types, we're begging you, skip them and just go right into the chapter because they'll just get on your nerves. However, the short intros at the beginning of each individual project, up at the top of the page, are usually pretty important. If you skip over them, you might wind up missing stuff that isn't mentioned in the technique itself. So, if you find yourself working on a technique, and you're thinking to yourself, "Why are we doing this?" it's probably because you skipped over that intro. So, just make sure you read it first, and then go to Step One. It'll make a difference—we promise.

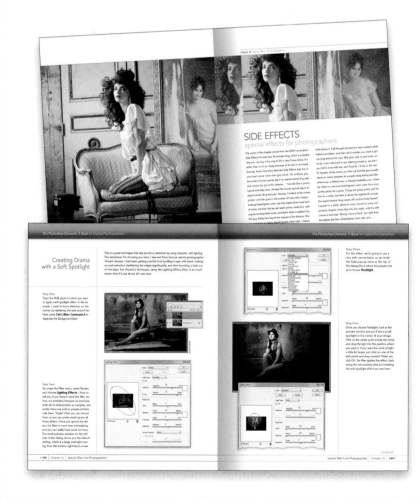

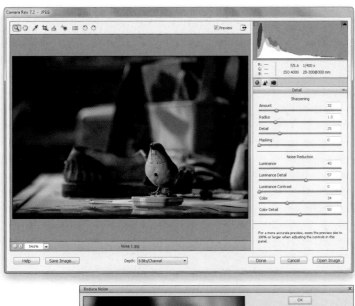

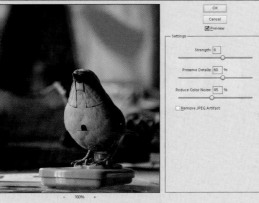

(5) There are things in Elements 11 and in Camera Raw that do the exact same thing.

For example, there's a way to reduce noise in a photo in Camera Raw and there's a way to do it in the Elements Editor, as well. And, they look almost identical. What this means to you is that some things are covered twice in the book. As you go through the book, and you start to think, "This sounds familiar," now you know why. By the way, in our own workflows, if we can do the exact same task in Camera Raw or the Editor, we always choose to do it in Camera Raw, because it's faster (there are no progress bars in Camera Raw) and it's non-destructive (so we can always change our minds later).

(6) Scott included his Elements 11 workflow, but don't read it yet.

At the end of Chapter 12, Scott included a special tutorial detailing his own Elements 11 workflow. But, please don't read it until you've read the rest of the book, because it assumes that you've read everything else in the book already, and understand the basic concepts, so it doesn't spell everything out (or it would be one really, really long drawn-out tutorial).

(Continued)

(7) What new stuff is in this book?

Once we started digging around Elements 11, we realized this is one of the biggest upgrades to it for photographers yet. So, in this edition of the book, we took out some of the old stuff and added more of the new stuff. For example, there's a brand new chapter on the different editing modes that shows you when you'd use each one. It seems like a small thing, but learning which editing mode is best for you can help a lot when you're trying to learn Elements. We also took your feedback (through emails and being out there teaching this stuff) and added a new chapter that covers one of the most important parts of Elements—layers. Finally, Elements 11 took a huge step forward in making selections. Selections are an important part of what we do when we want to edit specific parts of our photos, so we added plenty of things on the new technology in the Chapter 7.

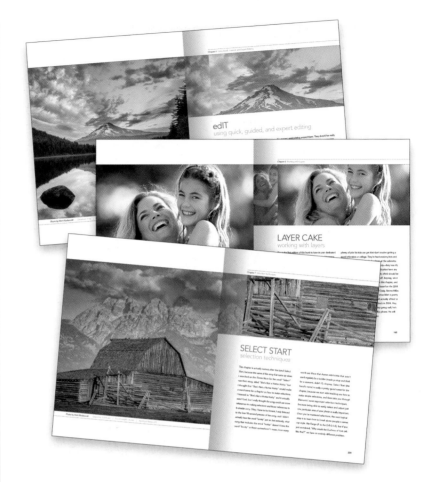

(8) Photography is evolving, Elements is evolving, and this book has to, too.

This is the first edition of this book that doesn't include a chapter on color correction, and that's because today we use Camera Raw (even if we don't shoot in RAW, because it works for JPEGs, TIFFs, and PSDs, too!). We spent years teaching Levels and Curves in books and podcasts, but honestly, today we really don't use them anymore. In fact, we had a hard time finding any photographers we know still using Levels, which just shows how Elements has evolved over time. So, although color correction and Levels aren't covered in their own chapter anymore, we do have a chapter on fixing common problems (Chapter 6), and some of them deal with color issues. The bulk of color correction, though, is now done with a couple sliders in Camera Raw.

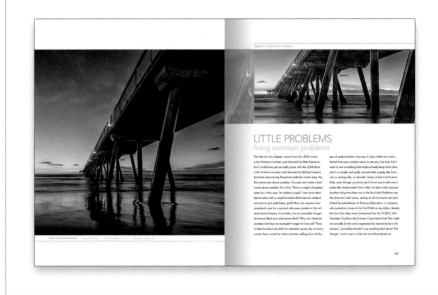

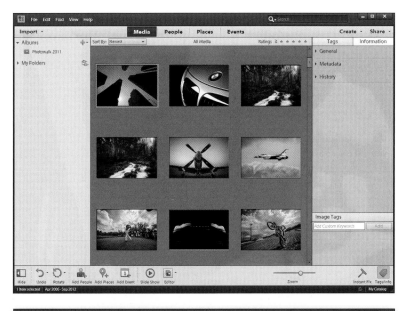

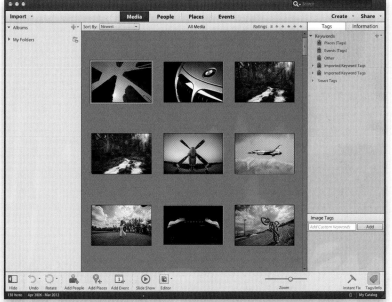

(9) This book is for Windows and Mac users.

Elements 11 is available for both Windows and Macintosh platforms, and the two versions are nearly identical. However, there are three keys on the Mac keyboard that have different names from the same keys on a PC keyboard, but don't worry, we give you both the Windows and Mac shortcuts every time we mention a shortcut (which we do a lot). Also, the Editor in Elements 11 is the same on both platforms, but the Organizer (where we sort and organize our images) was only made available on the Mac starting with Elements 9. As a result, there are some Organizer functions that still aren't available on the Mac yet, and we've noted it in the book wherever this is the case.

Okay, that's the scoop. Thanks for taking a few minutes to read this, and now it's time to turn the page and get to work.

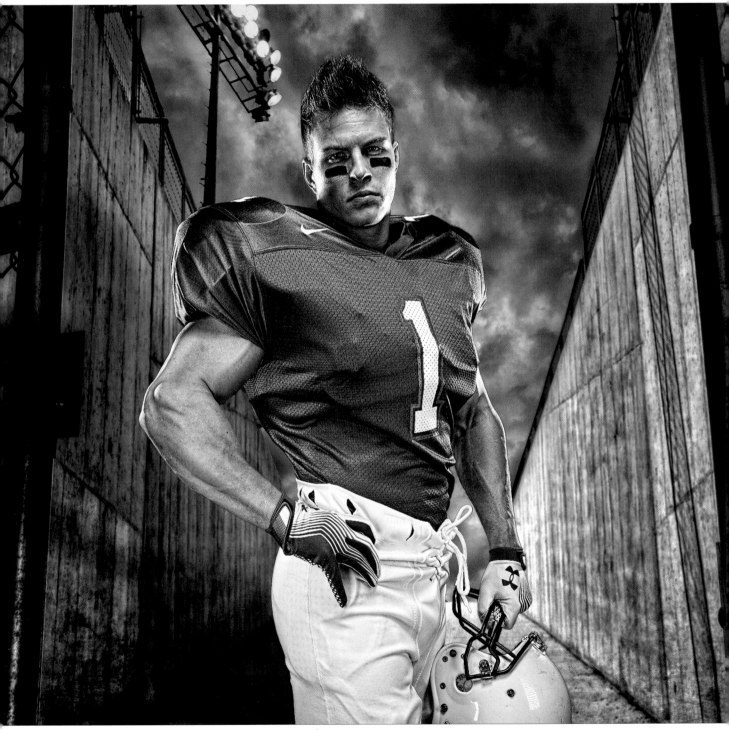

Photo by Scott Kelby   Exposure: 1/125 sec | Focal Length: 24 mm | Aperture Value: ƒ/14

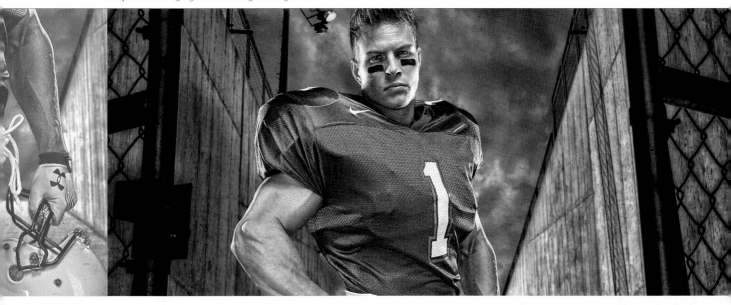

ORGANIZED CHAOS
managing photos using the organizer

If you're reading this chapter opener (and you are, by the way), it's safe to assume that you already read the warning about these openers in the introduction to the book (by the way, nobody reads that, so if you did, you get 500 bonus points, and a chance to play later in our lightning round). Anyway, if you read that and you're here now, you must be okay with reading these, knowing full well in advance that these have little instructional (or literary) value of any kind. Now, once you turn the page, I turn all serious on you, and the fun and games are over, and it's just you and me, and most of the time I'll be screaming at you (stuff like, "No, no—that's too much sharpening you goober!" and "Are you kidding me? You call that a Levels adjustment?" and "Who spilled my mocha Frappuccino?"), so although we're all friendly now, that all ends when you turn the page, because then we're down to business. That's why, if you're a meany Mr. Frumpypants type who feels that joking has no place in a serious book of learning like this, then you can: (a) turn the page and get to the discipline and order you crave, or (b) if you're not sure, you can take this quick quiz that will help you determine the early warning signs of someone who should skip all the rest of the chapter openers and focus on the "real" learning (and yelling). Question #1: When was the last time you used the word "poopy" in a sentence when not directly addressing or referring to a toddler? Was it: (a) During a morning HR meeting? (b) During a legal deposition? (c) During your wedding vows? Or, (d) you haven't said that word in a meaningful way since you were three. If you even attempted to answer this question, you're clear to read the rest of the chapter openers. Oh, by the way: pee pee. (Hee hee!)

Importing Your Photos

One of the major goals of Adobe Photoshop Elements is simply to make your life easier and the Photo Downloader is there to help do just that. Adobe has not only made the process of getting your photos from your digital camera into the Elements Organizer much easier, they also included some automation to make the task faster. Why? So you can get back to shooting faster. Here's how to import your photos and take advantage of this automation:

Step One:
When you attach a memory card reader to your computer (or attach your camera directly using a USB cable), the Elements Organizer – Photo Downloader standard dialog appears onscreen (if you have it set that way; by the way, it will also download photos from your mobile phone). The first thing it does is it searches the card for photos, and then it tells you how many photos it has found, and how much memory (hard disk space) those photos represent.

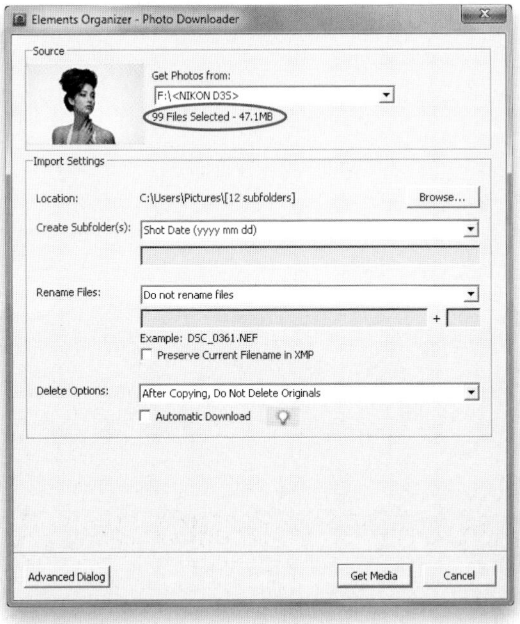

TIP: Import from Adobe Revel
If you use the Adobe Revel picture sharing service, Elements 11 will now let you import your photos directly from there: Go under the File menu and choose **Import From Adobe Revel**, or click on Import just below the menu bar and choose **From Adobe Revel**. Enter your account ID and password and you'll be connected to your Revel account, where you can import your photos into Elements.

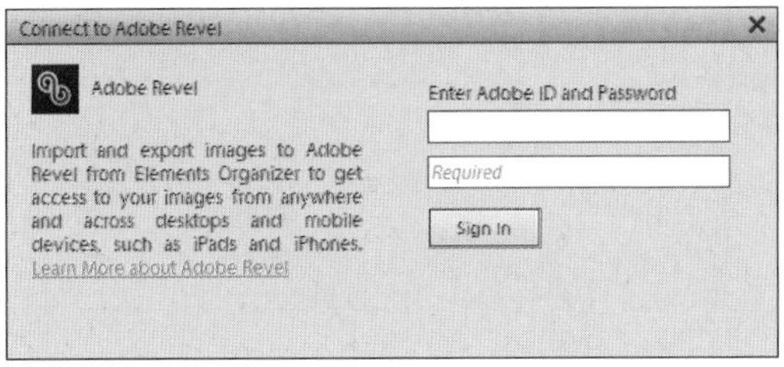

Step Two:
The Import Settings section is where you decide how the photos are imported. You get to choose where (on your hard disk) they'll be saved to, and you can choose to create subfolders with photos sorted by a custom name, today's date, when they were shot, and a host of attributes you can choose from the Create Subfolder(s) pop-up menu (as shown here).

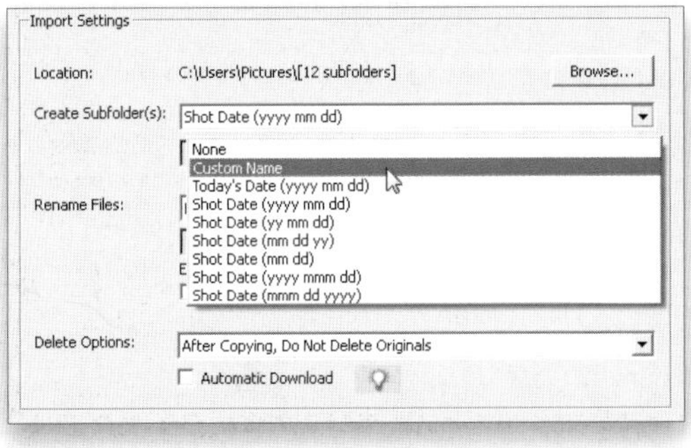

Step Three:

If you want to rename files as they're imported, you can do that in the next field down. You can use the built-in naming conventions, but I recommend choosing **Custom Name** from the Rename Files pop-up menu, so you can enter a name that makes sense to you. You can also choose to have the date the photo was shot appear before your custom name. Choosing Custom Name reveals a text field under the Rename Files pop-up menu where you can type your new name (you get a preview of how it will look). By the way, it automatically appends a four-digit number starting with 0001 at the end of your filename to keep each photo from having the same name.

TIP: Storing the Original Name

If you're fanatical (or required by your job) and want to store the original file-name, turn on the Preserve Current Filename in XMP checkbox and your original filename will be stored in the photo's metadata.

Step Four:

The last setting here is Delete Options. Basically, it's this: do you want the photos deleted off your memory card after import, or do you want to leave the originals on the card? What's the right choice? There is no right choice—it's up to you. If you have only one memory card, and it's full, and you want to keep shooting, well...the decision is pretty much made for you. You'll need to delete the photos to keep shooting. If you've got other cards, you might want to leave the originals on the card until you can make a secure backup of your photos, then erase the card later.

(Continued)

Step Five:

Beneath the Delete Options pop-up menu, is the Automatic Download check-box (this feature is currently only available in the PC version of Elements 11) and this feature is designed to let you skip the Photo Downloader. When you plug in a memory card reader, or camera, it just downloads your photos using your default preferences, with no input from you (well, except it asks whether you want to erase the original photos on the card or not). Now, where are these default preferences set? They're set in the Organizer's Preferences. Just go under the Organizer's Edit menu, under Preferences, and choose **Camera or Card Reader**. This brings up the Preferences dialog you see here.

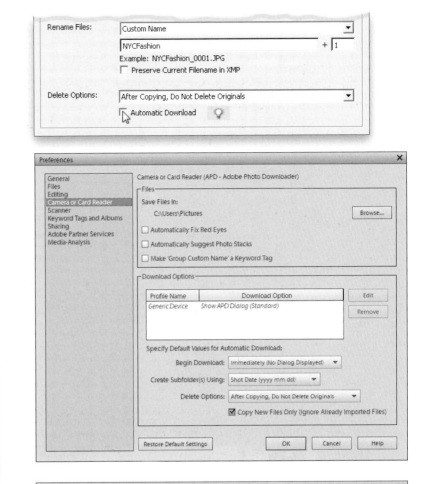

Step Six:

Here is where you decide what happens when you turn on the Automatic Download checkbox in the Photo Downloader. You get to choose a default location to save your photos (like your Pictures folder), and whether you want it to automatically fix any photos that it detects have red eye. You can also choose to have it automatically suggest photo stacks (it groups photos it thinks belong together), or make a keyword tag. You can have settings for specific cameras or card readers (if you want separate settings for your mobile phone, or a particular camera). At the bottom, you've got some other options (when to begin the downloading, if you're going to have subfolders, and your delete options). Click OK when the preferences are set the way you want them.

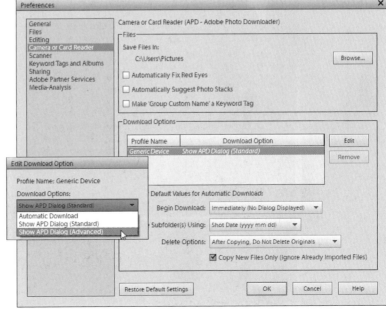

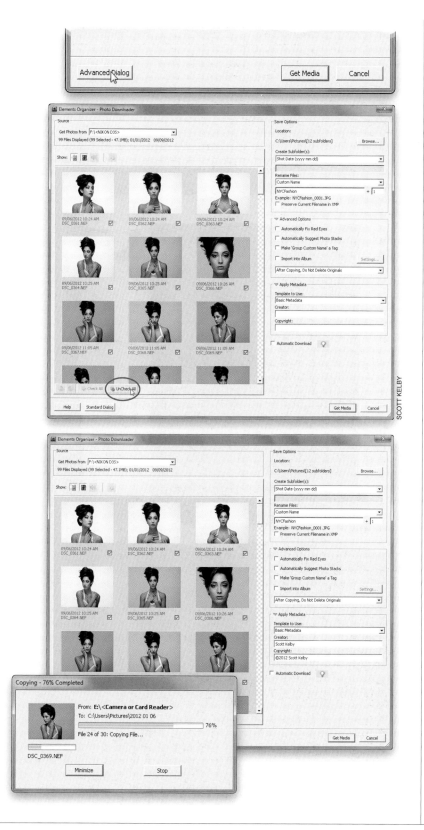

SCOTT KELBY

Step Seven:

Okay, back to the Photo Downloader. Now, at this point, all the photos on the card will be imported, but if you want to import just a few selected photos, then you'll need to click on the Advanced Dialog button at the bottom-left corner of the dialog (shown at the top). That expands the dialog and displays thumbnails of all the photos on the card. By default, every photo has a checkbox turned on below it, indicating that every photo will be imported. If you just want some of these photos imported, then you'll need to click the UnCheck All button at the bottom left of your thumbnails. This turns off all the photos' checkboxes, which enables you to then go and turn on the checkboxes below only the photos you actually want imported.

Step Eight:

When you look at the right side of the dialog, you'll see some familiar Save Options (the subfolder choice, renaming files), and in the Advanced Options section, you'll see choices to automatically fix red eyes, suggest photo stacks, make a tag, import into an album, and delete options. Another nice feature is the ability to embed metadata (like your name and your copyright info) directly into the digital file, just like your camera embeds information into your digital camera images. So, just type in your name and your copyright info, and these are embedded into each photo automatically as they're imported. This is a good thing. When you click Get Media, your photos are imported (well, at least the photos with a checkmark under them). If you want to ignore these advanced features and just use the standard dialog, click on the Standard Dialog button.

Backing Up Your Photos to a Disc or Hard Drive

When you think about backing up, I'd like you to consider this: it's not a matter of if your hard drive will crash, it's a matter of when. I've personally had new and old computers crash. So many times that now I'm totally paranoid about it. Sorry, but it's a harsh fact of computer life. You can protect yourself, though, by backing up your entire catalog to a disc or hard drive, and/or using an online backup, so your photos are protected in an off-site location. So even if your hard drive dies or your computer is lost, stolen, damaged in a fire, flood, or hurricane, you can retrieve your images.

Step One:
To back up your catalog to a hard drive or disc, you simply go under the Organizer's File menu and choose **Backup Catalog** (as shown here; currently in the Mac version of Elements 11, you can only back up to a hard drive).

TIP: Back Up to an External Hard Drive
We recommend backing up to an external hard drive. They're much larger than a CD, or even a DVD, and easier to manage. Plus, you can always take them with you or to a nice off-site location to really keep your backups safe. You can get a 500-GB external hard drive for around $80, and a 1-TB drive for around $100.

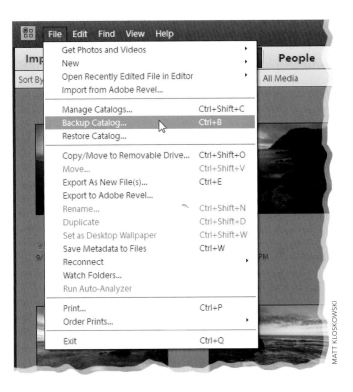

MATT KLOSKOWSKI

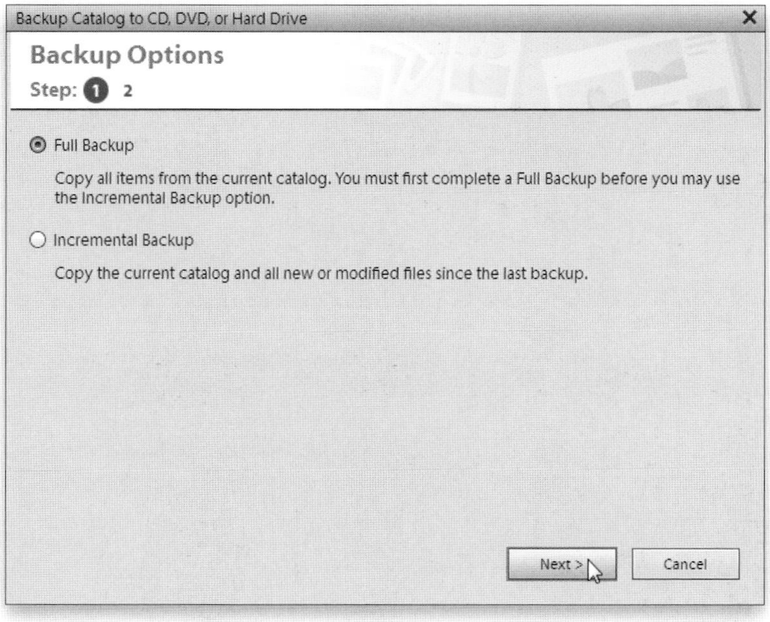

Backup Catalog to CD, DVD, or Hard Drive ✕

Backup Options
Step: ① 2

◉ Full Backup

    Copy all items from the current catalog. You must first complete a Full Backup before you may use the Incremental Backup option.

○ Incremental Backup

    Copy the current catalog and all new or modified files since the last backup.

[Next >]   [Cancel]

Step Two:
This brings up a dialog where you decide whether to do a Full Backup (you choose this the first time you back up your catalog), or an Incremental Backup (which is what you'll choose after your first backup, as it only backs up the files that have changed since your last backup, which is a big time saver). In this case, since this is your first time, choose Full Backup (as shown here), then click the Next button.

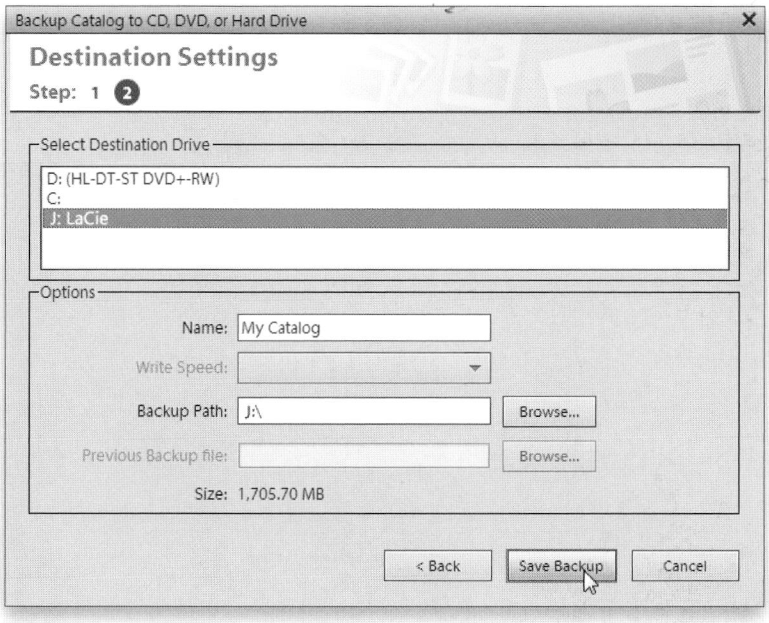

Backup Catalog to CD, DVD, or Hard Drive ✕

Destination Settings
Step: 1 ②

┌─ Select Destination Drive ──────────────
│ D: (HL-DT-ST DVD+-RW)
│ C:
│ **J: LaCie**
└──────────────────────────────

┌─ Options ───────────────────────────
│ Name: [My Catalog]
│ Write Speed: [　　　　　　　▾]
│ Backup Path: [J:\ ]　[Browse...]
│ Previous Backup file: [　　　　　　]　[Browse...]
│ Size: 1,705.70 MB
└──────────────────────────────

[< Back]   [Save Backup]   [Cancel]

Step Three:
When you click Next, the Destination Settings screen appears, which is basically where you tell Elements to back up your stuff to. If it's a DVD or CD, just insert a blank DVD or CD into your DVD/CD drive and choose that drive from the list. Give your disc a name, click the Save Backup button, and it does its thing. Same thing for a hard drive—just choose it from the list and click the Save Backup button.

Importing Photos from Your Scanner

If you're reading this and thinking: "But this is supposed to be a book for digital photographers. Why is he talking about scanning?" Then ask yourself this: "Do I have any older photos lying around that I wish were on my computer?" If the answer is "Yes," then this tutorial is for you. We'll take a quick look at importing scanned images into the Organizer.

Step One:
In the Elements Organizer, go under the File menu, under Get Photos and Videos, and choose **From Scanner**. By the way, in the Organizer, you can also use the shortcut **Ctrl-U** to import photos from your scanner or click on Import just below the menu bar and choose **From Scanner**. (*Note:* This feature is currently only available in the PC version of Elements 11.)

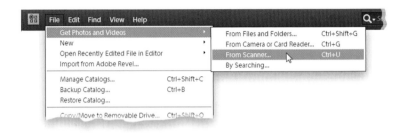

Step Two:
Once the Get Photos from Scanner dialog is open, choose your scanner from the Scanner pop-up menu. Choose a high Quality setting (I generally choose the highest quality, unless the photo is for an email to my insurance company for a claim—then I'm not as concerned), then click OK to bring in the scanned photo. See? Pretty straightforward stuff.

If you're the type that likes to squeeze every ounce of productivity out of your computer, then try this tutorial out. Elements lets you choose a folder that is "watched" by the Organizer. So whenever you put photos into that watched folder, they'll automatically be added into the Organizer. Yep, no interaction from you is needed at all. Here's how it works:

Automating the Importing of Photos by Using Watched Folders

Step One:
Go under the Organizer's File menu and choose **Watch Folders**. (*Note:* This feature is currently only available in the PC version of Elements 11.)

Step Two:
When the Watch Folders dialog appears, make sure the Watch Folders and Their Sub-Folders for New Files checkbox is turned on. In the Folders to Watch section, click the Add button, and then in the resulting dialog, navigate to any folders you want the Organizer to "watch" for the addition of new photos. Select the folder you want to watch, and then click OK. Continue to click the Add button and select more folders to watch. When you've selected all your folders, they will appear in the Folders to Watch section of the Watch Folders dialog. In the When New Files are Found in Watched Folders section, you have the choice of having the Organizer alert you when new photos are found in the watched folders (meaning you can choose to add them) or you can have them added automatically, which is what this feature is really all about. But if you're fussy about what gets added when (i.e., you're a control freak), at least you get an option.

Changing the Size of Your Photo Thumbnails

We all have our personal preferences. Some people like to cram as many photos onscreen at once as they can, while others like to see the photos in the Organizer's Media Browser at the largest view possible. Luckily, you have total control over the size they're displayed at.

Step One:
The size of your thumbnails is controlled by a slider below the right side of the Media Browser. Click-and-drag the Zoom slider to the right to make them bigger and to the left to make them smaller.

TIP: Jumping Up a Size
To jump up one size at a time, click on a thumbnail, then press-and-hold the **Ctrl (Mac: Command) key** and press the **+** (plus sign) **key**. To go down in size, press **Ctrl-–** (minus sign; **Mac: Command-–**).

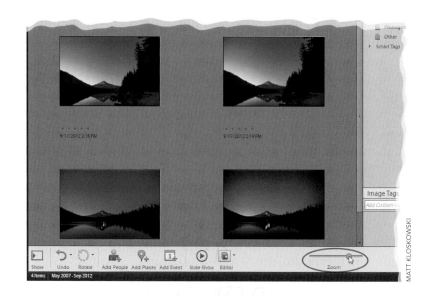

Step Two:
To jump to the largest possible view, just double-click on your thumbnail. At this large view, you can enter a caption directly below the photo by clicking on the placeholder text (which reads "Click here to add caption") and typing in your caption. (*Note:* If you don't see this text, go under the View menu and choose **Details**.) Press **Esc** to return to the grid view, or click on the Grid button in the top left of the Media Browser.

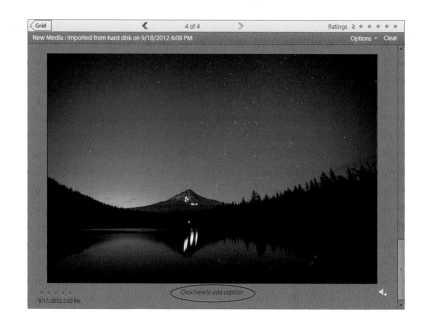

If you like seeing a super-big view of your photos, then use Elements' Full Screen View. It shows you a huge preview of a selected thumbnail without having to leave the Organizer. Here's how:

Seeing Full-Screen Previews

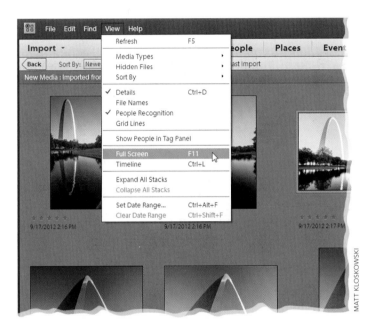

MATT KLOSKOWSKI

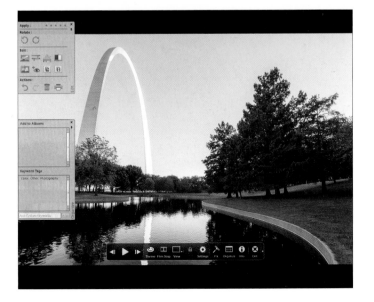

Step One:
To see a full-screen preview of your currently selected photo(s), go under the View menu, and choose **Full Screen** (or press **F11 [Mac: Command-F11]**).

Step Two:
This brings you into Full Screen view, and your photo should appear large onscreen with everything else black around it. This is really a way to launch into a slide show, but if you don't do anything here, you're simply just viewing your photos in a larger view. If you want to return to the Media Browser, press the **Esc key** on your keyboard. But wait, there's more.

(Continued)

Step Three:

Once your photo(s) appears full screen, there's a control palette at the bottom of the screen where you can control your viewing options—click the Play button to start moving through your photos and click the Pause button to stop. You can also click the Right Arrow and Left Arrow buttons to view the next or previous photo.

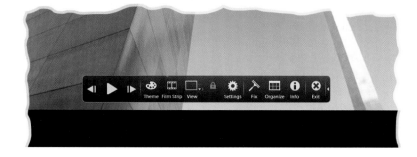

Step Four:

One more thing: Try clicking the Toggle Film Strip button on the control palette (or just press **Ctrl-F [Mac: Command-F]**). This opens a filmstrip view of your photos on the bottom of the screen. So you don't necessarily have to click the Right Arrow button or press the Right Arrow key a bunch of times to get to a photo that's 25 photos into your list. You can just scroll the filmstrip until you see it and click on it. Nifty, huh?

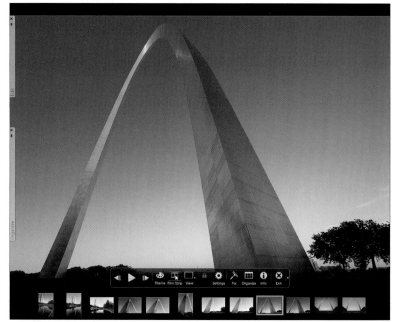

MATT KLOSKOWSKI

When photos are imported into the Organizer, the Organizer automatically sorts them by date. How does it know on which dates the photos were taken? The time and date are embedded into the photo by your digital camera at the moment the photo is taken (this info is called EXIF data). The Organizer reads this info and then sorts your photos automatically by date, putting the newest ones on top. You can change that, though, and you can choose whether or not to view your filenames.

Sorting Photos by Date and Viewing Filenames

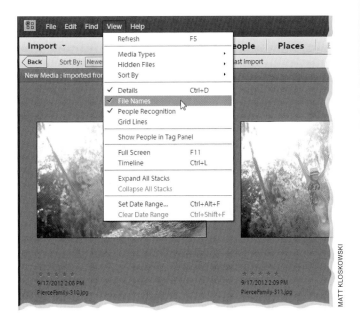

Step One:
By default, the newest photos are displayed first, so basically, your last photo shoot will be the first photos in the Organizer. You can see the exact date and time each photograph was taken by going under the View menu, and choosing **Details**. If you want to see the filenames, then under the View menu, choose **File Names**, as well.

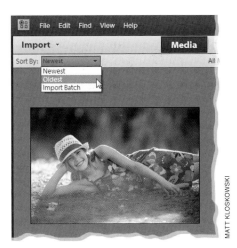

Step Two:
If you'd prefer to see your photos in reverse order (the oldest photos up top), then choose **Oldest** from the Sort By pop-up menu above the top left of the Media Browser. There you have it!

Adding Scanned Photos? Enter the Right Time & Date

Let's say that you have a scanner and you scan in a bunch of photos and import them into the Organizer. They're all going to show up on the date you scanned them, not the date they were taken. That's when you'll need to manually go in and enter the date. I know, you're wondering how you'll know what date the photos were taken. It could have been decades ago. Well, just getting close is a start. For example, if you see a guy wearing a tie-dyed shirt and socks pulled up to his knees, you can pretty much bet it was taken in the late '70s (at least you hope).

Step One:
First, get the photos from your scanner (see the "Importing Photos from Your Scanner" tutorial earlier in this chapter). Select all the photos you want to set the date for by Ctrl-clicking (Mac: Command-clicking) on each image (or Shift-clicking on the first and last images if they are contiguous) in the Media Browser. Then, go under the Organizer's Edit menu and choose **Adjust Date and Time of Selected Items** (or press **Ctrl-J [Mac: Command-J]**).

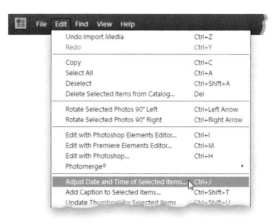

Step Two:
This brings up a dialog asking how you want to handle the date and time for these photos. For this example, select Change to a Specified Date and Time and click OK.

Step Three:
This brings up the Set Date and Time dialog, where you can use the pop-up menus to set your selected photos' date and time. Now these photos will appear sorted by the date you entered, rather than the date you imported them.

By default, the Organizer sorts your photos by date and time, with the most recent photos appearing at the top. You know and I know that it's hard to always remember when you took some of your favorite photos, though. With the Timeline, you can at least get pretty close. Let's say you're trying to find photos you took at an air show last spring. You may not remember exactly whether it was March or April, but by moving a slider you can hone in and find them really fast.

Finding Photos Fast by Their Month & Year

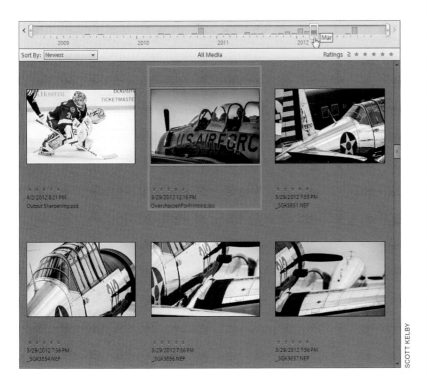

SCOTT KELBY

Step One:
First things first. You need to display the Timeline to use it. Go under the View menu and choose **Timeline** (or just press **Ctrl-L [Mac: Command-L]**). It'll appear right above the Media Browser. We're going to assume you're trying to find photos you took at an air show last spring (as mentioned above). You see those bars along the Timeline that look like the little bar charts from Microsoft Excel? Well, the higher the bar, the more photos that appear in that month. So click on any month in 2012 and the photos taken in that month will appear in the Media Browser. As you slide your cursor to the left (or right), you'll see each month's name appear. When you move to March, photos taken in March 2012 will appear. Take a quick look and see if any of those photos are the ones from the air show. If they're not in March, scroll on the Timeline to April, and those photos will be visible.

Tagging Your Photos (with Keyword Tags)

Although finding your photos by month and year is fairly handy, the real power of the Organizer appears when you assign tags (keywords) to your photos. This simple step makes finding the exact photos you want very fast and very easy. The first step is to decide whether you can use the pre-made tags that Adobe puts there for you or whether you need to create your own. In this situation, you're going to create your own custom tags.

Step One:
Start by finding the Tags palette in the Organizer (it's on the right side of the window). Adobe's default set of keyword tag categories will appear in a vertical list. Now, there are a few different ways to tag photos, so let's take a look at them all. In the end, they all do the same thing, just in a different way.

Step Two: The Really Easy Way
Let's start by tagging the really easy way. Type a tag name in the Add Custom Keywords text field at the top of the Image Tags palette (right below the Tags palette). Then in the Media Browser, click on the photo (Ctrl-click [Mac: Command-click] to select multiple photos) you want to assign this tag to and click the Add button to the right of the text field. The tag will automatically be created and applied to the selected photo(s).

TIP: Use an Existing Keyword Tag
Since the Image Tags text field dynami-cally displays existing keyword tags (in a pop-up menu) based on the letters you type, you can use it to assign an existing keyword tag to your photos instead of creating a brand new one.

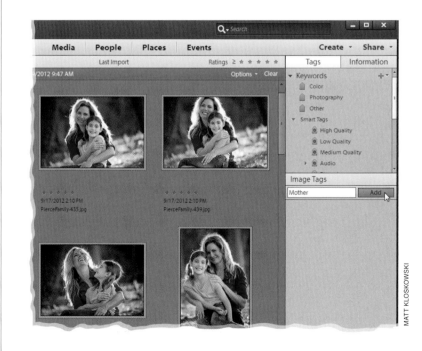

MATT KLOSKOWSKI

Step Three: The More Customized and Visual Way

The thing about Step Two is that it automatically creates your tag in the Other category. As you start tagging, you may want to categorize your tags and even create your own categories. So, let's start by creating a custom category (in this case, we're going to create a category for shots of friends). Click on the Create New Keyword Tag button (the little green plus sign) at the top right of the Tags palette and choose **New Category** from the pop-up menu. This brings up the Create Category dialog. Type in a name for your category (I typed "Friends"). Now choose an icon from the Category Icon list and then click OK. (The icon choices are all pretty lame, so we'll just choose the red tag icon here.)

Step Four:

To create your own custom tag, click on the Create New Keyword Tag button again and choose **New Keyword Tag**. This brings up the Create Keyword Tag dialog. Choose Friends from the Category pop-up menu (if it's not already chosen), then in the Name field, type in a name for your new tag (here I entered "Kate"). If you want to add additional notes about the photos, you can add them in the Note field, and you can choose a photo as an icon by clicking the Edit Icon button (there's more on choosing icons later in this chapter). Now click OK to create your tag.

(Continued)

Step Five:

Next, you'll assign this tag to all the photos from this shoot. In the Media Browser, scroll to the photos from that shoot. We'll start by tagging just one photo, so click on your new tag that appears in your Keywords list in the Tags palette and drag-and-drop that tag onto any one of the photos. That photo is now "tagged" and you'll see a small tag icon appear below the right side of the photo's thumbnail.

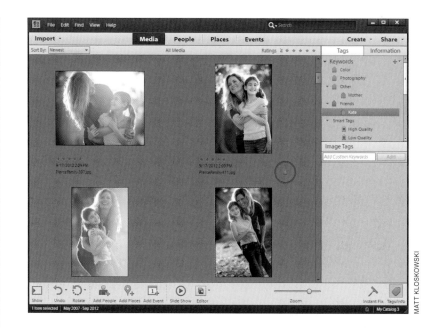

Step Six:

So at this point, we've only tagged one photo from this shoot. Drag-and-drop that same tag onto three more photos from the shoot, so a total of four photos are tagged. Now, in the Tags palette, hover your cursor over your new tag, and you'll see a small arrow to the right of the tag. Click on that arrow, and a search bar pops down at the top of the Media Browser with your tag already chosen in the Keywords column, and just those photos with that tag showing below the search bar. You can turn on the checkboxes for other criteria if you need to narrow your search further. To see all your photos again, click on the Back button that appears at the top left of the Media Browser. To start a new search, click the Clear button at the top right of the image results section. (Note: You can also search using the Search field at the top right of the Organizer window. Its pop-up menu allows you to search by visual similarity, for an object, and for duplicate photos, as well.)

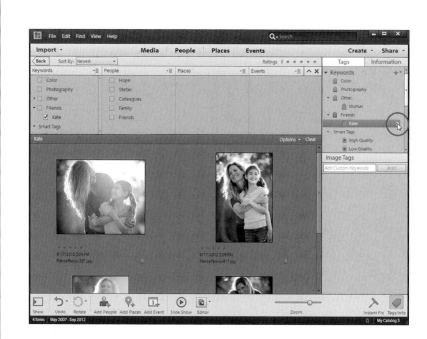

You saw how to tag your photos in the previous tutorial and I won't lie to you—it takes a little bit of time. However, there is a feature called Smart Tagging that does some auto-tagging for you. Now, it can't figure out that you were at Disney World and tag your photos with Disney tags, but there are a few useful Smart Tags to help you get started.

Auto Tagging with Smart Tags

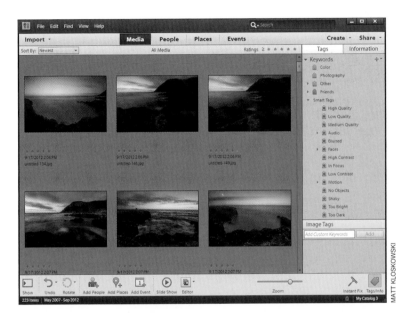

MATT KLOSKOWSKI

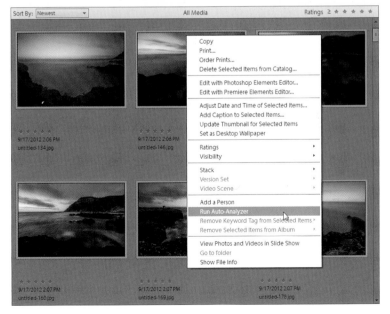

Step One:
Take a look at the Tags palette and, at the bottom of the tag category list, you'll see Smart Tags. When you click on the right-facing arrow to expand it, you'll see there are tags named High Quality, Faces, Too Bright, Too Dark, etc. There are also tags named Audio and Shaky, which are actually meant for video, if you're using Premier Elements.

Step Two:
To use Smart Tags, you've got to first let Elements analyze your photos. It's a snap, though. Just Ctrl-click (Mac: Command-click) on the photos in the Media Browser that you want to select, Right-click on any of the ones you just selected, and choose **Run Auto-Analyzer** from the pop-up menu. A progress bar will appear, so you'll know the Auto-Analyzer is doing something. This may take a few minutes depending on how many photos you select.

(Continued)

Step Three:

When the Auto-Analyzer is done running, go back to the Smart Tags in the Tags palette, and click on the small arrow to the right of one of the Smart Tags (I'll choose the Blurred tag here, since I used a long exposure in these to blur the water). Now, you'll see the photos that Elements has deemed are blurred. Like I said in the intro, the Smart Tags aren't the solution to everything, but they do give you a good starting point.

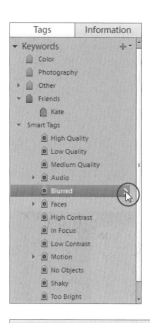

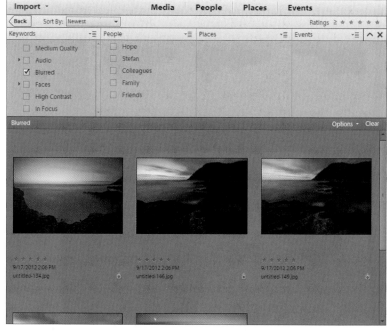

Okay, if you had to tag any more than a few photos, you've probably realized that dragging-and-dropping the tag onto each photo is a pain in the neck. If you had a whole photo shoot, that process would take forever and you'd probably be getting ready to send Adobe (or us for even showing you this feature) a nasty email. You'll be happy to know there are faster ways than this one-tag-at-a-time method. For example…

Tagging Multiple Photos

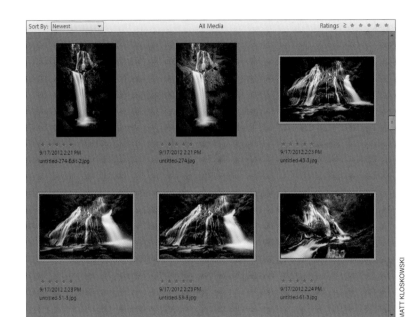

MATT KLOSKOWSKI

Step One:
To tag all the photos from your shoot at the same time, try this: First, click on any photo from the shoot. Then press-and-hold the Ctrl (Mac: Command) key and click on other photos from that particular shoot. As you click on them, they'll be-come selected (each selected photo will have a blue stroke around it). Or, if all the photos are contiguous, click on the first image in the series, press-and-hold the Shift key, and then click on the last image in the series to select them all.

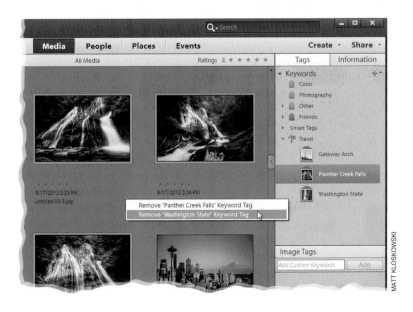

MATT KLOSKOWSKI

Step Two:
Now, drag-and-drop your chosen tag onto any one of those selected photos, and all of the selected photos will have that tag. If you want to see just the pho-tos from that shoot, you can click on the arrow to the right of that tag in the Tags palette and only photos with that tag will appear. By the way, if you decide you want to remove a tag from a photo, just Right-click on the tag icon below the photo and from the pop-up menu that appears, choose **Remove Keyword Tag**. If you have more than one tag applied (like the Panther Creek Falls [where I took these photos] keyword tag and the Washington State keyword tag), you can choose which tag you want removed.

Assigning Multiple Tags to One Photo

Okay, what if you want to assign a keyword tag to a photo, but you also want to assign other keyword tags (perhaps an "Upload to Website" tag and a "Make Prints" tag) to that photo, as well? Here's how:

Step One:

To assign multiple tags at once, first, of course, you have to create the tags you need, so go ahead and create your new tags by clicking on the Create New Keyword Tag button and choosing **New Keyword Tag** from the pop-up menu. Name them "Upload to Website," "Make Prints," and two others specific to this shoot. Now you have four tags you can assign. To assign all four tags at once, just press-and-hold the Ctrl (Mac: Command) key, then in the Tags palette, click on each tag you want to assign (Olympic National Park, Pacific Coast, Make Prints, and Upload to Website).

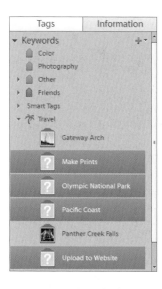

Step Two:

Then, click-and-drag those selected tags, and as you drag, you'll see you're dragging four tag icons as one group. Drop them onto a photo, and all four tags will be applied at once. If you want to apply the tags to more than one photo at a time, first press-and-hold the Ctrl (Mac: Command) key and click on all the photos you want to have all four tags. Then, go to the Tags palette, press-and-hold the Ctrl key again, and click on all the tags you want to apply. Drag those tags onto any one of the selected photos, and all the tags will be applied at once. Cool.

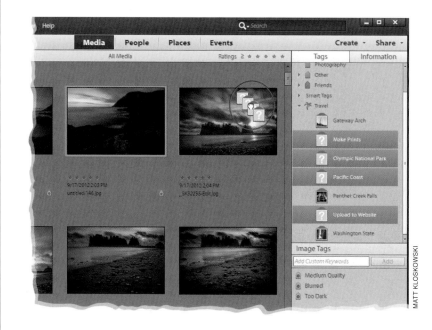

You're either going to think this is the coolest, most advanced technology in all of Elements, or you're going to think it's creepy and very Big Brother-ish (from the book by George Orwell, not the TV show). Either way, it's here to help you tag people easier because the Organizer can automatically find photos of people for you—as it has some sort of weird science, facial-recognition software built in (that at one point was developed for the CIA, which is all the more reason it belongs in Elements).

Tagging Images of People

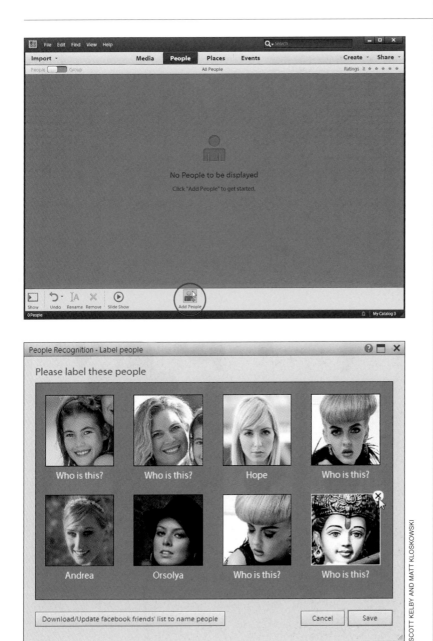

Step One:
Let's say you want to quickly find all the photos of your daughter. In the Organizer, at the top, click on People. If this is the first time you've searched for people, then click the Add People icon in the middle of the taskbar at the bottom of the window.

Step Two:
This brings up the People Recognition – Label People dialog with the images that contain a human face. Just click on the "Who is this?" link beneath one of the image thumbnails, type in a name to tag the photo with, and press Enter (Mac: Return). If this keyword doesn't already exist, this will create a new one. If Elements found something that isn't a person in a photo (like the statue in the bottom right here), just hover your cursor over the image, and click the X in the white circle at the top right. The thumbnail will be grayed out, will have the international symbol for No! in the top-right corner (a circle with a line through it), and will say "Excluded" beneath it. If multiple images contain the same people, there's no need to tag each image. Just click the Save button and the next time it asks you to add people's names, when you click below the thumbnail, you'll see the last three names you added. Just click on the one you want to add it to that thumbnail.

(Continued)

TIP: Use Your Facebook Friend List

When you set up Elements to be authorized to work with your Facebook account (to share your photos there), you'll also get an option to download your Facebook friend list (circled here). If you turn that option on, then your Facebook friends will appear in the list when you tag people. Each time you find people for tagging, you'll also get the chance to download or update your Facebook friend list by clicking on the link in the bottom left of the People Recognition – Label People dialog.

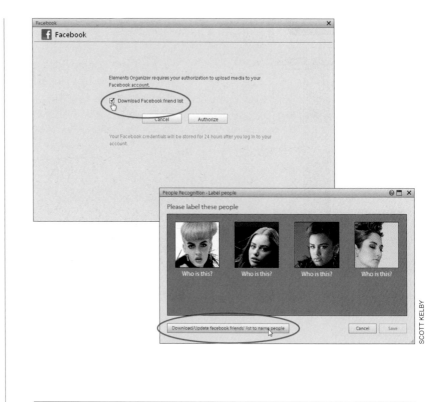

Step Three:

Once you've added some names and clicked Save, Elements will give you the option of tagging all the images of that person at once. When you click the Save button in the Label People dialog, the People Recognition – Confirm Groups of People dialog will appear. Here, you'll Ctrl-click (Mac: Command-click) on any images that you want to exclude from tagging. Then, hover over one of the selected thumbnails, and you'll see a down-facing arrow appear in the bottom right. Click on it and, in the pop-up menu, choose **Not [the person's name]**. (If you're not sure, you can choose to see the thumbnail at a larger size here, too.) This will gray out those thumbnails, so click Save, and it will bring up the next set of thumbnails to confirm. Once you've confirmed all the people you've named, it will take you back to Step Two by bringing up more thumbnails for you to name, until all people have been tagged.

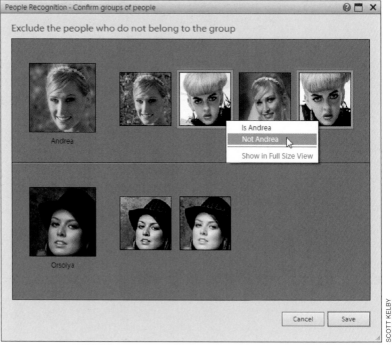

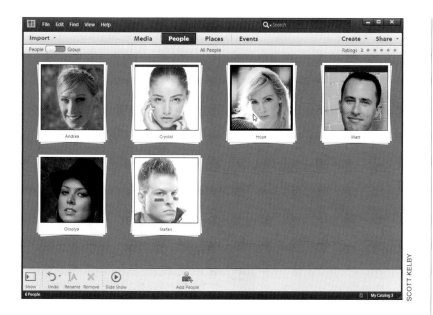

SCOTT KELBY

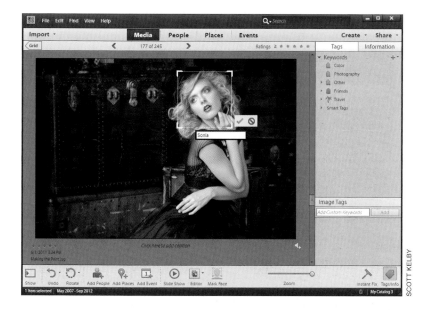

SCOTT KELBY

Step Four:
When you finish adding names to your people photos, the photos will be stacked by name, like you see here. If you move your cursor over a stack from left to right (or right to left), it will scroll through the images in your stack, so you don't have to open the stack to see the rest of the photos in it. If you double-click on a stack, it's like doing a search with that person's name, and shows you just the photos in that stack. Also, at the top left of the All People window is a switch. Click on it to see your photos by group. The Groups palette that appears on the right works much like the Tags palette. You can add new groups or use the default ones for Colleagues, Friends, and Family. Just drag-and-drop the group name onto the photo stack to add those photos to the group.

Step Five:
If Elements didn't recognize a face, you can always add it manually. In the Media Browser, double-click on the image with the person you want to tag, then click the Mark Face icon in the bottom task-bar. Click-and-drag the rectangle over the person's face, resize it by dragging any of the corner handles, and give 'em a name and click the green checkmark.

TIP: Train Elements to Find Faces
The more you tag and the more you use this face tagging technology, the better you train Elements to find faces. Each time you tag faces, it gets more and more accurate.

Choosing Your Own Icons for Keyword Tags

By default, a keyword tag uses the first photo you add to that tag as its icon. Most of the time, these icons are so small that you probably can't tell what the icon represents. That's why you'll probably want to choose your own photo icons instead.

Step One:
It's easier to choose an icon once you've created a keyword tag and tagged a few photos. Once you've done that, Right-click on your tag, and choose **Edit** from the pop-up menu. This brings up the Edit Keyword Tag dialog. In this dialog, click on the Edit Icon button to launch the dialog you see here on the right.

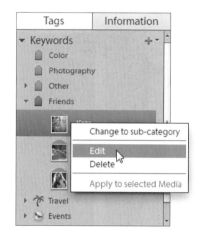

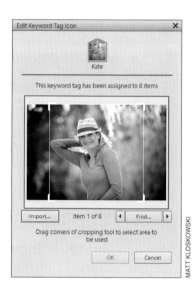

Step Two:
You'll see the first photo you tagged with this keyword in the preview window (this is why it's best to edit the icon after you've added tags to the photos). If you don't want to use this first photo, click the arrow buttons under the bottom-right corner of the preview window to scroll through your photos. Once you find the photo you want to use, click on the little cropping border (in the preview window) to isolate part of the photo. This gives you a better close-up photo that's easier to see as an icon. Then click OK in the open dialogs and that cropped image becomes your icon.

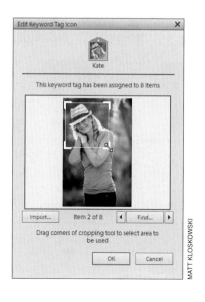

There will be plenty of times when you create a keyword tag or an album and later decide you don't want it anymore. Here's how to get rid of them:

Deleting Keyword Tags or Albums

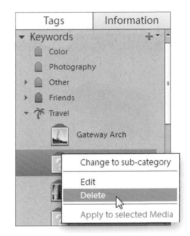

Step One:
To delete a keyword tag or album, Right-click on the keyword tag or album you want to delete in the Tags palette on the right side of the Organizer or under Albums on the left, and choose **Delete** from the pop-up menu.

Step Two:
If you're deleting a tag, it brings up a warning dialog letting you know that deleting the tag will remove it from all your photos and Saved Searches. If you want to remove that tag, click OK. If you've got an album selected, it asks if you're sure you want to delete the album. Click OK and it's gone. However, it does not delete these photos from your main catalog—it just deletes that album.

Seeing Your Photo's Metadata (EXIF Info)

When you take a photo with a digital camera, a host of information about that photo is embedded into the photo by the camera itself. It contains just about everything, including the make and model of the camera that took the photo, the exact time the photo was taken, what the f-stop setting was, what the focal length of the lens was, and whether or not the flash fired when you took the shot. You can view all this info (called Exchangeable Image File [EXIF] data—also known as metadata) from right within the Organizer. Here's how:

Step One:
To view a photo's EXIF data, click on the image in the Media Browser and then click on the Information palette's tab in the top right of the Organizer (if you don't see it, click on the Tags/Info icon on the right side of the taskbar at the bottom of the window) to open the palette.

TIP: Information Palette Shortcut
You can also just press **Alt-Enter (Mac: Option-Return)** to open and close the palette.

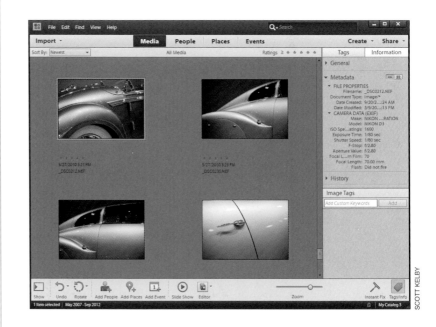

Step Two:
When the Information palette appears, you'll see a General section, a Metadata section, and a History section. Click on Metadata to expand the section. This shows an abbreviated version of the photo's EXIF data (basically, the make, model, ISO, exposure, shutter speed, f-stop, aperture, focal length of the lens, and the status of the flash). Of course, the camera embeds much more info than this. To see the full EXIF data, click on the Complete button (the right of the two buttons) to the right of the word "Metadata," and you'll get more information on this file than you'd probably ever want to know.

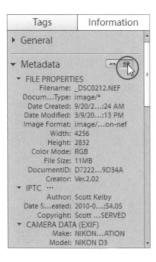

As soon as you press the shutter button, your digital camera automatically embeds information into your photos. But you can also add your own info if you want. This includes simple things like a photo caption (that can appear onscreen when you display your photos in a slide show), or notes for your personal use, either of which can be used to help you search for photos later, or you can add copyright and contact info.

Adding Your Own Info to Photos

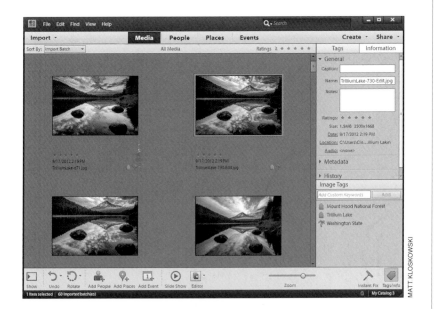

MATT KLOSKOWSKI

Step One:
First, click on the photo in the Media Browser that you want to add your own info to, and then click on the Information palette's tab on the top right to open it (or you can use the keyboard shortcut **Alt-Enter [Mac: Option-Return]**).

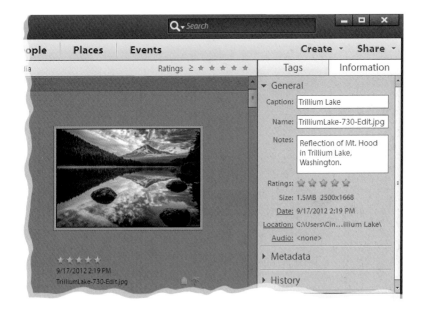

Step Two:
In the Information palette, you'll see General, Metadata, and History sections. By default, the General section is selected. In this section, the first field is for adding a caption (I know, that's pretty self-explanatory), and then the photo's filename appears below that. It's the third field down—Notes—where you add your own personal notes about the photo.

(Continued)

Step Three:

To add your copyright and contact info to your photos, you'll have to select multiple photos, so Ctrl-click (Mac: Command-click) on the photos you want to add this info to, and then click on the Information palette's tab on the right. In the palette, you'll see the number of photos you've selected, as well as an Add IPTC Information button. Click that button.

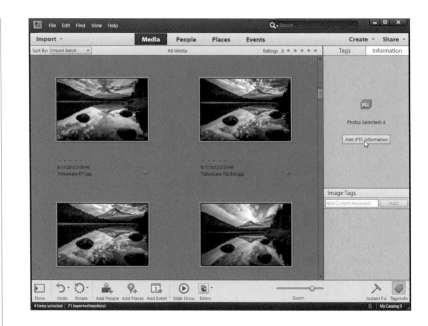

Step Four:

This brings up the Edit IPTC Information dialog (shown here). You'll see several IPTC metadata categories on the left-hand side. In the fields below each category, simply type in the information that you'd like to add to your photos (in the example shown here, I just added my basic copyright info in the IPTC Status section). Click Save, and that info will be added to all your selected photos.

Edit IPTC Information ✕

▼ IPTC Contact

Author: [_____] ● Append ○ Overwrite

Author Title: [_____]

▼ IPTC Image

City: [_____]

State/Province: [_____]

Country: [_____]

▼ IPTC Content

Headline: [_____]

Description: [_____]

Keywords: [_____] ● Append ○ Overwrite

Description Writer: [_____]

▼ IPTC Status

Document Title: [_____]

Instructions: [_____]

Credit: Matt Kloskowski

Source: www.mattk.com

Copyright: ©2012 Matt Kloskowski. All rights reserved.

Save   Cancel

Aside from actually doing things to fix your photos, finding them will be the most common task you do in Elements. If you've tagged them, then it's easy to find groups of photos. But finding just one photo can be a little harder (not really too hard, though). You first have to narrow the number of photos to a small group. Then you'll look through that group until you find the one you want. I know, it sounds complicated but it's really not. Here are the most popular searching methods:

Finding Photos

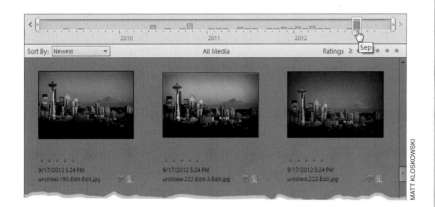

MATT KLOSKOWSKI

From the Timeline:

We saw this one earlier. The Timeline (from the View menu, choose **Timeline** to see it), which is a horizontal bar across the top of the Media Browser, shows you all the photos in your catalog. Months and years are represented along the Timeline. The years are visible below the Timeline; the small light blue bars above the Timeline are individual months. If there is no bar visible, there are no photos stored in that month. A short blue bar means just a few photos were taken that month; a tall bar means lots of photos. If you hover your cursor over a blue bar, the month it represents will appear. To see the photos taken in that month, click on the bar and only those photos will be displayed in the Media Browser. Once you've clicked on a month, you can click-and-drag the locator bar to the right or left to display different months.

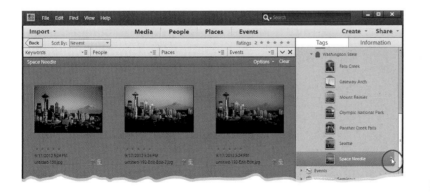

Using Keyword Tags:

If there's a particular shot you're looking for, and you've tagged all your shots with a particular tag, then just go to the Tags palette and click on the arrow to the right of that tag. Now only shots with that tag will appear in the Media Browser.

(Continued)

By Details (Metadata):

If you want to do a search with more options to really narrow down the results, then go under the Organizer's Find menu and choose **By Details (Metadata)**. In the resulting dialog, you pick your search criteria from pop-up menus, and you can add as many different lines of criteria as you'd like by clicking on the + (plus sign) button on the far-right side of each criteria line. Here, I searched for the keyword Seattle, but added more criteria, so it only searches for my 5-star images taken with my Nikon D800. You can also save this search by turning on the Save this Search Criteria as Saved Search checkbox at the bottom and giving the search a name. To use a saved search again, simply click on the magnifying glass icon in the search field at the top right of the Organizer, and choose **Saved Searches**.

By Caption or Note:

If you've added personal notes within tags or you've added captions to individual photos, you can search those fields to help you narrow your search. Just go under the Organizer's Find menu and choose **By Caption or Note**. Then, in the resulting dialog, enter the word(s) that you think may appear in the photo's caption or note, and click OK. Only photos that have that word in a caption or note will appear in the Media Browser.

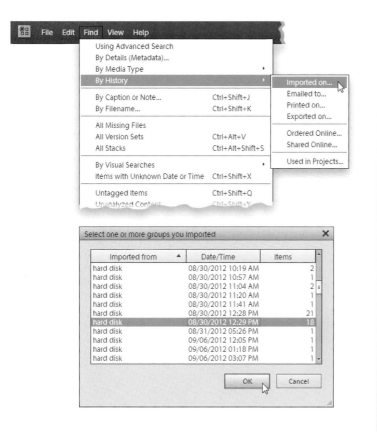

By History:

The Organizer keeps track of when you imported each photo and when you last shared it (via email, print, web-page, etc.); so if you can remember any of those dates, you're in luck. Just go under the Organizer's Find menu, under **By History**, and choose which attri-bute you want to search under in the submenu. (*Note:* Some of the options shown here are currently not available in the Elements 11 version for the Mac.) A dialog with a list of names or locations and dates will appear. Click on a date or name, click OK, and only photos that fit that criterion will appear in the Media Browser.

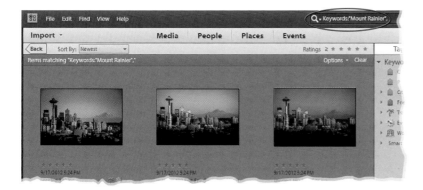

By Textual Information:

Elements has a Search field that basically lets you search all text information in a photo—not just keyword tags, but all of the metadata and stuff that gets stored with your photos. In fact, it's probably one of the most powerful and easiest ways to search, since you don't have to worry as much about what you're looking for and where to look for it. Just go to the Search field in the top right of the Organizer win-dow and type in your search terms. Here, I entered Mount Rainier and it found all of the photos taken with that in the note. I could have just as easily typed a key-word tag, part of a filename, or even my camera model.

Finding Duplicate Photos

If you're like most photographers out there, when you take a photo of someone (or something), you don't just take one. You take 18 or more. It's totally normal. We figure the more photos we take, the better chance we have that at least one photo will be exactly what we want. The problem comes when we're trying to organize our photos. We tend to build up huge libraries of photos that include a bunch of duplicates. I'm not talking exact filename duplicates (as if we imported the same photo twice), but duplicates in that one photo looks just like another. Well, Elements can help you find them.

Step One:

Let's say you took some photos of a friend and her daughter, and you wanted to quickly sort through them to find the best ones. Since they're portraits, chances are you probably shot a bunch in each pose, to make sure you had at least one good one of each. You only really need one keeper, right? In the Organizer, select the group of photos you want to search through (you can press **Ctrl-A [Mac: Command-A]** to Select All, click on an album, or just Ctrl-click [Mac: Command-click] on as many images as you want to sort through). Then, go under the Find menu, under By Visual Searches, and choose **Duplicate Photos**. Depending on how many photos you're looking through, it can take anywhere from a few seconds for 50 photos to a few minutes for a few thousand.

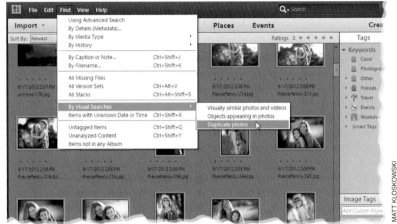

Step Two:

When Elements is done, you'll see the Visually Similar Photo Search dialog open. Elements will put each series of photos that it finds similar into suggested groups. For me, it was kinda hard to really see what was in each group, because the thumbnails are so small. Since we're going to actually do things with the photos in these series, you may want to increase the size of the thumbnails of the photos using the slider at the top right (circled here).

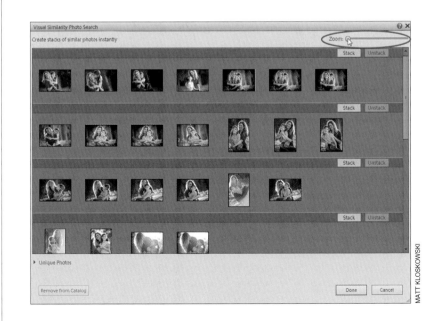

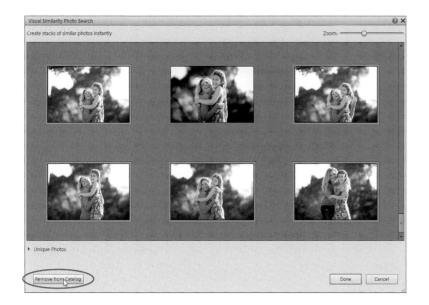

Step Three:

At this point, you've got two choices for what you can do with these suggested duplicate photos: First, you can look through the photos to find the best one from the series (which is why increasing the thumbnail size is important here), and then delete the rest, since you'll probably never use them. To do that, simply click on one of the photos (or Ctrl-click to select multiple ones) and click the Remove From Catalog button at the bottom left of the dialog (circled here). If you do that, Elements will give you the option to simply remove the photos from the catalog or remove them from the hard disk, as well. I also remove them from the hard disk altogether, since I don't need them anymore.

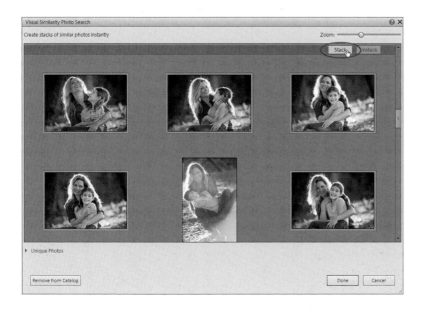

Step Four:

Your other option is to group the series of photos together in a stack. That way, when you're looking at them in the Organizer, you'll have fewer photos to look through since the entire series will be stacked. To stack the photos together, just click the Stack button above the right side of each group. Or, if you only want to stack certain photos from the group together, then select them first, and click the Stack button. When you're done stacking (or removing the photos from the catalog), just click the Done button in the lower-right corner to return to the Organizer.

Seeing an Instant Slide Show

Here's a scenario: You get back from a photo shoot and download your photos into the Organizer. You know you got some great shots and you just want to see them in a quick full-screen slide show. Nothing fancy. Just your photos, big onscreen. That's where the Full Screen option comes in. FYI...we've provided a video (on the book's companion website mentioned in the introduction) on how to show your work, where we look at how to create a rich, fully-featured slide show using another feature in Elements, but this one is a good trick to know.

Step One:
First, open the Organizer. Now press-and-hold the Ctrl (Mac: Command) key and click on each photo you want to appear in your slide show (if the photos are contiguous, you can click on the first photo, press-and-hold the Shift key, click on the last photo, and all the photos in between will be selected). Once the photos you want are selected, go to the View menu, and choose **Full Screen** from the pop-up menu (or just press **F11 [Mac: Command-F11]**).

Step Two:
This brings you into Full Screen view, where you'll see your photo large on-screen with a few pop-up palettes on the left and at the bottom of the image, and a filmstrip bar along the bottom of the screen. The Edit and Organize palettes on the left side will slide in and out of the screen as you move your cursor over them. They're basically there in case you want to make some quick edits or organizational changes as you see your photos large onscreen during the slide show.

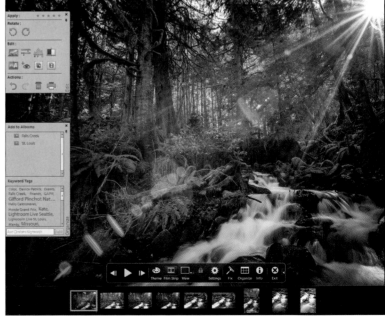

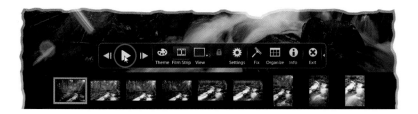

Step Three:

Your slide show won't start until you click the Play button in the control palette at the bottom of the image (or press the **Spacebar**, or **F5**). To stop your slide show (to pause), click the Pause button (the Play button toggles to the Pause button), and then to resume it, click Play/Pause again.

Step Four:

If you want to change the presentation options for your slide show, click the Settings button (the little gear) in the control palette. This brings up the Full Screen View Options dialog, where you choose the music for your slide show from the Background Music pop-up menu and how long each photo will appear onscreen from the Page Duration pop-up menu. It assumes you want any captions included, but you can turn that off by clicking on the Include Captions checkbox, and you can also have your slide show loop when it reaches the end by turning on the Repeat Slide Show checkbox. Click OK to close the dialog when you're done.

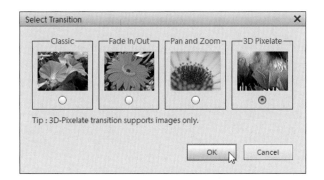

Step Five:

Okay, if you get anything out of this tutorial, this needs to be it: Toward the left end of the Control palette is the Theme button. When you click the button, it opens the Select Transition dialog. The first three are pretty self-explanatory (to me at least) but if you want to see a quick preview of them, just hover your cursor over the thumbnail and you'll see a quick animation of what the transition from slide to slide will look like. It's the last one, 3D Pixelate, that's crazy. You'll have to see it full screen to really appreciate it, so go ahead and click on the 3D Pixelate radio button, and then click OK.

(Continued)

Step Six:

Now click the Play button or hit the Spacebar or F5 key to start the slide show. Then watch in amazement as one photo transitions to another. I gotta warn you, though, if you've been drinking (alcohol, that is) it's really going to freak you out, and if you haven't been drinking, well, it's probably going to make you feel like you have been. After you kill an hour watching this (I'm serious, it's mesmerizing), go ahead and press the **Esc key** to get out of slide show mode or click on the Exit (X) button at the right end of the control palette to go back to Full Screen view.

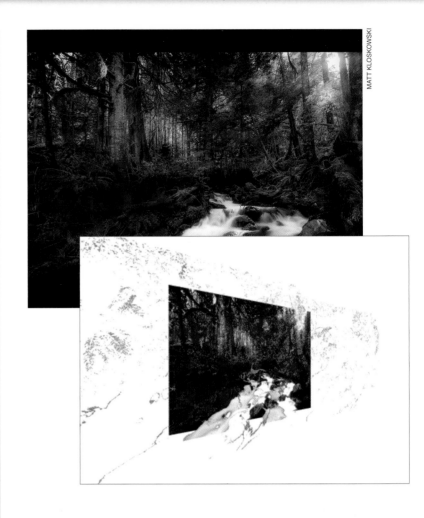

MATT KLOSKOWSKI

Step Seven:

There are extra controls at the right side of the control palette (click on the tiny right-facing arrow on the far right of the palette if you don't see them) for hiding/showing the Fix and Organize palettes, and opening the Information palette to add a caption or note. I usually keep them hidden and just display the slide show controls.

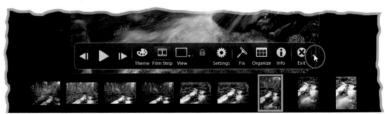

Step Eight:

To get out of Full Screen view and return to the Organizer, press the **Esc key** again on your keyboard, or click the Exit button in the control palette.

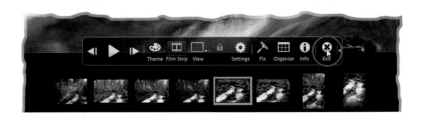

When you see a great photo opportunity do you take just one shot? Probably not, right? Most times you snap off a few (or 10, if you're like me), just to make sure you have several to choose from. But when you get back to your computer, you've got to make sure you do just that—choose the best ones and delete the rest. Because if you don't, you'll then have a bunch of similar-looking photos cluttering your screen, and you'll never really know which one to go to. Here's a way to help:

Comparing Photos

Step One:
First, open the Organizer. To compare (or review) photos side by side, press-and-hold the Ctrl (Mac: Command) key and click on all the photos you want to compare. Then, go under the View menu and choose **Full Screen** (or press **F11 [Mac: Command-F11]**). This brings up the same Full Screen view we saw in the last tutorial.

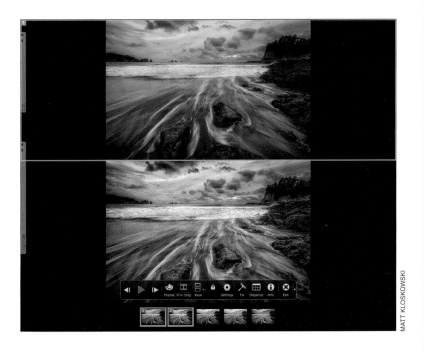

Step Two:
When Full Screen View mode opens, to place the first and second photos you selected side by side onscreen, click on the View button in the control palette and choose the side-by-side or above-and-below view. The first photo (on the top) has the number 1 in its upper left-hand corner, and the second photo (the one being compared) is noted as number 2 when clicked on.

MATT KLOSKOWSKI

(Continued)

Step Three:

Visually compare these two photos. You want the one that looks best to remain onscreen so you can compare other selected photos to it, right? To do that, click-and-drag anywhere on the "bad" photo, and a blue highlight will appear around that photo, indicating that this is the one that will change. In this example, I thought the first photo looked better, so I clicked-and-dragged on photo number 2 (on the bottom).

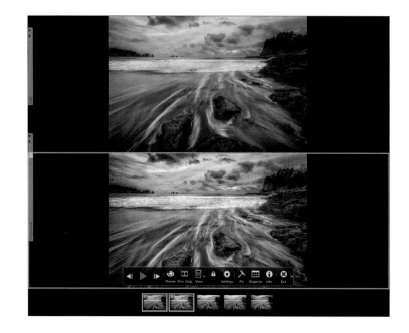

Step Four:

Now go to the control palette, click on the Next Media-Right Arrow button, and the photo on the bottom will be replaced with your next photo in that series. Again, review which of these two looks the best, then click-and-drag on the photo that looks worst (that way, you can replace it with another photo you want to compare). Click the Next Media-Right Arrow button to compare the next photo (and so on). To back up and review a previous photo, click the Previous Media-Left Arrow button in the control palette.

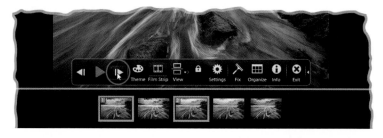

Step Five:

Besides this above-and-below mode, there's also an option that lets you see your photos side by side (which you might like for comparing photos in portrait orientation). To change to that mode, click on the View icon again to get the other view options, and from the pop-up menu that appears, choose the side-by-side view. Cycle through the images as you did before—just repeat Steps Three and Four until you find the photo you like best. When you're finished, press the **Esc key** on your keyboard or click the Exit (X) button in the control palette.

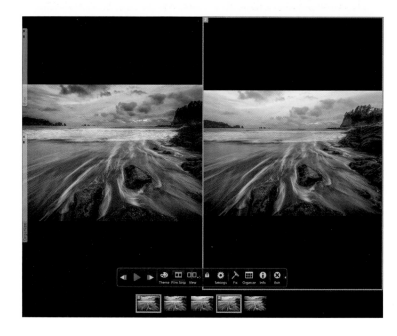

Reducing Clutter by Stacking Your Photos

I love stacks, because as much as I try to compare my photos and get rid of the ones that I have duplicates of, I inevitably wind up with several photos that look the same. Well, there's a feature called stacking and it works just like its real-world counterpart does—it stacks several photos on top of each other and you'll just see the top one. So if you have 20 shots of the same scene, you don't have to have all 20 cluttering up your Media Browser. Instead, you can have just one that represents all of them with the other 19 underneath it.

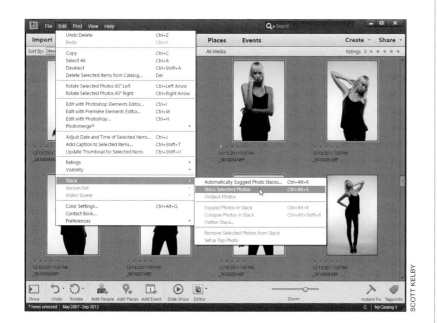

SCOTT KELBY

Step One:
With the Organizer open, press-and-hold the Ctrl (Mac: Command) key on your keyboard and click on all the photos you want to add to your stack (or if the images are contiguous, simply click on the first image in the series, press-and-hold the Shift key, and click on the last image in the series). Once they're all selected, go under the Organizer's Edit menu, under Stack, and choose **Stack Selected Photos** in the submenu.

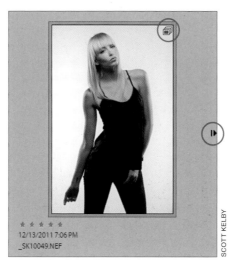

SCOTT KELBY

Step Two:
No dialog appears, it just happens—your other photos now are stacked behind the first photo you selected (think of it as multiple layers, and on each layer is a photo, stacked one on top of another). You'll know a photo thumbnail contains a stack because a Stack icon (which looks like a little stack of paper) will appear in the upper-right corner of your photo. You'll also see a right-facing arrow to the right of the image thumbnail.

(Continued)

Step Three:

Once your photos are stacked, you can view these photos at any time by clicking on the photo with the Stack icon, and then going under the Edit menu, under Stack, and choosing **Expand Photos in Stack**, or just clicking on the right-facing arrow to the right of the image thumbnail. This is like doing a Find, where all the photos in your stack will appear in the Media Browser within a gray shaded area so you can see them without unstacking them. Then, to collapse the stack, just click on the left-facing arrow that appears to the right of the last image thumbnail in the stack.

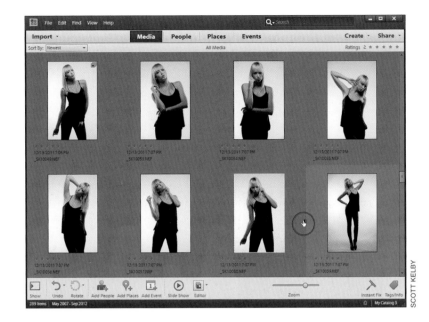

Step Four:

If you do want to unstack the photos, select the photo with the Stack icon in the Media Browser, then go under the Edit menu, under Stack, and choose **Unstack Photos**. If you decide you don't want to keep any of the photos in your stack, select the photo with the Stack icon in the Media Browser, go back under the Edit menu, under Stack, and choose **Flatten Stack**. It's like flattening your layers—all that's left is that first photo. However, when you choose to flatten, you will have the choice of deleting the photos from your hard disk or not.

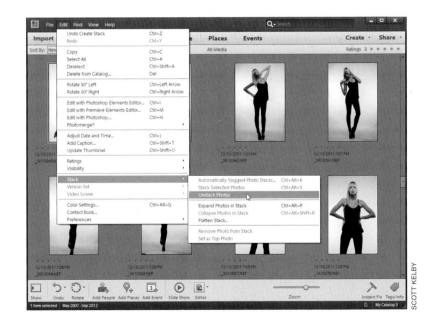

Places in the Organizer is new to Elements 11. It's a new way for you to view your photos based on where they were taken. It works great if you use your cell phone to take a lot of photos (which many people do nowadays), because your phone typically embeds location info right into the photo. But it doesn't stop there. If you have a photo that doesn't have the location info in it, it's really simple to add it after the fact, so you can see all your photos on a map.

Places: Viewing Your Photos on a Map

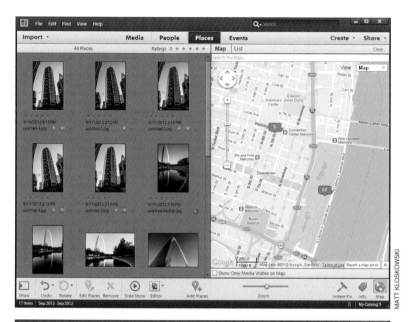

MATT KLOSKOWSKI

Step One:
In the Organizer, click on Places at the top of the window to switch to the Map view of your photos. In this example, I already have photos with location info in them, so Elements shows the photos on the left and shows where they were taken on the map on the right.

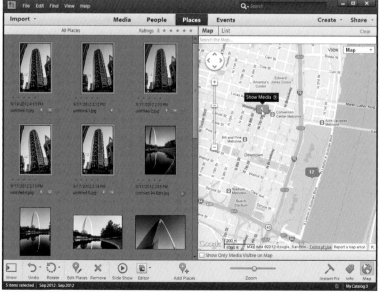

Step Two:
As you look at the map, you'll see exactly how many photos were taken in each location. If you click on one of the locations on the map, Elements will automatically select those photos in the Media Browser on the left side. If you want to see only the photos taken in that location in the Media Browser, choose **Show Media**, which pops up when you click on the location.

(Continued)

Step Three:

This is a really good way to create an album based on places you've visited, because Elements does a lot of the work for you. Just click on a location on the map and all of the photos will automatically be selected for you. Then, click on the Create New Album button (the green plus sign) at the top left of the window (if you don't see Albums, click on the Show icon at the bottom left of the window), choose **New Album**, give it a descriptive name, and you're ready to go.

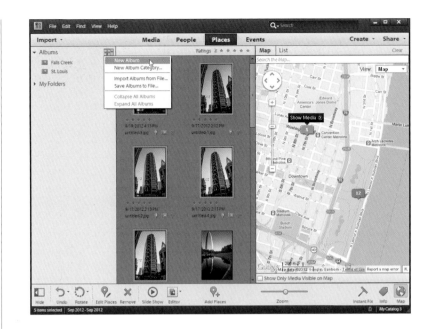

Step Four:

But what happens if you have photos without location or GPS info in them? Just click the Add Places icon in the middle of the taskbar at the bottom of the window (make sure none of your photos that are already on the map are selected). That opens the Add Places dialog, where you'll see all your photos with no GPS info associated with them in a filmstrip along the top.

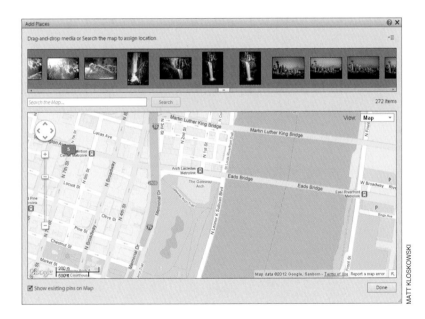

MATT KLOSKOWSKI

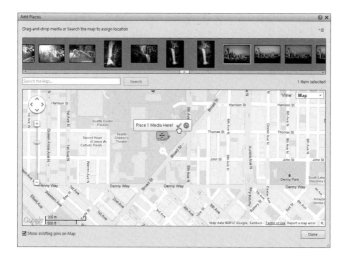

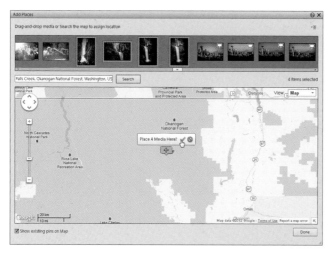

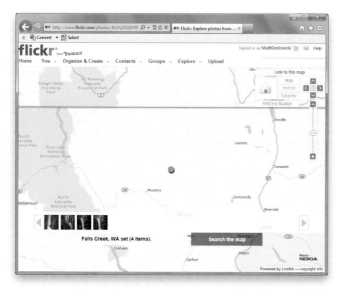

Step Five:

To associate a photo with a place, you can do one of two things: First, you could just drag-and-drop the photo from the filmstrip onto the map to add it to a location (or Ctrl-click [Mac: Command-click] on several photos to select them, then drag-and-drop all of them onto the map at once). When it appears on the map, just click the little green checkmark to confirm that that is indeed where you want it to go.

Step Six:

If you can't find the exact location on the map, then try searching for it. Select the photos you're going to add to that location, then type in the location in the Search the Map field below the left side of the filmstrip, and click the Search button. Depending on how specific you are in your location, you may get one or more suggestions that pop down from the Search the Map field. If so, just click on the correct one, and the location will show up on the map, with Elements asking if you want to place those photos in that location. Just click that little green checkmark to associate your selected photos with that location. You gotta love this stuff, huh?

Step Seven:

What's really cool is that now that you have GPS info associated with your photos, any time you share them on places like Flickr or Facebook (or any other photo sharing service that supports GPS info), your locations will automatically travel along with your images, so you won't have to add the locations again on each site.

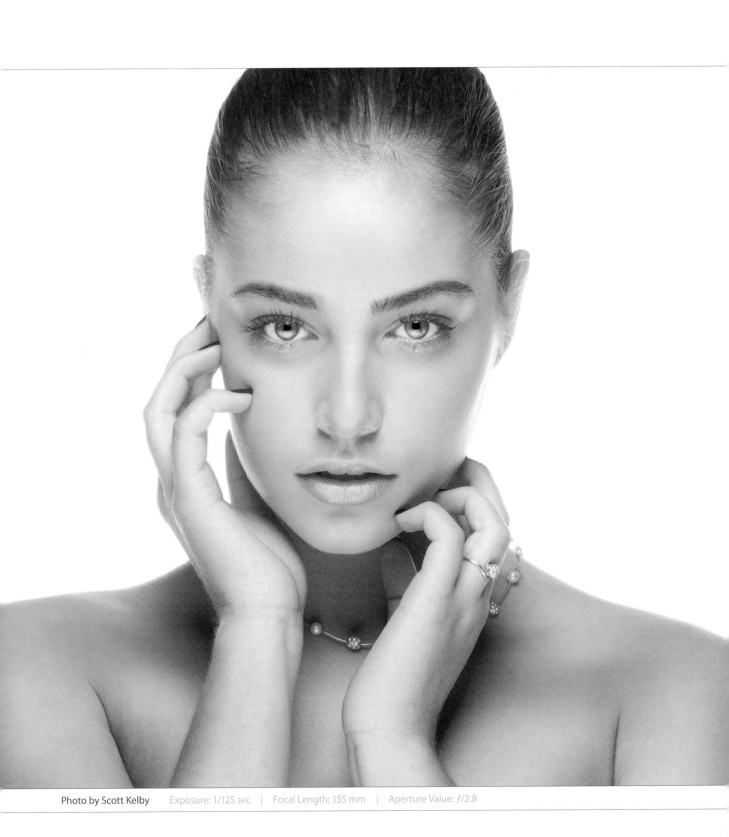

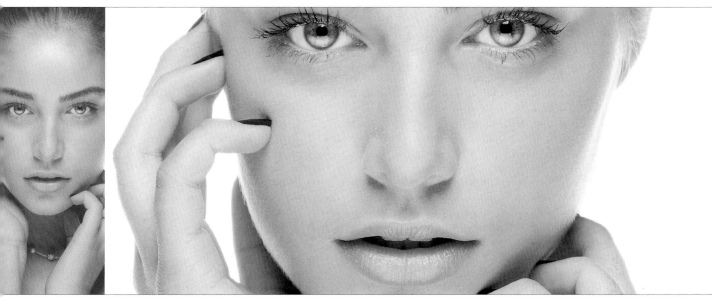

RAW JUSTICE
processing your images using camera raw

When I searched The Internet Movie Database (IMDb) for movies or TV shows containing the word "Raw," I was pleasantly surprised to find out just how many choices I actually had. However, I went with the 1994 movie *Raw Justice*, but I don't want you to think for one minute that I was influenced in any way by the fact that the star of the movie was Pamela Anderson. That would be incredibly shallow of me. Like any serious movie buff, I was drawn to this movie by what drew most of the audience to this movie: actor Robert Hays (who could forget his role in 2007's *Nicky's Birthday Camera* or the Michael Tuchner–directed film *Trenchcoat*?). Of course, the fact that Stacey Keach was in the movie was just the icing on the cake, but everybody knows the real draw of this flick clearly was Hays. However, what I found most puzzling was this: in the movie poster, Pamela Anderson totally dominates the poster with a large, full-color, ¾-length pose of her wearing a skimpy black dress, thigh-high boots, and holding a pistol at her side, but yet the other actors appear only as tiny black-and-white, backscreened head-shots. I have to admit, this really puzzles me, because while Pamela Anderson is a fine actress—one of the best, in fact—I feel, on some level, they were trying to fool you into watching a movie thinking it was about Pamela Anderson's acting, when in fact it was really about the acting eye candy that is Hays. This is called "bait and switch" (though you probably are more familiar with the terms "tuck and roll" or perhaps "Bartles & Jaymes"). Anyway, I think, while "Raw Justice" makes a great title for a chapter on processing your images in Camera Raw, there is no real justice in that this finely crafted classic of modern cinematography wound up going straight to DVD.

Opening Your Photos into Camera Raw

Although Adobe Camera Raw was created to process photos taken in your camera's RAW format, it's not just for RAW photos, because you can process your JPEG, TIFF, and PSD photos in Camera Raw, as well. So even though your JPEG, TIFF, and PSD photos won't have all of the advantages of RAW photos, at least you'll have all of the intuitive controls Camera Raw brings to the table.

Step One:

We'll start with the simplest thing first: opening a RAW photo from the Organizer. If you click on a RAW photo to select it in the Organizer, then click on the down-facing arrow to the right of the Editor icon (on the taskbar at the bottom of the window) and choose **Photo Editor** from the pop-up menu, it automatically takes the photo over to the Elements Editor and opens it in Camera Raw.

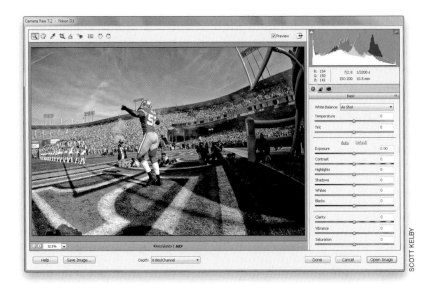

Step Two:

To open more than one RAW photo at a time, go to the Organizer, Ctrl-click (Mac: Command-click) on all the photos you want to open, then choose an option from the Editor icon's pop-up menu (as shown here, or just press **Ctrl-I [Mac: Command-I]**). It follows the same scheme—it takes them over to the Editor and opens them in Camera Raw. On the left side of the Camera Raw dialog, you can see a filmstrip with all of the photos you selected.

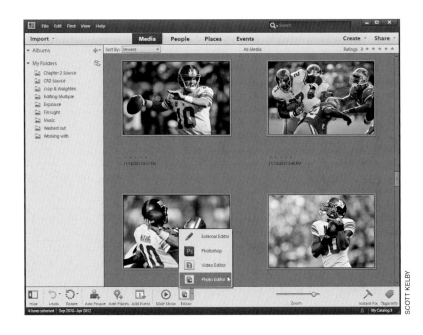

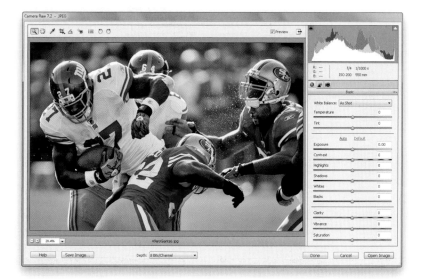

Step Three:

Okay, so opening RAW photos is pretty much a no-brainer, but what if you want to open a JPEG, TIFF, or PSD in Camera Raw? Go under the Editor's File menu and choose **Open As (Mac: Open)**. In the Open As (Mac: Open) dialog, navigate to the photo you want to open and click on it once. When you click on a JPEG, TIFF, or PSD, if you choose JPEG, TIFF, or Photoshop in the Open As (Mac: Format) pop-up menu at the bottom, it will open in the Elements Editor like any other JPEG, TIFF, or PSD. So to open this JPEG, TIFF, or PSD in Camera Raw instead, you have to choose **Camera Raw** from the Open As pop-up menu (as shown here).

Step Four:

When you click the Open button, that JPEG, TIFF, or PSD is opened in the Camera Raw interface, as shown here (notice how JPEG appears up in the title bar, just to the right of Camera Raw 7.2?). *Note:* When you make adjustments to a JPEG, TIFF, or PSD in Camera Raw and you click either the Open Image button (to open the adjusted photo in Elements) or the Done button (to save the edits you made in Camera Raw), unlike when editing RAW photos, you are now actually affecting the pixels of the original photo. Of course, there is a Cancel button in Camera Raw and even if you open the photo in Elements, if you don't save your changes, the original photo remains untouched. Also, if you have a layered PSD file open in Camera Raw and you click the Open Image button, Elements will flatten your layers as it opens the photo.

Miss the JPEG Look? Try Applying a Camera Profile

If you've ever looked at a JPEG photo on the LCD screen on the back of your digital camera, and then wondered why your RAW image doesn't look as good, it's because your camera adds color correction, sharpening, contrast, etc., to your JPEG images while they're still in the camera. But when you choose to shoot in RAW, you're telling the camera, "Don't do all that processing—just leave it raw and untouched, and I'll process it myself." But, if you'd like that JPEG-processed look as a starting place for your RAW photo editing, you can use Camera Raw's Camera Profile feature to get you close.

Step One:

As I mentioned above, when you shoot in RAW, you're telling the camera to pretty much leave the photo alone, and you'll do all the processing yourself using Camera Raw. Each camera has its own brand of RAW, so Adobe Camera Raw applies a Camera Profile based on the camera that took the shot (it reads the embedded EXIF data, so it knows which camera you used). Anyway, if you click on the Camera Calibration icon (the icon on the right above the right-side Panel area), you'll see the built-in default Camera Profile (Adobe Standard) used to interpret your RAW photo.

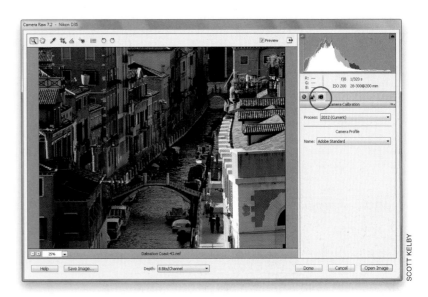

Step Two:

If you click-and-hold on the Name pop-up menu at the top of the panel, a menu pops up with a list of profiles for the camera you took the shot with (as seen here, for images taken with a Nikon digital camera). Adobe recommends that you start by choosing **Camera Standard** (as shown here) to see how that looks to you.

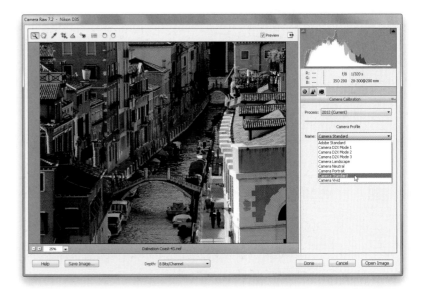

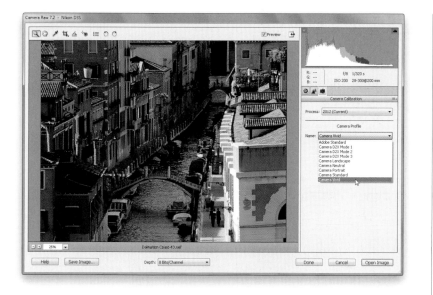

Step Three:

Depending on the individual photo you're editing, Camera Standard might not be the right choice, but as the photographer, this is a call you have to make (in other words, it's up to you to choose which one looks best to you). I usually wind up using either Camera Standard, Camera Landscape, or Camera Vivid for images taken with a Nikon camera, because I think Landscape and Vivid look the most like the JPEGs I see on the back of my camera. But again, if you're not shooting Nikon, Landscape or Vivid won't be one of the available choices (Nikons have eight picture styles and Canons have five). If you don't shoot Canon or Nikon, then you'll only have Adobe Standard, and possibly Camera Standard or one other, to choose from, but you can create your own custom profiles using Adobe's free DNG Profile Editor utility, available from Adobe at http://labs.adobe.com.

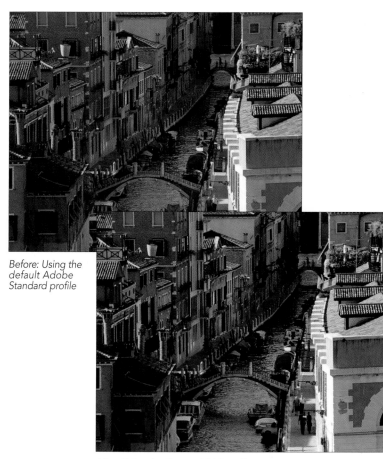

Before: Using the default Adobe Standard profile

After: Using the Camera Vivid profile

Step Four:

Here's a before/after with only one thing done to this photo: I chose Camera Vivid (as shown in the pop-up menu in Step Three). Again, this is designed to replicate color looks you could have chosen in the camera, so if you want to have Camera Raw give you a similar look as a starting point, this is how it's done. Also, since Camera Raw allows you to open more than one image at a time (in fact, you can open hundreds at a time), you could open a few hundred images, then click the Select All button that will appear at the top-left corner of the window, change the camera profile for the first-selected image, and then all the other images will have that same profile automatically applied. Now, you can just click the Done button.

Updating to the Latest Camera Raw Editing Features (Not for New Users)

Okay, this is only for those who have been using Camera Raw in previous versions of Elements, because if this is the first time you'll be using it, this won't affect you at all, so you can skip this. Here's why: in Elements 11, Adobe dramatically improved the math and controls for the Basic panel, so if you have RAW images you edited in earlier versions of Camera Raw, when you open them in Elements 11's updated version of Camera Raw, you'll have the choice of keeping the old look (and old controls) or updating to the new, vastly improved Basic panel controls (called the 2012 process version).

Step One:
Even before you bought this book, you probably heard that Camera Raw now has a different set of sliders that offer more powerful, and overall just better, control over your images. But, when you open a RAW image in Elements 11's Camera Raw that you previously edited in an earlier version of Camera Raw, you might be surprised to see that all the sliders look exactly the same as they did before. That's because Adobe didn't want to change the way your already-processed photo looks without your permission, so at this point, your image looks the same (and so do Camera Raw's sliders—the Fill Light and Recovery sliders are still there).

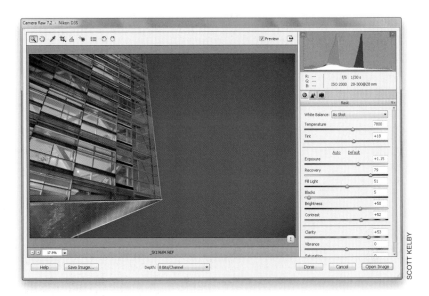

Step Two:
However, the processing technology being used on your photo at this point is actually out-of-date. If fact, it's either old technology from 2010, or it's actually processing technology from back in 2003. Adobe calls these "process versions"—if you go to the Camera Calibration panel and click on the Process pop-up menu (as shown here), you can choose from the three different versions (the 2010 version improved the sharpening and noise reduction quality pretty dramatically).

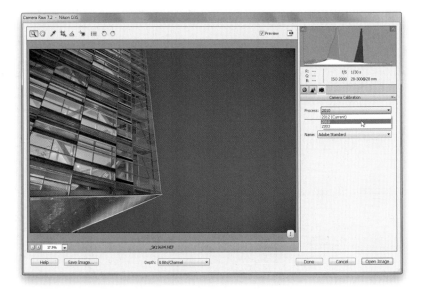

SCOTT KELBY

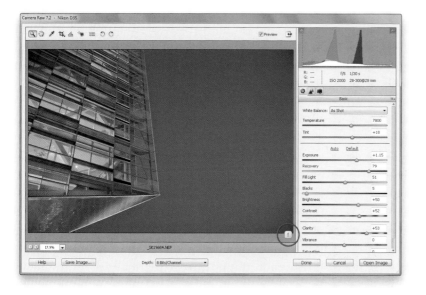

Step Three:

Of course, you could choose the 2012 (Current) process version from that pop-up menu and your image will be updated to the current processing power, and all the new, improved sliders will appear in the Basic panel. But, I'd only do that if I were charging by the hour, because there's a much quicker way to do it. When you open an image edited in a previous version of Camera Raw, you'll see a warning icon in the bottom-right corner of the Preview area (actually, it's an exclamation point, shown circled here in red). To instantly update to the latest version, just click directly on that exclamation point and it's updated.

TIP: Getting Fill Light & Recovery Back

If you ever decide that you just can't live without the old Fill Light and/or Recovery sliders, just go to the Camera Calibration panel and from the Process pop-up menu up top, choose **2010**, and they instantly reappear (but you'll be using the old processing technology now, as well).

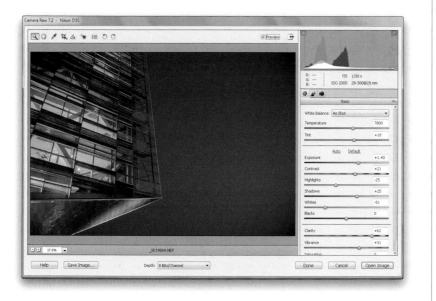

Step Four:

Now your image is updated to the latest processing technology, and it's been my experience that just by converting to the new process version, my photos look instantly better (well, in the vast majority of cases—in some cases, they look the same, but I've never had one I thought looked worse). However, if you didn't apply any Basic panel adjustments to your image previously, there's nothing for it really to update, so you're not going to notice a change when you update. In this image, once I updated to the 2012 process version, I was able to increase the Clarity more (without creating halos), and I bumped up the Exposure a bit, too.

The Essential Adjustments: White Balance

If you've ever taken a photo indoors, chances are the photo came out with kind of a yellowish tint. Unless, of course, you took the shot in an office, and then it probably had a green tint. Even if you just took a shot of somebody in a shadow, the whole photo probably looked like it had a blue tint. Those are white balance problems. If you've properly set your white balance in the camera, you won't see these distracting tints (the photos will just look normal), but most people shoot with their cameras set to Auto White Balance, and well…don't worry, we can fix it really easily in Camera Raw.

Step One:
On the right side of the Camera Raw window, there's a section for adjusting the white balance. Think of this as "the place we go to get rid of yellow, blue, or green tints that appear on photos." There are three ways to correct this, and we'll start with choosing a new white balance from the White Balance pop-up menu. By default, Camera Raw displays your photo using your camera's white balance setting, called As Shot. Here, I had been shooting indoors under regular lighting, so my white balance had been set to Tungsten, but then I went into the studio and didn't change my white balance, so the first few shots came out with a heavy bluish tint (as seen here—yeech!).

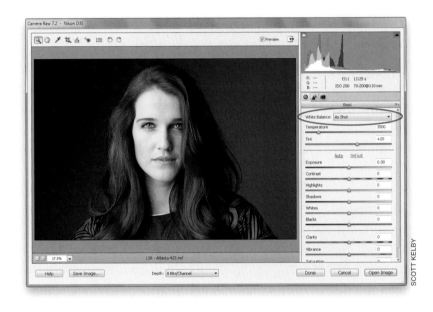

Step Two:
To change the white balance, click on the White Balance pop-up menu and choose a preset. Just choose the preset that most closely matches what the lighting situation was when you originally took the photo. Here, I tried each preset and Flash seemed to look best—it removed the bluish tint and made the background gray again. *Note:* You will only get this complete list of white balance presets (Cloudy, Shade, etc.) when working with RAW images. If you open a JPEG, TIFF, or PSD in Camera Raw, your only preset choice (besides As Shot and creating a custom white balance) is Auto.

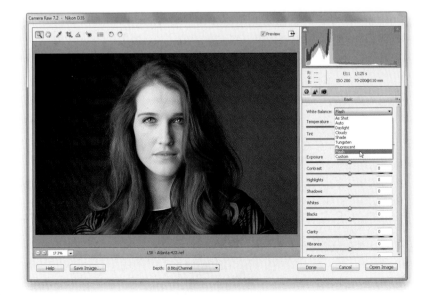

SCOTT KELBY

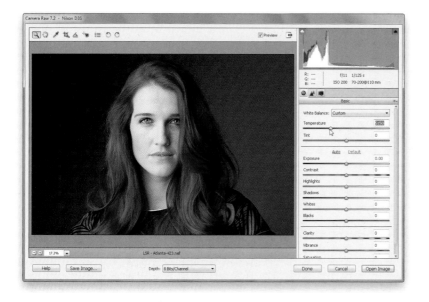

Step Three:

Although the Flash setting is the best of the built-in presets here, if you don't think it's right on the money, then you can simply use it as a starting point (hey, at least it gets you in the ballpark, right?). So, I would choose Flash first, and if I thought this made her a bit too yellow, I would then drag the Temperature slider to the left (toward the blue side of the slider) to cool the photo back down just a little bit. In this example, the Flash preset was close, but made it a little too yellow, so I dragged the Temperature slider a little bit toward blue, to 5150 (as shown here).

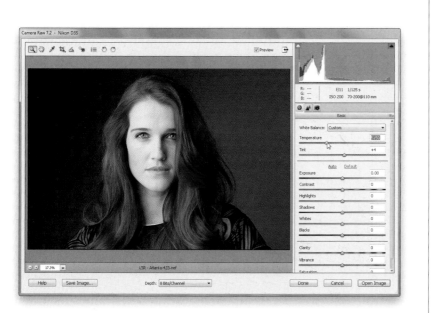

Step Four:

The second method of setting your white balance is to use just the Temperature and Tint sliders (although most of the time you'll only use the Temperature slider, as most of your problems will be too much [or too little] yellow or blue). The sliders themselves give you a clue on which way to drag (on the Temperature slider, blue is on the left and it slowly transitions over to yellow). This makes getting the color you want so much easier—just drag in the direction of the color you want. By the way, when you adjust either of these sliders, your White Balance pop-up menu changes to Custom (as shown).

(Continued)

Step Five:

The third method, using the White Balance tool, is perhaps the most accurate because it takes a white balance reading from the photo itself. You just click on the White Balance tool **(I)** in the toolbar at the top left (it's circled in red here), and then click it on something in your photo that's supposed to be a light gray (that's right—you properly set the white balance by clicking on something that's light gray). So, take the tool and click it once on the background to the right of her hair (as shown here) and it sets the white balance for you. If you don't like how it looks (maybe it's still too blue), then just click on a different light gray area until it looks good to you. (It looked a little dark here, so I bumped up the Exposure a little, too.)

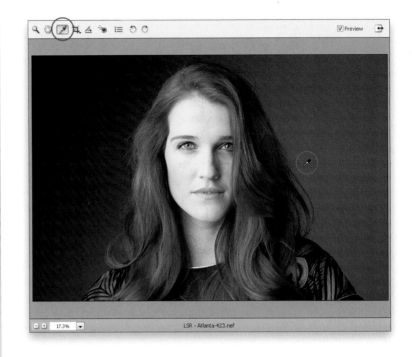

Step Six:

Now, here's the thing: although this can give you a perfectly accurate white balance, it doesn't mean that it will look good (for example, people usually look better with a slightly warm white balance). White balance is a creative decision, and the most important thing is that your photo looks good to you. So don't get caught up in that "I don't like the way the white balance looks, but I know it's accurate" thing that sucks some people in—set your white balance so it looks right to you. You are the bottom line. You're the photographer. It's your photo, so make it look its best. Accurate is not another word for good. Okay, I'm off the soapbox, and it's time for a tip: Want to quickly reset your white balance to the As Shot setting? Just double-click on the White Balance tool up in the toolbar (as shown here).

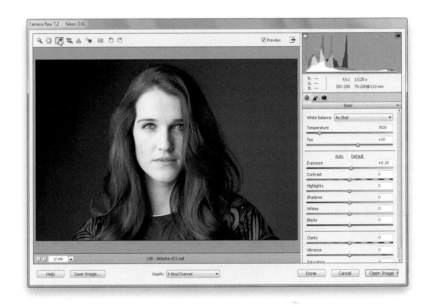

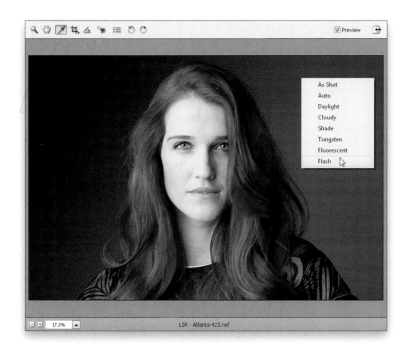

Step Seven:

One last thing: once you have the White Balance tool, if you Right-click within your photo, a White Balance preset pop-up menu appears under your cursor (as shown here), so you can quickly choose a preset.

Step Eight:

Here's a before/after so you can see what a difference setting a proper white balance makes (by the way, you can see a quick before/after of your white balance edit by pressing **P** on your keyboard to toggle the Preview on/off).

TIP: Using a Gray Card

To help you find that neutral light gray color in your images, we've included an 18% gray card for you in the back of this book (it's perforated so you can tear it out). Just put this card into your scene (or have your subject hold it), take the shot, and when you open the image in Camera Raw, click the White Balance tool on the card to instantly set your white balance.

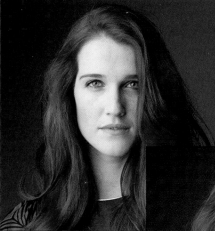

Before: The As Shot white balance has a bluish tint

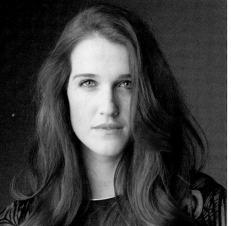

After: With one click of the White Balance tool, everything comes together

The Essential Adjustments: Exposure

The next thing I fix (after adjusting the white balance) is the photo's exposure. Now, some might argue that this is the most essential adjustment of them all, but if your photo looks way too blue, nobody will notice if the photo's underexposed by a third of a stop, so I fix the white balance first, then I worry about exposure. However, exposure in Camera Raw isn't just the Exposure slider. It's actually five sliders: Exposure (midtones), Blacks (deep shadows), Shadows (regular shadows), Highlights (well-named), and Whites (extreme highlights).

Step One:

I recommend (and so does Adobe) starting with the top tonal slider in the Basic panel (Exposure) and working your way down through the other sliders in order, which is a different workflow than in previous versions of Camera Raw, where it didn't matter too much which slider you moved when. However, in Elements 11, it works best if you start by getting the Exposure (midtones) set first, and then if things look kind of washed out, adding some Contrast (the Contrast slider in Elements 11 is way, way better than the one in previous versions, which I generally avoided). This photo, well, it's a mess. Taken in harsh, unflattering light, it needs some serious Camera Raw help.

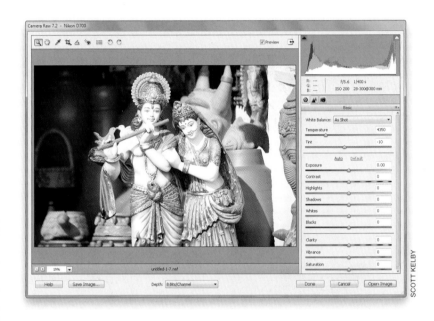

Step Two:

Start by adjusting the Exposure slider. This photo is way overexposed, so drag it to the left to darken the midtones and the overall exposure. Here, I dragged it over to –1.25 (it looks a lot better already), but the image is still kind of flat looking, and that's why your next step should be to adjust the contrast (by the way, although you can drag the Contrast slider to the left to make things less contrasty, I can't remember an occasion where I wanted my image to look more flat, so I don't drag to the left. Ever. But, hey, that's just me).

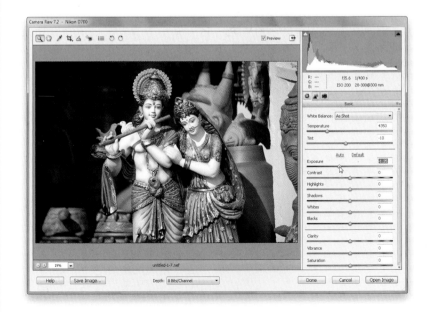

SCOTT KELBY

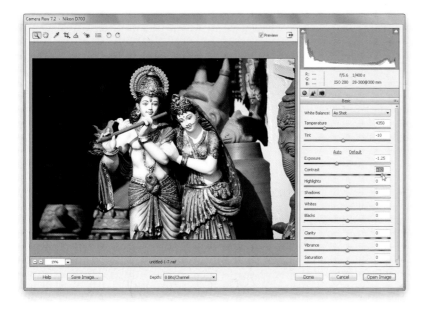

Step Three:

In previous versions of Camera Raw, when I saw an image looking flat like this one did back in Step Two, I would reach for the Blacks slider, but in Elements 11, now you increase the contrast using the Contrast slider, which makes the bright areas brighter and the dark areas darker (here, I dragged it to the right to +82, which helped deal with the flat, low-contrast look). These two steps—adjusting the Exposure and then the Contrast slider (if necessary)—should be your starting points every time. This top-down approach helps, because the other sliders build off this exposure foundation, and it will keep you from having to constantly keep tweaking slider after slider. So, think of these two as the foundation of your exposure, and the rest are kind of optional based on the image you're working on.

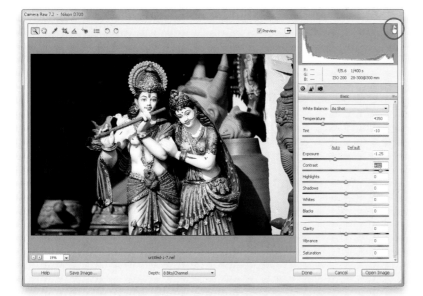

Step Four:

Before we go any further, increasing our contrast to where we wanted it created a highlight clipping problem (part of our photo got so bright that it won't have any detail in that area at all. It's blown out. If all that sounds bad, well, that's 'cause it is). Luckily, Camera Raw gives you a warning if you're clipping, in the upper-right corner of the histogram. See that triangle? That's the highlight clipping warning (although I just call it "the white triangle of death"; the one in the upper-left corner is the shadow clipping warning). Now, if you do see a white triangle, don't freak out. First, go up and click directly on that white triangle and the areas that are clipping will appear in red (look on her arm). We do this to find out if what's clipping is an area of important detail, or if it's like a tiny highlight on a chrome bumper or something meaningless in the background of your image.

(Continued)

Step Five:

If that red highlight shows over an area you feel has important detail (her arm and the other areas you could see clipping in the last step certainly seem important to me), go to the Highlights slider and drag it to the left until the red areas disappear (here, I dragged the Highlights slider to the left to –18). For those of you upgrading from an earlier version of Camera Raw, I kind of hesitate to say this replaces the Recovery slider, because there's more going on than just that, due to the way Adobe reworked the Exposure slider. Now when you adjust the Exposure slider, there's less chance of clipping than ever before, so it's kind of like the Exposure slider has some built-in Recovery power, too! That being said, I still look to the Highlights slider to recover clipped highlights first, and then if that doesn't do the trick, I try lowering the Exposure amount, but I rarely have to do that.

TIP: The Color Warning Triangles

If you see a red, yellow, magenta, etc., highlight or shadow clipping warning triangle (rather than white), it's not great, but it's not nearly as bad as white. It means you're clipping just that one color channel (and there's still detail in the other channels).

Step Six:

The next slider down, Shadows, is another one you only use if there's a problem (just like the Highlights slider), and in this case, the problem is we can't see any detail in the upper-left corner of the photo. We can see that something's there, but we can't see exactly what. That's when you reach for the Shadows slider—drag it to the right to brighten the shadows (like I did here, where I dragged it over to +87) and look how you can now see the pottery in the background.

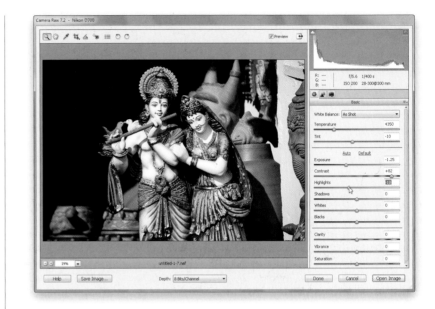

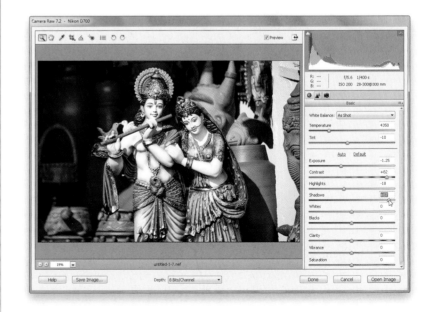

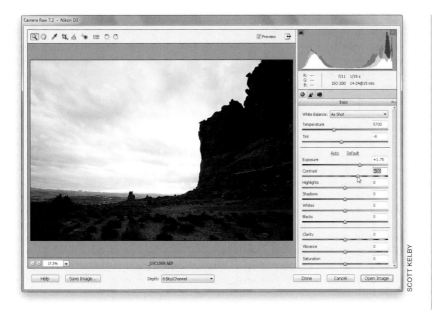

SCOTT KELBY

Step Seven:

Before we leave the Shadows slider, we need to switch to another image for just a moment (we'll come back to the other image shortly), because I want to point out that one of the most common times you'll use the Shadows slider is when your subject is backlit like this one, where the sky is pretty well exposed, but the foreground is really dark. When I was standing there, of course, my eye compensated perfectly for the two vastly different exposures, but our cameras still aren't as sophisticated as the human eye, so we get shots that look like this. In previous versions of Camera Raw, I'd reach for the Fill Light slider to fix this problem, but it created its own problems (if you bumped it way up, your image started to look a bit HDR-like, but not in a good way). Now, in Elements 11, the Shadows slider works with the Exposure slider to give you better results than the old Fill Light slider alone could give. Start by bumping up the Exposure, and then the Contrast (the Shadows slider will work much better when you tweak these first).

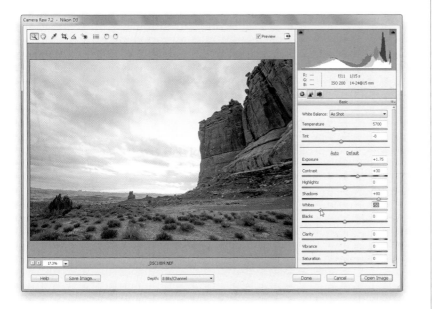

Step Eight:

Now, drag the Shadows slider way over to the right to open up those rocks and the foreground, so the whole image looks more balanced (here, I dragged over to +80). That overprocessed Fill Light look from previous versions of Camera Raw is gone. Instead, we have a much more natural-looking edit. Believe it or not, bumping the Shadows up this much created some highlight clipping (I saw the white highlight warning triangle appear in the upper-right corner), but that's an easy fix—I just dragged the Whites slider to the left (to –58, as shown here) to reduce the brightest highlights. Now we can jump back to our original image.

(Continued)

Step Nine:

The last two essential exposure sliders are the Whites and Blacks. If you're used to working with Levels in Elements, you'll totally get these, because they're like setting your highlight and shadow points (or your white and black points). Most of the time, if I use the Whites slider (which controls the brightest highlights), I find myself dragging it to the right to make sure the whites are nice and bright white (and not light gray). But in this instance, I was using the Whites slider to pull the whites back a bit (to help hide the fact that it was shot in harsh, direct daylight), so I dragged it to the left (to darken the whites) to –28. I also increased the deepest shadows by dragging the Blacks slider to the left just a little bit (here, I dragged over to –10). I still use this slider if, near the end of the editing process, I think the color needs more oomph, as this helps the colors look saturated and less washed out. Here's a before/after, but I did add two last finishing touches, which were to increase the Clarity a little (more on this coming up on page 66) and I increased the Vibrance amount a bit. Again, I recommend doing all of this in a top-to-bottom order, but just understand that not every image will need an adjustment to the Highlights and Shadows—only mess with those if you have a problem in those areas. Otherwise, skip 'em.

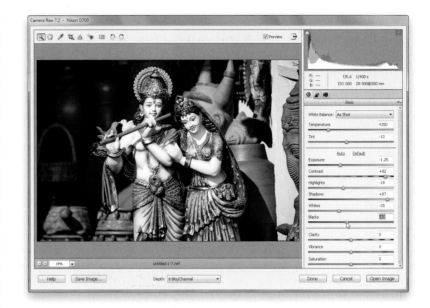

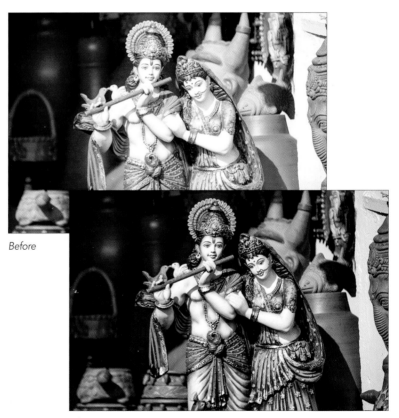

Before

After

If you're not quite comfortable with manually adjusting each image, Camera Raw does come with a one-click Auto function, which takes a stab at correcting the overall exposure of your image (including contrast, shadows, highlights, etc.), and at this point in Camera Raw's evolution, it's really not that bad. If you like the results, you can set up Camera Raw's preferences so every photo, upon opening in Camera Raw, will be auto adjusted using that same feature.

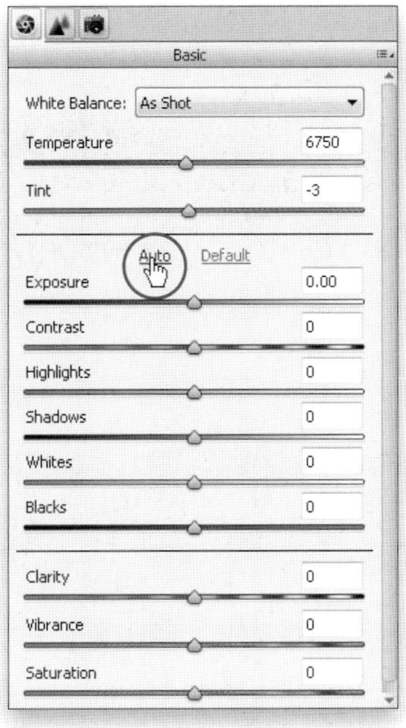

Letting Camera Raw Auto Correct Your Photos

Step One:
Once you have an image open in Camera Raw, you can have Camera Raw take a stab at setting the overall exposure (using the controls in the Basic panel) for you by clicking on the Auto button (shown circled in red here). In older versions of Camera Raw, this Auto correction feature was…well…let's just say it was less than stellar, but it has gotten much better since then, and now it does a somewhat decent job (especially if you're stuck and not sure what to do), so click on it and see how it looks. If it doesn't look good, no sweat—just press **Ctrl-Z (Mac: Command-Z)** to Undo.

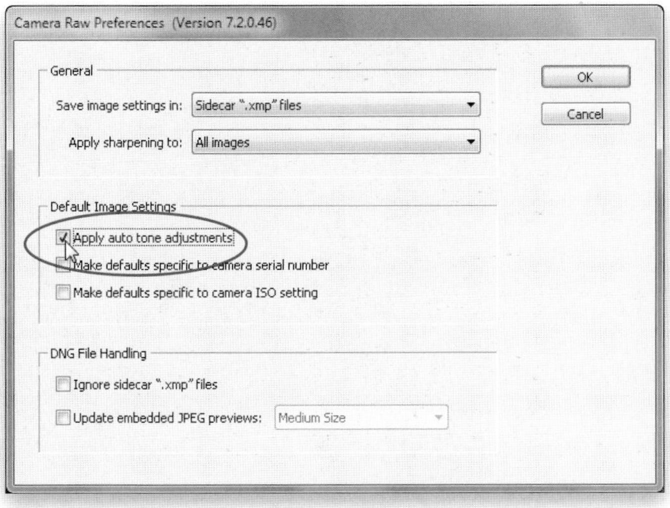

Step Two:
You can set up Camera Raw so it automatically performs an Auto Tone adjustment each time you open a photo—just click on the Preferences icon up in Camera Raw's toolbar (it's the third icon from the right), and when the dialog appears, turn on the checkbox for Apply Auto Tone Adjustments (shown circled here), then click OK. Now, Camera Raw will evaluate each image and try to correct it. If you don't like its tonal corrections, then you can just click on the Default button, which appears to the right of the Auto button (the Auto button will be grayed out because it has already been applied).

Adding Punch to Your Images with Clarity

This is one of my favorite features in Camera Raw, and whenever I show it in a class, it never fails to get "Ooohhs" and "Ahhhhs." I think it's because it's just one simple slider, yet it does so much to add "snap" to your image. The Clarity slider (which is well-named) basically increases the midtone contrast in a way that gives your photo more punch and impact, without actually sharpening the image. I add lots of Clarity anytime I want to enhance the texture in an image, and it works great on everything from landscapes to cityscapes, from travel photos to portraits of men—anything where emphasizing texture would look good.

Step One:
The Clarity slider is found in the bottom section of the Basic panel in Camera Raw, right above the Vibrance and Saturation sliders. (Although its official name is Clarity, I heard that at one point Adobe engineers considered naming it "Punch" instead, as they felt using it added punch to the image.) To clearly see the effects of Clarity, first zoom in to a 100% view by double-clicking on the Zoom tool up in the toolbar (it looks like a magnifying glass). In the example shown here, I only zoomed to 25% so you could see more of the image.

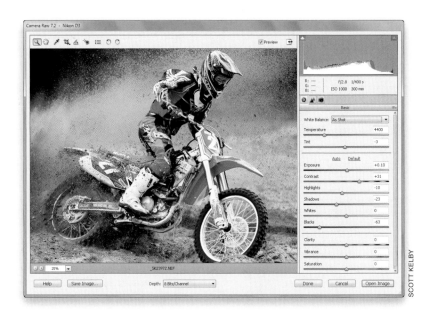

Step Two:
Using the Clarity control couldn't be easier—drag the slider to the right to increase the amount of punch (midtone contrast) in your image (compare the top and bottom images shown here). Here, I dragged it over to +100, which is something you really couldn't get away with in earlier versions of Camera Raw (you'd get horrible halos around everything), but in Elements 11, you can crank that puppy up and it looks awesome! Any image I edit where I want to emphasize the texture (landscapes, cityscapes, sports photos, etc.) gets between +25 and +50 Clarity, but now you can crank it up even higher in most cases (as seen here).

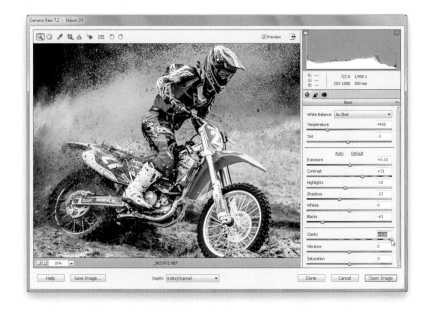

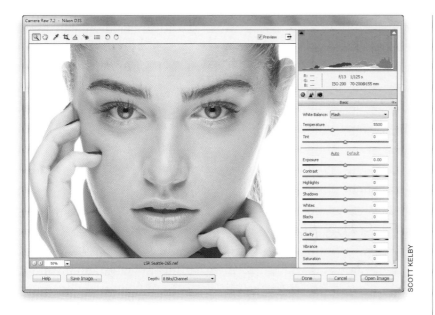

Step Three:
Of course, there are subjects where you don't want to emphasize texture (like women and children), and in those cases, I don't apply any positive Clarity. However, you can also use the Clarity control in reverse—to soften skin. This is called adding negative Clarity, meaning you can apply less than 0 (zero) to reduce the midtone contrast, which gives you a softening effect. Here's an original image without any negative Clarity applied.

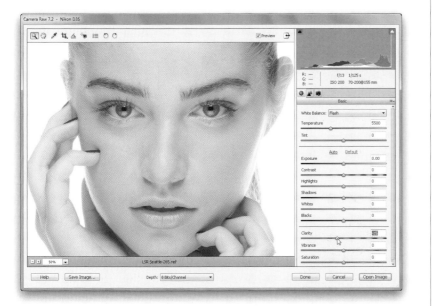

Step Four:
Now drag the Clarity slider to the left (which gives you a negative amount of Clarity), and take a look at how much softer our subject's skin looks. Everything else in the image looks softer too, so it's an overall softening, but in the chapter on retouching (Chapter 8), you'll learn how to apply softening just to your subject's skin, while leaving the rest of the image sharp.

Making Your Colors More Vibrant

Besides the White Balance control, there's only one other adjustment for color that you want to use to make your colors more vibrant, and that's the Vibrance slider. Rather than making all your colors more saturated (which is what the Saturation slider does), the Vibrance slider is smarter—it affects the least saturated colors the most, it affects the already saturated colors the least, and it does its darndest to avoid flesh tones as much as possible. It's one very savvy slider, and since it came around, I avoid the Saturation slider at all costs.

Step One:

Here's an image where the colors are kind of flat and dull. If I used the Saturation slider, every color in the image would get the same amount of saturation, so I do my best to stay away from it (in fact, the only time I use the Saturation slider anymore is when I'm removing color to create a color tint effect or a black-and-white conversion).

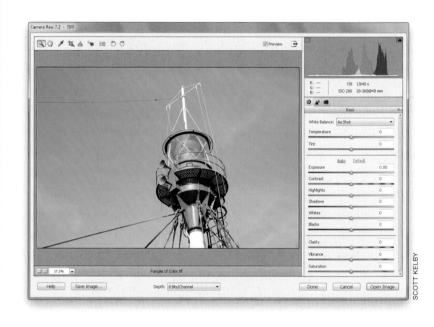

Step Two:

Drag the Vibrance slider to the right, and you'll notice the colors become more vibrant (it's a well-named slider), but without the color becoming cartoonish, which is typical of what the Saturation slider would do. You'll notice in the image here that the color isn't "over the top" but rather subtle, and maybe that's what I like best about it.

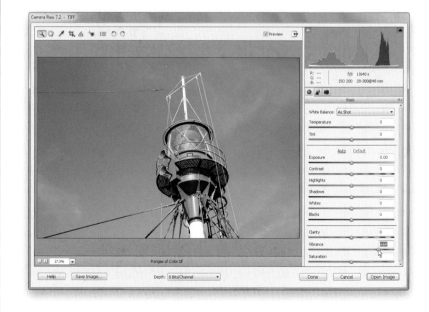

SCOTT KELBY

There are some distinct advantages to cropping your photo in Camera Raw, rather than in Elements itself, and perhaps the #1 benefit is that you can return to Camera Raw later and return to the uncropped image. (Here's one difference in how Camera Raw handles RAW photos vs. JPEG, TIFF, and PSD photos: this "return to Camera Raw later and return to the uncropped image" holds true even for them, as long as you haven't overwritten the original JPEG, TIFF, or PSD file. To avoid overwriting, when you save the JPEG, TIFF, or PSD, in Elements, change the filename.)

Cropping and Straightening

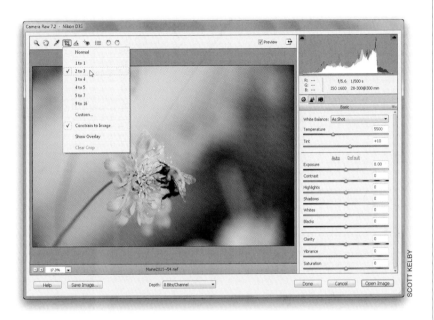

Step One:
The fourth tool in Camera Raw's toolbar is the Crop tool. By default, it pretty much works like the Crop tool in Elements (you click-and-drag it out around the area you want to keep), but it does offer some features that Elements doesn't—like access to a list of preset cropping ratios. To get them, click-and-hold on the Crop tool and a pop-up menu will appear (as shown here). The Normal setting gives you the standard drag-it-where-you-want-it cropping. However, if you choose one of the cropping presets, then your cropping is constrained to a specific ratio. For example, choose the 2-to-3 ratio, click-and-drag it out, and you'll see that it keeps the same aspect ratio as your original uncropped photo.

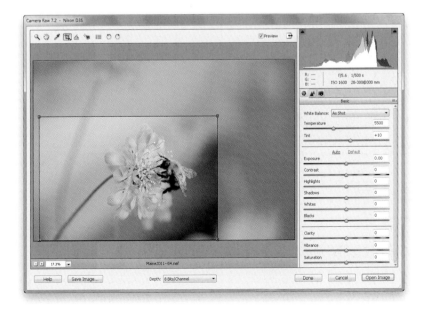

Step Two:
Here's the 2-to-3-ratio cropping border dragged out over my image. The area that will be cropped away appears dimmed, and the clear area inside the cropping border is how your final cropped photo will appear. If you reopen this RAW photo later and click on the Crop tool, the cropping border will still be visible onscreen, so you can move it, resize it, or remove it altogether by simply pressing the **Esc key** or the **Backspace (Mac: Delete) key** on your keyboard (or by choosing **Clear Crop** from the Crop tool's pop-up menu).

(Continued)

Step Three:

If you want your photo cropped to an exact size (like 8x10", 13x19", etc.), choose **Custom** from the Crop tool's pop-up menu. You can choose to crop by pixels, inches, centimeters, or a custom ratio. In our example, we're going to create a custom crop so our cropped photo winds up being exactly 8x10", so choose **Inches** from the pop-up menu (as shown here), then type in your custom size. Click OK, click-and-drag out the Crop tool, and the area inside your cropping border will be exactly 8x10".

Step Four:

Once you click on the Open Image button in Camera Raw, the image is cropped to your specs and opened in the Editor (as shown here). If, instead, you click on the Done button, Camera Raw closes and your photo is untouched, but it keeps your cropping border in position for the future.

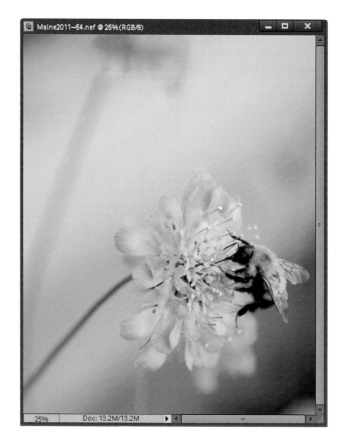

Step Five:

If you save a cropped JPEG, TIFF, or PSD photo out of Camera Raw (by clicking on the Save Image button on the bottom left of the Camera Raw window), the only option is to save it as a DNG (Digital Negative) file. DNG files open in Camera Raw, so by doing this, you can bring back those cropped areas if you decide to change the crop. Your original JPEG, TIFF, or PSD will also keep the cropping border if you simply click the Done button, or once you open the cropped photo in the Editor, save it from there with a new filename. Just open the original photo in Camera Raw again, and click on the Crop tool to see the border.

Step Six:

If you have a number of similar photos you need to crop the same way, you're going to love this: First, select all the photos you want to crop (either in the Organizer or on your computer), then open them all in Camera Raw. When you open multiple photos, they appear in a vertical filmstrip along the left side of Camera Raw (as shown here). Click on the Select All button (it's above the filmstrip) and then crop the currently selected photo as you'd like. As you apply your cropping, look at the filmstrip and you'll see all the thumbnails update with their new cropping instructions. A tiny Crop icon will also appear in the bottom-left corner of each thumbnail, letting you know that these photos have been cropped in Camera Raw.

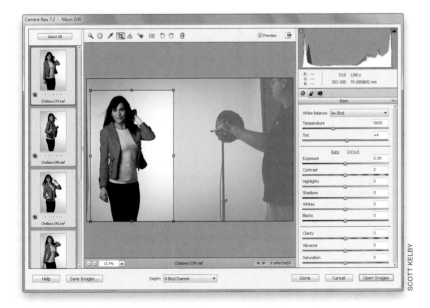

SCOTT KELBY

(Continued)

Step Seven:

Another form of cropping is actually straightening your photos using the Straighten tool. It's a close cousin of the Crop tool because what it does is essentially rotates your cropping border, so when you open the photo, it's straight. In the Camera Raw toolbar, choose the Straighten tool (it's immediately to the right of the Crop tool, and shown circled here in red). Now, click-and-drag it along the horizon line in your photo (as shown here). When you release the mouse button, a cropping border appears and that border is automatically rotated to the exact amount needed to straighten the photo.

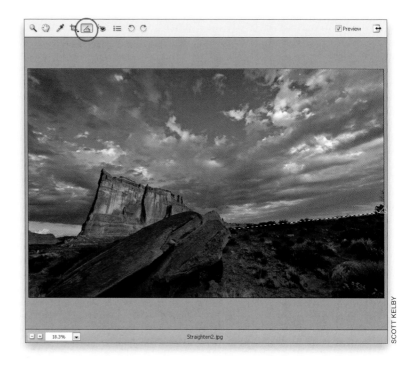

Step Eight:

You won't actually see the rotated photo until you click on another tool (which I've done here) or open it in Elements (which means, if you click Save Image or Done, Camera Raw closes, and the straightening information is saved along with the file. So, if you open this file again in Camera Raw, that straightening crop border will still be in place). If you click Open Image, the photo opens in Elements, but only the area inside the cropping border is visible, and the rest is cropped off. Again, if this is a RAW photo (or you haven't overwritten your JPEG, TIFF, or PSD file), you can always return to Camera Raw and remove this cropping border to get the original uncropped photo back.

TIP: Canceling Your Straightening

If you want to cancel your straightening, just press the **Esc key** on your keyboard, and the straightening border will go away.

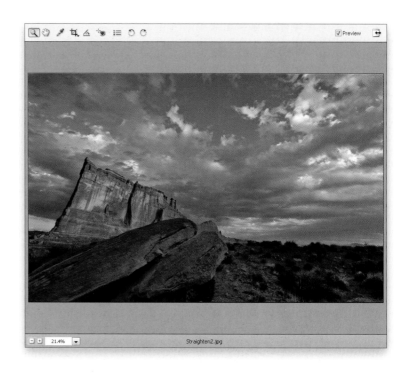

One of the coolest things about Camera Raw is the ability to apply changes to one photo, and then have those same changes applied to as many other similar images as you'd like. It's a form of built-in automation, and it can save an incredible amount of time in editing your shoots.

Editing Multiple Photos at Once

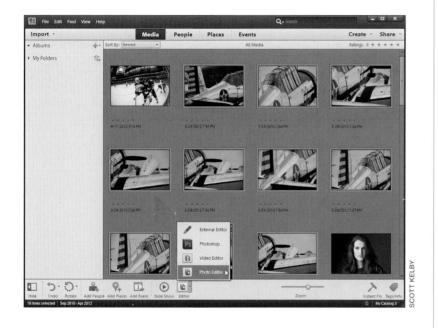

Step One:
Start off in the Organizer by selecting a group of RAW photos that were shot in the same, or very similar, lighting conditions (click on one photo, press-and-hold the Ctrl [Mac: Command] key, and click on the other photos), then open these images in Camera Raw.

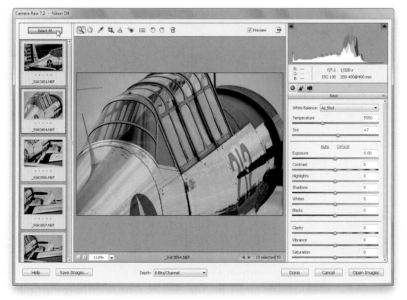

Step Two:
The selected photos will appear along the left side of the Camera Raw window. First, click on the photo you want to edit (this will be your target photo—the one all the adjustments will be based upon), then click the Select All button at the top left of the window to select all the other images (as shown here).

(Continued)

Step Three:

Go ahead and adjust the photo the way you'd like. You can see the settings I used here, for this photo. You'll notice that the changes you make to the photo you selected first are being applied to all the photos in the Camera Raw filmstrip on the left (you can see their thumbnails update as you're making adjustments).

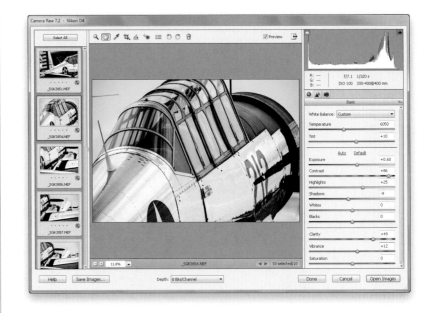

Step Four:

When you're done making adjustments, you have a choice to make: (a) if you click the Open Images button, all of your selected images will open in the Elements Editor (so if you're adjusting 120 images, you might want to give that some thought before clicking the Open Images button), or (b) you can just click the Done button, which applies all your changes to the images without opening them in Elements. So, your changes are applied to all the images, but you won't see those changes until you open the images later (I usually choose [b] when editing lots of images at once). That's it—how to make changes to one image and have them applied to a bunch of images at the same time.

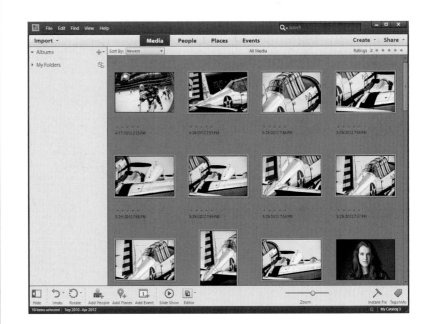

Adobe created DNG (an open archival format for RAW photos) because, at this point in time, each camera manufacturer has its own proprietary RAW file format. If, one day, one or more manufacturers abandon their proprietary format for something new (like Kodak did with their Photo CD format), will we still be able to open our RAW photos? With DNG, it's not proprietary—Adobe made it an open archival format, ensuring that your negatives can be opened in the future, but besides that, DNG brings another couple of advantages, as well.

The Advantages of Adobe's DNG Format for RAW Photos

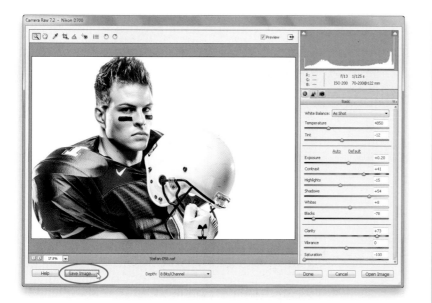

Step One:
There are three advantages to converting your RAW files to Adobe DNG: (1) DNG files are generally about 20% smaller. (2) DNG files don't need an XMP sidecar file to store Camera Raw edits, metadata, and keywords—the info's embedded into the DNG file, so you only have one file to keep track of. And, (3) DNG is an open format, so you'll be able to open them in the future (as I mentioned in the intro above). If you have a RAW image open in Camera Raw, you can save it as an Adobe DNG by clicking the Save Image button (as shown here) to bring up the Save Options dialog (seen in the next step). *Note:* There's really no advantage to saving TIFF, JPEG, or PSD files as DNGs, so I only convert RAW photos.

Step Two:
When the Save Options dialog appears, in the middle of the dialog, you'll see the File Extension pop-up menu is set to DNG (shown here). Below that, under Format: Digital Negative, is a set of options for saving your DNGs.

(Continued)

Step Three:

New in Elements 11 is the Embed Fast Load Data checkbox, which uses a smaller embedded RAW preview that makes switching between images faster (I turn this feature on). Below that is a somewhat controversial option, but if used in the right way, I think it's okay. It uses a JPEG-like lossy compression (meaning there is a loss in quality), but the trade-off (just like in JPEG) is that your file sizes are dramatically smaller (about 25% of the size of a full, uncompressed RAW file). So, if there's a loss of quality, why would you use this? Well, I wouldn't use it for my Picks (the best images from a shoot—ones I might print, or a client might see), but what about the hundreds the client rejected or you don't like? Those might (it's your call) be candidates to be compressed to save drive space. It's something to consider. If you do want to do it, turn on that checkbox, then choose (from its pop-up menu) which option is most important to you: saving the same physical dimensions (pixel size) or file size (megapixels). Once you've made your choices, click Save, and you've got a DNG.

TIP: Setting Your DNG Preferences

With Camera Raw open, press **Ctrl-K (Mac: Command-K)** to bring up Camera Raw's Preferences dialog. There are two preferences in the DNG File Handling section: Choose Ignore Sidecar ".xmp" Files only if you use a different RAW processing application (other than Camera Raw or Lightroom), and you want Camera Raw to ignore any XMP files created by that application. If you turn on the Update Embedded JPEG Previews checkbox (and choose your preferred preview size from the pop-up menu), then any changes you make to the DNG will be applied to the preview, as well.

Sharpening in Camera Raw

In Elements, we have pro-level sharpening within Camera Raw. So when do you sharpen here, and when in Elements? I generally sharpen my photos twice—once here in Camera Raw (called "capture sharpening"), and then once in Elements at the very end of my editing process, right before I save the final image for print or for the web (called "output sharpening"). Here's how to do the capture sharpening part in Camera Raw:

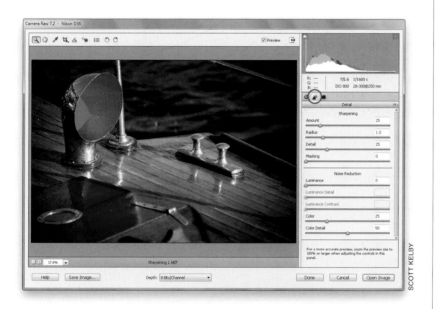

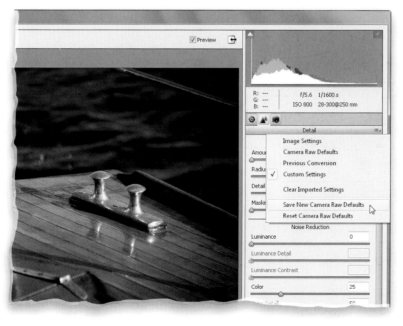

Step One:

When you open a RAW image in Camera Raw, by default it applies a small amount of sharpening to your photo (not the JPEGs, TIFFs, or PSDs—only RAW images). You can adjust this amount (or turn if off altogether, if you like) by clicking on the Detail icon (circled here in red), or using the keyboard shortcut **Ctrl-Alt-2 (Mac: Command-Option-2)**. At the top of this panel is the Sharpening section, where by a quick glance you can see that sharpening has already been applied to your RAW photo. If you don't want any sharpening applied at this stage (it's a personal preference), then simply click-and-drag the Amount slider all the way to the left, to lower the amount of sharpening to 0 (zero), and the sharpening is removed.

Step Two:

If you want to turn off this "automatic-by-default" sharpening (so image sharpening is only applied if you go and manually add it yourself), first set the Sharpening Amount slider to 0 (zero), then go to the Camera Raw flyout menu and choose **Save New Camera Raw Defaults** (as shown here). Now, RAW images taken with that camera will not be automatically sharpened.

(Continued)

Step Three:

Before we charge into sharpening, there's one more thing you'll want to know: if you don't actually want sharpening applied, but you'd still like to see what the sharpened image would look like, you can sharpen just the preview, and not the actual file. Just press **Ctrl-K (Mac: Command-K)** while Camera Raw is open, and in the Camera Raw Preferences dialog, choose **Preview Images Only** from the Apply Sharpening To pop-up menu (as shown here), and then click OK to save this as your default. Now the sharpening only affects the preview you see here in Camera Raw, but when you choose to open the file in Elements, the sharpening is not applied.

Step Four:

This may seem kind of obvious (since it tells you this right at the bottom of the Detail panel, as seen in Step One), but so many people miss this that I feel it's worth repeating: before you do any sharpening, you should view your image at a 100% size view, so you can see the sharpening being applied. A quick way to get to a 100% size view is simply to double-click directly on the Zoom tool (the one that looks like a magnifying glass) up in Camera Raw's toolbar. This zooms you right to 100% (you can double-click on the Hand tool later to return to the normal Fit in Window view).

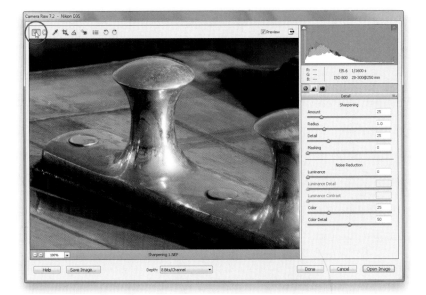

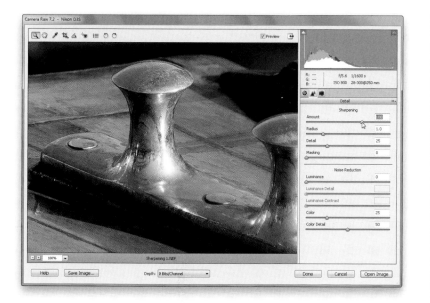

Step Five:

Now that you're at a 100% view, just for kicks, drag the Amount slider all the way to the right so you can see the sharpening at work (then drag it back to its default of 25). Again, dipping into the realm of the painfully obvious, dragging the Amount slider to the right increases the amount of sharpening. Compare the image shown here, with the one in Step Four (where the Sharpening Amount was set to the default of 25), and you can see how much sharper the image now appears, since I dragged it to 100.

TIP: Switch to Full Screen

To have Camera Raw expand to fill your entire screen, click the Full Screen icon to the right of the Preview checkbox, at the top of the window.

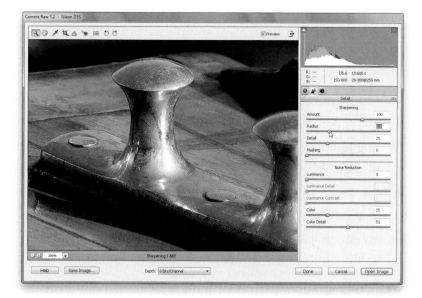

Step Six:

The next slider down is the Radius slider, which determines how far out the sharpening is applied from the edges being sharpened in your photo. I leave my Radius set at 1 most of the time. I use less than a Radius of 1 if the photo I'm processing is only going to be used on a website, in video editing, or something where it's going to be at a very small size or resolution. I only use a Radius of more than 1 when the image is visibly blurry and needs some "emergency" sharpening, or if it has lots of detail (like this photo, where I pushed the Radius to 1.2). If you decide to increase the Radius amount above 1 (unlike the Unsharp Mask filter, you can only go as high as 3 here), just be careful, because your photo can start to look oversharpened. You want your photo to look sharp, not sharpened, so be careful out there.

(Continued)

Step Seven:

The next slider down is the Detail slider, which is kind of the "halo avoidance" slider (halos occur when you oversharpen an image and it looks like there's a little halo, or line, traced around your subject or objects in your image, and they look pretty bad). The default setting of 25 is good, but you'd raise the Detail amount (dragging it to the right) when you have shots with lots of tiny important detail, like in landscapes, cityscapes, or the photo here, where I dragged it to 78. Otherwise, I leave it as is. By the way, if you want to see the effect of the Detail slider, make sure you're at a 100% view, then press-and-hold the Alt (Mac: Option) key, and you'll see your preview window turn gray. As you drag the Detail slider to the right, you'll see the edges start to become more pronounced, because the farther you drag to the right, the less protection from halos you get (those edges are those halos starting to appear).

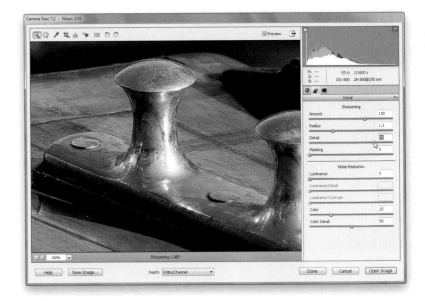

Step Eight:

I'm going to change photos to show you the Masking slider. This one's easier to understand, and for many people, I think it will become invaluable. Here's why: When you apply sharpening, it gets applied to the entire image evenly. But what if you have an image where there are areas you'd like sharpened, but other softer areas that you'd like left alone (like the photo here, where you want to keep her skin soft, but have her eyes, lips, etc., sharpened)? If we weren't in Camera Raw, you could apply the Unsharp Mask filter to a duplicate layer, add a layer mask, and paint away (cover) those softer areas, right? Well, that's kind of what the Masking slider here in Camera Raw does—as you drag it to the right, it reduces the amount of sharpening on non-edge areas. The default Masking setting of 0 (zero) applies sharpening to the entire image. As you drag to the right, the non-edge areas are masked (protected) from being sharpened.

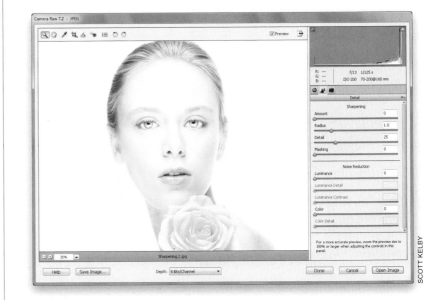

SCOTT KELBY

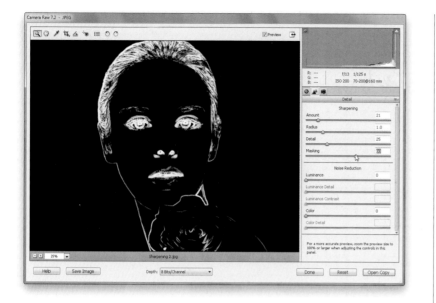

Step Nine:

All four sliders in the Sharpening section of the Detail panel let you have a live preview of what the sharpening is affecting—just press-and-hold the Alt (Mac: Option) key as you drag; your screen will turn grayscale, and the areas that the slider you're dragging will affect appear as edge areas in the Preview area. This is particularly helpful in understanding the Masking slider, so press-and-hold the Alt key and drag the Masking slider to the right. When Masking is set to 0, the screen turns solid white (because sharpening is being evenly applied to everything). As you drag to the right, in the preview (shown here), the parts that are no longer being sharpened turn black (those areas are masked). Any areas you see in white are the only parts of the photo receiving sharpening (perfect for sharpening women, because it avoids sharpening their skin, but sharpens the things you want sharp, like the eyes, hair, eyebrows, lips, edges of her face, and so on). Below is a before/after of our boat deck shot, with these settings—Amount: 100, Radius: 1, Detail: 78, Masking: 0.

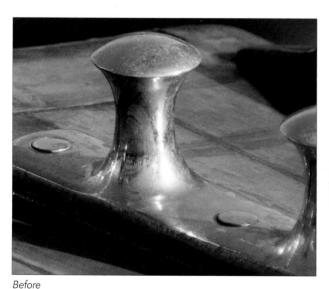

Before

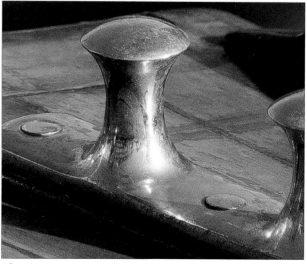

After

Reducing Noise in Noisy Photos

This is, hands down, not only one of the most-requested features by photographers, but one of the best since the last Camera Raw upgrade. Now, if you're thinking, "But Scott, didn't Elements and Camera Raw both have built-in noise reduction before?" Yes, yes they did. And did it stink? Yes, yes it did. But, does the current noise reduction rock? Oh yeah! What makes it so amazing is that it removes the noise without greatly reducing the sharpness, detail, and color saturation. Plus, it applies the noise reduction to the RAW image itself (unlike most noise plug-ins).

Step One:

Open your noisy image in Camera Raw (the Noise Reduction feature works best on RAW images, but you can also use it on JPEGs, TIFFs, or PSDs, as well). The image shown here was shot at a high ISO using a Nikon D3S, which didn't do a very good job in this low-light situation, so you can see a lot of color noise (those red, green, and blue spots) and luminance noise (the grainy looking gray spots).

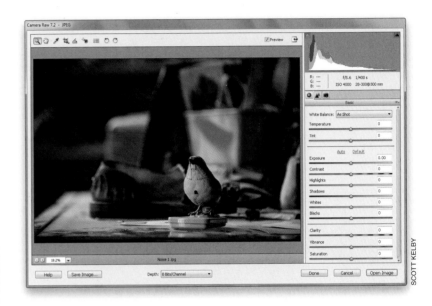

Step Two:

Sometimes it's hard to see the noise until you really zoom in tight, so zoom in to at least 100%, and there it is, lurking in the shadows (that's where noise hangs out the most). Click on the Detail icon (it's the middle icon at the top of the Panel area) to access the Noise Reduction controls. I usually get rid of the color noise first, because that makes it easier to see the luminance noise (which comes next). Here's a good rule of thumb to go by when removing color noise: start with the Color slider over at 0 (as shown here) and then slowly drag it to the right until the moment the color noise is gone. *Note:* A bit of color noise reduction is automatically applied to RAW images—the Color slider is set to 25—but, for JPEGs, TIFFs, or PSDs, the Color slider is set to 0.

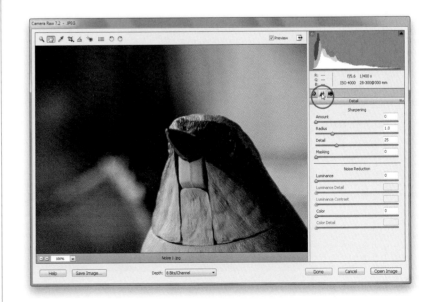

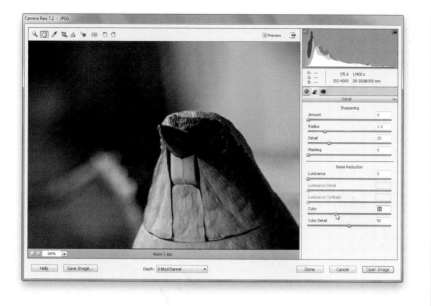

Step Three:

So, click-and-drag the Color slider to the right, but remember, you'll still see some noise (that's the luminance noise, which we'll deal with next), so what you're looking for here is just for the red, green, and blue color spots to go away. Chances are that you won't have to drag very far at all—just until that color noise all turns gray. If you have to push the Color slider pretty far to the right, you might start to lose some detail, and in that case, you can drag the Color Detail slider to the right a bit, though honestly, I rarely have to do this for color noise.

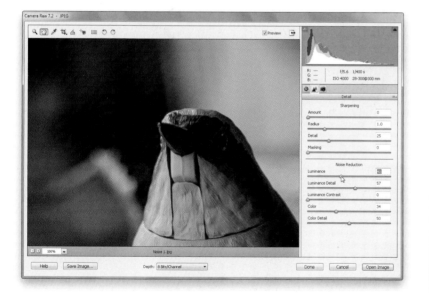

Step Four:

Now that the color noise is gone, all that's left is the luminance noise, and you'll want to use a similar process: just drag the Luminance slider to the right, and keep dragging until the visible noise disappears (as seen here). You'll generally have to drag this one farther to the right than you did with the Color slider, but that's normal. There are two things that tend to happen when you have to push this slider really far to the right: you lose sharpness (detail) and contrast. Just increase the Luminance Detail slider if things start to get too soft (but I tend not to drag this one too far), and if things start looking flat, add the missing contrast back in using the Luminance Contrast slider (I don't mind cranking this one up a bit, except when I'm working on a portrait, because the flesh tones start to look icky). You probably won't have to touch either one all that often, but it's nice to know they're there if you need them.

(Continued)

Step Five:

Rather than increasing the Luminance Detail a bunch, I generally bump up the Sharpening Amount at the top of the Detail panel (as shown here), which really helps to bring some of the original sharpness and detail back. Here's the final image, zoomed back out, and you can see the noise has been pretty much eliminated, but even with the default settings (if you're fixing a RAW image), you're usually able to keep a lot of the original sharpness and detail. A zoomed-in before/after of the noise reduction we applied here is shown below.

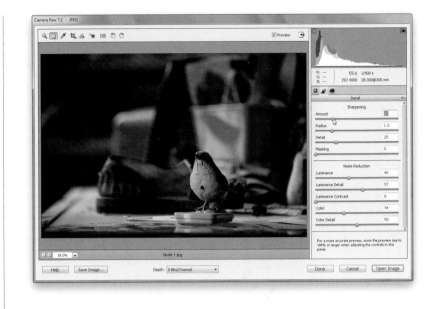

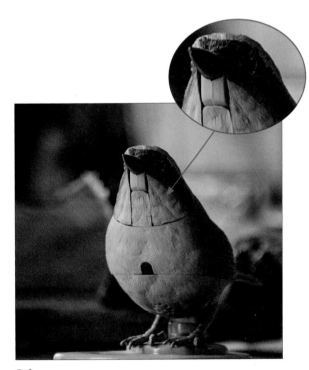

Before

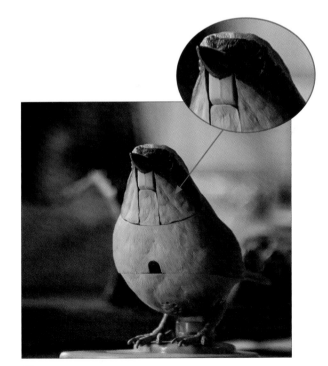

After

Camera Raw has its own built-in Red Eye Removal tool, and there's a pretty good chance it might actually work. Although, if it were me, I might be more inclined to use the regular Red Eye tool in Elements itself, which actually works fairly well, but if you're charging by the hour, this might be a fun place to start. Here's how to use this tool, which periodically works for some people, somewhere. On occasion. Perhaps.

Removing Red Eye in Camera Raw

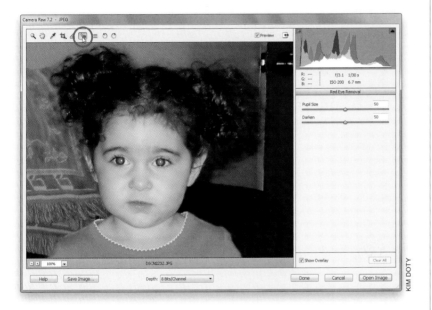

KIM DOTY

Step One:
Open a photo in Camera Raw that has the dreaded red eye (like the one shown here). To get the Red Eye Removal tool, you can press the letter **E** or just click on its icon up in Camera Raw's toolbar (as shown here).

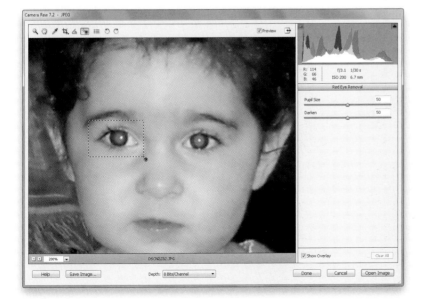

Step Two:
You'll want to zoom in close enough so you can see the red-eye area pretty easily (as I have here, where I just simply zoomed to 200%, using the zoom level pop-up menu in the bottom-left corner of the Camera Raw window). The way this tool works is pretty simple—you click-and-drag the tool around one eye (as shown here) and as you drag, it makes a box around the eye (seen here). That tells Camera Raw where the red eye is located.

(Continued)

Step Three:

When you release the mouse button, theoretically it should snap down right around the pupil, making a perfect selection around the area affected by red eye (as seen here). You'll notice the key word here is "theoretically." If it doesn't work for you, then press **Ctrl-Z (Mac: Command-Z)** to undo that attempt, and try again. Before you do, try to help the tool along by increasing the Pupil Size setting (in the Red Eye Removal panel on the right) to around 100 (as I did here).

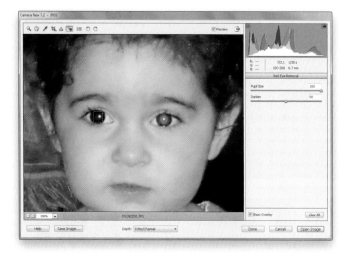

Step Four:

Once that eye looks good, go over to the other eye, drag out that selection again (as shown here), and it does the same thing (the before and after are shown below). One last thing: if the pupil looks too gray after being fixed, then drag the Darken amount to the right (as I have here). Give it a try on a photo of your own. It's possible it might work.

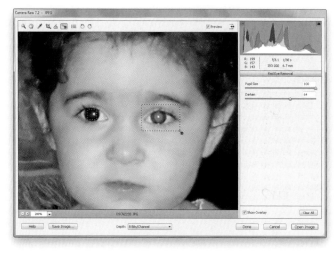

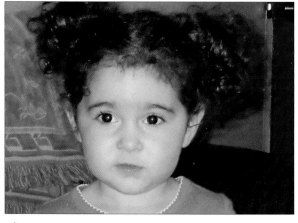

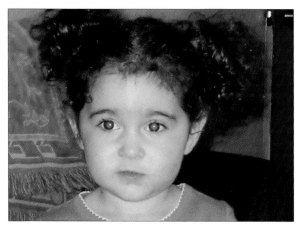

Before

After

As good as today's digital cameras are, there are still some scenes they can't accurately expose for (like backlit situations, for example). Even though the human eye automatically adjusts for these situations, your camera is either going to give you a perfectly exposed sky with a foreground that's too dark, or vice versa. Well, there's a very cool trick (called double processing) that lets you create two versions of the same photo (one exposed for the foreground, one exposed for the sky), and then you combine the two to create an image beyond what your camera can capture!

The Trick for Expanding the Range of Your Photos

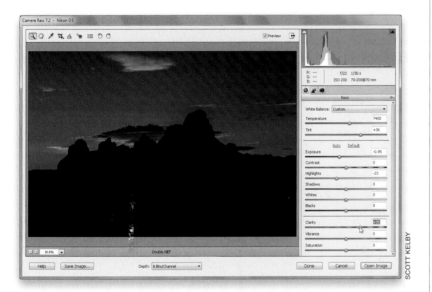

SCOTT KELBY

Step One:
Open an image with an exposure problem in Camera Raw. In our example here, the camera properly exposed for the sky, so the foreground is too dark. Of course, or goal is to create something our camera can't—a photo where both the foreground and sky are exposed properly. Let's start by darkening the sky a little by dragging the Exposure slider to the left to –0.85 and dragging the Highlights slider to –23. Then, drag the Temperature and Tint sliders a little to the right to warm the color of the sky, and then increase the Clarity to +35 (it makes the clouds look a little more interesting). Now, click Open Image to create the first version of your photo.

Step Two:
In the Elements Editor, go under the File menu, choose **Save As**, and rename and save this adjusted image. Then go back under the File menu, and under **Open Recently Edited File**, choose the same photo you just opened. It will reopen in Camera Raw. The next step is to create a second version of this image that exposes for the foreground, even though it will make the sky very light.

(Continued)

Step Three:

Reset the sliders you moved in the first step by double-clicking on their little nubs, and then let's start by making the rocks visible. Drag the Shadows slider all the way to the right, and now at least you can see them, but it's still not enough, so you'll have to bump up the Exposure slider, as well (here, I've dragged it over to +1.00). The rocks look kind of "flat" contrast-wise, so bump up the Contrast a bit, too (let's go to +28). Lastly, since these are rocks, and we want to accentuate their texture, let's crank the Clarity up to around +40, and then make the little bit of color that's there more vibrant by increasing the Vibrance to around +37. When it looks good to you, click the Open Image button to open this version of the photo in the Editor.

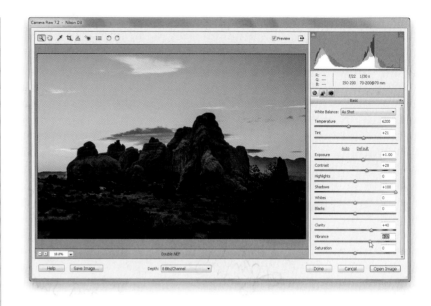

Step Four:

Now you should have both versions of the image open in the Editor: one exposed for the foreground and one exposed for the sky. (*Note:* This is easier if your windows are floating. To do that, in Elements' General Preferences, turn on the checkbox for Allow Floating Documents in Expert Mode, and then go under the Window menu, under Images, and choose **Float All in Windows**.) Arrange the image windows so you can see both onscreen at the same time (with the lighter photo in front). Press **V** to get the Move tool, press-and-hold the Shift key, click on the lighter image, and drag-and-drop it on top of the good sky version. The key to this part is holding down the Shift key while you drag between documents, which perfectly aligns the lighter image (that now appears on its own layer in the Layers palette) with the darker version on the Background layer. (This exact alignment of one identical photo over another is referred to as being "pin-registered.") You can now close the lighter document without saving, as both versions of the image are contained within one document.

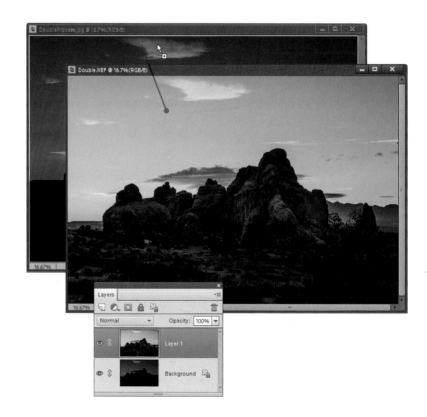

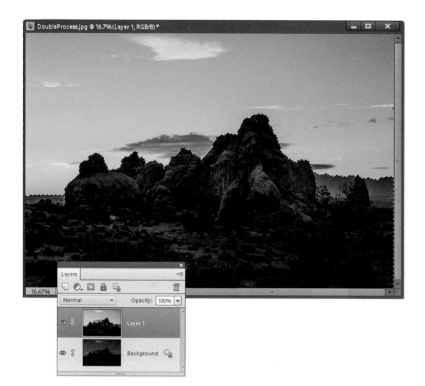

Step Five:
You now have two versions of your photo, each on a different layer—the darker sky version on the bottom layer and the brighter one exposed for the rocks in the foreground on the layer directly on top of it—and they are perfectly aligned, one on top of the other. This is why we call it "double-processing," because you have two versions of the same image, each processed differently. Now what we need to do is combine these two different layers (with different exposures) into one single image that combines the best of both. We'll combine the images with a layer mask (to learn more about layer masks, see Chapter 5), but rather than painstakingly painting it, we can cheat and use the Quick Selection tool **(A)**. So, get it from the Toolbox and paint over the rocks and foreground, and it selects them for you in just a few seconds (as shown here).

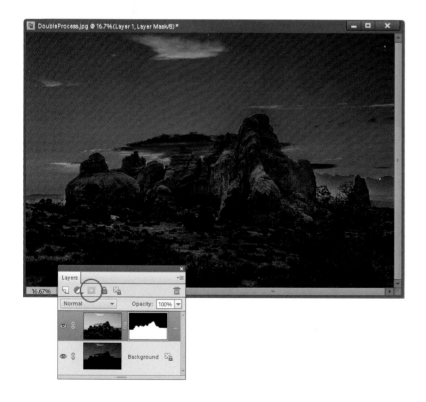

Step Six:
Go to the Layers palette and click on the Add Layer Mask icon at the top of the palette (shown circled here in red). This converts your selection into a layer mask, which hides the light sky and reveals the darker sky layer in its place (as seen here). It still needs some tweaking (for sure), but at least now you can see what we're aiming for—the brighter foreground rocks from one layer blended with the darker sky from the other layer.

(Continued)

Step Seven:

Now, you're going to lower the Opacity of this top layer (the brighter rocks layer), so it blends in a little better with the darker sky layer. Here, I've lowered it to 77%, and the colors match much better. Well, except for those blue mountain areas on either side of the base of the rocks, which look kind of funky. They're too bright, and a bit "glowy." We're going to have to fix that. Uggh!

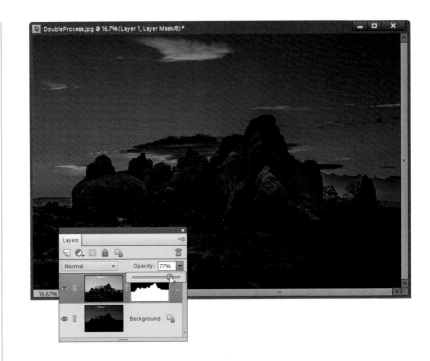

Step Eight:

Press the letter **B** to get the Brush tool, then click on the Brush thumbnail in the Tool Options Bar and choose a medium-sized, soft-edged brush from the Brush Picker. Also, to help blend this a little better, lower the Opacity of the brush (in the Tool Options Bar) to just 50%. Now, press **D**, then **X** to set your Foreground color to black, start painting over those blue mountain areas on the sides of the photo, and it paints back in 50% of the darker image, so it helps to hide those areas without making them solid black. If you make a mistake, press X again to switch your Foreground color to white and paint over your mistake to erase the spillover.

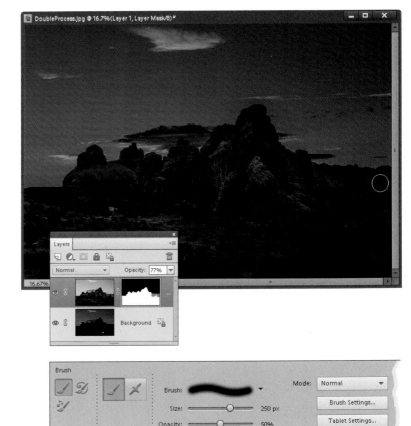

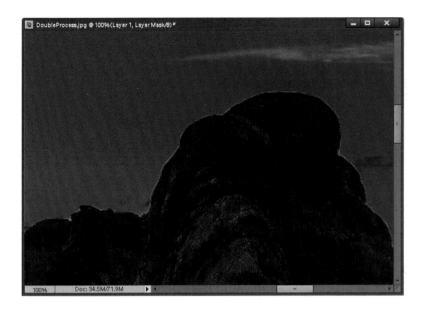

Step Nine:

Now, we have a pretty common problem to deal with here: along the edge, where the brighter rocks meet the darker sky, there's a little bit of a white fringe happening (I zoomed in here to 100%, so you can see it better). Luckily, that's fairly easy to fix, without having to take a tiny brush and paint all along that edge (which is how we used to do it, and we still sometimes do that for a little touch-up, but this isn't a little touch-up).

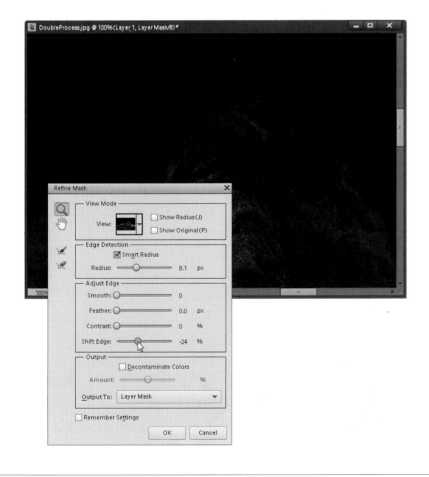

Step 10:

We're going to shift the edge of our mask a few pixels, so you don't see that white edge fringe any longer, and we'll let Elements do all the heavy lifting. Go under the Select menu and choose **Refine Edge**. This brings up the Refine Mask dialog you see here. First, to make seeing this white edge easier, from the View pop-up menu up top, choose **On Black** and now it really stands out, so you can see it clearly for what you're going to do next. In the Edge Detection section, turn on the Smart Radius checkbox and drag the Radius slider to the right until the white edge is almost gone (I dragged to 8.1). Then, under Adjust Edge, drag the Shift Edge slider to the left (as shown here) until the white edge disappears (as you see here, where I dragged to –24), then click OK. See, that was fairly easy. Again, if after doing this, you still notice a white pixel or two here or there, just take a very small brush (you're still at 50% Opacity with this brush) and simply paint over it to hide it.

(Continued)

Step 11:

Now, let's finish this baby off. Go to the Layers palette and, from the flyout menu at the top right, choose **Flatten Image** to flatten the image down to one layer. The image looks a little dark overall, so press **Ctrl-L (Mac: Command-L)** to bring up the Levels dialog, and bring back some of the overall highlights by dragging the white Input Levels highlights slider (right below the far-right side of the histogram) to the left to brighten things up. A before/after of our double-processing is shown below.

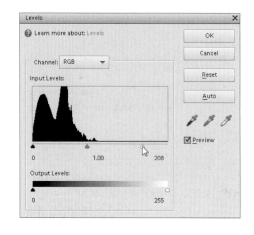

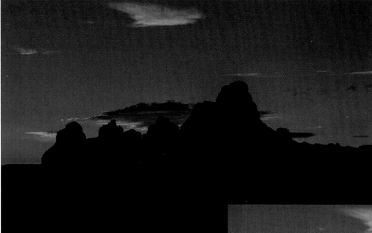

Before

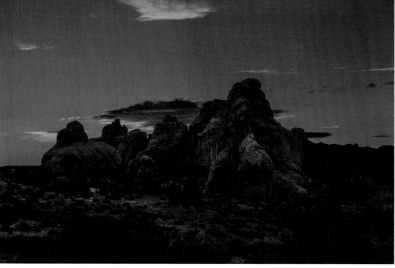

After

One of the easiest ways to make great black-and-white photos (from your color images) is to do your conversion completely within Camera Raw. You're basically just a few sliders away from a stunning black-and-white photo and then all you have left to do is finish off the image by opening it in Photoshop Elements and adding some sharpening. Here's how it's done:

Black & White Conversions in Camera Raw

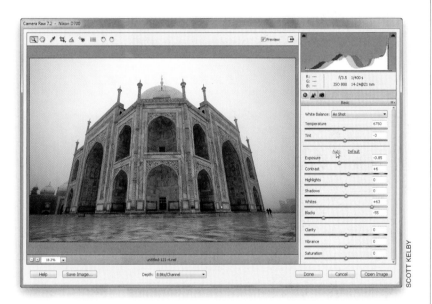

SCOTT KELBY

Step One:
Start by opening a photo you want to convert to black and white. This is one of the rare times I start by clicking the Auto button (you know, the button beneath the Tint slider that looks like a web link), because it usually pumps up the exposure about as high as it can go without too much clipping (if any). So, start there—click the Auto button. Here, it adjusted the Exposure, along with Contrast, Whites, and Blacks.

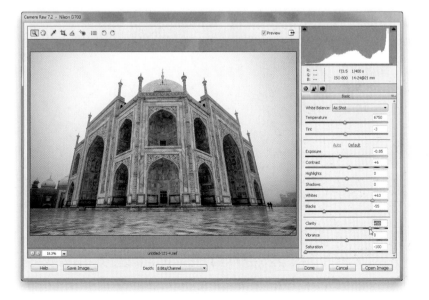

Step Two:
Now we're going to work from the bottom of the Basic panel up. The next step in converting to black and white is to remove the color from the photo. Go to the Saturation slider and drag it all the way to the left. Although this removes all the color, it usually makes for a pretty flat-looking (read as: lame) black-and-white photo. So, go up two sliders to the Clarity slider and drag it over quite a bit to the right to really make the midtones snap (I dragged over to +58).

(Continued)

Step Three:

Now you're going to add extra contrast by (you guessed it) dragging the Contrast slider to the right until the photo gets real contrasty (as shown here). It's important that you set this slider first—before you set the Blacks slider—or you'll wind up setting the blacks, then adjusting the contrast, and then lowering the Blacks slider back down. That's because what the Contrast slider essentially does is makes the darkest parts of the photo darker, and the brightest parts brighter. If the blacks are already very dark, then you add contrast, it makes them too dark, and you wind up backing them off again. So, save yourself the extra step and set the contrast first.

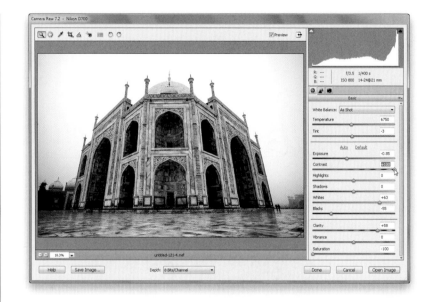

Step Four:

The insides of the arches are kind of dark, so drag the Shadows slider to the right to lighten those areas a bit (I dragged to +41). Also, the sky looks really white, so let's pull back those highlights by dragging the Highlights slider to the left (here, I dragged to –43). That's it—the quickest way to convert to black and white (and get a nice high-contrast look) right within Camera Raw.

TIP: Change the White Balance

Another thing you might try for RAW images is going through each of the White Balance presets (in the White Balance pop-up menu) to see how they affect your black-and-white photo. You'll be amazed at how this little change can pay off (make sure you try Fluorescent and Tungsten—they often look great in black and white).

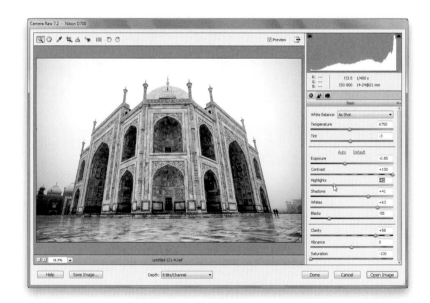

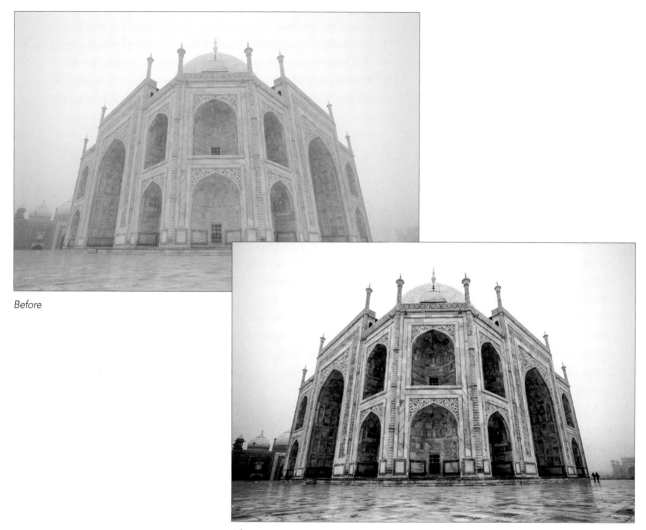

Before

After

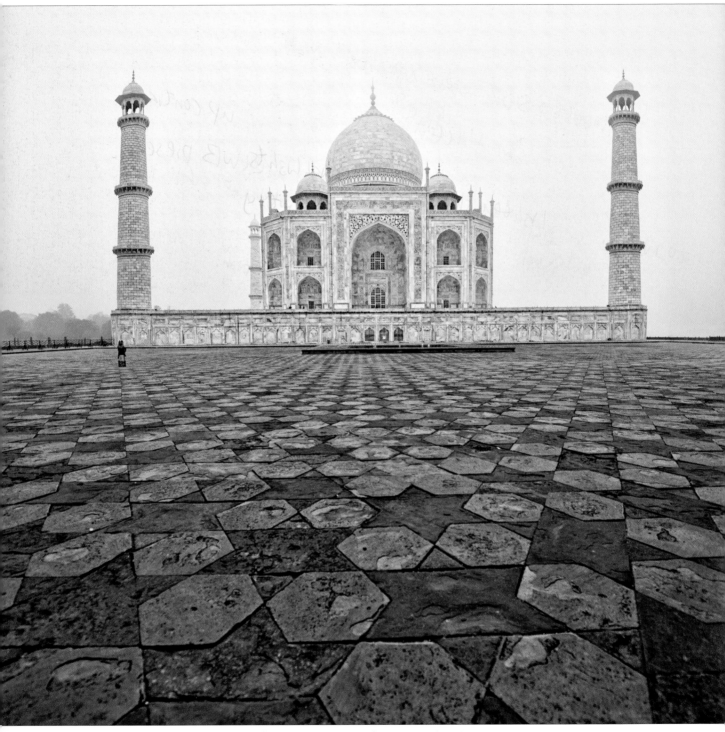

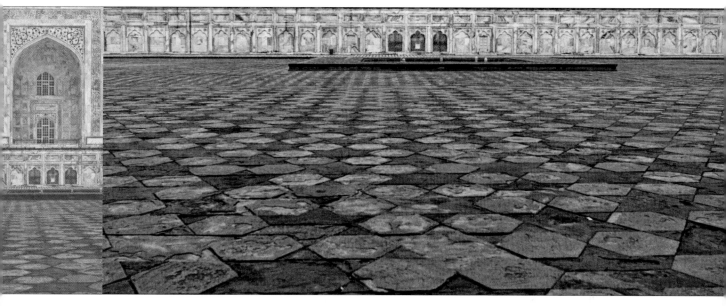

SCREAM OF THE CROP
how to resize and crop photos

I love the title of this chapter—it's the name of an album from the band Soulfarm (tell me that Soulfarm wouldn't make a great name for a horror movie!). Anyway, I also found a band named Cash Crop, which would make a great title, too, but when I looked at their album, every song was marked with the Explicit warning. I listened to a 90-second preview of the first track (which was featured in the original motion picture soundtrack for the movie *Sorority Row*), and I immediately knew what kind of the music they did. Naughty, naughty music. Anyway, while I was listening, and wincing from time to time as F-bombs exploded all around me, I realized that someone at the iTunes Store must have the full-time job of listening to each song and choosing the 90-second preview. I imagine, at this point, that person has to be 100% completely numb to hearing things like the F-bomb, the S-missile, and the B-grenade (which means

they could totally do a stint as Joe Pesci's nanny). But, I digress. The "Scream of the Crop" title (which would make a great title for a movie about evil corn) is almost ideal for this chapter, except for the fact that this chapter also includes resizing. So, I thought, what the heck, and searched for "resize" and found a song called "Undo Resize" by electronic ambient artist DJ Yanatz Ft. The Designers, and it literally is an 8:31 long background music track with two European-sounding women whispering the names of menu commands from Adobe products. Stuff like "Select All," "Fill," "Distort," "Snap to Grid," and so on. I am not making this up (I listened to the free 90-second preview). It was only 99¢, which is a bargain for 8+ minutes of menu commands set to music. Normally, this many minutes of menu commands set to music would be more like, I dunno, $1.29 or so.

Basic Cropping

After you've sorted your images in the Organizer, one of the first editing tasks you'll probably undertake is cropping a photo. There are a number of different ways to crop a photo in Elements. We'll start with the basic garden-variety options, and then we'll look at some ways to make the task faster and easier.

Step One:
Open the image you want to crop in the Elements Editor, and then press the letter **C** to get the Crop tool (you could always select the tool directly from the Toolbox, but I only recommend doing so if you're charging by the hour).

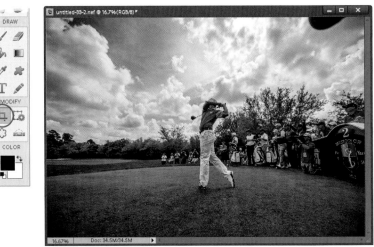

SCOTT KELBY

Step Two:
Click within your photo and drag out a cropping border. By default, you'll see a grid appear within your border. This feature lets you crop photos based on some of the popular composition rules that photographers and designers use. We'll go over this feature more in a moment, so for now click on the None icon on the left end of the Tool Options Bar. The area to be cropped away will appear dimmed (shaded). You don't have to worry about getting your cropping border right when you first drag it out, because you can edit it by dragging the control handles that appear in each corner and at the center of each side.

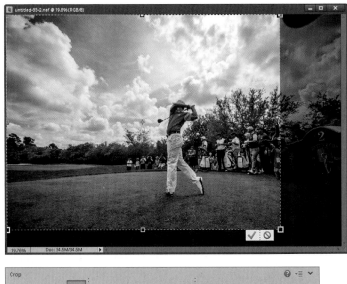

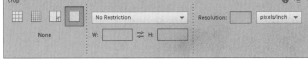

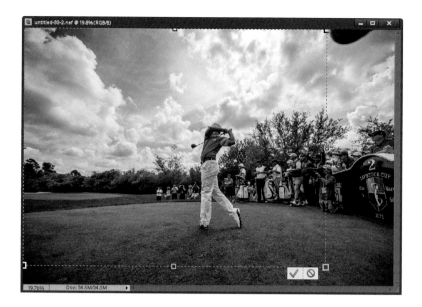

TIP: Turn Off the Shading
If you don't like seeing your photo with the cropped-away areas appearing shaded (as in the previous step), you can toggle this shading feature off/on by pressing the **Forward Slash key (/)** on your keyboard. When you press the Forward Slash key, the border remains in place but the shading is turned off.

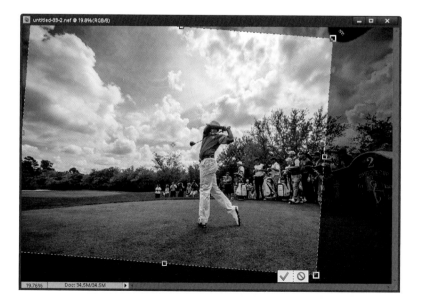

Step Three:
While you have the cropping border in place, you can rotate the entire border. Just move your cursor outside the border, and your cursor will change into a double-headed arrow. Then, click-and-drag, and the cropping border will rotate in the direction that you drag. (This is a great way to save time if you have a crooked image, because it lets you crop and rotate at the same time.)

(Continued)

Step Four:

Once you have the cropping border where you want it, click on the green checkmark icon at the bottom corner of your cropping border, or just press the **Enter (Mac: Return) key** on your keyboard. To cancel your crop, click the red international symbol for "No Way!" at the bottom corner of the cropping border, or press the **Esc key** on your keyboard.

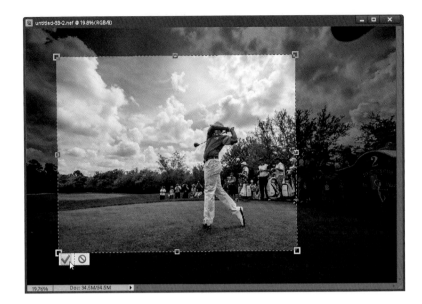

Step Five:

Like I mentioned, Elements 11 includes overlay features to help you crop your photos. The one you'll use the most is called the Rule of Thirds (and is the default overlay). It's essentially a trick that photographers sometimes use to create more interesting compositions. Basically, you visually divide the image you see in your camera's viewfinder into thirds, and then you position your horizon so it goes along either the top imaginary horizontal line or the bottom one. Then, you position the subject (or focal point) at the intersections of those lines (as you'll see in the next step). But if you didn't use the rule in the viewfinder, no sweat! You can use this overlay feature to achieve it. There are also two other options in the overlay icons: (1) Grid, which is useful for straightening horizons and (2) Golden Ratio, which is used for more of a "spiral" composition.

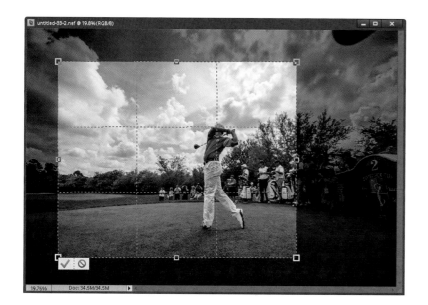

Step Six:
So, click on the Rule of Thirds icon and then click within your photo and drag out a cropping border. When you drag the cropping border onto your image, you'll see the Rule of Thirds overlay appear over your photo. Just position your image's horizon along one of the horizontal grid lines, and be sure your focal point (the golfer's head, arms, and club, in this case) falls on one of the intersecting points (the top-right intersection, in this example).

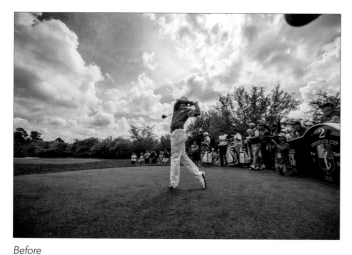

Before

After

Auto-Cropping to Standard Sizes

If you're outputting photos for clients, chances are they're going to want them in standard sizes so they can easily find frames to fit. If that's the case, here's how to crop your photos to a predetermined size (like a 5x7", 8x10", etc.):

Step One:

Open an image in the Elements Editor that you want to crop to be a perfect 5x7" for a vertical image, or 7x5" if your image is horizontal. Press **C** to get the Crop tool, then go to the Tool Options Bar and click on the words "No Restriction" in the pop-up menu. From the list of preset crop sizes, choose **5x7 in**. (*Note:* To hide the Rule of Thirds overlay grid, click on the None icon on the left side of the Tool Options Bar.)

TIP: Swapping Fields

The Width and Height fields are populated based on the type of image you open—7x5" for horizontal images and 5x7" for vertical images. If you opened a horizontal image, but your crop is going to be vertical (tall), you'll need to swap the figures in the Width and Height fields by clicking on the Swaps icon between the fields in the Tool Options Bar (as shown here).

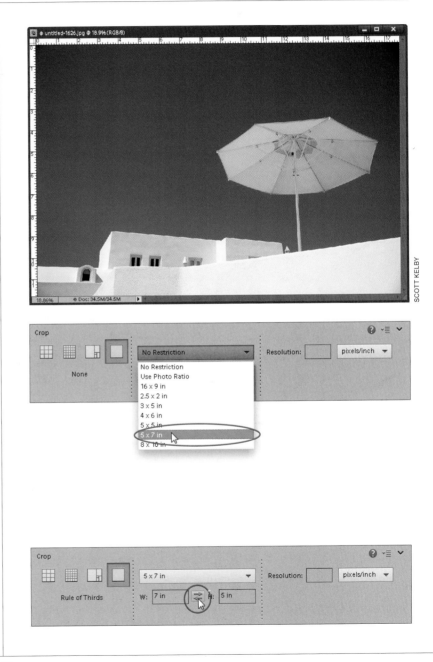

SCOTT KELBY

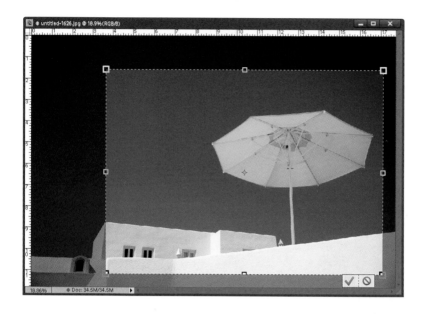

Step Two:
Now click-and-drag the Crop tool over the portion of the photo that you want to be 7x5" (if your image is vertical, Elements will automatically adjust your border to 5x7"). While dragging, you can press-and-hold the Spacebar to adjust the position of your border, if needed.

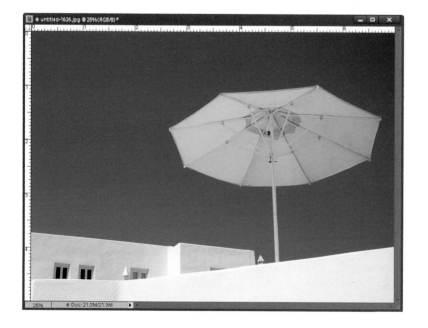

Step Three:
Once it's set, press the **Enter (Mac: Return) key** and the area inside your cropping border will become 7x5" (as shown here).

TIP: Crop with an Action
You can also use the new Actions palette (found under the Window menu) in Elements 11 to crop your photos. In the palette, they are in the Resize and Crop folder. Simply open the image you want to crop, click on the cropping action you want to run, then click on the Play Selection icon at the top right of the palette, and—BAM!—your image is cropped and ready to go.

Cropping to an Exact Custom Size

Okay, now you know how to crop to Elements' built-in preset sizes, but how do you crop to a nonstandard size—a custom size that you determine? Here's how:

Step One:

Open the photo that you want to crop in the Elements Editor. (I want to crop this image to 8x6".) First, press **C** to get the Crop tool. In the Tool Options Bar, you'll see fields for Width and Height. Enter the size you want for Width, followed by the unit of measure you want to use (e.g., enter "in" for inches, "px" for pixels, "cm" for centimeters, "mm" for millimeters, etc.). Next, press the **Tab key** to jump over to the Height field and enter your desired height, again followed by the unit of measure.

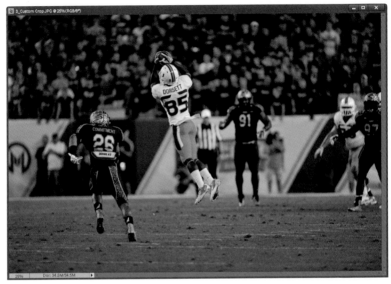

SCOTT KELBY

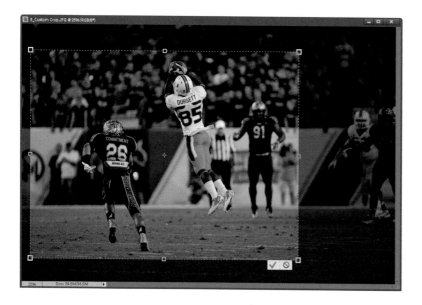

Step Two:
Once you've entered these figures in the Tool Options Bar, click within your photo with the Crop tool and drag out a cropping border. (*Note:* To hide the Rule of Thirds overlay grid, click on the None icon on the left side of the Tool Options Bar.) You'll notice that as you drag, the border is constrained to an 8x6" aspect ratio; no matter how large of an area you select within your image, the area within that border will become your specified size. When you release your mouse button, you'll still have both side handles and corner handles visible, but the side handles will act like corner handles to keep your size constrained.

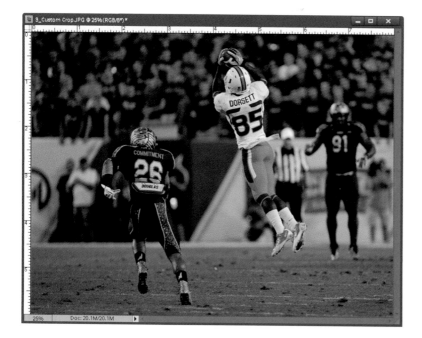

Step Three:
Once your cropping border is onscreen, you can resize it using the corner handles or you can reposition it by moving your cursor inside the border. Your cursor will change to a Move arrow, and you can now click-and-drag the border into place. You can also use the **Arrow keys** on your keyboard for more precise control. When it looks right to you, press **Enter (Mac: Return)** to finalize your crop or click on the checkmark icon at the bottom right of your cropping border. Here, I made the rulers visible (**Ctrl-Shift-R [Mac: Command-Shift-R]**) so you could see that the image measures exactly 8x6".

(Continued)

TIP: Clearing the Fields

Once you've entered a Width and Height in the Tool Options Bar, those dimensions will remain there. To clear the fields, just choose **No Restriction** from the pop-up menu above the Width and Height fields. This will clear the fields, and now you can use the Crop tool for freeform cropping (you can drag it in any direction—it's no longer constrained to your specified size).

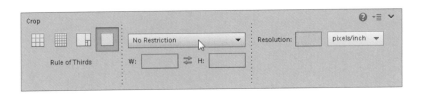

COOLER TIP: Changing Dimensions

If you already have a cropping border in place, you can change your dimensions without re-creating the border. All you have to do is enter the new sizes you want in the Width and Height fields in the Tool Options Bar, and Elements will resize your cropping border.

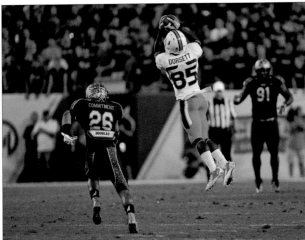

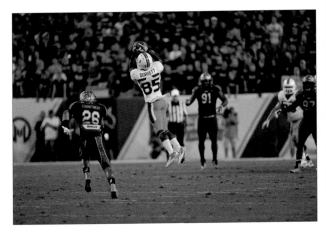

Before

After

Cropping into a Shape

Elements has a cool feature that lets you crop your photo into a pre-designed shape (like putting a wedding photo into a heart shape), but even cooler are the edge effects you can create by cropping into one of the pre-designed edge effects that look like old Polaroid transfers. Here's how to put this feature to use to add visual interest to your own photos.

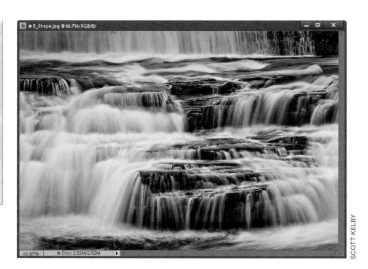

SCOTT KELBY

Step One:
In the Elements Editor, open the photo you want to crop into a pre-designed shape, and press the letter **Q** to get the Cookie Cutter tool.

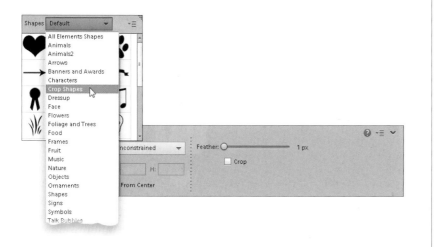

Step Two:
Now, go down to the Tool Options Bar and click on the shape thumbnail. This brings up the Custom Shape Picker, which contains the default set of 30 shapes. To load more shapes, click on the Shapes pop-up menu at the top of the Picker and a list of built-in shape sets will appear. From this list, choose **Crop Shapes** to load the edge-effect shapes, which automatically crop away areas outside your custom edges.

(Continued)

Step Three:

Once you select the custom edge shape you want to use in the Custom Shape Picker, just click-and-drag it over your image to the size you want it. When you release the mouse button, your photo is cropped to fit within the shape. *Note:* I like Crop Shape 10 (which is shown here) for something simple, and Crop Shape 20 for something a little wilder. The key thing here is to experiment and try different crop shapes to find your favorite.

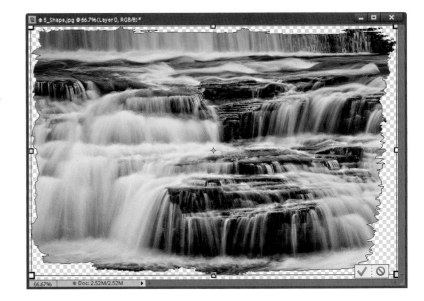

Step Four:

You'll see a bounding box around the shape, which you can use to resize, rotate, or otherwise mess with your shape. To resize your shape, press-and-hold the Shift key (or choose Defined Proportions from the pop-up menu to the right of the shape thumbnail in Tool Options Bar) to keep it proportional while you drag a corner handle. To rotate the shape, move your cursor outside the bounding box until your cursor becomes a double-sided arrow, and then click-and-drag. As long as you see that bounding box, you can still edit the shape. When it looks good to you, press **Enter (Mac: Return)** and the parts of your photo outside that shape will be permanently cropped away.

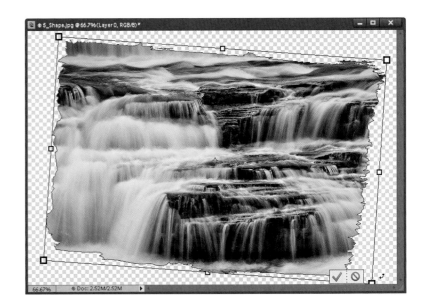

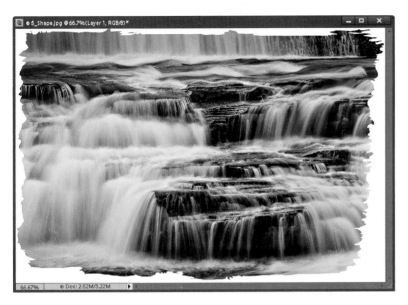

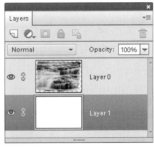

TIP: Tightly Crop Your Image
If you want your image area tightly cropped, so it's the exact size of the shape you drag out, just turn on the Cookie Cutter's Crop checkbox (in the Tool Options Bar) before you drag out your shape. Then when you press Enter to lock in your final shape, Elements will tightly crop the entire image area to the size of your shape. *Note:* The checker-board pattern you see around the photo is letting you know that the background around the shape is transparent. If you want a white background behind the shape, click on the Create a New Layer icon at the top of the Layers palette, and then drag your new layer below the Shape layer. Press **D**, then **X** to set your Foreground color to white, then press **Alt-Backspace (Mac: Option-Delete)** to fill this layer with white.

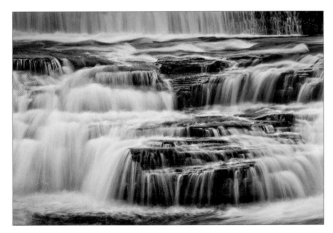

Before

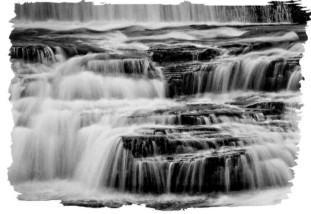

After

Using the Crop Tool to Add More Canvas Area

I know the heading for this technique doesn't make much sense—"Using the Crop Tool to Add More Canvas Area." How can the Crop tool (which is designed to crop photos to smaller sizes) actually make the canvas area (white space) around your photo larger? That's what I'm going to show you.

Step One:

In the Elements Editor, open the image to which you want to add additional blank canvas area. Press the letter **D** to set your Background color to its default white. (*Note:* If you want to add a different color canvas, like black, then go under the File menu, under New, and choose **Blank File** to open the New dialog. At the bottom, change the Background Contents pop-up menu to **Background Color**, then click OK. Close the new document, and set your Background color to whatever color you want the canvas to be.)

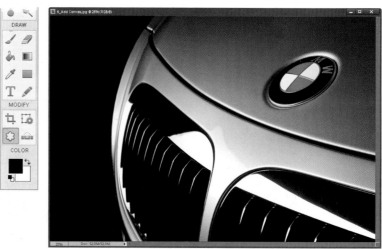

Step Two:

If you're in Maximize Mode or tabbed viewing, press **Ctrl--** (minus sign; **Mac: Command--**) to zoom out a bit (so your image doesn't take up your whole screen). If your image window is floating, click-and-drag out the bottom corner of the document window to see the gray desktop area around your image. (To enter Maximize Mode, click the Maximize Mode icon in the top-right corner of the image window. To enter tabbed viewing, go under the Window menu, under Images, and choose **Consolidate All to Tabs**.)

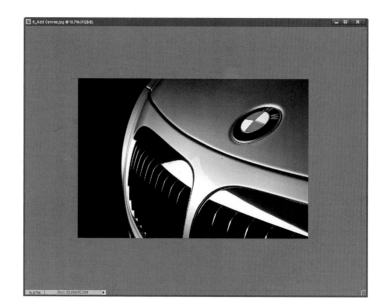

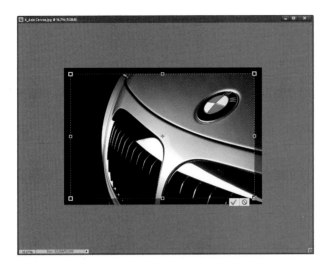

Step Three:
Press the letter **C** to switch to the Crop tool and drag out a cropping border to any random size (it doesn't matter how big or little it is at this point).

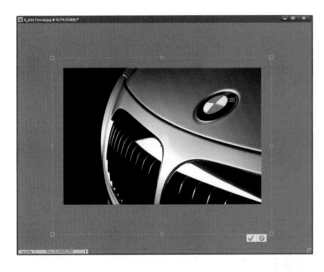

Step Four:
Next, grab any one of the side or corner handles and drag outside the image area, out into the gray area that surrounds your image. The cropping border extending outside the image is the area that will be added as white canvas space, so position it where you want to add the blank canvas space.

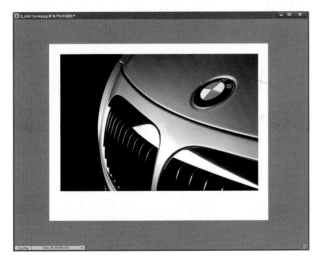

Step Five:
Now, just press the **Enter (Mac: Return) key** to finalize your crop, and when you do, the area outside your image will become white canvas area.

Auto-Cropping Gang-Scanned Photos

A lot of photographers scan photos using a technique called "gang scanning." That's a fancy name for scanning more than one picture at a time. Scanning three or four photos at once with your scanner saves time, but then you eventually have to separate these photos into individual documents. Here's how to have Elements do that for you automatically:

Step One:
Place the photos you want to "gang scan" on the bed of your flatbed scanner. In the Organizer, you can scan the images by going under the File menu, under Get Photos and Videos, and choosing **From Scanner** (they should appear in one Elements document). In the dialog that appears, select where and at what quality you want to save your scanned document. (*Note:* This feature is currently not available in the Elements 11 version for the Mac, so you'll need to use your scanner's software.)

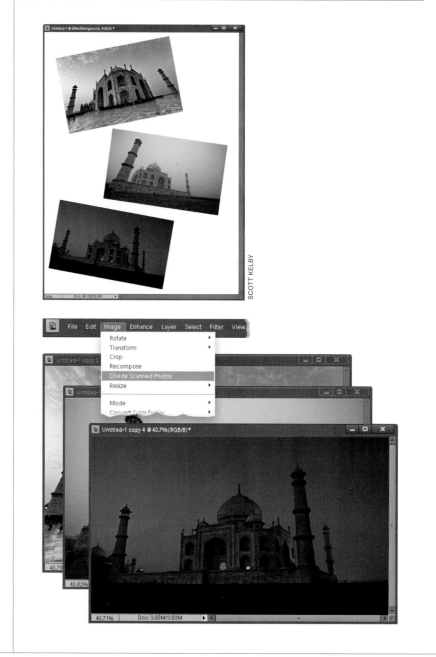

SCOTT KELBY

Step Two:
Once your images appear in one document in the Editor, go under the Image menu and choose **Divide Scanned Photos**. It will immediately find the edges of the scanned photos, straighten them if necessary, and then put each photo into its own separate document. Once it has "done its thing," you can close the original gang-scanned document, and you'll be left with just the individual documents.

In Elements, there's a simple way to straighten photos, but it's knowing how to set the options for the tool that makes your job dramatically easier. Here's how it's done:

Straightening Photos with the Straighten Tool

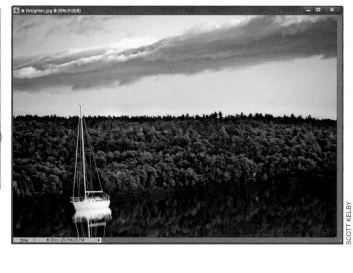

Step One:
Open the photo that needs straightening (the photo shown here looks like the horizon is sloping down to the left). Then, choose the Straighten tool from the Toolbox (or just press the **P key**).

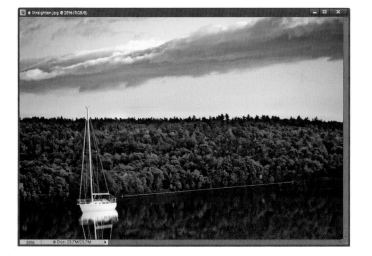

Step Two:
Take the Straighten tool and drag it along an edge in the photo that you think should be perfectly horizontal, like a horizon line (as shown here).

(Continued)

Step Three:

When you release the mouse button, the image is straightened, but as you see here, the straightening created a problem of its own—the photo now has to be re-cropped because the edges are showing a white background (as the image was rotated until it was straight). That's where the options (which I mentioned in the intro to this technique) come in. You see, the default setting does just what you see here—it rotates the image and leaves it up to you to crop away the mess. However, Elements can do the work for you (as you'll see in the next step).

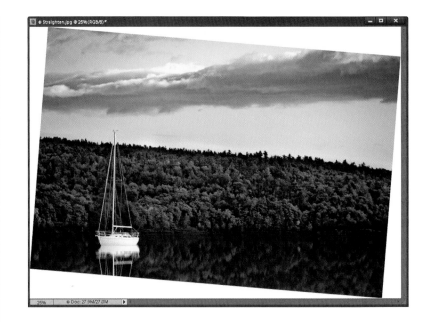

Step Four:

Once you click on the Straighten tool, go down to the Tool Options Bar and click on the Remove Background icon.

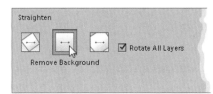

Step Five:

Now when you drag out the tool and release the mouse button, not only is the photo straightened, but the annoying white background is automatically cropped away, giving you the clean result you see here.

TIP: Straightening Vertically

In this example, we used the Straighten tool along a horizontal plane, but if you wanted to straighten the photo using a vertical object instead (like a column or light pole), just click with the Straighten tool, then press-and-hold the Ctrl (Mac: Command) key before you drag it, and that will do the trick.

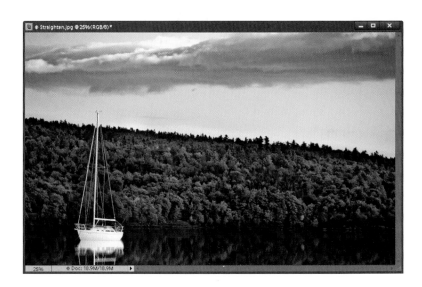

Resizing Digital Camera Photos

If you're more familiar with resizing scanned images, you'll find that resizing images from digital cameras is a bit different, primarily because scanners create high-resolution images (usually 300 ppi or more), but the default setting for most digital cameras usually produces an image that is large in physical dimension, but lower in ppi (usually 72 ppi). The trick is to decrease the physical size of your digital camera image (and increase its resolution) without losing any quality in your photo. Here's the trick:

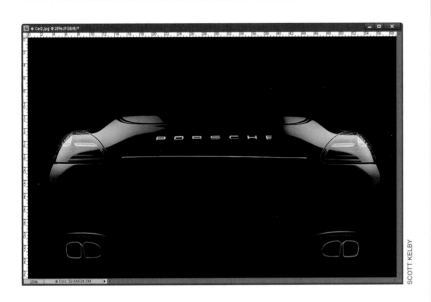

SCOTT KELBY

Step One:
Open the digital camera image that you want to resize. Press **Ctrl-Shift-R (Mac: Command-Shift-R)** to make Elements' rulers visible. Check out the rulers to see the approximate dimensions of your image. As you can see from the rulers in the example here, this photo is around 37x59".

Step Two:
Go under the Image menu, under Resize, and choose **Image Size** to bring up the Image Size dialog. In the Document Size section, the Resolution setting is 72 pixels/inch (ppi). A resolution of 72 ppi is considered low resolution and is ideal for photos that will only be viewed on-screen (such as web graphics, slide shows, etc.). This res is too low, though, to get high-quality results from a color inkjet printer, color laser printer, or for use on a printing press.

(Continued)

Step Three:

If we plan to output this photo to any printing device, it's pretty clear that we'll need to increase the resolution to get good results. I wish we could just type in the resolution we'd like it to be in the Resolution field (such as 200 or 240 ppi), but unfortunately, this "resampling" makes our low-res photo appear soft (blurry) and pixelated. That's why we need to make sure the Resample Image checkbox is turned off (as shown here). That way, when we type in the setting that we need in the Resolution field, Elements automatically adjusts the Width and Height fields for the image in the exact same proportion. As your Width and Height decrease (with Resample Image turned off), your Resolution increases. Best of all, there's absolutely no loss of quality. Pretty cool!

Step Four:

Here I've turned off Resample Image, then I typed 240 in the Resolution field (for output to a color inkjet printer—I know, you probably think you need a lot more resolution, but you don't. In fact, I never print with a resolution higher than 240 ppi). At a resolution of 240 ppi here, I can actually print a photo that is almost 18 inches wide by around 11 inches high.

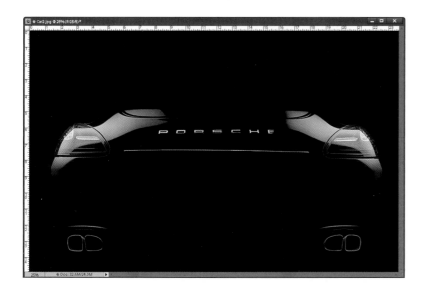

Step Five:

Here, I've lowered the Resolution setting to 180 ppi. (Again, you don't need nearly as much resolution as you'd think, but 180 ppi is pretty much as low as you should go when printing to a color inkjet printer.) As you can see, the Width of my image is now around 23" and the height is almost 15". Best of all, we did it without damaging a single pixel, because we were able to turn off Resample Image.

Step Six:

When you click OK, you won't see the image window change at all—it will appear at the exact same size onscreen. But now look at the rulers—you can see that your image's dimensions have changed. Resizing using this technique does three big things: (1) it gets your physical dimensions down to size (the photo now fits on a 16x24" sheet); (2) it increases the resolution enough so you can output this image on a color inkjet printer; and (3) you haven't softened or pixelated the image in any way—the quality remains the same—all because you turned off Resample Image. *Note:* Do not turn off Resample Image for images that you scan on a scanner—they start as high-res images in the first place. Turning off Resample Image is only for photos taken with a digital camera at a low resolution.

Resizing and How to Reach Those Hidden Free Transform Handles

What happens if you drag a large photo onto a smaller photo in Elements? (This happens all the time, especially if you're collaging or combining two or more photos.) You have to resize the photo using Free Transform, right? Right. But here's the catch—when you bring up Free Transform, at least two (or, more likely, all four) of the handles that you need to resize the image are out of reach. You see the center point, but not the handles you need to reach to resize. Here's how to get around that hurdle quickly and easily:

Step One:
Open two different-sized photos in the Elements Editor. Use the Move tool **(V)** to drag-and-drop the larger photo on top of the smaller one (if you're in tabbed viewing, drag one image onto the other image's thumbnail in the Photo Bin). To resize a photo on a layer, press **Ctrl-T (Mac: Command-T)** to bring up the Free Transform command. Next, press-and-hold the Shift key to constrain your proportions (or turn on the Constrain Proportions checkbox in the Tool Options Bar), grab one of the Free Transform corner handles, and (a) drag inward to shrink the photo, or (b) drag outward to increase its size (not more than 20%, to keep from making the photo look soft and pixelated). But wait, there's a problem. The problem is—you can't even see the Free Transform handles in this image.

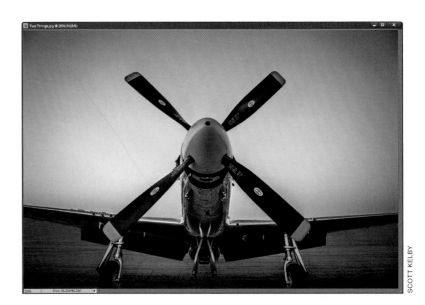

SCOTT KELBY

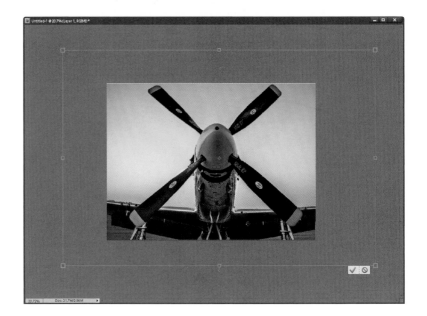

Step Two:
To instantly have full access to all of Free Transform's handles, just press **Ctrl-0** (zero; **Mac: Command-0**), and Elements will instantly zoom out of your document window and surround your photo with gray desktop, making every handle well within reach. Try it once, and you'll use this trick again and again. *Note:* You must choose Free Transform first for this trick to work.

There is a different set of rules we use for maintaining as much quality as possible when making an image smaller, and there are a couple of different ways to do just that (we'll cover the two main ones here). Luckily, maintaining image quality is much easier when sizing down than when scaling up (in fact, photos often look dramatically better—and sharper—when scaled down, especially if you follow these guidelines).

Making Your Photos Smaller (Downsizing)

Downsizing photos where the resolution is already 300 ppi:
Although earlier we discussed how to change image size if your digital camera gives you 72-ppi images with large physical dimensions (like 24x42" deep), what do you do if your camera gives you 300-ppi images at smaller physical dimensions (like a 10x6" at 300 ppi)? Basically, you turn on Resample Image (in the Image Size dialog—go under the Image menu, under Resize, and choose **Image Size**), then simply type the desired size (in this example, we want a 4x6" final image size), and click OK (don't change the Resolution setting, just click OK). The image will be scaled down to size, and the resolution will remain at 300 ppi. *IMPORTANT:* When you scale down using this method, it's likely that the image will soften a little bit, so after scaling you'll want to apply the Unsharp Mask filter to bring back any sharpness lost in the resizing (look at the sharpening chapter [Chapter 11] to see what settings to use).

(Continued)

Making one photo smaller without shrinking the whole document:

If you're working with more than one image in the same document, you'll resize a bit differently. To scale down a photo on a layer, first click on that photo's layer in the Layers palette, then press **Ctrl-T (Mac: Command-T)** to bring up Free Transform. Press-and-hold the Shift key to keep the photo proportional (or turn on the Constrain Proportions checkbox in the Tool Options Bar), grab a corner handle, and drag inward. When it looks good to you, press the **Enter (Mac: Return) key**. If the image looks softer after resizing it, apply the Unsharp Mask filter (again, see the sharpening chapter).

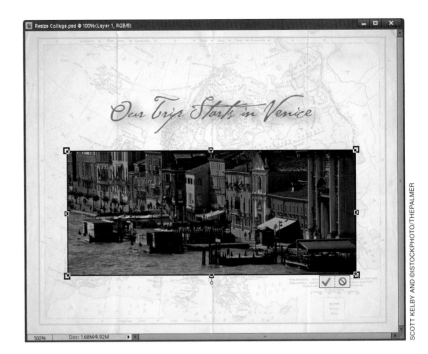

Resizing problems when dragging between documents:

This one gets a lot of people, because at first glance it just doesn't make sense. You have two documents, approximately the same size, side-by-side onscreen. But when you drag a 72-ppi photo (of sunflowers, in this case) onto a 300-ppi document (Untitled-1), the photo appears really small. Why is that? Simply put: resolution. Although the documents appear to be the same size, they're not. The tip-off that you're not really seeing them at the same size is found in the title bar of each photo. For instance, the photo of the sunflowers is displayed at 100%, but the Untitled-1 document is displayed at only 25%. So, to get more predictable results, make sure both documents are at the same viewing size and resolution (check in the Image Size dialog).

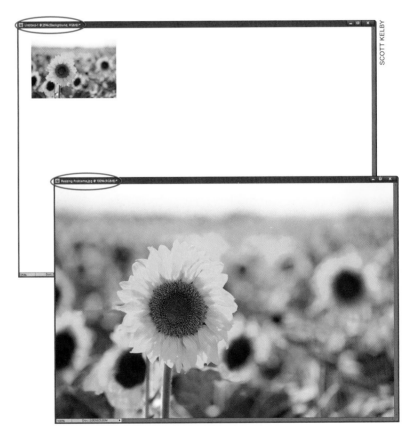

Elements has a pretty slick little utility that lets you take a folder full of images and do any (or all) of the following automatically at one time: (1) rename them; (2) resize them; (3) change their resolution; (4) color correct and sharpen them; and (5) save them in the file format of your choice (JPEG, TIFF, etc.). If you find yourself processing a lot of images, this can save a ton of time. Better yet, since the whole process is automated, you can teach someone else to do the processing for you, like your spouse, your child, a neighbor's child, passersby, local officials, etc.

Automated Saving and Resizing

Step One:
In the Elements Editor, go under the File menu and choose **Process Multiple Files**.

Step Two:
When the Process Multiple Files dialog opens, the first thing you have to do is choose the folder of photos you want to process by clicking on the Browse button in the Source section of the dialog. Then, navigate to the folder you want and click OK (Mac: Choose). If you already have some photos open in Elements, you can choose Opened Files from the Process Files From pop-up menu (or you can choose Import to import files). Then, in the Destination section, you decide whether you want the new copies to be saved in the same folder (by turning on the Same as Source checkbox), or copied into a different folder (in which case, click on the section's Browse button and choose that folder).

(Continued)

How to Resize and Crop Photos | Chapter 3 | 121

Step Three:

The next section is File Naming. If you want your files automatically renamed when they're processed, turn on the Rename Files checkbox, then in the fields directly below that checkbox, type the name you want these new files to have and choose how you want the numbering to appear after the name (a two-digit number, three-digit, etc.). Then, choose the number with which you want to start numbering images. You'll see a preview of how your file naming will appear just below the document name field (shown circled here).

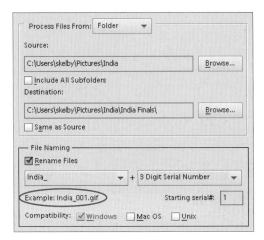

Step Four:

In the Image Size section, you decide if you want to resize the images (by turning on the Resize Images checkbox), and you enter the width and height you want for your finished photos. You can also choose to change the resolution. If you want to change their file type (like from RAW to JPEG Max Quality), you choose that in the bottom section—File Type. Just turn on the Convert Files To checkbox, and then choose your format from the pop-up menu.

Step Five:

On the top-right side of the dialog, there is a list of Quick Fix cosmetic changes you can make to these photos, as well, including Auto Levels (to adjust the overall color balance and contrast), Auto Contrast (this is kind of lame if you ask me), Auto Color (it's not bad), and Sharpen (it works well). Also on the right is a Labels section, where you can add a custom watermark or a caption to these photos. Now, just click OK and Elements does its thing, totally automated based on the choices you made in this dialog. How cool is that!

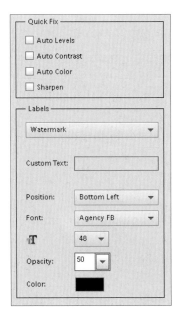

You really have to see this feature in action but, in a nutshell, you can resize one part of your image, while the important parts stay intact. For example, let's say you took a photo of some rock climbers that you want to print out as a 10x8. But when you go to print it, you realize you're going to have to crop it (since the 10x8 aspect ratio is not what your camera shoots in) and cut out a key part of the photo. With the Recompose tool, you can resize the background, without resizing the rock climbers. Like I said, you gotta see it in action.

Resizing Just Parts of Your Image Using the Recompose Tool

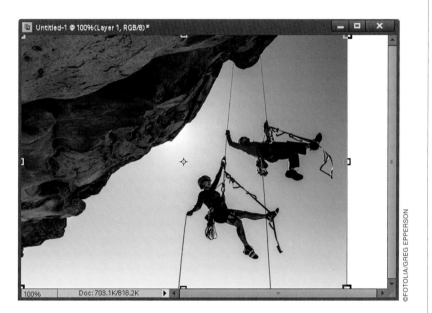

©FOTOLIA/GREG EPPERSON

Step One:
One of the things I use the Recompose tool for most is making digital camera images fit in traditional photography sizes (like 8x10", 5x7", 4x6", etc.). You always have to crop the image, or leave white space, when resizing it to fit in one of these standard sizes (as shown here, where I dragged a digital camera image into a 10x8" document and then used Free Transform **[Ctrl-T; Mac: Command-T]** to position it). When you position it so you see the full image, it leaves a huge gap on the right.

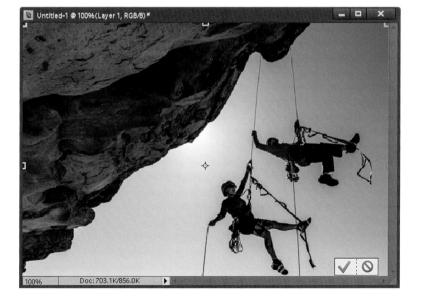

Step Two:
Rather than leaving the gap, most folks try to just resize the photo (again, using Free Transform), so it fills the full 10x8" area, but you can see what happens when you do that—you no longer see the full image as you composed it. In our case—worse yet—it clips off part of the photo at the bottom.

(Continued)

Step Three:

Since the resizing from Step Two doesn't work, we'll go back to what we did in Step One, which at least gives you the full image, as you shot it. You could try just stretching the image by, again, using Free Transform—when the resizing handles appear, grab the right-side handle and drag to the right, as shown here—but that distorts everything and stretches out the rock climbers, so this really isn't an option either for most images.

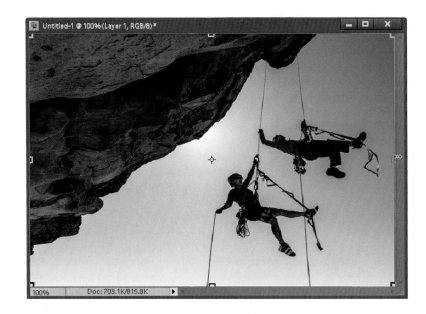

Step Four:

This is where the Recompose tool comes in handy. Select the Recompose tool **(W)** from the Toolbox. The way the tool works is you tell Elements which areas of the photo you want to make sure it preserves and which areas of the photo are okay to remove/squish/expand/get rid of. This is all done using the four options at the left end of the Tool Options Bar (circled in red here at the bottom).

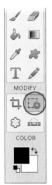

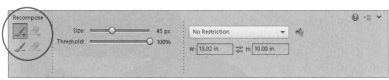

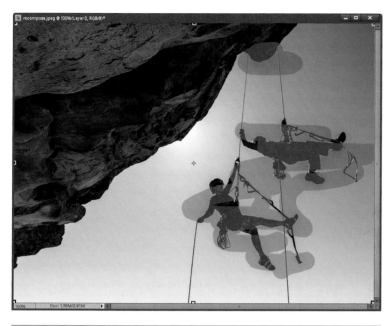

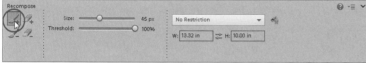

Step Five:

First, switch back over to your original image, then click on the Mark for Protection icon (the brush with the plus sign), and paint some loose squiggly lines over the areas of the photo you want to make sure Elements protects. These are the important areas that you don't want to see transformed in any way (here I painted over the rock climbers, their ropes, and the rocks right above them). If you make a mistake and paint on something you didn't want to, just use the tool's corresponding Erase option to the right of the Mark for Protection option.

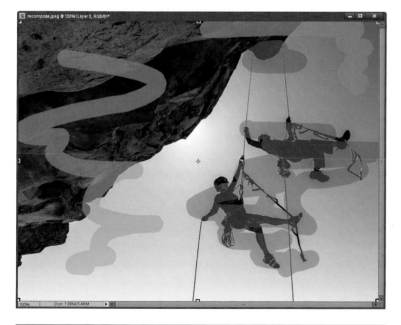

Step Six:

Now you have to tell Elements what parts of the photo are okay to get rid of. Click on the Mark for Removal icon in the Tool Options Bar (the brush with the minus sign) and paint some lines over the non-essential areas of the photo. No need to go crazy here, a couple of quick brush strokes will do just fine.

(Continued)

Step Seven:

Click on the right-middle handle and drag inward, until the Width setting in the Tool Options Bar reads 10 inches. You'll notice that it changes the appearance of the rock on the left, but not in a way that makes it look unnatural. Now, if you keep dragging inward (beyond what we've dragged here), it will start distorting other parts of the photo, so you can't just drag forever. Luckily, you see a live onscreen preview as you're dragging, so you'll know right away how far you can drag. Next, drag the top-middle handle downward until the Height setting in the Tool Options Bar reads 8 inches. When you've dragged far enough, press the **Enter (Mac: Return) key** to lock in your change and you've got your 10x8. Now, let's look at another way to use the Recompose tool.

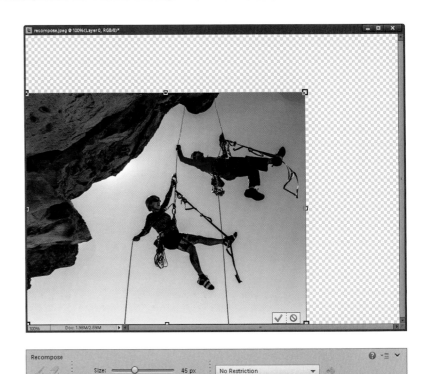

TIP: Use the Preset Pop-Up Menu

The Recompose tool has a preset pop-up menu in the Tool Options Bar with some common print sizes, so when you select one of them, it automatically recomposes your photo to that specific size.

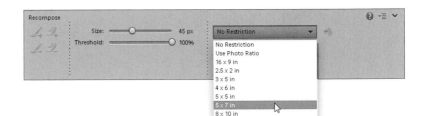

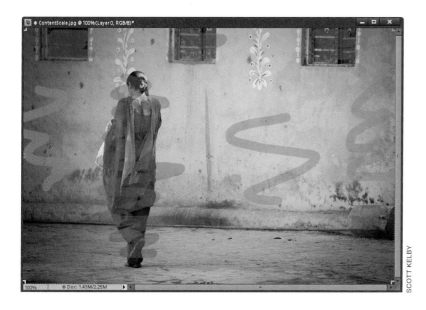

SCOTT KELBY

Step Eight:
Since you can make the Recompose tool aware of your subject, you can use it in other ways. For example, let's say you wanted the three windows here to be closer together, so you have a smaller image for your layout without cropping it. Click on the Mask for Protection icon in the Tool Options Bar, and paint over the woman and windows. Then, click on the Mark for Removal icon and paint on the wall, like I did here.

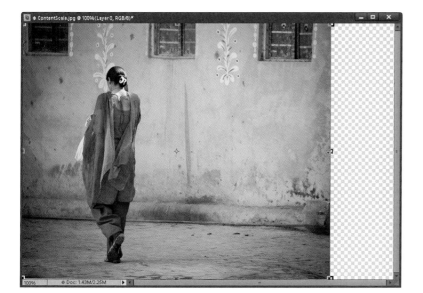

Step Nine:
Now, click on the right-side handle and drag over toward the left to squeeze the photo, making it narrower. Again, Elements does a good job of removing the space between the windows without making them look like they were squished, and without distorting the woman, either. As you can see, I can get away with plenty of squeezing here in this example, but even if you can't, I've got a trick for you in the next step.

(Continued)

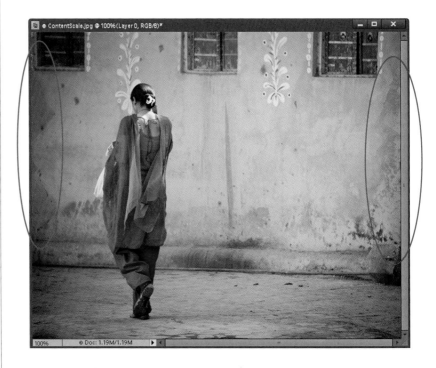

TIP: Protecting Skin Tones

I wanted to point out another Recompose tool option and that is an icon in the Tool Options Bar with a little person (shown circled here in red). You turn this Highlight Skin Tones option on when you have people in the photo you're about to resize, and it tells the Recompose tool to automatically highlight people's skin tones for protection so they don't get, well, recomposed. Now, Elements will try to avoid those areas. It doesn't always work, but it usually helps.

Step 10:

Press **Enter (Mac: Return)** to lock in your recomposition, then press the **C key** to switch to the Crop tool, and crop away the excess background. Now, if you look closely enough, you'll see the Recompose tool made a jagged line and some deformities on the wall along the edges of the photo (while it's a bit hard to see this here in print, you should be able to see it better on your computer screen). If this ever happens to you, don't feel like you have to abandon the Recompose tool altogether because of a small area. Instead, we can always try some of the retouching tools to clean that area up.

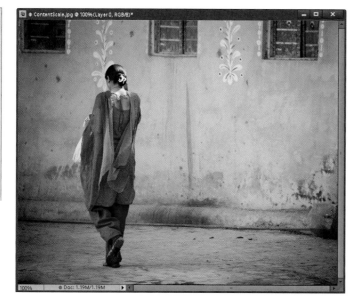

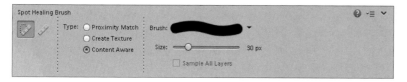

Step 11:

I think the Spot Healing Brush tool **(J)** will work great here, so go ahead and select it from the Toolbox. In the Tool Options Bar, set the Type to **Content Aware**, so it will fix the problem with the surrounding area. Now, paint over those dark areas to remove them. You may need to paint a few times, so you don't get repeating patterns.

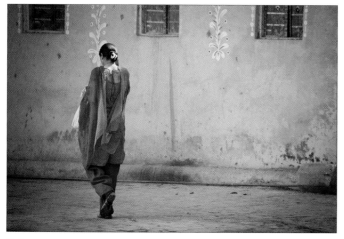

Before

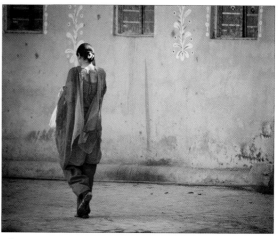

After

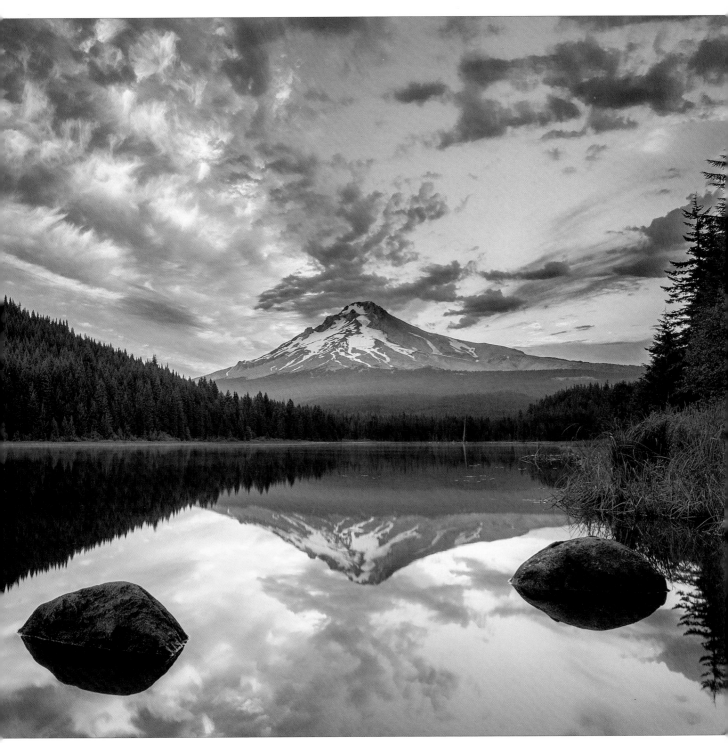

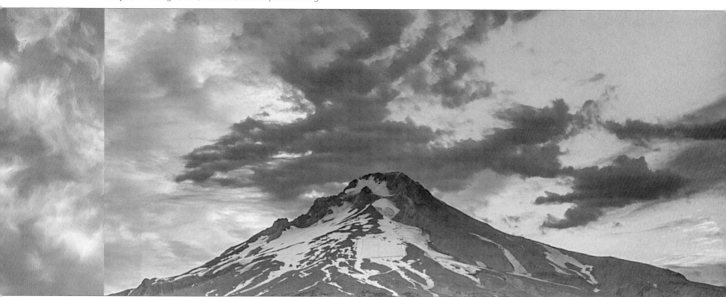

edIT
using quick, guided, and expert editing

Man, did I luck out on the name of this chapter: edIT. It's actually named after the popular DJ, producer, and musician, and that right there is enough for me, especially since he gets to work with hip-hop artists and rappers. I love rappers, because they use such colorful phrases—stuff you usually only hear from fans at a Redskins football game when a receiver is wide open in the flat and drops a ball thrown right into his hands. But when the fans say it, they're yelling, which can really get on your nerves. In a rap song, even though they're saying the same things, since it's set to music, it just floats by. In fact, a lot of times, when you're listening to rap, they'll say something and you stop and think, "Did he really just say what I thought he said?" but you try to convince yourself that's not what you heard because nobody dropped an easy pass. I always wonder what rappers have to be so angry about. They're rich, successful entrepreneurs, and everybody obviously wants to hang out with them and go to "da club" and drink Cristal and look thoroughly bored at all the women gesticulating around them. They should be really happy, one would think, but often they sound very grumpy, which always strikes me as odd for millionaire celebrity rappers, which I assume DJ edIT produces or mixes. By the way, a "mix," I believe, is what you add to gin (like juice) when you're chillin' with your posse in your crib (which must mean you have small children sleeping in your home). Anyway, I thought I would help out by writing some positive, non-angry, upbeat lyrics that edIT can show to his rapper friends so they'll sound more like the happy millionaire celebrities that they are. Please don't laugh—this is my first rap for my peeps and my crew, so I'm just rappin' lyrical for me, and one for my homies. (See, that's rap talk, right?) Okay, here goes: "I was having lots of fun at Busch Gardens today. I rode an awesome roller coaster and didn't have to pay. I drove there in my new limo and the driver's real nice. And we're listening to some snappy tunes from cool Vanilla Ice." See? Rap can be happy and super-edgy, too! Peace out. Word. Wikki-wikki.

Which Editing Mode Do I Use: Quick, Guided, or Expert?

Before we jump into using the different editing modes in Elements, I wanted to give you a quick overview of what those modes are and which one may be right for you. The main thing to keep in mind, though, is that you may actually use multiple editing modes. If you're just starting out, then Quick mode is a great place to begin. But, even beginners may need to jump to Expert mode for some things (trust me, you don't have to be an expert either) in the end. So keep an open mind and just know that although you may like one editing mode best, the others are at least worth looking at.

Quick Mode:

If you're a beginner and just starting out, then I think Quick edit mode is a great place to start (click on Quick at the top of the Editor window). Ever hear the saying: You don't know what you don't know? To me, that's why Quick mode is there. It not only nicely lays out which things you'll most likely do to your photos (in the Palette Bin on the right side of the window), but it provides them in a good order, too. There are also some tools in the Toolbox on the left side of the window, but I stay away from these most of the time because, well, they kinda take away from the point of Quick edit mode. If you're in Quick mode, then try to forget about the tools—just keep it simple and work with the options provided on the right (we'll take a look at Quick mode in the next tutorial).

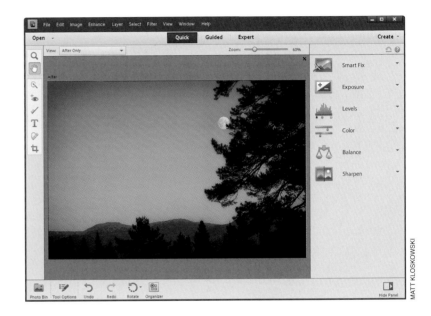

MATT KLOSKOWSKI

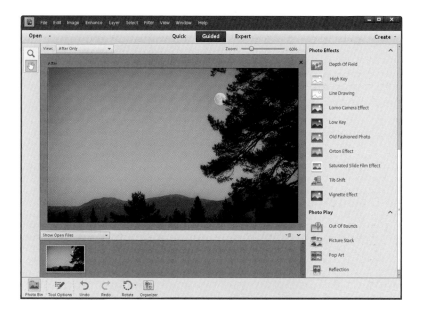

Guided Mode:

Guided edit mode (click on Guided at the top of the Editor window) is for applying special effects (for me, at least). They appear under Photo Effects and Photo Play on the right. There's also a Touchups section at the top right, and they're kinda like built-in tutorials—Elements walks you through the steps involved. But if you're reading this book, isn't that kinda the reason why you bought it? Guided mode is really just a place between Quick mode and Expert mode. So, if you've moved past Quick mode, then your best bet is to jump straight to Expert mode (it's really not that hard), unless you want to do one of the special effects (like turning your photo into a line drawing) in Guided mode. We'll take a quick look at Guided mode later in this chapter, and for some other Guided mode special effects, check out Chapter 10.

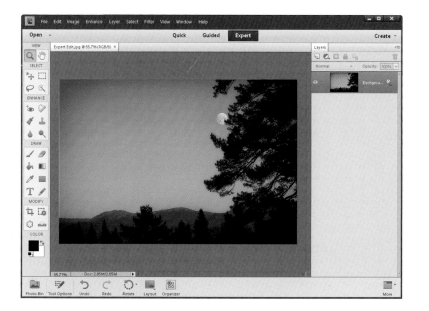

Expert Mode:

Expert mode (click on Expert at the top of the window) is the traditional Elements Editor. It's been around since the beginning and looks a lot like Elements' big brother, Photoshop. Here, you can use layers, all the tools, lots of menus, adjustments, layer masks, etc. It's what most of this book is based on. Don't let the name fool you—once you've moved past Quick mode, Expert mode is really the place you need to be. Quick mode is great for global changes to a photo (like if the whole photo is too dark), but once you get to the point where you want to start changing only parts of a photo, making selections, retouching, and working non-destructively, then Expert mode is the place to be. We'll look a little more at Expert mode at the end of this chapter, and throughout the book.

Photo Quick Fix
in Quick Mode

Quick edit mode is kinda like a stripped down version of Expert mode. If you're new to Elements, it's not a bad place to start. I'm usually against "quick" modes and "auto-fix" stuff, but the way they've implemented this in Elements 11 is actually really nice, and I think it works great for beginners.

Step One:

Open a photo and click on Quick at the top of the Editor window. First things first: forget about the left side of the window. The tools in the Toolbox make using Quick mode too much like using Expert mode (but without all of the options that Expert mode has). So, if you find that you need the tools here, you're better off going into Expert mode to do what you need to do.

Step Two:

In the preview area of Quick mode, you can see side-by-side, before-and-after versions of the photo you're correcting (before on the top or left; after on the bottom or right). To see this view, from the View pop-up menu above the top left of the preview area, select **Before & After (Horizontal or Vertical)**. In the Palette Bin on the right side of the window is a group of nested palettes offering tonal and lighting fixes you can apply to your photo. Start with the Smart Fix palette at the top. Click on the Auto button and Smart Fix will automatically analyze the photo and try to balance the overall tone (adjusting the shadows and highlights), while fixing any obvious color casts while it's at it. In a lot of cases, this feature does a surprisingly good job. There's also a slider within the Smart Fix palette that you can use to increase (or decrease) the effect, or you can click on the thumbnails beneath the slider.

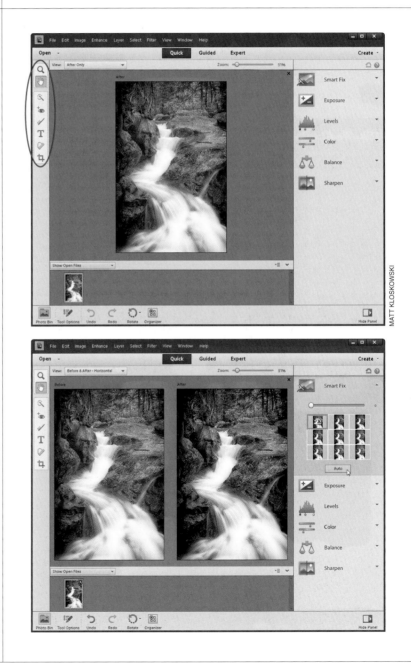

MATT KLOSKOWSKI

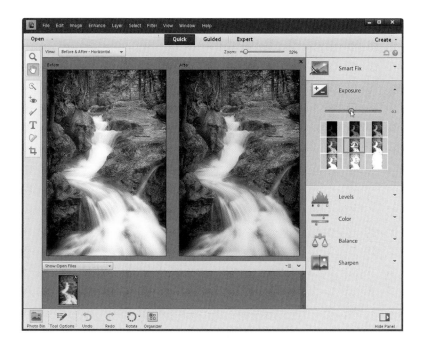

Step Three:

If you're not happy with the Smart Fix results, don't try to stack more "fixes" on top of it. Instead, click the Reset Panel icon (the curved arrow above a straight line that appears above the top right of the Palette Bin) to reset the photo to how it looked when you first entered Quick mode. Now, let's take a look at each setting individually: First, click on Exposure to open its palette. The Exposure setting is like the heavy hitter—if the whole photo is too dark or too bright, then this is where to go. You'll see its palette also has a slider and thumbnails right below it. They're different ways of doing the same thing. If you like using the thumbnails, just click on the one that looks closest to how bright or dark you'd like your photo to be. As you do that, you'll see the slider move each time. Usually, though, I just drag the slider (as shown here) until I'm happy with the overall exposure.

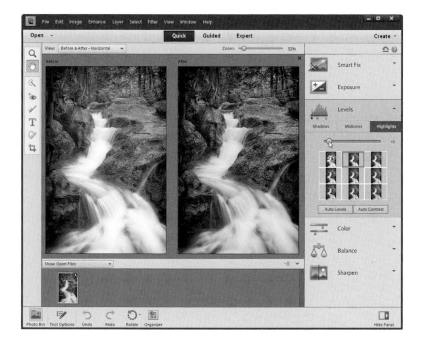

Step Four:

More often than not, just adjusting the exposure won't fix the whole photo. You'll usually end up in the next palette, which is Levels. Here you can choose to work on the shadows, midtones, or highlights separately. The Shadows slider is particularly helpful because we tend to lose a lot of detail in the shadows. Drag it to the right a little bit, and watch how it opens up the dark shadow areas in your photo (mainly in the rocks in this photo). The Highlights slider will add some detail back to the water here, as well. For this one, I increased the Shadows slider to 2, the Midtones slider to 30, and the Highlights slider to 10. I tend to stay away from the Auto Levels and Auto Contrast buttons, because chances are, if Smart Fix didn't work well, then neither will they.

(Continued)

Step Five:

The next palette down, Color, has only really one setting that I think is worthwhile. You'll see at the top of the palette you can control the Saturation, Hue, and Vibrance. The Saturation adjustment adds or removes color saturation in the whole photo. It's worth trying out and maybe even clicking the Auto button. Sometimes the photo looks good, but most of the time, the Vibrance setting is the most useful here. While Saturation adds color to everything in the photo, Vibrance tends to only add color saturation to the colors that need it, while leaving the other colors alone, so you don't get that fakey look. It's also great on portraits because it tends to leave skin tones alone and only adds color saturation to everything else.

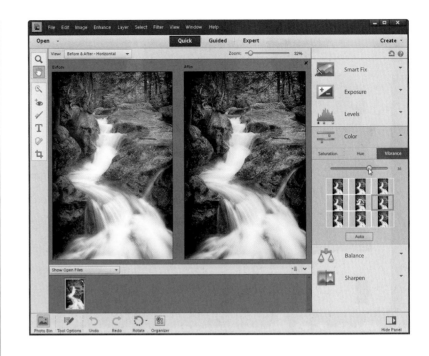

Step Six:

While the Color palette helps us fix the overall color saturation in a photo, the Balance palette right below helps remove color casts (like when an indoor photo looks really yellow). It's pretty simple to use to control the temperature and the tint in the photo. I'll warn you ahead of time, though, small adjustments here make *big* changes, so be careful. The Temperature adjustment lets you add more blue or more yellow/red to a photo. Basically, adding blue removes yellow and adding more yellow removes blue. Photos taken indoors at night are perfect candidates for this since they tend to look really yellow, so dragging the slider toward blue helps balance (hence the name of this palette) the photo. You can also control the Tint (greens and magentas), but honestly, you won't notice much of a problem there in most cases. But if you do, it works the same—adding more green removes magenta, and adding more magenta removes a greenish color cast.

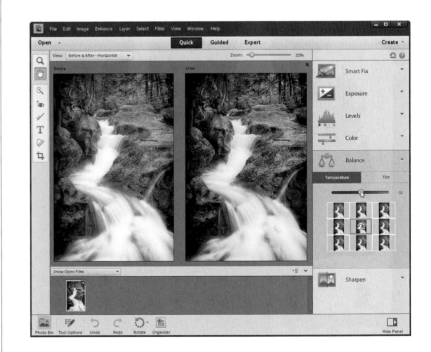

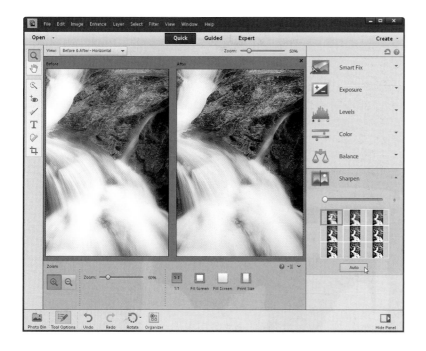

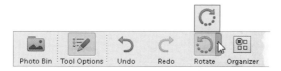

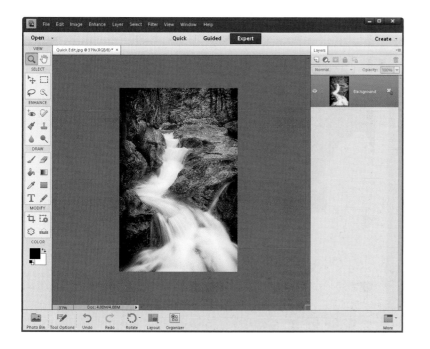

Step Seven:
The final step here is to sharpen your photo. I always click on the Zoom tool in the Toolbox, and zoom in a little further, so I can see the details. Then, just click the Auto button in the Sharpen palette and watch the results. If the photo isn't sharp enough for you, drag the slider to the right to increase the amount of sharpening. But, be careful, because oversharpening can ruin the photo by becoming too obvious, and it can introduce color shifts and halos around objects.

Step Eight:
There are a couple other things you can do while you're here in Quick mode (basically, think of this as a "one-stop shop" for quickly fixing images). Below the preview area is an icon you can click on to rotate your photo (this photo doesn't need to be rotated, but hey, ya never know). And, I know I told you to forget about the Toolbox on the left, but there is a Crop tool there, so if you need to do a quick crop you can do it here.

Step Nine:
Okay, so you've color corrected, fixed the contrast, sharpened your image, and even cropped it down to size (if it needed it). So, how do you leave Quick mode and return to Expert mode? Just click on Expert at the top of the window (the same place you went to, to get into Quick mode). It basically applies all the changes to your photo and returns you to the normal Expert editing mode.

Special Effects in Guided Mode (the Only Time to Use It)

When you use Guided mode, it walks you through a bunch of popular editing options, like cropping, enhancing colors, retouching, and sharpening. As I mentioned at the beginning of this chapter, they're kind of like built-in tutorials in Elements—they don't do all of the work for you, they just explain to you what tools you should use and the order in which to use them. However, there are some other options in Guided mode that can be more useful, because they can help you to easily create some special effects. (*Note:* We look at some other Guided mode special effects in Chapter 10.)

Step One:

Open a photo and click on Guided at the top of the Editor window. The Palette Bin on the right is broken up into three sections: Touchups, Photo Effects, and Photo Play. Forget about the Touchups section. In fact, there's a little upward-facing arrow you can click on to collapse that section. (Again, the options there are basically tutorials with guided walk-throughs, but they're the kinds of things we cover in this book. So, if you weren't reading this book [which you are, by the way], then that would be a good section to check out. Since you are reading this book [I'm psychic, you know], I'd stick with the tutorials in the book you just paid for.)

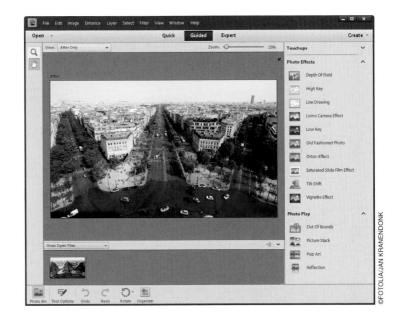

Step Two:

This brings us to the Photo Effects section. You could do some of these effects in Expert mode if you wanted to, but you'd have to use a bunch of tools, dialogs, layers, and filters to do them. So, if the effect you want is here, it's not a bad place to get to know. Here, we'll look at the Tilt-Shift effect, since it's new in Elements 11. The rest of the effects pretty much work exactly the same—remember, this is "Guided" mode, so Elements will walk you through each step. The Tilt-Shift effect simulates the use of a tilt-shift lens and makes a photo look like a miniature model. It's been a popular effect lately. So, go ahead and click on Tilt-Shift to start.

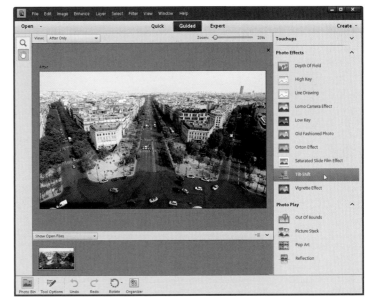

©FOTOLIA/JAN KRANENDONK

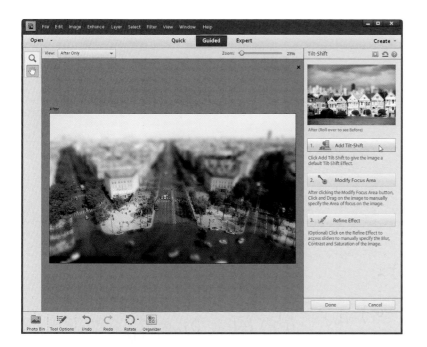

Step Three:
Photos taken from up high (looking down on a street or city) tend to look best for this effect. In the Tilt-Shift palette, click on the Add Tilt-Shift button and you'll see that Elements blurs your photo, but keeps a sharp area of focus in the middle. Depending on the individual photo you're editing, this may or may not look good right from the start (usually not). Read on and you'll see how you can customize it.

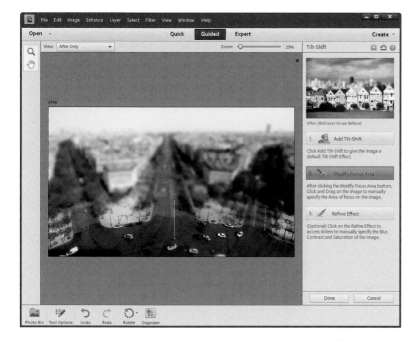

Step Four:
Let's say you don't like where it put the focus area in the photo. Just click on the next button down, Modify Focus Area, and you can change it. Click-and-drag over another area that you want to keep in focus, and Elements will redraw the effect to blur everything but the area you dragged over.

(Continued)

Step Five:

By now you can see what I was talking about earlier when I said Guided mode is like a tutorial. It's not doing anything that you couldn't do elsewhere in Elements, but it just guides you through it here. Now, there's one more button at the bottom called Refine Effect, which lets you customize the amount of blur in the photo. When you click on it, you'll see three new sliders appear. The Blur slider controls the amount of blur added for the Tilt-Shift effect. You can increase it a little, but I wouldn't go much above 30–40 because it starts looking too funky. Below that are Contrast and Saturation, but I rarely mess around with those—if anything, maybe increase the Contrast slider to 10–15 and Saturation to around 10, but that's it. When you're done, click the Done button at the bottom-right of the window and it'll take you right back to the main Guided mode window.

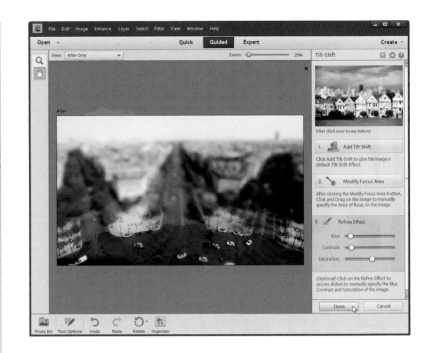

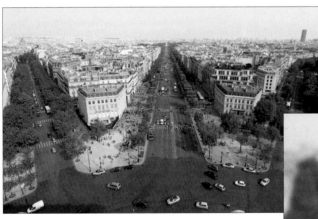

Before

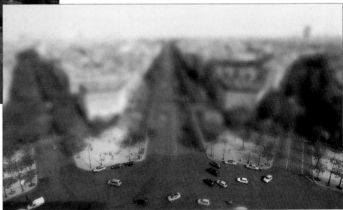

After

Okay, I know the third editing mode is called "Expert" mode, but don't let the name fool you—it's not just for experts. In fact, most of what you'll do in this book is done in Expert mode because, let's face it, that's where all the cool stuff is. You go into Expert mode when you want to do things like retouching photos, or adding text, or modifying just a specific portion of a photo, because it's got a ton of features like layers, layer masks (which are covered in Chapter 5), and much more. So, get it out of your mind that Expert mode is just for experts. It's for you, even if you're not a seasoned pro at Elements.

A Quick Look at Expert Mode (It's Not Just for Experts!)

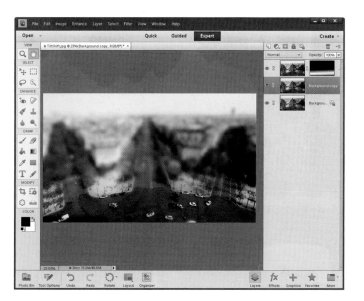

Step One:
Open an image and then click on Expert at the top of the Editor window, which will take you into the full Elements Editor (if you're not already there) with all the bells and whistles. By the way, if you were to go into Expert mode after applying a Guided edit (like we did in the previous tutorial), you'd actually see all the layers and effects that Elements has applied, as shown here in the Layers palette for the previous tutorial's photo.

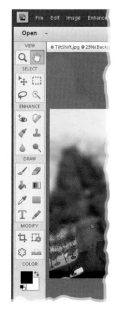

Step Two:
Over on the left side of the window, one of the first things you'll notice is that there are a bunch of tools in the Toolbox. These tools are broken up into categories: View, Select, Enhance, Draw, Modify, and Color. As a photographer using Elements (which I assume you are, since you bought this book), you won't use the Draw tools much (except for the Brush tool) and you won't use the Modify tools much either (except for cropping and straightening). But, you'll use the Select and Enhance tools plenty.

(Continued)

Step Three:

Go ahead and click on one of the tools in the Toolbox. It can be any tool, so just click around a few times and then look at the bottom of the window beneath the preview area. You'll see a context-sensitive Tool Options Bar appear for each tool (here, I clicked on the Quick Selection tool). Since most tools have different settings, you'll notice it changes based on which tool you click on. This is a really important area, so make sure you get accustomed to it. (*Note:* To hide/show the Tool Options Bar, press **F5**.)

TIP: Getting to Tools Quickly

If you're going to be using Expert mode a lot, then it's a good idea to get used to the keyboard shortcuts for the most commonly used tools. If you hover your cursor over each tool in the Toolbox, you'll see a tool tip appear with the name of the tool followed by its one-letter keyboard shortcut.

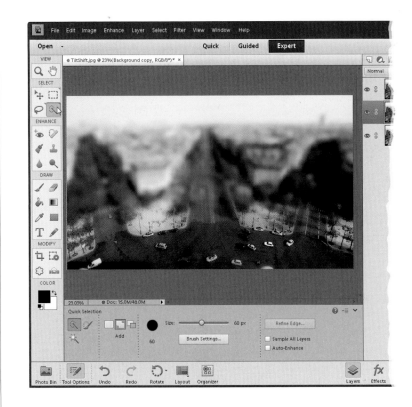

Step Four:

Now look over at the bottom-right of the window. There are five icons there. Click on the Layers icon to open/close the Layers palette on the right side of the window. Layers are one of the key elements to working inside of Expert mode and there's actually a whole chapter devoted to them (Chapter 5). For now, just know that you should probably keep that palette open all the time, since you'll be using it a lot. Click on the More icon to access some of the other palettes. As for the other icons, you (as a photographer, at least) probably won't use them as much. (*Note:* To undock the Layers palette from the right side of the window, choose **Custom Workspace** from the More icon's pop-up menu, then click on the Layers palette's tab and drag it out of the nested palettes. This will minimize the size of the palette, giving you more room in your work area.)

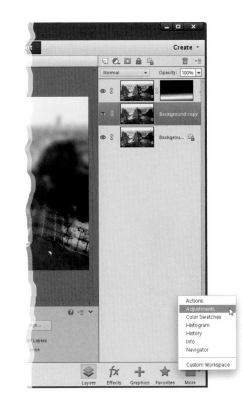

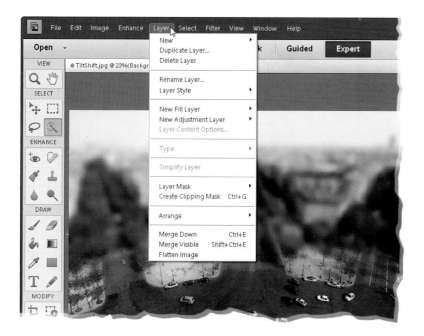

Step Five:

Finally, don't forget the menu bar at the very top of the window. That's the launch pad for a lot of the things we'll do in the book. So, for example, if you read "Go to the Layer menu," that means to go to the Layer menu up in the menu bar. And, if you read something like "Go to the Layers palette," that means to go to the palette we just talked about in Step Four.

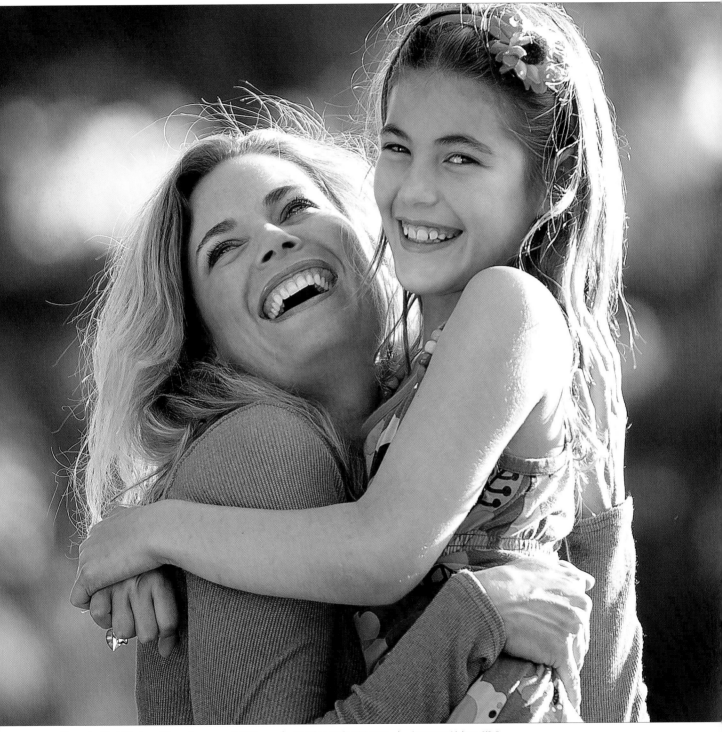

Photo by Matt Kloskowski   Exposure: 1/250 sec | Focal Length: 200 mm | Aperture Value: ƒ/2.8

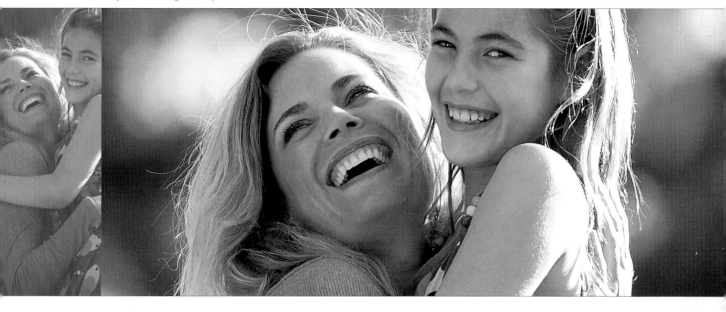

LAYER CAKE
working with layers

This is the first edition of this book to have its own dedicated chapter just on layers. Luckily, Matt (my co-author) happens to be an absolute expert on layers (his book, *Layers: The Complete Guide to Photoshop's Most Powerful Feature*, is one of the best-selling Photoshop books ever), so I asked Matt to write this chapter. Even though it's just one chapter, he cherry-picked the most important stuff from his book and added it here, which is awesome, except that now you're going to feel like you don't need to actually buy Matt's book, because you've already got the best of it here, and so adding this chapter actually cost Matt money. I don't know if I mentioned this, but Matt has two young children and a wife, and probably a cat, but we're not really that close (it might be a goldfish or something. Really, who pays attention to that stuff?). Anyway, the important thing here isn't the stuff that Matt is giving up for you—after all, there are plenty of jobs his kids can get that don't involve getting a good education or college. They're hard-working kids and I'm certain they'll find good jobs down at the asbestos mine (kids eat that stuff like it's cotton candy—they love it!), so don't let Matt's messed-up personal situation have any effect on how much you enjoy this chapter, which should be plenty after Matt's sacrifice on your behalf. Anyway, since I felt bad, I let Matt choose the name for this chapter, and he chose "Layer Cake," which he says is based on the 2004 movie of the same name starring Daniel Craig, Sienna Miller, and Michael Gambon, and I believe it, since Matt is pretty broke. I imagine the last time he could actually afford to go to the movies with his family was back in 2004. Hey, good news, though: I hear if things keep going well, he's thinking of getting a Motorola Razr flip phone. He will so love finally having a cellular phone.

Layer Basics

This tutorial is only meant for those of you who don't really understand why you would use layers. If you already know why layers are important, then skip this and go straight to the next one, where we dive right into building things with layers. So, let's talk a little bit about layers and how they're the foundation of everything you do in Elements. Think of it this way: you'd never dream of drawing on a printed photograph with a black marker and then expect to go back and erase that drawing, would you? Well, that's exactly what you're doing if you don't use layers in Elements and you work on the original image.

Step One:

Picture this: you're holding a printed photo of me. Why? Because I didn't think it was right to do what I'm about to do to a portrait of someone else. Seriously, though, it can be any printed photo. The point is, imagine you set that photo down on the desk, grabbed a black marker, and started drawing on it—fake eyeglasses, a mustache, and maybe even a funny beard.

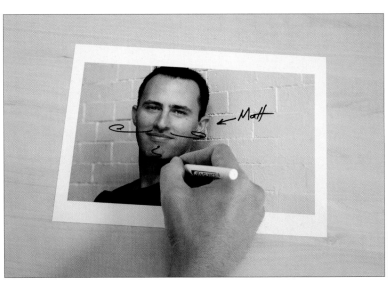

Step Two:

Now, what would happen if you grabbed a damp towel and tried to erase what you just drew? One of two things would most likely happen: (a) you would start to erase the drawing marks, but you'd probably start to ruin the photo under them, as well, or (b) you wouldn't be able to erase anything (if you used a permanent marker) and you'd be stuck with a pretty funny-looking photo.

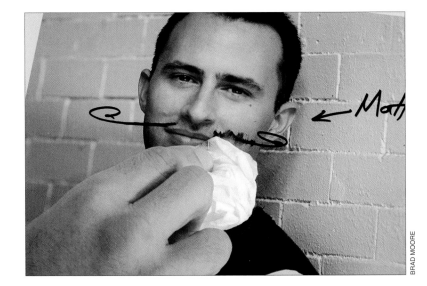

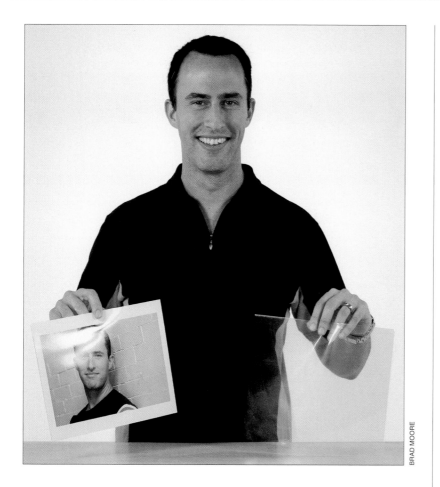

BRAD MOORE

Step Three:
Let's take this example one step further. Back up to the point where you have a photo that you want to draw over. This time, though, you also have a piece of transparent paper.

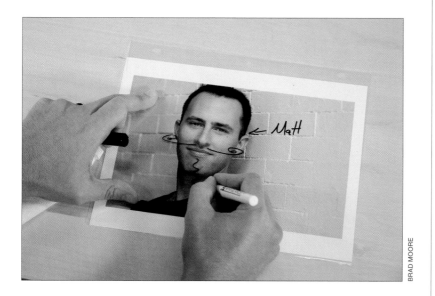

BRAD MOORE

Step Four:
Now when you place the photo down on the desk and get ready to draw, you place the transparent piece of paper over it. Just like before, imagine taking a black marker and drawing over the photo. However, unlike before, you're not drawing directly on the photo it-self—instead, you're drawing on the transparent paper. It looks the same, though, right?

(Continued)

Step Five:

After you see the final result, you'll probably decide that I look much better without a mustache. Once again, try erasing what you just drew with that damp cloth. Now it's a breeze. Or, if you're unhappy with the entire project, then just toss the transparent piece of paper into the garbage and start over again. By using that transparent piece of paper, you've gained a tremendous amount of flexibility.

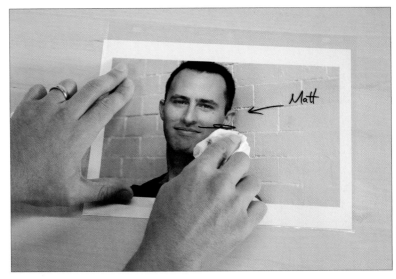

Step Six:

Okay, enough imagining. I promise we'll actually be using Elements for the rest of the chapter. Go ahead and open a photo in the Editor by clicking on the File menu and choosing **Open** (or just press **Ctrl-O [Mac: Command-O]**). Navigate to the photo you want (or just use the photo of me), click on it, and click Open. Now you'll see the photo, but more importantly, notice the Layers palette (if you don't see it, just go under the Window menu and choose **Layers**). You should notice that there's only one layer in the Layers palette—it's called Background.

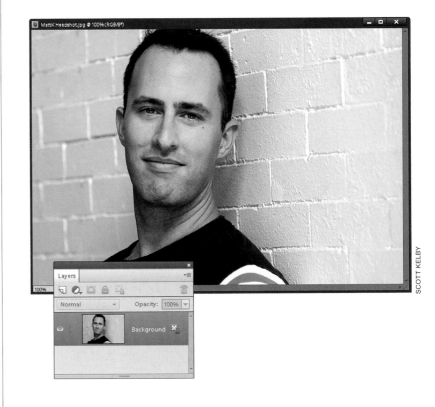

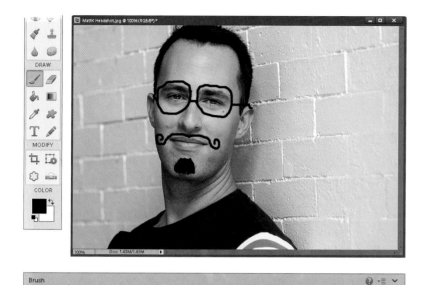

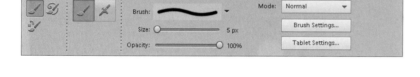

Step Seven:

Select the Brush tool from the Toolbox (or just press **B**), then click on the Brush thumbnail down in the Tool Options Bar to open the Brush Picker, and select a small, hard-edged brush. Press the letter **D** to set your Foreground color to black and start painting on the photo. Have at it—a funny face with glasses, a mustache, whatever you want!

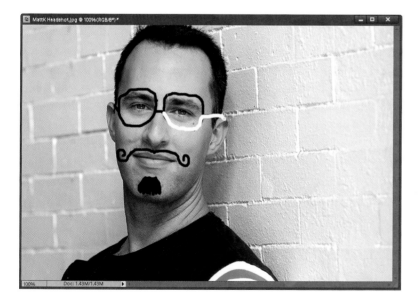

Step Eight:

After you're done painting on the photo, you'll inevitably think it looked much better before the vandalism (sorry, I meant to say artwork). So, select the Eraser tool **(E)** from the Toolbox and try to erase those brush strokes away. See what happens? Not only do you erase away the black brush strokes, but the underlying photo is erased, as well (you see white here because my Background color is set to white). Not good, but as you can imagine, there's a better way to do this. Go ahead and close this image, but make sure you don't save the changes.

(Continued)

Step Nine:

Let's bring this example back around to the photo with the transparent piece of paper. Remember how well it worked to isolate our drawing on the transparent piece of paper? Well, layers give us the same benefit. Open a new image (or use the same one of me) and click on the Create a New Layer icon at the top of the Layers palette (circled in red here). You'll see a new layer, named Layer 1, now appears on top of the Background layer. This new layer is just like that transparent piece of paper.

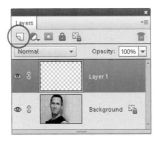

Step 10:

Press B to select the Brush tool again, like you did in Step Seven. Click once on Layer 1 in the Layers palette to make sure it's selected (you've got to click on a layer to select it in the Layers palette. If you don't, then you may be working on the wrong layer. Always look for the layer that is highlighted in color. That is the current or active layer and the one that you'll be editing). Then, start painting on it just like before. Everything should look and act exactly the same.

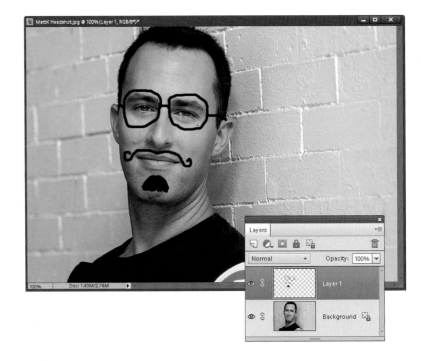

Step 11:

Finally, to bring this example back around full circle, select the Eraser tool again and erase away any of those brush strokes. You'll see that you can easily erase them without affecting the original photo. That's because you created your changes on a separate, blank layer on top of the photo. You never touched the original photo, just the layer on top of it.

There you have it my friends—the totally basic introduction to layers. Don't forget to stop by the website (mentioned in the book's introduction) to download the images to follow along with. Now, roll your sleeves up and get ready—we've got some really cool stuff ahead.

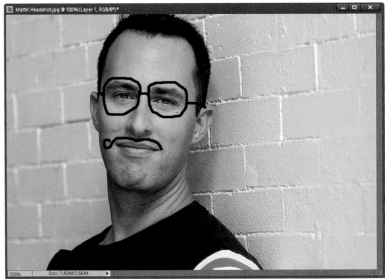

Using Multiple Layers

The main idea behind this tutorial is to use multiple images and get used to the way layer stacking works. Working with one image is great, but you'll get an even better understanding of layers when you start bringing multiple images into one Elements document. There are going to be plenty of times where you want to take a layer from one image and add it into another image you're working on. A great example would be blending multiple photos together to create some type of collage.

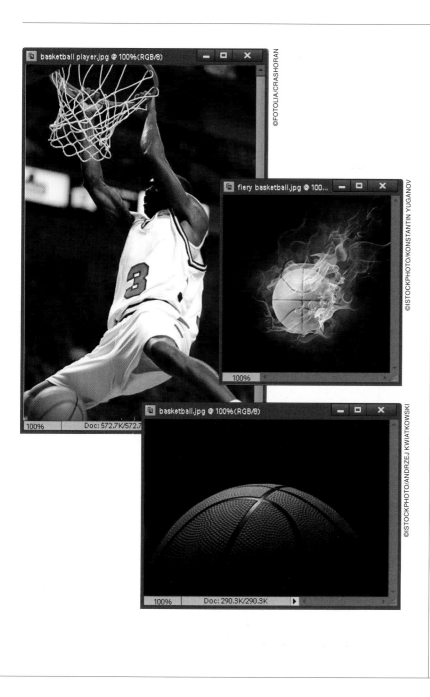

Step One:
First off, open the photos that you'd like to combine into one image. Click on the File menu and choose **Open**. Then navigate to each photo and click Open. Here, we're going to combine three photos, so I've opened all three and can see them in my workspace. *Note:* To float all three image windows, press **Ctrl-K (Mac: Command-K)** to open the General Preferences, and turn on the Allow Floating Documents in Expert Mode checkbox. Then, you can go under the Window menu, under Images, and choose **Float All in Windows**.

(Continued)

Step Two:

Now let's create a brand new document to hold what we're about to create. Go under the File menu, under New, and choose **Blank File**. For this example, we're going to create a promo card for a basketball team. I want my new document to be 7" tall by 5" wide, so from the Preset pop-up menu, choose **Photo**, then from the Size pop-up menu, choose **Portrait, 5x7**. Since we're just displaying this onscreen, change the resolution to 72 ppi. If we were going to print this, we'd probably use something between 240 ppi and 300 ppi. Click OK to create the new blank document.

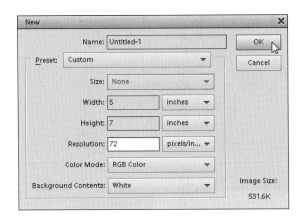

Step Three:

We need to get the photos into the new blank document now. There are a couple ways to do this and each have their place. First, let's try the one I use the most—copy-and-paste: Click on the photo of the half-basketball to bring it to the front and make it the active document. Go under the Select menu and choose **All** to select the entire image. Copy this selection by going under the Edit menu and choosing **Copy**. Now, click over to the blank document and paste the copied photo into it by going under the Edit menu and choosing **Paste**. By the way, we're not going to use the Edit menu for these anymore. The keyboard shortcuts for Copy and Paste are **Ctrl-C (Mac: Command-C)** and **Ctrl-V (Mac: Command-V)**, respectively, and they work a lot faster.

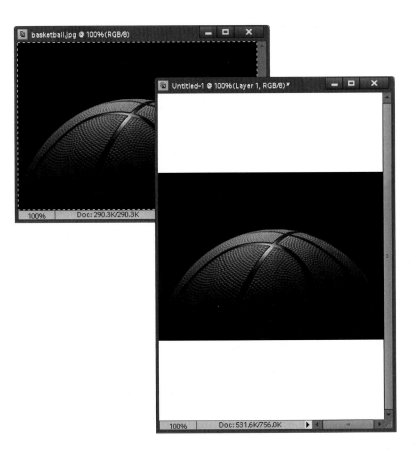

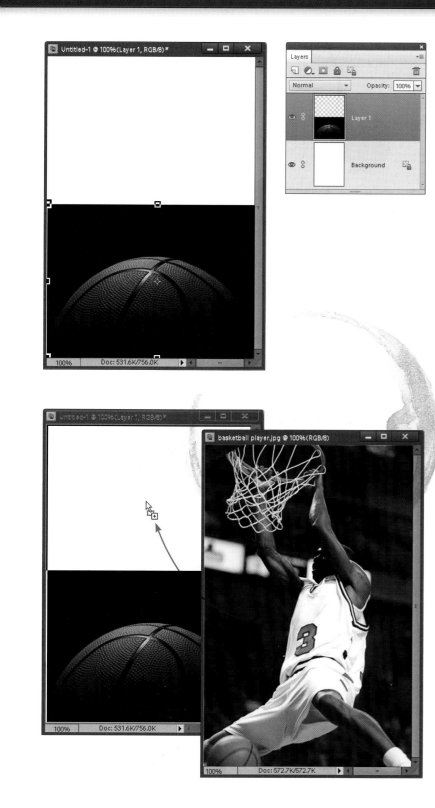

Step Four:

Right after you paste the image, you should see a new layer called Layer 1 appear in the Layers palette right above the Background layer. By default, Elements automatically creates a new layer whenever you paste something into an image. This is a good thing, because it forces us to work on multiple layers. Now, select the Move tool from the Toolbox (or just press **V**), click on the pasted image, and drag it toward the bottom of the document (press-and-hold the Shift key while you drag to keep the layer on the same vertical or horizontal line).

Step Five:

Let's bring another photo into the new document. Before, we used copy-and-paste, but there's another way: you can also click-and-drag images into other documents. Position the new document window and the photo of the basketball player so you can see both next to each other. Click once on the player photo to make it the active document, and with the Move tool, click-and-hold on the player photo, and drag it over into the new document (that's why you need to be able to see both of them). Once your cursor is over the new document, release the mouse button and this photo will appear as a new layer. Use the Move tool to center it in the document.

(Continued)

Step Six:

Go ahead and bring the last photo (the basketball with the flames photo) into the new document. I recommend the copy-and-paste method, since it's easier for me, but feel free to use whichever way works best for you. Once it's there, use the Move tool to move it to the top left of the image, like you see here.

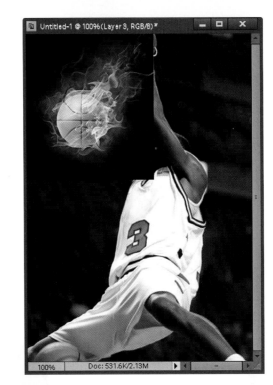

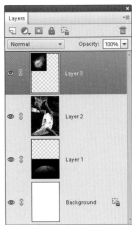

Step Seven:

Close the original three photos. We don't need them open anymore because we've copied their contents into layers in our new document. (The layers in our new image are not connected to their originals. No matter what you do here, you won't affect the originals.) Now, notice how the basketball player on Layer 2 totally hides the basketball on Layer 1? That's because Layer 2 is on top of Layer 1. Let's swap them by clicking on Layer 1 in the Layers palette and dragging it above Layer 2. Now, you'll see the contents of Layer 1 on top of Layer 2. One more thing: we're going to work on Layer 3 last, so let's hide it by clicking on the little Eye icon to the left of the layer's thumbnail in the Layers palette (circled here in red).

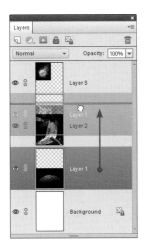
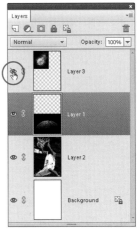

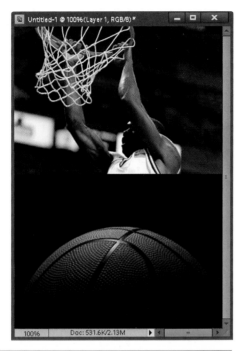

Step Eight:

Now, we're going to blend these layers together, so select the Eraser tool from the Toolbox (or just press **E**). In the Tool Options Bar, click on the Brush thumbnail to open the Brush Picker, and choose a soft-edged brush. Set the Size to something large (like 175 pixels). Also, set the Opacity to 30%. By using a lower opacity setting, we'll be able to lightly erase away parts of the photos that are on top of each other and give the illusion that they're blending together, since you'll see whatever is below them. If we used a 100% setting, you'd see some obvious seams and erase marks. The lower opacity will allow us to blend things better.

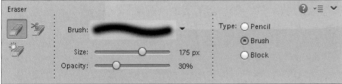

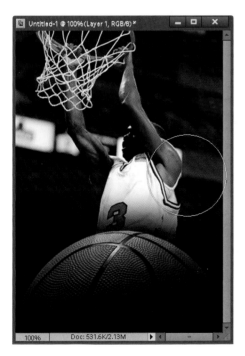

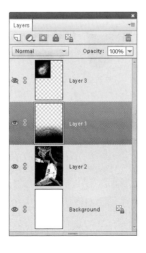

Step Nine:

With Layer 1 (the half-basketball) active in the Layers palette, start erasing away the left, top, and right part of the black background of the photo—just a few clicks with the Eraser tool should do it. Remember, though, you're working with a tool that's set to one-third strength (the Opacity setting), so you're only erasing a little bit at a time. The more times you click, the more you'll erase. So, just keep erasing and you'll reveal the contents of Layer 2 (the basketball player), which is below it in the layer stack (press the **Left Bracket key** to decrease the size of your brush as you get closer to the basketball). This makes the two photos blend together.

(Continued)

Step 10:

Go back and make the image on Layer 3 visible again (click on the Eye icon to the left of the layer's thumbnail again) and do the same thing to the basketball with flames that we just did in Step Nine (be sure to click on Layer 3 in the Layers palette first to make it active). Make your brush size smaller and erase away the black area around the basketball, along with some of the flames, so only the basketball shows over the net and not its black background. Since it's on top of Layer 2 in the layer stack, wherever you erase, you'll be revealing the photo on that layer. Again, this blends them together, making it look like the photos were smoothly merged together. Use the Move tool to reposition it, if necessary.

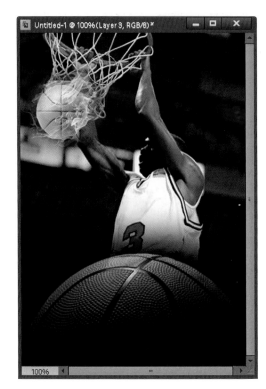

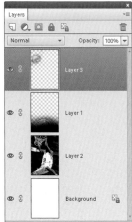

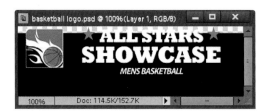

Step 11:

Finally, let's bring in a finishing logo. Open the image that has the graphics and logo that you want to add. So far, we've been opening JPEG images and dragging them in, but you can just as easily open other types of files, too, including Photoshop (PSD) files. Here, I've got a PSD file that has a logo on its own layer.

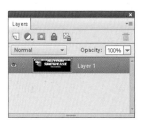

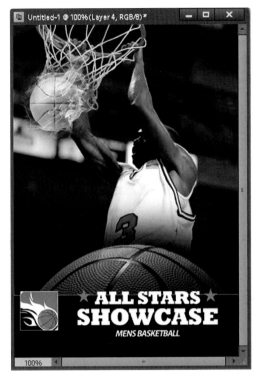

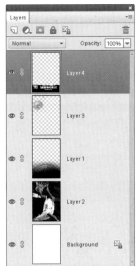

Step 12:

Go back to your new image and make sure the top layer in your Layers palette (Layer 3) is active (this is important, because when you bring the logo over to this document, it will appear above whichever layer is active in your Layers palette. So, save time by clicking on the layer you want it to appear above). Now, click-and-drag (or copy-and-paste) the logo from the other image into your new image. It'll appear at the very top of the layer stack, ready to be positioned where you need it. Here, I moved it to the bottom of the image.

Final

Step Five:

Click on the small Eye icon to the left of the texture layer's thumbnail to hide that layer and, with the new blank layer you just added at the bottom active (high-lighted), add a white-to-black radial gradient. To do this, select the Gradient tool from the Toolbox **(G)**, click on the down-facing arrow to the right of the Gradient thumbnail in the Tool Options Bar, and choose the Black, White gradient from the Gradient Picker (the third gradient from the left in the top row). Now, click on the Radial Gradient icon (it's the second icon to the right of the Mode pop-up menu), turn on the Reverse checkbox (also in the Tool Options Bar), then starting in the middle of your document, just drag from left to right to add a gradient to the bottom layer.

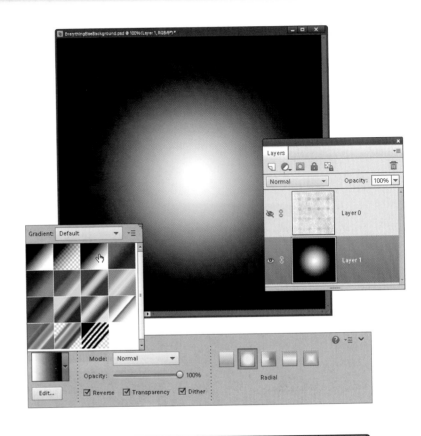

Step Six:

Next, we're going to use the gradient to give our background texture some depth and dimension. Click on the texture layer's Eye icon again to make it visible. We just added a gradient, but we don't see it anymore because the texture layer now hides it. The Opacity setting, though, will let us blend the two together. So, click on the top texture layer to make it active and then move your cursor over the word "Opacity" in the top right of the Layers palette. You'll see two little arrows appear on either side of the hand cursor. If you click-and-drag your cursor to the left, you'll decrease the Opacity setting, allowing you to see through the texture to the gradient below. Here, I set the Opacity to 85%.

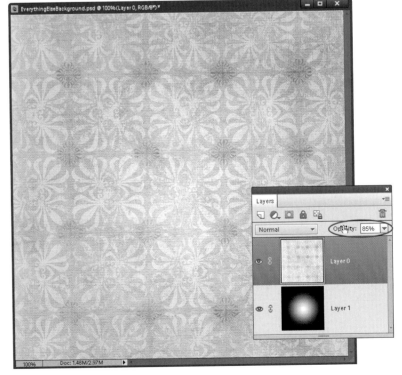

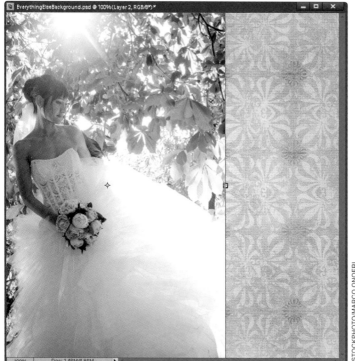

©ISTOCKPHOTO/MARCO ONOFRI

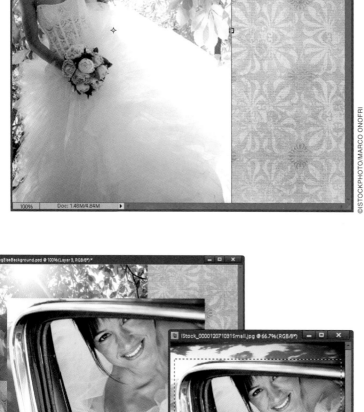

©ISTOCKPHOTO/MARCO ONOFRI

Step Seven:

Open the photos that are going to be included on the album page. (*Note:* This is easiest if you turn on the Allow Floating Documents in Expert Mode checkbox in Elements' General Preferences. Then, you can click on the Layout icon at the bottom of the window and choose **All Floating**.) Here, I'm going to use three photos of a couple on their wedding day. Let's start with the photo of the bride alone. Position the photo so you can see both it and the texture (album) image. Then, with the Move tool **(V)**, click-and-hold on the photo, then drag it into your album image, and place it toward the left. As you can see, it happens to pretty much fit right in and is a good size for what we're looking for. That's not always the case, though, so read on to the next step.

Step Eight:

Let's move on to the next photo. I know that I want two small square photos toward the right of this layout, and just by looking at this image of the bride in the car window, you can tell it's not going to work, because it's not square. So, instead of bringing the entire photo in, let's just take a selection. Grab the Rectangular Marquee tool **(M)**, press-and-hold the Shift key (which keeps your selection square), and make a square selection over the area you want (if it's not in the right place at first, simply click-and-drag inside the selection to move it). Now, press **Ctrl-C (Mac: Command-C)** to Copy and then click on the album image and press **Ctrl-V (Mac: Command-V)** to Paste that selected area into the album layout. You'll see only the selected part of the photo is placed and it's on its own layer.

(Continued)

Step Nine:

We got lucky with the first photo of the bride—it was the exact size we wanted. But, I'll be the first to tell you that it will never happen again. More often than not, you'll have to resize the images you add. In this case, the photo of the bride in the car window is still too big. The best way to resize precisely is to press **Ctrl-T (Mac: Command-T)** to go into Free Transform, click on the Scale icon near the left end of the Tool Options Bar, and then enter the exact width and height settings you want. In this case, enter 188 px for the W(idth) setting and 188 px for the H(eight) setting. Don't forget to actually type the "px" (for pixels) after 188 or bad things will happen. Press **Enter (Mac: Return)** when you're done.

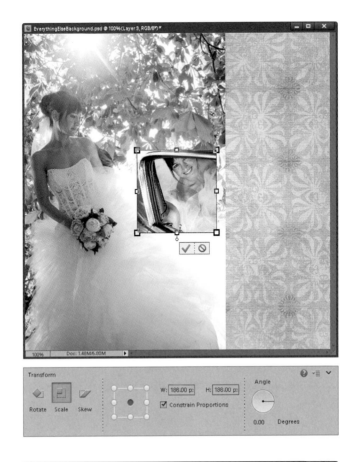

Step 10:

Now we need to bring the third photo into the wedding album image. Make a square selection of only the part of the photo where you can see the couple kissing, then copy-and-paste the selection into the wedding album image, just like we did with the last one. Resize it just like in the previous step, so it's exactly 188x188 pixels in size. Finally, use the Move tool to position it somewhere below the other one (no need to be exact, because we'll take care of aligning them in the next step).

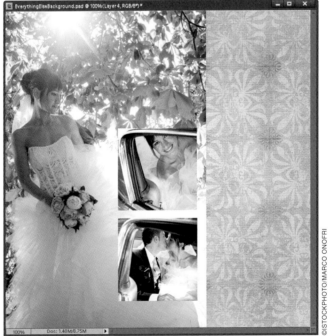

©ISTOCKPHOTO/MARCO ONOFRI

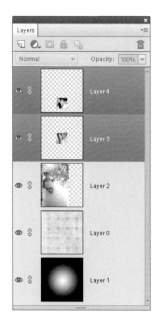

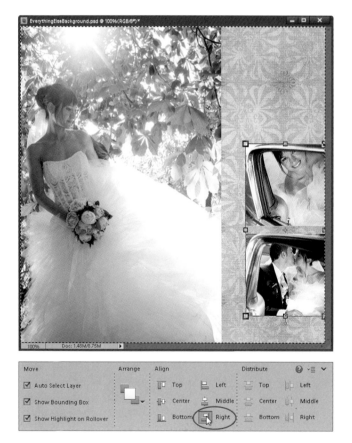

Step 11:

As you can see, the two small photos we just added to the album image probably aren't perfectly aligned. We could try to precisely align each one of them with the Move tool, but it's way too hard to really be exact when you're just eyeballing it. Instead, let's use the Align Layers options. First, we need to select the layers we want to align in the Layers palette. So, click on one of the small photo layers in the Layers palette and then Ctrl-click (Mac: Command-click) on the other small photo layer to select multiple layers. You'll be able to tell that both are selected because they'll be highlighted with a color (the layers not selected will not be highlighted).

Step 12:

Now, you need to tell Elements where to align the layers. First, press **Ctrl-A (Mac: Command-A)** to select the whole canvas, so Elements sees a selection edge around the entire album image. Then, with the Move tool still selected, you'll see some Align choices in the middle of the Tool Options Bar. Click on the Right icon to align the selected layers to the right side of the selection. This pushes the two photos up against the right edge of the album image. It's automatic, so there's no manual effort required on your part.

(Continued)

Step 13:

Remember how you selected the two photo layers back in Step 11? Let's say you decide you want to move those two smaller photos somewhere else in the album image. Since they're both still selected, there's a temporary link between the two layers and any moves you make will affect both at the same time. Press **Ctrl-D (Mac: Command-D)** to remove your selection from the entire image, and then, using the Move tool, click-and-drag one of the photos toward the left, so it's not right up against the right edge of the image (I like this placement better actually). The other photo will follow right along. When you're done, just click on one of the layers in the Layers palette to deselect the other.

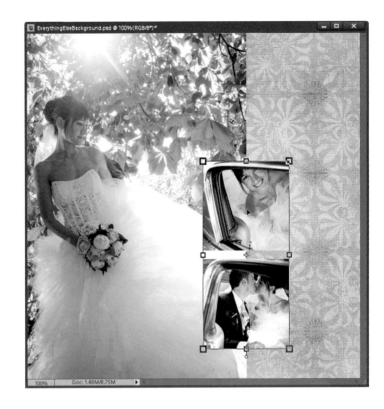

Step 14:

If you want to create a more permanent connection between the two layers, so that every time you move one of them, the other follows, Elements lets you create a link between them that lasts even after you click on another layer to do something else. To create this link, select both of the smaller photo layers, just like we did before. Then, click on the Link Layers icon at the left of either layer (next to the Eye icon and circled here). Now, click on one of the layers, so only that one is active, and then use the Move tool to move one photo, and both of them will move together. With this permanent link, from now on, you'll only have to select one layer to move and the other(s) will follow.

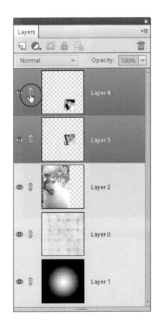

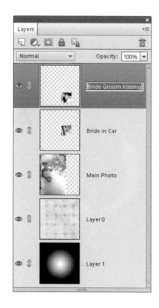

Step 15:

Let's take a break from copying, pasting, and moving for a minute. As your Layers palette starts growing, you should name your layers to keep things organized. Just double-click on the layer name in the Layers palette, the name will highlight, and you can then type a new name (as seen here for the three photo layers).

Step 16:

Now, back to our album page. Let's add a white stroke around the small photos. Click on the Bride in Car layer in the Layers palette to make it the active layer, then press-and-hold the Ctrl (Mac: Command) key and click on the layer's thumbnail. This puts a selection around whatever is on that layer. Click on the Create a New Layer icon at the top of the palette to create a new layer on top of this layer. From the Edit menu, choose **Stroke (Outline) Selection**. Set the Width to 3 px, the Color to white (click on the swatch), the Location to Inside, and click OK. Press Ctrl-D to Deselect and you'll see a white stroke around the photo. Go ahead and rename this stroke layer something descriptive, too.

(Continued)

Step 17:

Let's add the same stroke to the other square photo. Repeat the same steps: click on the layer, Ctrl-click on the layer thumbnail, add a new layer, then add your stroke. When the Stroke dialog opens, it should already have the correct settings, so just click OK. Now, deselect and re-name your layer.

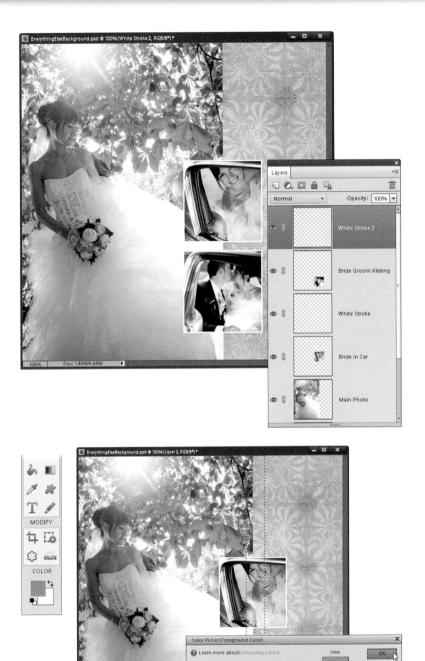

Step 18:

Next, let's add some simple colored rectangles to the background. Click on the background texture layer in the Layers palette to make it the active layer, then click on the Create a New Layer icon to add a new layer above the background texture, but below the large photo of the bride. Using the Rectangular Marquee tool, make a tall, thin selection to the right of the main bride photo. Click on the Foreground color swatch at the bottom of the Toolbox to open the Color Picker and set the color to R: 137, G: 160, B: 165. Click OK to close the Color Picker.

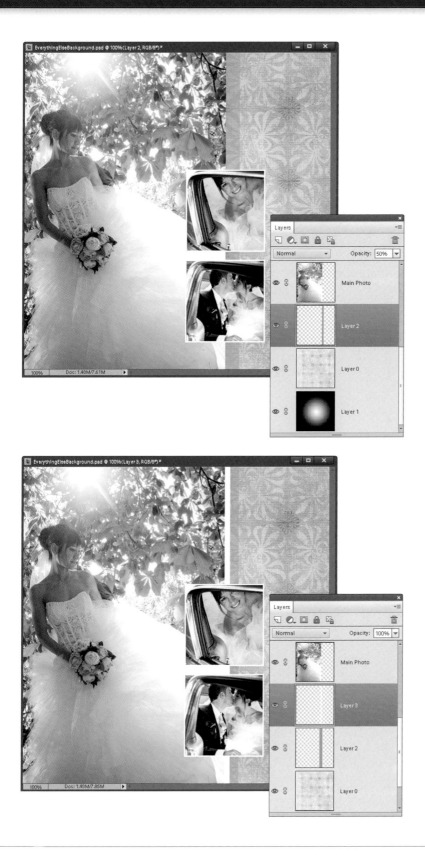

Step 19:

Now, press **Alt-Backspace (Mac: Option-Delete)** to fill that selection with the Foreground color. Since the color appears a little obtrusive as it is, let's make it a bit more subtle. At the top right of the Layers palette, reduce the Opacity setting of this layer to 50% (we did this earlier in the project with the texture background for the gradient layer we added below it), then deselect.

Step 20:

Click on the Create a New Layer icon again to add one more new layer on top of the current rectangle layer. Then, create another thin rectangular selection (thinner than the first one and to its left) with the Rectangular Marquee tool. Press **D**, then **X** to set your Foreground color to white, and press Alt-Backspace to fill that selection with white. Deselect, and now you've got some extra color and a nice way to separate that large photo from the background.

(Continued)

Step 21:

Another task to do often is delete any layers that aren't needed or that you just don't like. For example, let's say you don't like the teal rectangle you added a few steps back. You could click on the little Eye icon to the left of the layer thumbnail to turn it off, but that still leaves the layer. To delete it permanently, click on that layer and drag it onto the Trash icon at the top right of the Layers palette (as shown here). Once you know you want something removed, deleting layers is a good habit to get into as you're working, because it helps keep file size to a minimum and Elements running faster overall. Plus, it cuts down on clutter in the Layers palette. I kinda like it with the teal rectangle, so I'm not going to delete it, but I wanted to show you how it's done.

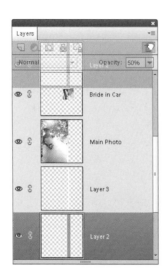

Step 22:

Finally, I'd merge any layers that don't need to stay editable. You see, every layer you have in the Layers palette takes up space in your file and your computer's memory. Plus, too many layers are just plain hard to deal with. Who wants an image with 20, 30, or even more layers in it? So I merge (flatten) layers often when I know I don't need to change something. A great example here would be the small square photos and their stroke layers. To merge them, select both layers first (as seen here). Then from the Layers palette's flyout menu, choose **Merge Layers**. This squishes both layers into one. You won't be able to edit the stroke independently of the photo it was around anymore, but you probably don't care at this point. That's it! The über layers project is complete. The only thing left to do is save the image as a PSD file, so you can reopen it later and still edit all of the layers if you need to.

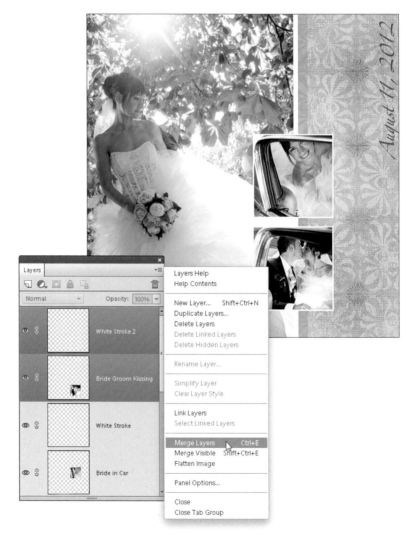

Blending layers is the next level of merging your images together. There are a lot of ways to blend layers together that go beyond simply changing the opacity. One of those ways is called blend modes. It's like opacity on steroids, and the effects you can get with blend modes are unlike any other effects you'll find in Elements. That said, I gotta tell ya, there are a lot of blend modes in Elements. My goal here is to show you only those you really need to know about. Most of the blend modes will probably never get used, so we're just going to concentrate on the ones that you're going to use often.

Layer Blend Modes for Photographers

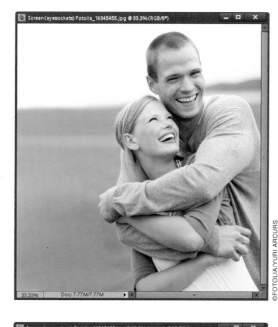

©FOTOLIA/YURI ARCURS

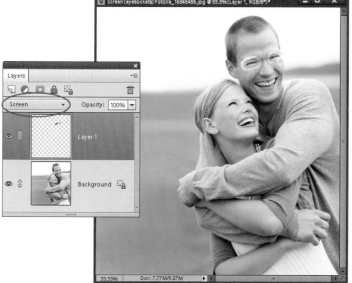

Step One:
One of the first ways you'll see blend modes can help with photos is when you have a photo with a dark or under-exposed area. In our example here, we have a really common problem with portraits taken outdoors. The eye socket area of the person on the right shows up a little shadowy compared to the rest of his face. Because of the shape of our forehead and face, an overhead light source doesn't reach the eyes as much as other areas. Again, this is a really common problem that a blend mode can help with.

Step Two:
Grab the Lasso tool **(L)** and make a quick selection around the eye sockets (select one eye, then press-and-hold the Shift key while you select the other eye to add it to the original selection). Press **Ctrl-J (Mac: Command-J)** to duplicate the selection onto its own layer, so now you'll have two layers in the Layers palette. Then, at the top left of the palette, change the blend mode of the top layer to **Screen**. Because Screen is a lightening blend mode, it has the effect of lightening everything on that layer.

TIP: Use a Shortcut for Screen
You can use the keyboard shortcut **Alt-Shift-S (Mac: Option-Shift-S)** to switch to the Screen blend mode quickly.

(Continued)

Step Three:

Yeah, I know. He looks like a raccoon now. You could stop here if you wanted a good prank to play on your friends, but let's assume you want to move on. Get the Eraser tool (**E**), then click on the Brush thumbnail in the Tool Options Bar, and choose a small, soft-edged brush from the Brush Picker. Click-and-drag to erase away the areas that don't need the lightening effect. Finally, try reducing the Opacity of the layer to about 50% to help it blend in better with the original layer below it.

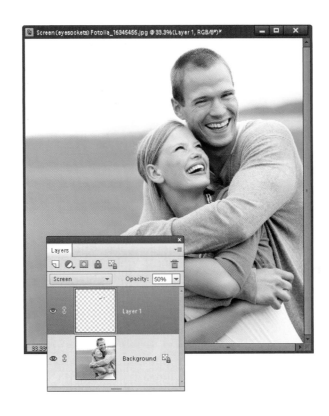

Step Four:

Another problem that blend modes can help with is when you have a bright, faded area in a photo. Here I've opened a photo where the sky looks good, but the buildings are too bright. The first step is to duplicate the Background layer by pressing Ctrl-J.

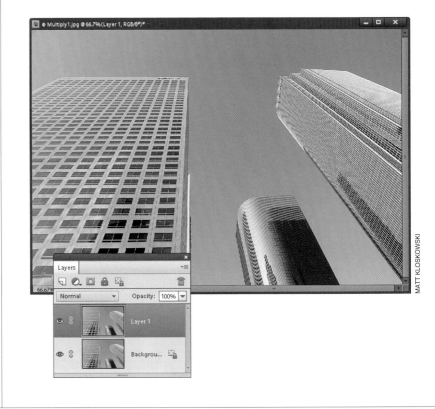

MATT KLOSKOWSKI

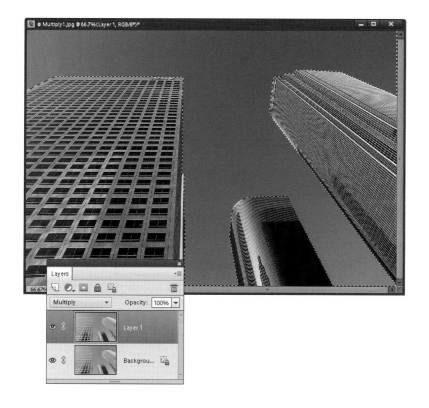

Step Five:
Change the blend mode of the duplicate layer to **Multiply**. Since Multiply is a darkening blend mode, this darkens everything in the photo. It may look just fine like that, so feel free to leave it alone. However, in this photo I think it made the sky look too saturated and dark. So, get the Magic Wand tool (press **A** until you have it) and click on the sky to select it. You may have to Shift-click again elsewhere in the sky to add other areas if the entire sky wasn't selected the first time.

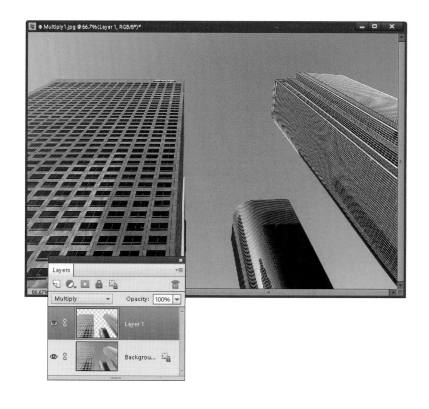

Step Six:
Press the **Backspace (Mac: Delete) key** to remove (or erase) the sky, then press **Ctrl-D (Mac: Command-D)** to Deselect. The darkening effect of the Multiply blend mode should now just affect the buildings, so they have a little more punch to them. Feel free to reduce the opacity if the effect is too dark.

(Continued)

Step Seven:

Here's another example of what Multiply can be used for: Open one of those cool, grungy black frame images, and you'll find most of them have white in the middle where a photo is supposed to go. To start, press **Ctrl-A (Mac: Command-A)** to put a selection around the entire frame image.

Step Eight:

Press **Ctrl-C (Mac: Command-C)** to Copy the frame, then open another image and press **Ctrl-V (Mac: Command-V)** to Paste it into that image. Press **Ctrl-T (Mac: Command-T)** if you need to resize it to fit the photo. Then, change blend mode of the frame layer to Multiply, and Photoshop will automatically drop out the white and leave you with just the black frame around the photo. No selections, no nuthin'.

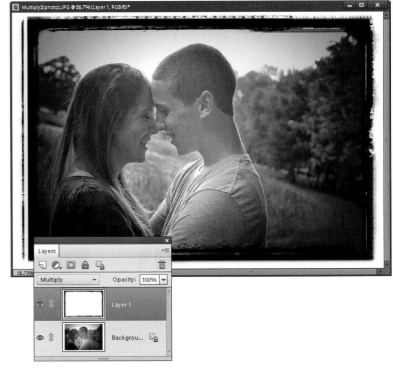

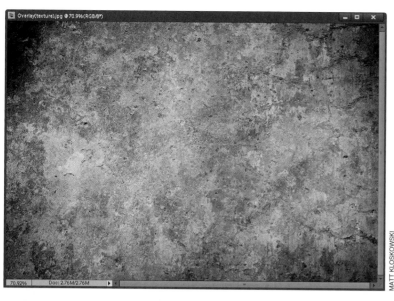

MATT KLOSKOWSKI

MATT KLOSKOWSKI

Step Nine:

As you'll see in Chapter 10, when you have a photo with a bright sky and a dark foreground, you can use a gradient to act like a graduated neutral density gradient filter. You simply change the gradient layer's blend mode to Overlay or Soft Light. Well, here's a totally different example to improve your photos with the Overlay or Soft Light blend mode: Open a photo and a texture image. It could be something you've downloaded or created in Elements, or you could just take a photo of a wall. Copy-and-paste the texture image into the photo. Change the texture layer to **Overlay** (or Soft Light), and it gives the photo a very rugged and faded style, as seen here.

The Power of Layer Masks

One of the things that Elements never had that the full version of Photoshop did was layer masks. It was always one of the big features that people liked more about the full version of Photoshop. Well, a couple versions ago, Adobe decided to add layer masks to Elements. Yup, the same layer masks as Photoshop. These things are a huge help when it comes to working on your photos. Whether it's retouching, color correction, sharpening—you name it—layer masks play a key role. We'll give you a quick introduction here, but you'll see them pop up plenty of times throughout the book.

Step One:
In order to really take advantage of layer masks, you need to have at least two layers. So, go ahead and open two images that you'd like to combine in some way. In this example, we're going to put the photo of the motocross rider into the computer screen and make it look like a part of him, and his bike, are actually coming out of the screen.

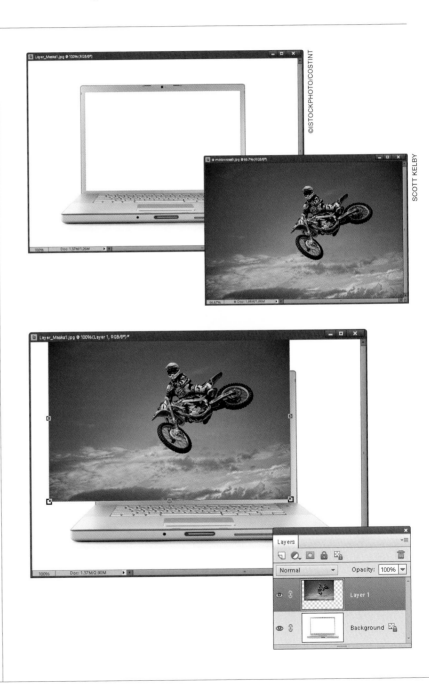

Step Two:
Click on the photo of the motocross rider, press **Ctrl-A (Mac: Command-A)** to Select All, then press **Ctrl-C (Mac: Command-C)** to copy the photo. Switch over to the photo of the laptop, and press **Ctrl-V (Mac: Command-V)** to paste the motocross rider on top of the laptop screen on a separate layer. Press **Ctrl-T (Mac: Command-T)** to go into Free Transform (if you can't see the edges of the photo or the control handles, press **Ctrl-0** [zero; **Mac: Command-0**]). With the Constrain Proportions checkbox turned on in the Tool Options Bar, grab a corner handle and drag inward to make the image smaller, then move it so the bottom-right corner of the photo meets the white space at the bottom-right corner of the screen. Once you've got the motocross rider positioned like you see here, press **Enter (Mac: Return)** to lock in your changes, and close the original photo of him, so you're left with only the document with two layers.

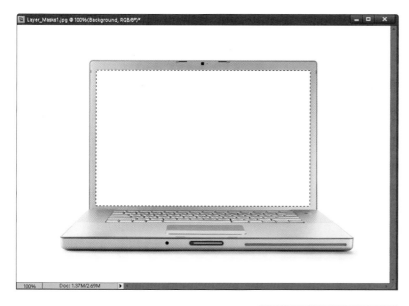

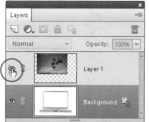

Step Three:

There are two main ways to work with layer masks: selections and brushes. Let's look at selections first. Hide the top layer (the motocross rider) by clicking on the Eye icon to the left of it in the Layers palette (it's circled here in red), so you only see the laptop. Click on the Background layer, and use the Rectangular Marquee tool **(M)** to make a selection of the white area inside the laptop screen.

Step Four:

Now unhide the photo of the motocross rider by clicking on the Eye icon again, and click on that layer to target it. When working with layer masks, a selection tells Elements that you want to keep that portion of a layer and hide the rest of it. Notice I said hide, not delete. Give it a try. Click on the Add Layer Mask icon at the top of the Layers palette (shown circled here) and see what happens.

(Continued)

Step Five:

You should now see only the rectangular area (that was previously selected) of the photo. Again, when you have a selection active, a layer mask tells Elements that you want to keep the selected area visible and hide everything that isn't selected. In our case, a portion of the layer with the motocross rider on it was selected, so that stays visible. But his head, part of one arm, and part of the rear fender on his bike were hidden (again, not deleted—just hidden for now).

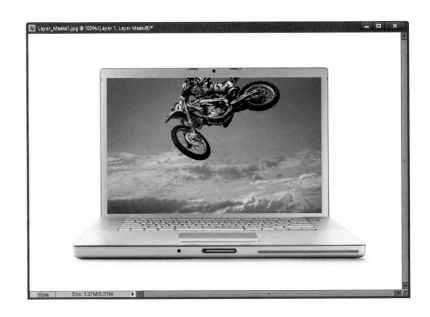

Step Six:

Now take a look at the layer itself. Notice it has a black-and-white thumbnail next to the image thumbnail? That's the layer mask. The layer mask is the same size as the layer. The white part of the thumbnail corresponds to the rectangular portion of the photo (the motocross rider) that we see. The black part corresponds to the area we don't see. In other words, white shows you whatever is on the layer that the layer mask is attached to and black hides that part of the layer and shows you whatever is below it in the layer stack (in this case, the laptop).

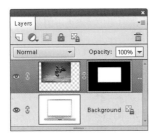

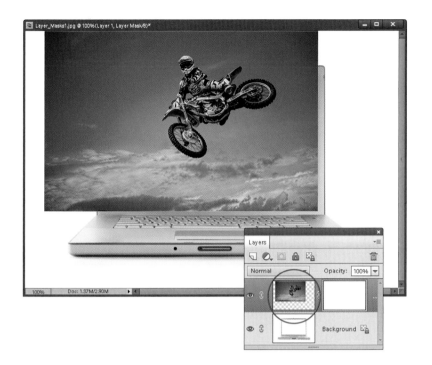

Step Seven:

The biggest advantage of layer masks is that nothing is permanent. Even though it looks like we've deleted the sky around the motocross rider, it's still there. Go ahead and look at the layer thumbnail (circled here) and you'll see it looks exactly the same. Nothing was deleted—just hidden. Layer masks are non-destructive and always give you a way out. Just to demonstrate really quickly, click once on the layer mask thumbnail (not the layer thumbnail) to select it. Then go under the Edit menu and choose **Fill Layer**. Set the Use pop-up menu to **White** and click OK to fill the whole mask with white again. Things are back to normal, as if nothing ever happened.

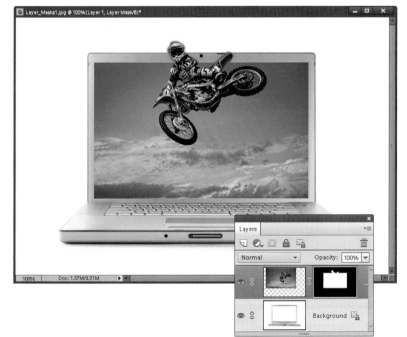

Step Eight:

Press **Ctrl-Z (Mac: Command-Z)** to undo that last step, so the black-and-white layer mask is back again. Let's take a look at the other main way to work with layer masks: adjusting them after the fact with brushes. In our example, the motocross rider's head and arm, and his bike's rear fender are cut off. We can fine-tune the mask to show them, though. Remember, layer masks just care about one thing: black and white. It doesn't matter how black and white get there. Earlier, we did it with a selection, but you can also use a brush to get the ultimate flexibility and control over the mask. Click on the mask thumbnail, then get the Brush tool **(B)**, click on the Brush thumbnail in the Tool Options Bar and choose a small, soft-edged brush from the Brush Picker. Press **D** to set your Foreground color to white (remember, white allows us to keep whatever is on this layer visible) and paint over the areas that aren't showing (his head and arm, and the rear fender). You'll see them reappear, because they weren't permanently gone in the first place.

(Continued)

Step Nine:

Why all the trouble? If you're asking yourself, why not just erase away the unwanted areas instead of adding a layer mask, then read on. If not, skip to the next step. So, what would happen if we erased away the sky with the Eraser tool, and then we erased some more sky? At some point, maybe we'd erase away part of his head or arm. But then we'd continue to erase away sky until we got to the point where we were done, and we'd realize we'd erased part of his head. Well, each one of those clicks of the mouse when we erase is a history state. They build up, so we'd have to undo all the work we did to get back to the point where we inadvertently erased his head. Needless to say, that'd be a big pain in the neck. Plus, since layer masks are part of the layer, we can save our image as a PSD file and open it again tomorrow (or at some later date) and change it. Layer masks allow us to be non-destructive in our editing, so we can always come back and change something later if we need to.

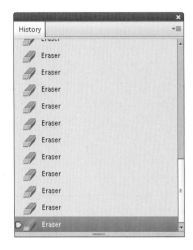

Step 10:

You can see in Step Eight that I went a little overboard with the white brush and brought back parts of the sky, too. No sweat. Remember that black and white thing? We were painting with white to bring areas back into view, so if we switch to black, the opposite will happen. Press the letter **X** on your keyboard to switch your Foreground color to black. Then, press **Ctrl-+ (Mac: Command-+)** to zoom in if you need to, and paint on the mask again to hide those sky areas and reveal the laptop and white background behind his head and fender.

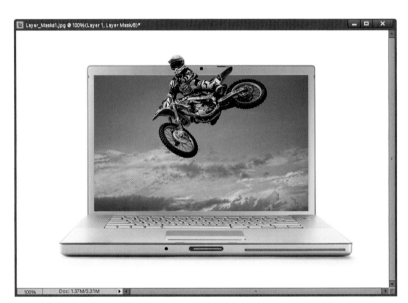

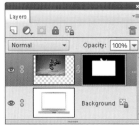

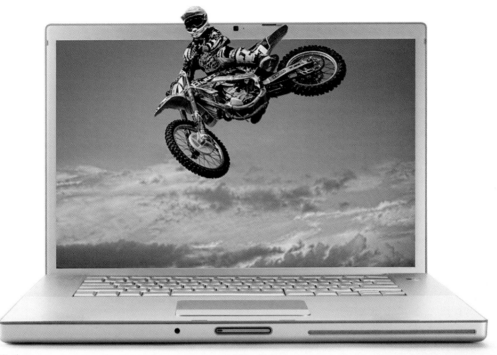

Final

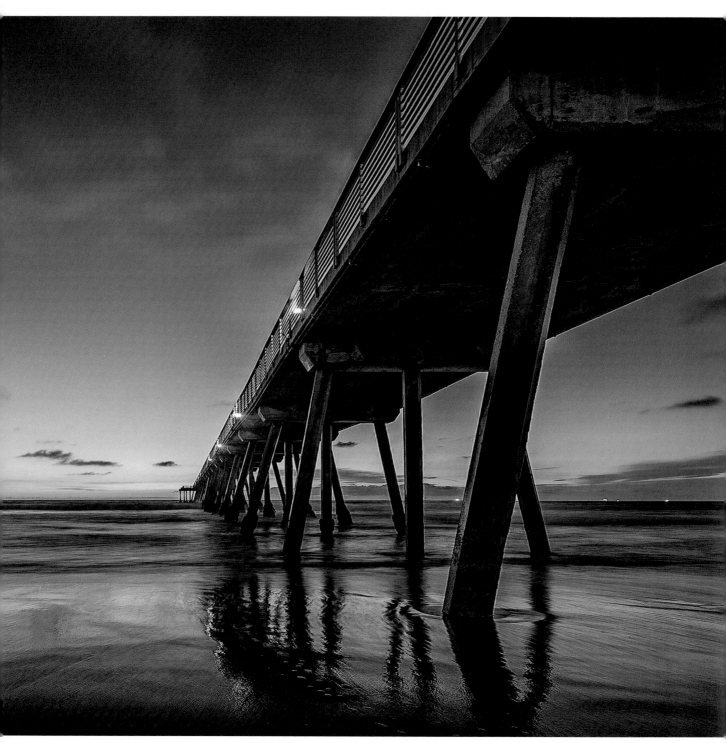

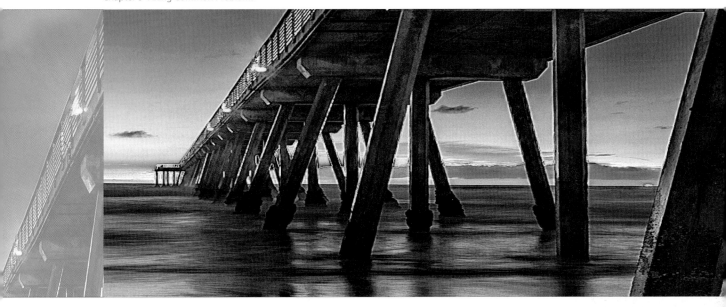

LITTLE PROBLEMS
fixing common problems

The title for this chapter comes from the 2009 movie *Little Problems* (written and directed by Matt Pearson), but I could have just as easily gone with the 2008 short *Little Problems* (written and directed by Michael Lewen), but there was one big thing that made the choice easy: the first movie was about zombies. You just can't make a bad movie about zombies. It's a lock. Throw a couple of hapless teens (or in this case "an unlikely couple") into some desolate location with a couple hundred flesh-starved undead, and you've got gold baby, gold! Now, has anyone ever wondered, even for a second, why every zombie in the rich and colorful history of zombies, has an insatiable hunger for human flesh and only human flesh? Why can't there be zombies that have an insatiable hunger for broccoli? Then, in their bombed-out shell of a desolate vacant city, on every corner there would be other zombies selling broccoli the size of azalea bushes. Anyway, it's just a little too coincidental that every zombie wants to eat you, but they don't want to eat something that might actually keep them alive, and is in ample and easily reproducible supply, like broccoli, or spring rolls, or chowder. Nope, it has to be human flesh, even though you know and I know (say it with me) it tastes like chicken (well, that's what I've been told, anyway). Another thing that drew me to the first Little Problems was the director's last name, seeing as all my books are published by subsidiaries of Pearson Education, a company who somehow chose to hire Ted Waitt as my editor, despite the fact that they were forewarned by the DCBGC (the Desolate City Broccoli Growers' Consortium) that Ted might not actually be the strict vegetarian he claimed to be in his resume. I probably shouldn't say anything bad about Ted, though. I don't want to bite the hand that feeds me.

Adjusting Flesh Tones

So what do you do if someone in your photo has a red face? This is one of the most common people-photo problems out there. You can try this quick trick for getting your flesh tones in line by removing the excess red. This one small adjustment can make a world of difference.

Step One:
Open a photo that needs red removed from the flesh tones. If the whole image appears too red, skip this step and move on to Step Three. However, if just the flesh-tone areas appear too red, get the Quick Selection tool **(A)** and click on all the flesh-tone areas in your photo (press-and-hold the **Alt [Mac: Option] key** to remove any areas that were selected that shouldn't have been). Here, only her face and neck were too red, because they were in the shade.

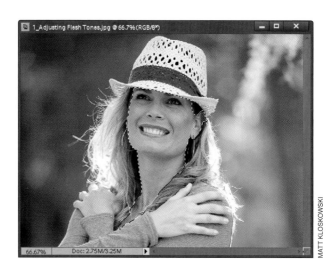

Step Two:
Go under the Select menu and choose **Feather**. Enter a Feather Radius of about 3 pixels, then click OK. By adding this feather, you're softening the edges of your selection, preventing a hard, visible edge from appearing around your adjustments.

Step Three:
Click on the Create New Adjustment Layer icon at the top of the Layers palette, and choose **Hue/Saturation** from the pop-up menu. Then, in the Hue/Saturation adjustments palette, click on the Channel pop-up menu near the top and choose **Reds**, so you're only adjusting the reds in your photo (or in your selected areas if you put a selection around the flesh tones).

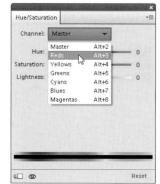

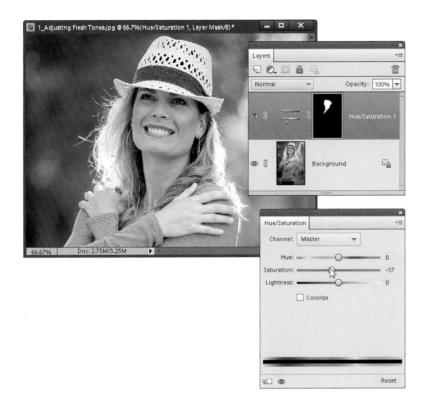

Step Four:
The rest is easy—you're simply going to reduce the amount of saturation, so the flesh tones appear more natural. Drag the Saturation slider to the left to reduce the amount of red (I moved mine to –17, but you may have to go farther to the left, or not as far, depending on how red your skin color is). The changes are live, so you'll be able to see the effect of reducing the red as you lower the Saturation slider. Also, if you made a selection of the flesh tone areas, once you create the adjustment layer, it will hide the selection border from view and create a layer mask with your selection. When the flesh tones look right, you're done.

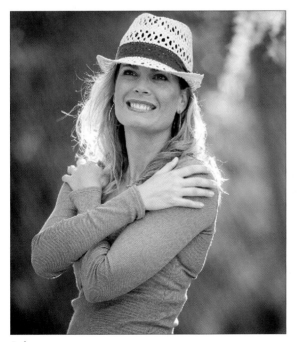

Before

After

Fixing Shots with a Dull Gray Sky

This technique really comes in handy when shooting outdoor scenes because it lets you enhance the color in one particular area of the photo (like dull gray skies), while leaving the rest of the photo untouched. Real estate photographers often use this trick because they want to present a house on a bright, sunny day, but the weather doesn't always cooperate. It works great for travel photos too, when maybe the weather wasn't so great but you can't easily go back to the location. With this technique, a blah sky can become a beautiful blue sky in just seconds.

Step One:
Here's a shot where the sky is really blah. Not totally 100%, but close enough. Also, the clouds are a little dark, so even if you went into Camera Raw and lowered the exposure, those darkish clouds would look like rain clouds, and you'd have a whole different problem to deal with (an underexposed photo with the buildings in the shadows). So, this technique will work pretty well for this image. You'll start by making a selection of the sky and your first thought might be to use the Magic Wand tool. Now, if the sky was just a flat sky with no clouds, that would probably work out okay, but in this case (a sky with clouds), you're much better off using the Quick Selection tool (it'll select that sky in all of 5 seconds). So, get the Quick Selection tool **(A)** from the Toolbox, click it on the far-left side of the sky, then drag it over to the right side, and—BAM!— it's selected (as shown here).

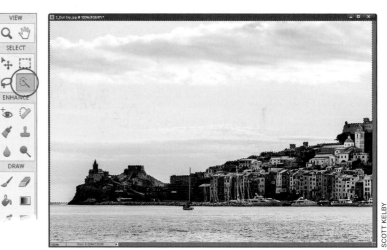

SCOTT KELBY

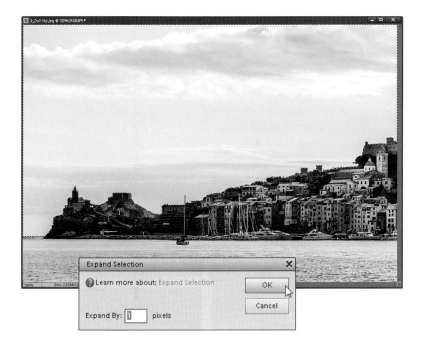

Step Two:

When I make a selection like this, to make sure it didn't miss any little areas, I usually expand (grow) the selection outward by a pixel or two (that way, it kind of "digs-in" to the city a little and eliminates any little gaps that would be a giveaway you tweaked the sky). To do this, go under the Select menu, under Modify, and choose **Expand**. When the dialog appears, if it's a really high-resolution image, use 2 pixels. If it's a 6- or 8-megapixel image (or smaller), just use 1 pixel, then click OK (you might not see anything onscreen when you do this—you just have to trust that it actually expanded outward by a pixel or two).

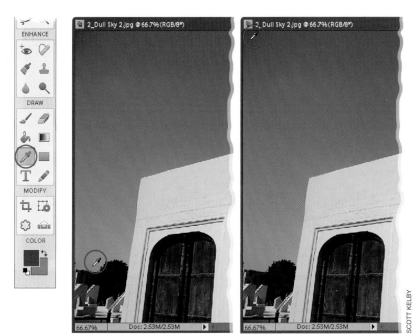

Step Three:

To get a realistic color for the sky, we're going to open another photo that already has a nice sky color (you can download this same photo, and most of the key photos used in this book, at the web address listed in the introduction at the front of the book). Once you open the image, switch to the Color Picker tool **(I)**, and click once on the brightest blue area in the image (as shown here) to make that your Foreground color. Now, press the letter **X** to swap your Foreground and Background colors, then click the tool on the darkest blue in the photo (higher in the sky), so that now your Foreground is a darker blue, and your Background is a lighter blue.

(Continued)

Step Four:

Go back to the original image, then go to the Layers palette and add a new, blank layer by clicking on the Create a New Layer icon at the top of the palette. Switch to the Gradient tool **(G)**, click on the down-facing arrow next to the Gradient thumbnail in the Tool Options Bar, and make sure the Foreground to Background gradient is selected in the Gradient Picker. Click on the Linear (far left) icon on the right side of the Tool Options Bar, and then click-and-drag your gradient from the top of the photo down to the bottom of the sky (the light blue color should be at the bottom of the gradient). This fills the new layer with a gradient made up of your Foreground and Background colors (as seen here). For some images, you can leave this gradient as is (or maybe just lower the layer opacity a little to let it blend in), but I think it usually looks a little too fakey, which is why there are two more steps.

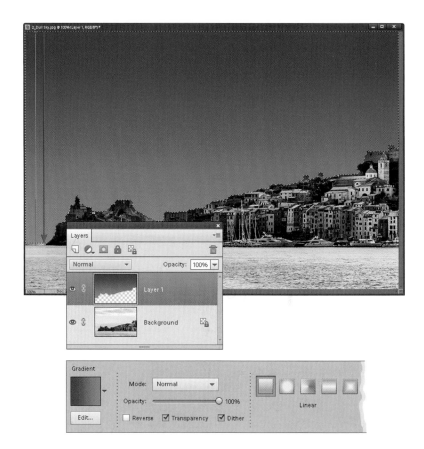

Step Five:

First, press **Ctrl-D (Mac: Command-D)** to Deselect, then go to the Layers palette and change the layer's blend mode from Normal to **Color** (shown here), just to see how the color itself looks. In this case, it looks a bit too cyan and fakey, so we'll have to take it another step further (don't worry—it's easy), but at least we can see that we're in the ballpark (so to speak).

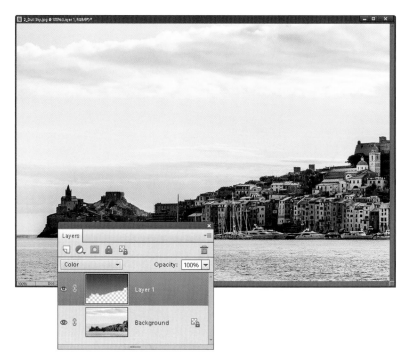

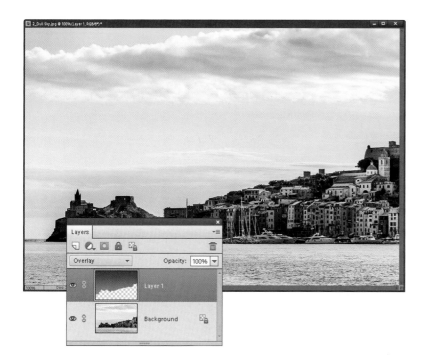

Step Six:

There are two layer blend modes that add contrast to our layer: Soft Light and Overlay. Let's try both of those. When you try Soft Light, you can see its effect is more subtle, and Overlay (shown here) is more contrasty (and in this case, that's what I'd go with, because it looks darker, but not at all over-the-top. If you want a really dramatic sky, try Color Burn, and then lower the layer's Opacity to around 50%). If you're not sure which one you want, switch to the Hand tool (H), and just press **Shift-+** (plus sign) to toggle through all the different layer blend modes until you find one you like. A before and after are shown below (it's subtle, but it's supposed to be).

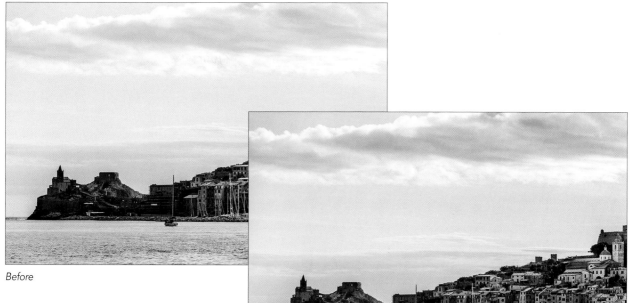

Before

After

Using the Smart Brush Tool to Select and Fix at the Same Time

Photoshop Elements includes a brush tool that lets you fix problem areas (as well as create some pretty cool effects) with just a brush stroke. It's called the Smart Brush tool, and it helps keep you from making complicated selections and then having to fix them in a separate step. Instead, you choose which effect you want to apply and just brush away. Let's check it out.

Step One:
Open a photo that has an area you want to enhance or fix. There's actually a huge list of things you can do with this brush, but let's concentrate on one area for now—the sky. A big digital image problem is that the sky never seems to look as vibrant and dramatic as it does when we're there photographing it. Well, the Smart Brush tool has an option to help fix this, so go ahead and select it from the Toolbox (it's the large paint brush icon in the Enhance section) or just press the **F key**.

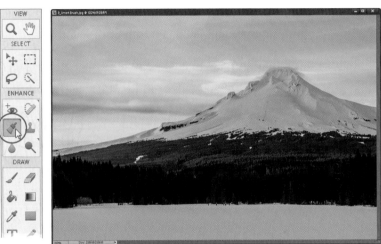

MATT KLOSKOWSKI

Step Two:
Once you select the tool, click on the thumbnail near the left side of the Tool Options Bar to open the Preset Picker. As you change the Presets pop-up menu and scroll through the Preset Picker, you'll see what I meant in Step One—there are indeed a bunch of things you can do here. Let's go ahead and choose **Nature** from the pop-up menu, though, to narrow it down. Then click on the thumbnail in the top left, which makes dull skies bluer.

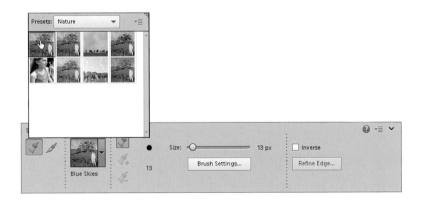

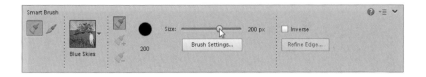

Step Three:

Now the main thing to remember about this tool is that it is still a brush, which means it has settings just like all other brushes (size, hardness, spacing, etc.). So, using the Size slider in the Tool Options Bar, choose a size that'll help you paint over the area fairly quickly. In this example, I'm using a 200-pixel brush for the sky.

Step Four:

The rest is pretty simple—just click-and-drag on the sky to paint the effect on the photo. By the way, notice how Elements automatically started adding the Blue Skies effect to parts of the sky that you haven't even painted over yet? That's where the "smart" part of this brush comes into play. It automatically examines your photo for areas similar to what you have painted on and adds them to the selection.

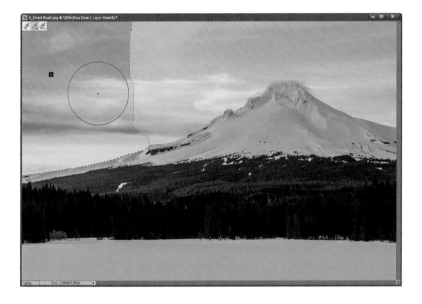

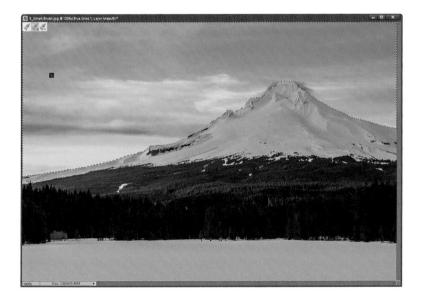

Step Five:

Now, keep brushing on the sky to get the rest of it. Each time you click, you're adding to the selection, so there's no need to press-and-hold any keys or change tools to widen the effect to other parts of the photo.

(Continued)

Step Six:

Okay, this brush is pretty cool, right? But it's not perfect. There will inevitably come a time (probably sooner than later) where the "smartness" of the brush isn't as smart as it thinks it is, and it bleeds into a part of the photo you didn't want it to (like where the exposed rocks are on the left side of the mountain, as seen in Step Five). When that happens, press-and-hold the **Alt (Mac: Option) key** to put the brush into subtract mode. Then paint over the areas you didn't want to apply the effect to (as shown here). Again, Elements will do a lot of the work for you and wipe away the areas, even if you don't paint directly on them. *Note:* Decrease the size of your brush and zoom in on the area, if needed, to help remove it from the selection.

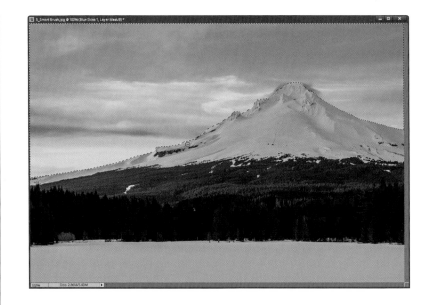

Step Seven:

Here's another really cool part about the Smart Brush tool: it's non-destructive to your photo. This means you can always go back and change (or even delete) the effects. You'll see this in two ways: First, you'll notice that the Smart Brush tool automatically adds a new adjustment layer to the Layers palette. If you ever find the effect is too harsh, you can always reduce the opacity of the layer to reduce the effect.

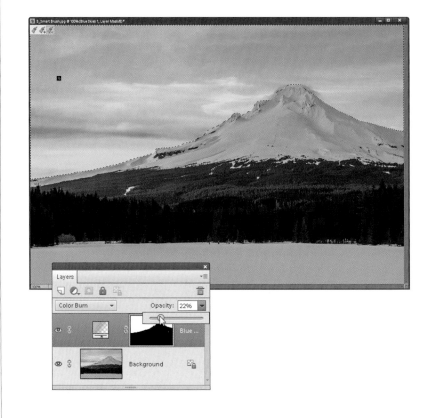

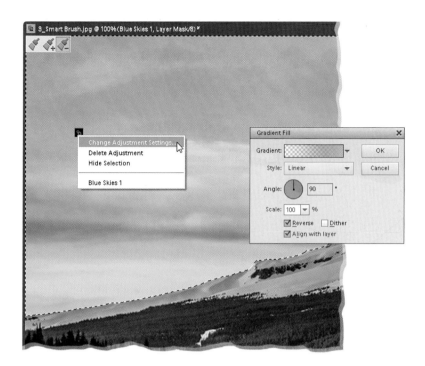

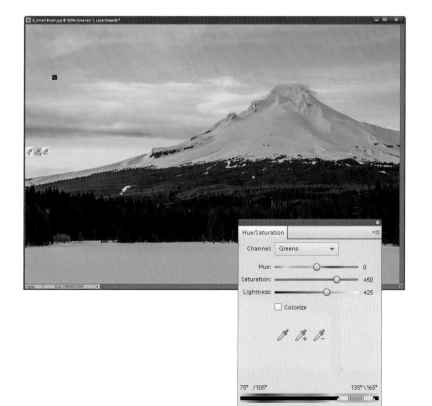

Step Eight:

Also, you may have noticed a tiny red box on your photo where you started to paint with the Smart Brush tool. This is the adjustment marker, letting you know you've applied a Smart Brush adjustment to the photo. If you Right-click on it, you'll see you can delete it if you want or you can change the adjustment settings. Choosing Delete Adjustment does just what you think it does—the adjustment will be removed totally. But try choosing **Change Adjustment Settings** instead. It brings up the Adjustments palette or dialog with the controls for whatever adjustment Elements used to achieve your effect. If you're familiar with that Adjustments palette or dialog, you can always try tweaking the settings. In this case, Gradient was used, so the Gradient Fill dialog appeared.

Step Nine:

You can also add multiple Smart Brush adjustments to different parts of the photo. If you notice, the sky looks a lot better, but now the foreground looks a little flat in comparison. Press **Ctrl-D (Mac: Command-D)** to Deselect the current Smart Brush adjustment in the sky. Then, go to the Preset Picker in the Tool Options Bar and, under the Nature presets in the pop-up menu, click on the second thumbnail in the second row, which intensifies foliage. Now, paint on the foreground to add some contrast to the trees. To bring some more color out in them, I Right-clicked on the adjustment marker for the trees and chose Change Adjustment Settings to get to the Adjustments palette options that were used for the effect. It brought up the Hue/Saturation controls, where I chose **Yellows** from the Channel pop-up menu, and increased the Saturation to +45. Then, I chose **Greens** from the pop-up menu, and increased the Saturation to +50 and the Lightness to +25.

(Continued)

Step 10:

One more thing: the Smart Brush tool is so smart that you can not only change the adjustment settings, but you can also totally change the Smart Brush adjustment you've applied. For example, let's say we want to see what the Cloud Contrast adjustment looks like. Just click back on your Blue Skies layer in the Layers palette, then in the Preset Picker, click on the second thumbnail in the top row of the Nature presets and Elements will swap out the Blue Skies adjustment with the Cloud Contrast one. If you like it, then keep it; if not, then just click back on the first preset you chose or try a new one altogether. Once you're finished, just choose **Flatten Image** from the Layers palette's flyout menu.

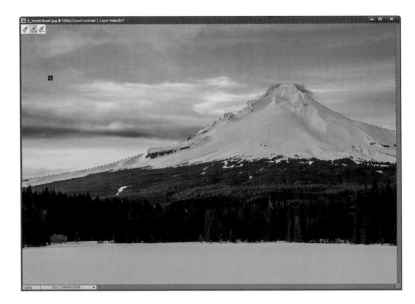

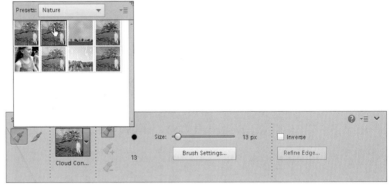

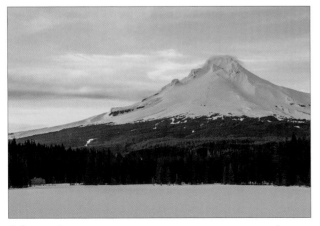

Before

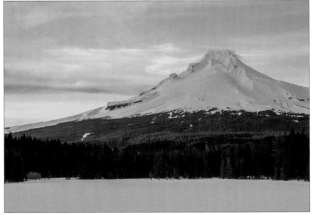

After (with the Blue Skies preset)

Sometimes we don't get to shoot in perfect weather. Especially when you're traveling—you don't get to pick the day, time, or weather forecast. It has happened to me a hundred times. I get somewhere cool and I've got gray skies. Well, there's a sweet little adjustment in Elements that can take those gray skies and make them look pretty darn cool and dramatic. And more often than not, when you apply this and show it to people, they'll comment on how good the sky looks.

Adding Contrast to Cloudy Skies

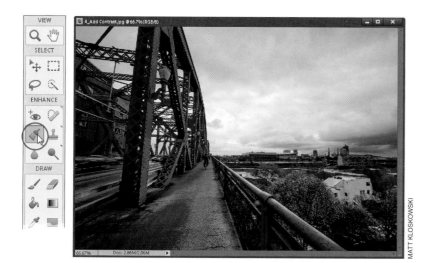

Step One:
Open a photo where you've got some cloudy gray skies. I took the photo here on a trip to Portland, which has no shortage of cloudy skies at certain times of the year :-) Then, select the Smart Brush tool from the Toolbox (it's the large paint brush icon in the Enhance section) or just press the **F key**. (*Note:* For more on the Smart Brush tool, see the previous tutorial.)

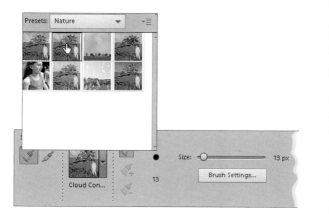

Step Two:
Once you have the tool selected, click on the thumbnail on the left side of the Tool Options Bar to open the Preset Picker. From the Presets pop-up menu, choose **Nature**, and then click on the second thumbnail in the top row, which adds contrast to cloudy skies.

(Continued)

Step Three:

Now, choose a brush size using the Size slider (also in the Tool Options Bar), paint over the sky, and you'll start to see all the details that you knew were there when you took the photo start to come out (be sure to click on the areas of sky behind the bridge).

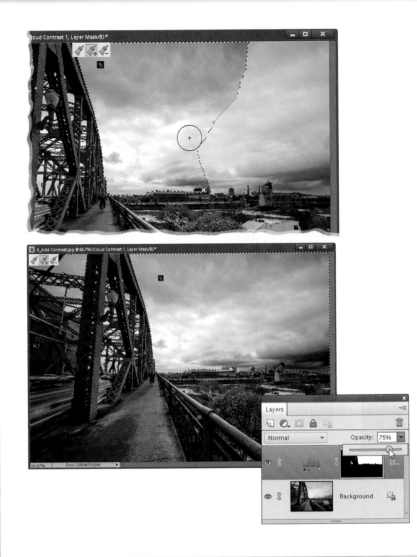

Step Four:

Like most of the Smart Brush tool adjustments, sometimes the default adjustment is too strong. If that's the case, just go to the Layers palette and reduce the Opacity setting to 50%–75%, depending on how strong you want it to look. Not bad, eh? It does a great job of taking an ordinary photo and turning it into something way more dramatic.

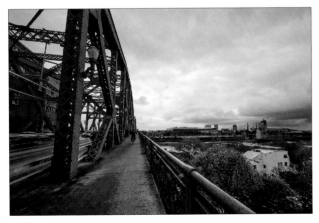

Before

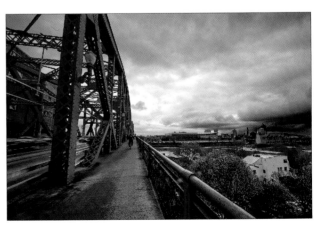

After

Before you go any further, this is one of those circumstances mentioned in the beginning of the book, in the introduction on page xvi. Remember the whole topic about how Elements has changed over the years, and the way we work on our photos is very different today than it was say, five years ago? This is a perfect example. Elements 11 has added the hands-down best way to remove noise in your photos, but it's in Camera Raw (see Chapter 2). So, if you're thinking about using this filter, just know that there's a much better way to remove noise in Camera Raw. If you already have the photo open in the Editor and you're not in the mood to reopen it in Camera Raw, then this filter is an alternative (but not really a good one).

Removing Digital Noise

Step One:
Open the photo that was taken in low lighting (or using a high ISO setting) and has visible digital noise. This noise will be most obvious when viewed at a magnification of 100% or higher (noise appears throughout this photo, but is most visible on the trees, ground, and water, although it's hard to see at the small size of the image here). *Note:* If you view your photos at smaller sizes, you may not notice the noise until you make your prints.

MATT KLOSKOWSKI

Step Two:
Go under the Filter menu, under Noise, and choose **Reduce Noise**. The default settings usually aren't too bad, but if you're having a lot of color aliasing (dots or splotchy areas of red, green, and blue), like we have here, drag the Reduce Color Noise slider to the right. If it still looks splotchy, try dragging the Preserve Details slider to the left.

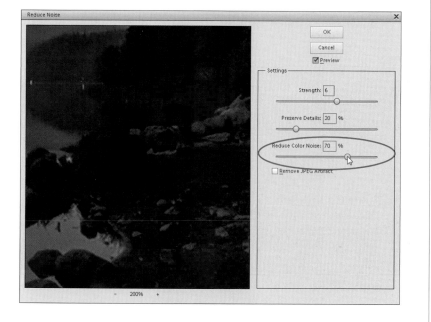

(Continued)

Step Three:
One thing to watch out for when using this filter is that, although it can reduce noise, it can also make your photo a bit blurry, and the higher the Strength setting and the higher the amount of Reduce Color Noise, the blurrier your photo will become. If the noise is really bad, you may prefer a bit of blur to an incredibly noisy photo, so you'll have to make the call as to how much blurring is acceptable, but to reduce the amount of blur a bit, drag the Preserve Details slider to the right.

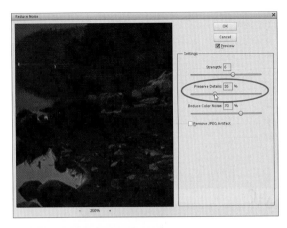

TIP: See a Before/After
To see an instant before/after of the Reduce Noise filter's effect on your photo without clicking the OK button, click your cursor within the Reduce Noise dialog's preview window. When you click-and-hold within that window, you'll see the before version without the filter (zoom in if you need to). When you release the mouse button, you'll see how the photo will look if you click the OK button.

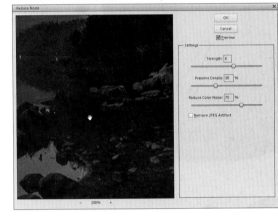

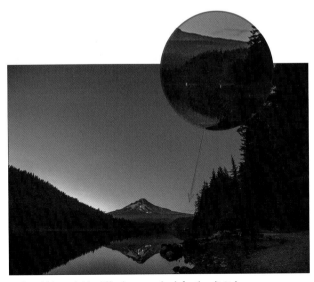

Before (although it's difficult to see, look for the digital noise in the trees, ground, and water)

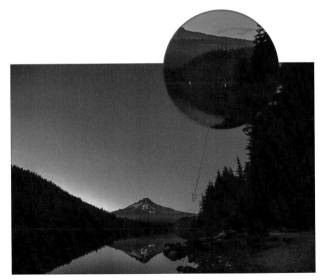

After (noise removed using a slight blur from the Reduce Noise filter)

I've got some bad news and some good news (don't you hate it when people start a conversation like that?). The bad news first (yeah, I like it that way, too): Elements' Dodge and Burn tools are kind of lame. The pros don't use them and, after you read this tutorial, I hope you won't either. The good news... there is a great method the pros do use to dodge and burn and it's totally non-destructive. It's flexible and really quite easy to use. See, isn't it better to end on a good note (with the good news, that is)?

Focusing Light with Digital Dodging and Burning

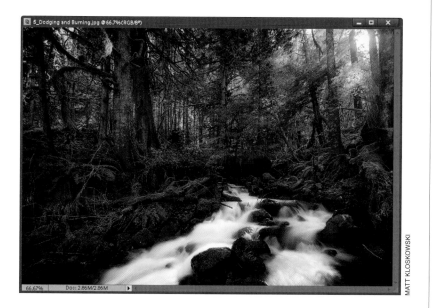

Step One:

In this tutorial, we're going to dodge areas to add some highlights, then we're going to burn in the background a bit to darken some of those areas. Start by opening the photo you want to dodge and burn.

Step Two:

Go to the Layers palette, click on the down-facing arrow at the top right, and from the flyout menu, choose **New Layer** (or just Alt-click [Mac: Option-click] on the Create a New Layer icon at the top of the palette). This accesses the New Layer dialog, which is needed for this technique to work.

(Continued)

Step Three:
In the New Layer dialog, change the Mode to **Overlay**, then right below that, turn on the checkbox for Fill with Overlay-Neutral Color (50% Gray). This is normally grayed out, but when you switch to Overlay mode, this choice becomes available. Click the checkbox to turn it on, then click OK.

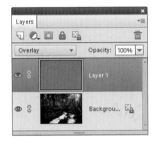

Step Four:
This creates a new layer, filled with 50% gray, above your Background layer. (When you fill a layer with 50% gray and change the Mode to Overlay, Elements ignores the color. You'll see a gray thumbnail in the Layers palette, but the layer will appear transparent in your image window.)

Step Five:
Press **B** to switch to the Brush tool, and choose a medium, soft-edged brush from the Brush Picker (which opens when you click on the Brush thumbnail in the Tool Options Bar). While in the Tool Options Bar, lower the Opacity to approximately 30%.

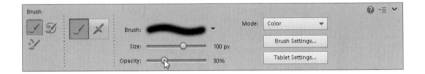

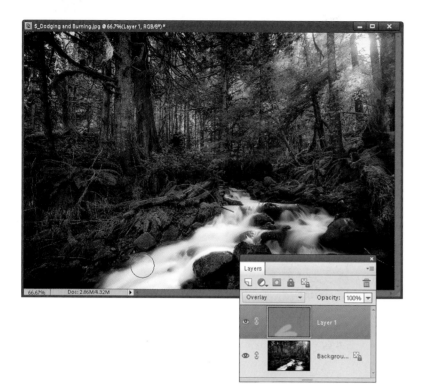

Step Six:

Press **D**, then **X** to set your Foreground color to white and begin painting over the areas that you want to highlight (dodge). As you paint, you'll see light gray strokes appear in the thumbnail of your gray transparent layer, and in the image window, you'll see soft highlights.

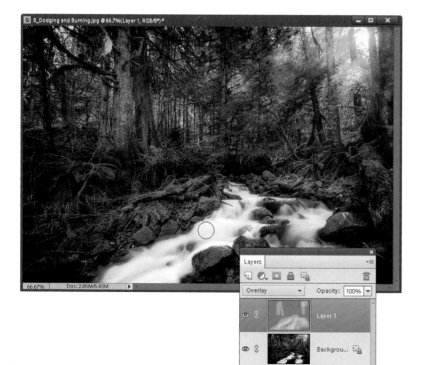

Step Seven:

If your first stab at dodging isn't as intense as you'd like, just release the mouse button, click again, and paint over the same area. Since you're dodging at a low opacity, the highlights will "build up" as you paint over previous strokes. If the highlights appear too intense, just go to the Layers palette and lower the Opacity setting of your gray layer until they blend in.

(Continued)

Step Eight:

If there are areas you want to darken (burn) so they're less prominent (such as the background or the greenery on the left and in the center, where I'm painting here), just press **D** to switch your Foreground color to black and begin painting in those areas. Okay, ready for another dodging-and-burning method? Good, 'cause I've got a great one.

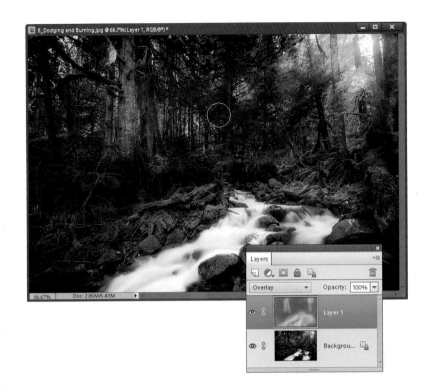

Alternate Technique:

Open the photo that you want to dodge and burn, then just click on the Create a New Layer icon in the Layers palette and change the blend mode to **Soft Light**. Now, set white as your Foreground color and you can dodge right on this layer using the Brush tool set to 30% Opacity. To burn, just as before, switch to black. The dodging and burning using this Soft Light layer appears a bit softer and milder than the previous technique, so you should definitely try both to see which one you prefer.

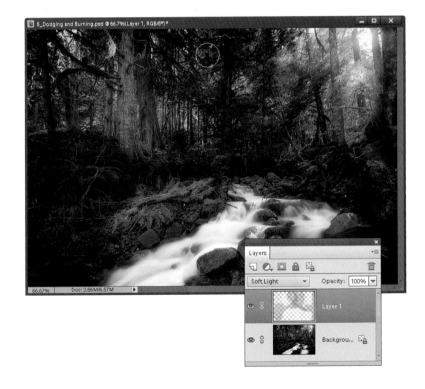

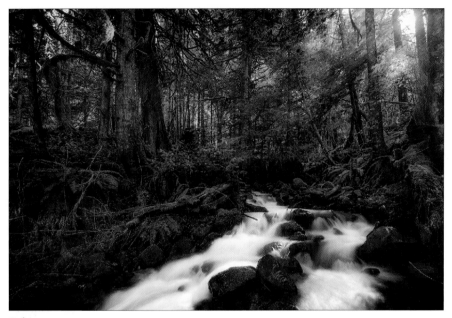

Before

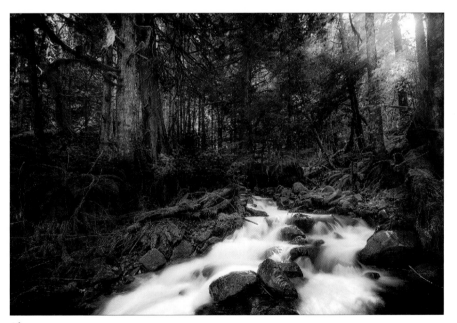

After

Opening Up Shadow Areas That Are Too Dark

One of the most common problems you'll run into with your digital photos is that the shadow areas are too dark. Fortunately for you, since it is the most common problem, digital photo software like Elements has gotten really good at fixing this problem. Here's how it's done:

Step One:
Open the photo that needs to have its shadow areas opened up to reveal detail that was "lost in the shadows."

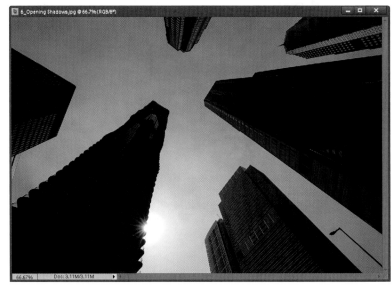

MATT KLOSKOWSKI

Step Two:
Go under the Enhance menu, under Adjust Lighting, and choose **Shadows/Highlights**.

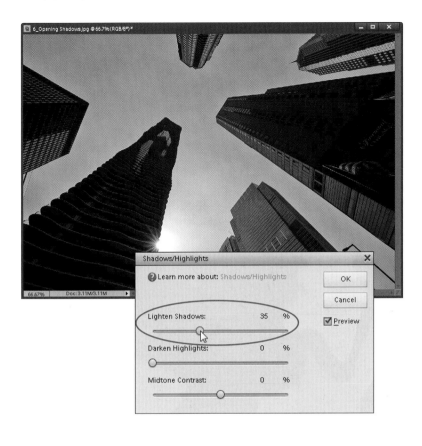

Step Three:

When the dialog appears, it already assumes you have a shadow problem (sadly, most people do but never admit it), so it automatically opens up the shadow areas in your document by 35% (you'll see that the Lighten Shadows slider is at 35% by default [0% is no lightening of the shadows]). If you want to open up the shadow areas even more, drag the Lighten Shadows slider to the right. If the shadows appear to be opened too much with the default 35% increase, drag the slider to the left to a setting below 35%. When the shadows look right, click OK. Your repair is complete.

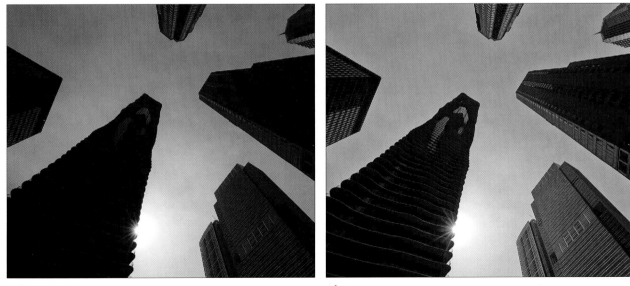

Before   *After*

Fixing Areas That Are Too Bright

Although most of the lighting problems you'll encounter are in the shadow areas of your photos, you'll be surprised how many times there's an area that is too bright (perhaps an area that's lit with harsh, direct sunlight, or you exposed for the foreground but the background is now overexposed). Luckily, this is now an easy fix, too!

Step One:

Open the photo that has highlights that you want to tone down a bit. *Note:* If it's an individual area (like the sun shining directly on your subject's hair), you'll want to press the **L key** to switch to the Lasso tool and put a loose selection around that area. Then go under the Select menu and choose **Feather**. For low-res, 72-ppi images, enter 2 pixels and click OK. For high-res, 300-ppi images, try 8 pixels.

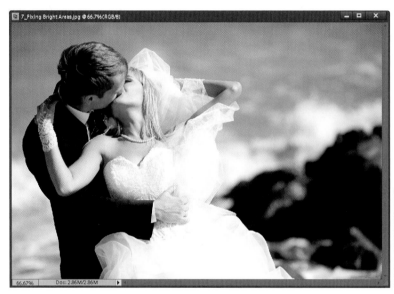

Step Two:

Now go under the Enhance menu, under Adjust Lighting, and choose **Shadows/Highlights**.

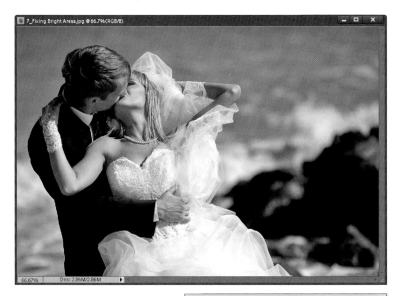

Step Three:
When the dialog appears, drag the Lighten Shadows slider to 0% and drag the Darken Highlights slider to the right, and as you do, the highlights will decrease, bringing back detail and balancing the overall tone of your (selected) highlights with the rest of your photo. (You'll mainly see it in the dress, veil, skin tones, and background here. They have lots more detail now.) Sometimes, when you make adjustments to the highlights (or shadows), you can lose some of the contrast in the midtone areas (they can become muddy or flat looking, or they can become oversaturated). If that happens, drag the Midtone Contrast slider (at the bottom of the dialog) to the right to increase the amount of midtone contrast, or drag to the left to reduce it. Then click OK. *Note:* If you made a selection, you'll need to press **Ctrl-D (Mac: Command-D)** to Deselect when you're finished.

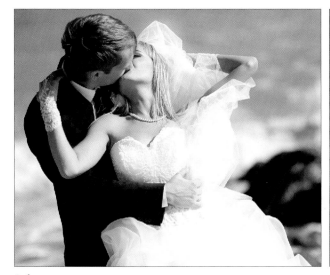

Before

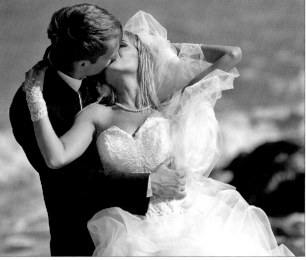

After

When Your Subject Is Too Dark

Sometimes your subject is too dark and blends into the background: maybe there just wasn't enough light, or you forgot to use fill flash, or a host of other reasons that could have caused this. You could go and retake the photo if you realize it right away. However, you don't always realize it immediately, so you'll need to get Elements to help out. For those times, there's a really clever way in Elements to essentially paint your light onto the subject after the fact.

Step One:
Open a photo where the subject(s) of the image appears too dark.

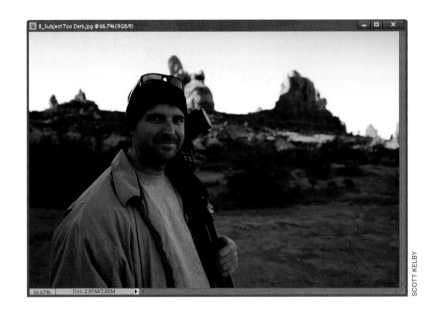

Step Two:
Click on the Create New Adjustment Layer icon at the top of the Layers palette (shown circled here), and choose **Levels**. This will add a Levels adjustment layer above your Background layer, and open the Levels adjustments palette.

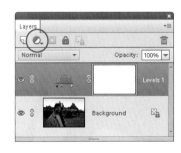
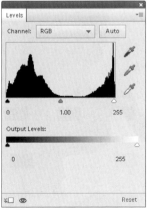

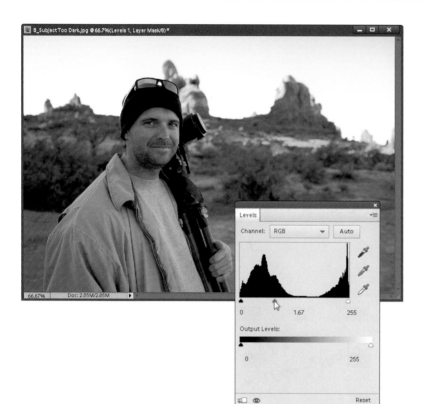

Step Three:
Drag the middle gray Input Levels slider (under the histogram) to the left until your subject(s) looks properly exposed. (*Note:* Don't worry about how the background looks—it will probably become completely blown out, but you'll fix that next—for now, just focus on making your subject look right.) If the midtones slider doesn't bring out the subject enough, you may have to increase the highlights as well, so drag the far-right (white) Input Levels slider to the left to increase the highlights.

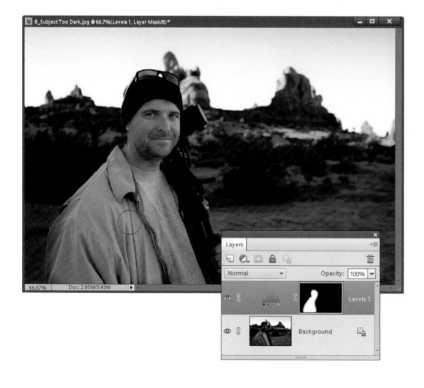

Step Four:
When your subject looks properly exposed, press **D** to set your Foreground color to white and your Background color to black. Then press **Ctrl-Backspace (Mac: Command-Delete)** to fill the layer mask with black and remove the brightening of the photo. Press **B** to switch to the Brush tool and click on the Brush thumbnail in the Tool Options Bar to open the Brush Picker, where you'll choose a soft-edged brush. Now, you'll paint (on the layer mask) over the areas of the image that need a fill flash with your newly created "Fill Flash" brush. The areas you paint over will appear lighter, because you're "painting in" the lightening of your image on this layer.

(Continued)

Step Five:

Continue painting until it looks as if you had used a fill flash. If the effect appears too intense, just lower the opacity of the adjustment layer by dragging the Opacity slider to the left in the Layers palette (as shown here).

TIP: Try the Smart Brush Tool Instead

The Smart Brush tool (covered earlier in this chapter) has a Portrait preset called Lighten Skin Tones that also works pretty well in cases like this.

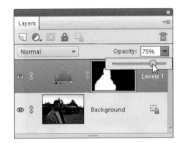

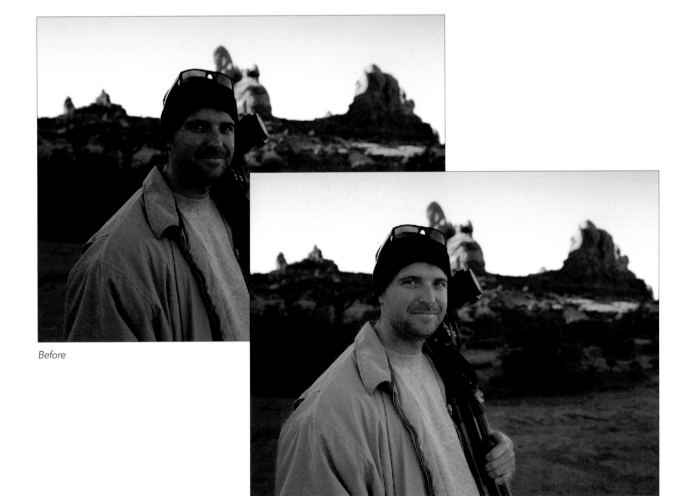

Before

After

If you just finished shooting an indoor event with lots of flash and low light, chances are you're going to have a ton of photos with red eyes. If you know this ahead of time, then the feature you're about to see comes in very handy. You can set up Elements to automatically remove red eye as your photos are being imported into the Organizer. No interaction by you is needed. Just let Elements do its work and by the time you see your photos onscreen, you'll never even know red eye existed.

Automatic Red-Eye Removal

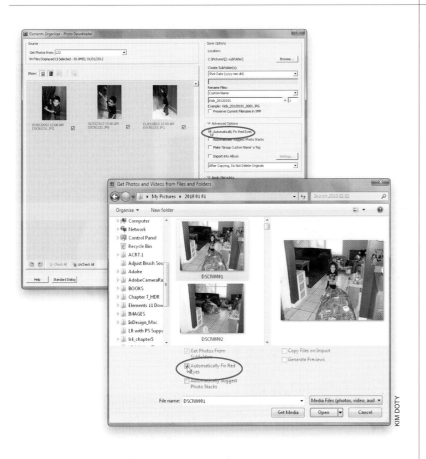

KIM DOTY

Step One:
First, we'll start with the fully automatic version, which you can use when you're importing photos into the Organizer. Here's how it works: When importing photos from your camera, the Elements Organizer – Photo Downloader dialog appears. On the right side of the dialog, in the Advanced Options section, there's a checkbox for Automatically Fix Red Eyes (if your dialog doesn't look like this, click on the Advanced Dialog button at the bottom). If you think some of the photos you're about to import will have red eye, just turn on this checkbox (shown circled here), and then click the Get Media button to start the importing and the red-eye correction. If you're importing photos already on your computer, you'll have the same option in the Get Photos and Videos from Files and Folders dialog.

Step Two:
Once you click the Get Media button, the Getting Media dialog will appear. In this dialog, there's a status bar indicating how many photos are being fixed. It also shows you a preview of each photo it's importing.

(Continued)

Step Three:

Once the process is complete, it automatically groups the original with the fixed version in a Version Set (you'll see an icon at the top right of the image thumbnail), so if you don't like the fix (for whatever reason), you still have the original. You can see both versions of the file by Right-clicking on the photo (in the Organizer) and in the pop-up menu, under Version Set, choosing **Expand Items in Version Set** (or by just clicking on the right-facing arrow to the right of the image thumbnail).

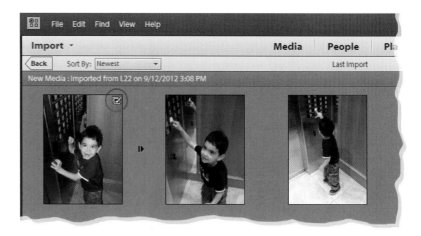

Step Four:

Here is one of the photos with red eye and with it automatically removed.

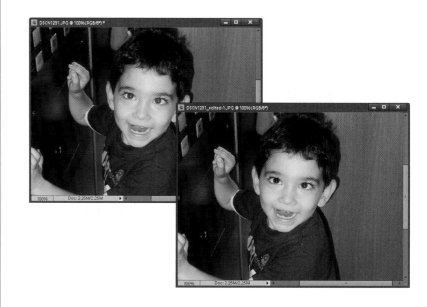

Step Five:

This really isn't a step; it's another way to get an auto red eye fix, and that's by opening an image in the Editor, in Expert mode or Quick mode, and then going under the Enhance menu and choosing **Auto Red Eye Fix**. You can also use the keyboard shortcut **Ctrl-R (Mac: Command-R)**. Either way, it senses where the red eye(s) is, removes it automatically, and life is good.

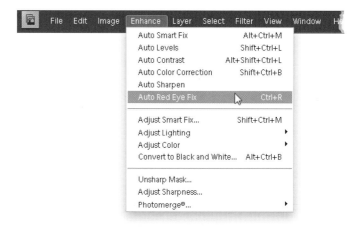

When you use the flash on your digital point-and-shoot camera (or even the on-camera flash on a digital SLR), do you know what you're holding? It's called an A.R.E.M. (short for automated red-eye machine). Yep, that produces red eye like it's going out of style. Studios typically don't have this problem because of the equipment and positioning of the flashes, but sometimes you don't have a choice—it's either an on-camera flash or a really dark and blurry photo. In those cases, just accept the red eye. Become one with it and know that you can painlessly remove it with a couple of clicks in Elements.

Instant Red-Eye Removal

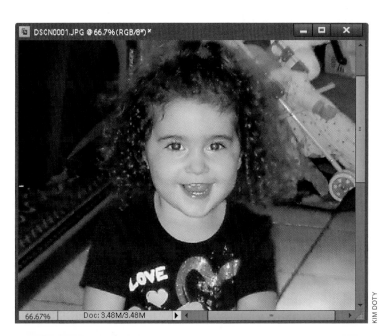

KIM DOTY

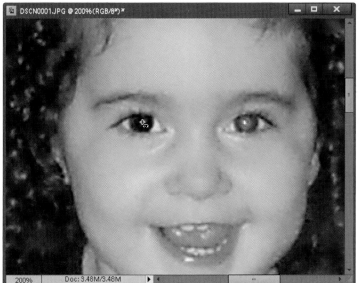

Step One:
Open a photo where the subject has red eye.

Step Two:
Press **Z** to switch to the Zoom tool (it looks like a magnifying glass in the Toolbox) and drag out a selection around the eyes (this zooms you in on the eyes). Now, press the letter **Y** to switch to the Red Eye Removal tool (its Toolbox icon looks like an eye with a tiny crosshair cursor in the left corner). There are two different ways to use this tool: click or click-and-drag. We'll start with the most precise, which is click. Take the Red Eye Removal tool and click it once directly on the red area of the pupil. It will isolate the red in the pupil and replace it with a neutral color. Instead, now you have "gray" eye, which doesn't look spectacular, but it's a heck of a lot better than red eye.

(Continued)

Step Three:

If the gray color that replaces the red seems too "gray," you can adjust the darkness of the replacement color by going to the Tool Options Bar and adjusting the Darken amount. To get better results, you may have to adjust the Pupil Radius setting so that the area affected by the tool matches the size of the pupil. This is also done in the Tool Options Bar when you have the Red Eye Removal tool selected. Now, on to the other way to use this tool (for really quick red-eye fixes).

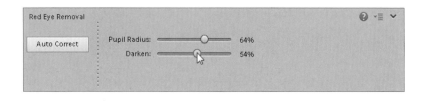

Step Four:

If you have a lot of photos to fix, you may opt for this quicker red-eye fix—just click-and-drag the Red Eye Removal tool over the eye area (putting a square selection around the entire eye). The tool will determine where the red eye is within your selected area (your cursor will change to a timer), and it removes the red. Use this "drag" method on one eye at a time for the best results.

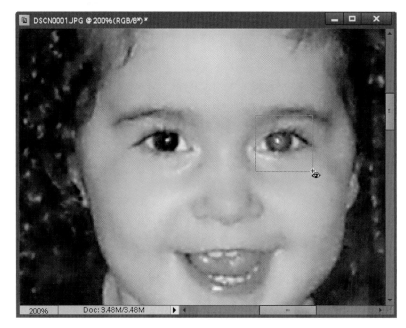

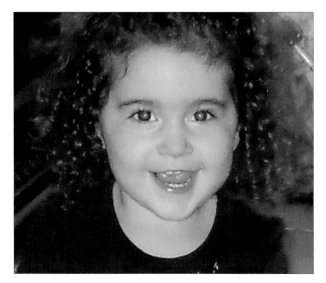

Before

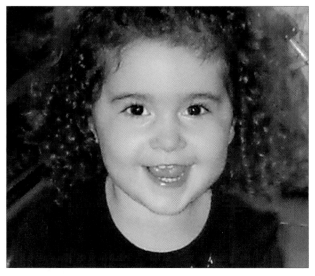

After

Fixing Problems Caused by Your Camera's Lens

Back in Elements 5, Adobe introduced a filter called the Correct Camera Distortion filter. It is pretty much a one-stop shop for repairing the most common problems caused by the camera's lens, including pincushion and barrel distortion, horizontal and vertical perspective problems, and edge vignetting.

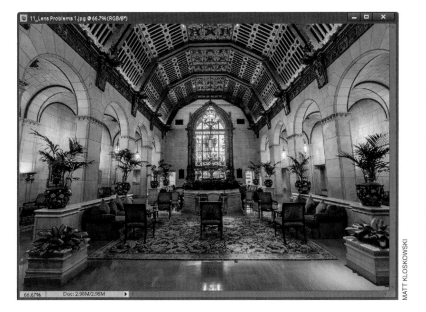

MATT KLOSKOWSKI

Problem One:
Perspective Distortion

Step One:
The first problem we're going to tackle is perspective distortion. In the example shown here, I captured this photo with a 14–24mm lens, so the vertical walls appear at an angle.

Step Two:
To fix this problem (caused by the lens), go under the Filter menu and choose **Correct Camera Distortion**. When the dialog appears, turn off the Show Grid checkbox near the bottom right of the preview window (it's on by default), then go to the Perspective Control section (on the center-right side of the dialog) and drag the Vertical Perspective slider to the left until the walls start to look straight.

(Continued)

Step Three:

When you make this correction, the filter pinches the bottom third of your photo inward, which actually leaves transparent gaps along the bottom and lower-side edges of your photo (you see the checkerboard in these areas). The Scale slider at the bottom of the dialog in the Edge Extension section is what takes care of these edge gaps caused by the perspective repair. By default, in Elements 11, it is set at 100%, eliminating the edge gaps, but if you drag the slider to the left, you'll see them come back as you see the parts of your photo it cropped off.

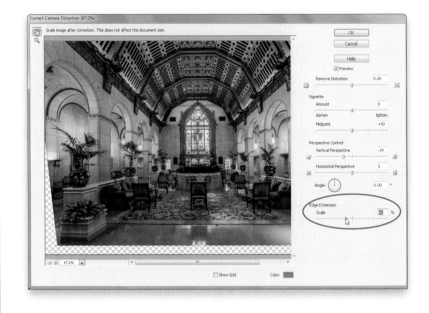

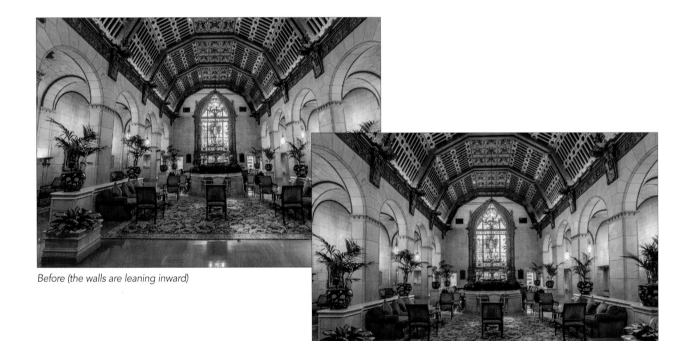

Before (the walls are leaning inward)

After (the perspective distortion is corrected)

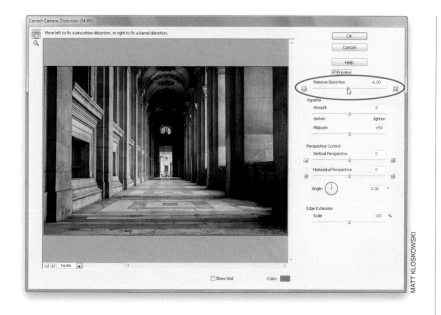

Problem Two:
Pincushion Distortion

Step One:
Another common lens correction problem is called pincushion distortion, where the sides of your photo appear to curve inward (see the Before photo below, where the wall and pillars seem to bow inward).

Step Two:
So, open the Correct Camera Distortion filter again, but this time you're going to drag the Remove Distortion slider (in the top right of the dialog) slowly to the left to straighten out the photo. To remove barrel distortion, which makes your photo look bloated or rounded, drag the slider to the right to "pucker" the photo inward from the center. As with the perspective correction, your photo is automatically scaled up to remove any gaps.

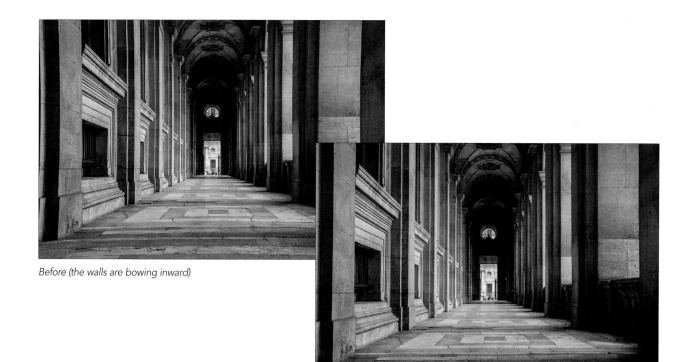

Before (the walls are bowing inward)

After (the pincushion distortion is corrected)

(Continued)

Problem Three:
Lens Vignetting

Step One:
Vignetting is a lens problem where the corners of your photo appear darkened (see the Before photo below). To remove this problem, go back to the Correct Camera Distortion filter.

Step Two:
In the Vignette section at the center-right side of the dialog, drag the Amount slider to the right, and as you do, you'll see the edges brighten. Keep dragging the slider until the edges match the brightness of the rest of the photo. The Midpoint slider (just below the Amount slider), determines how far into the photo your corner brightening will extend. In this case, you have to retract it just a little bit by dragging the slider to the right, then click OK.

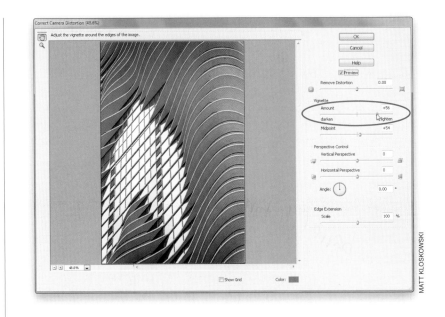

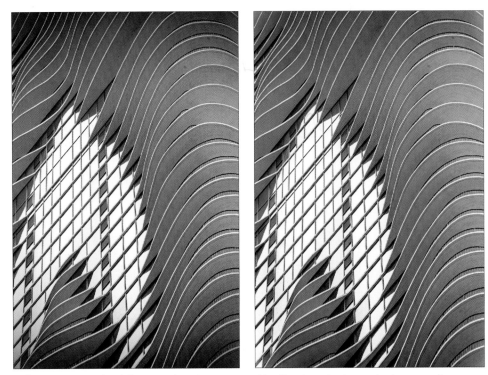

Before (you can see the dark vignetted areas in the corners)

After (the vignetting is completely removed)

Group shots can be a challenge. Everyone has to be looking and smiling at the right time. If one person isn't, then you have to shoot it again. The real problem comes from the fact that you really can't tell if everyone has their eyes open or is looking the right way from the small LCD on the back of your camera. So you get back and upload your photos only to find out that not one of them has everyone looking and smiling the way that they need to be. No sweat, with Elements' Group Shot feature. As long as you have a few photos to choose from, you can create the perfect group photo afterward.

The Elements Secret to Fixing Group Shots

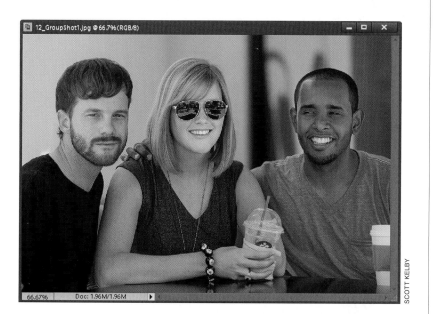

Step One:
Here's a group shot where one of the subjects (the guy on the right) is kind of squinting and looking away.

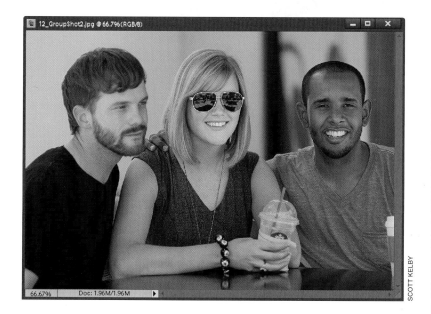

Step Two:
If you've ever taken group shots before, you're guilty of photographing until your group threatens to riot or otherwise destroy your gear. Chances are, you took more photos of the same group before such threats ensued. So here's another shot where the guy on the right looks great. But, we can't use this shot, because now the guy on the left is looking away (and he's a bit out of focus, as well). No problem. We're going to use the Group Shot feature to give us the best of both worlds and combine these photos.

(Continued)

Step Three:

At this point, you should have both photos open in the Editor. So, go under the Enhance menu, under Photomerge®, and choose **Photomerge® Group Shot**.

Note: A quick rule of thumb when using the Group Shot feature is to pick the best photo of the group as the first photo selected. See, Elements uses the first photo as the bottommost layer in the Layers palette. You'll see in a few steps, that makes it easier for us to go back later and restore the best parts of the photo with the Eraser tool.

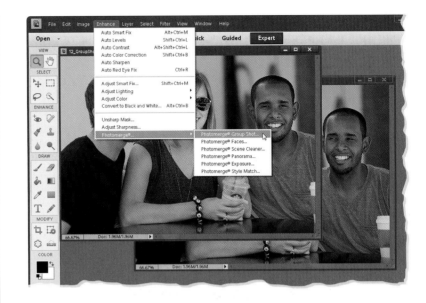

TIP: Using More Photos

Even though I'm only using two photos here, you can use the Group Shot feature with up to 10 photos of the same group. So, if everyone is looking the wrong way, not smiling, or has their eyes closed at some point, you'll have a better chance of fixing the photo with more than two shots.

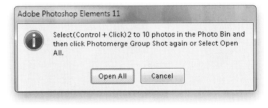

Step Four:

A dialog will open (shown above) asking you to go back and select from two to 10 photos from the Project Bin or to select Open All. Since these are the only two photos I have open in the Editor, I just clicked Open All and Elements switched to Guided mode, and opened my images in the Photomerge Group Shot window.

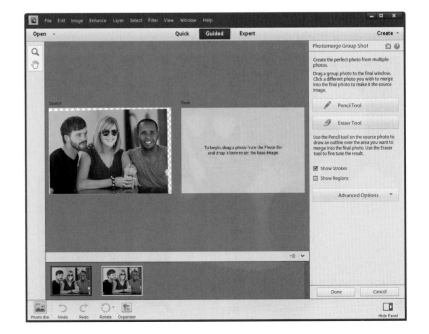

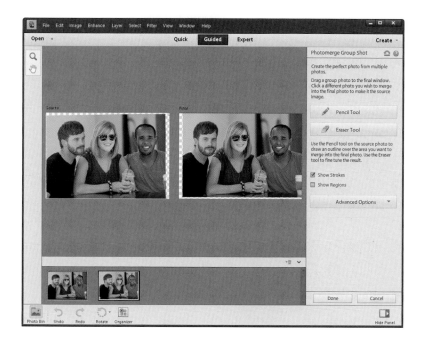

Step Five:

The first thing you need to do here is set up the photos as a source and a final. In the example here, I wanted the good photo where the guy on the right was looking straight (but the guy on the left was looking away) on the Source side (if it wasn't, I would've just clicked on its thumbnail down in the Project Bin). Then, I went to the Project Bin and clicked-and-dragged the thumbnail of the photo where the guy on the right was looking away and squinting (but the guy on the left was looking straight) to the Final side. So basically, what I want to do is take the guy on the right from the Source side (the one where he's looking straight and his eyes are open) and use him to replace the guy on the Final side (where he's looking away and his eyes are squinted).

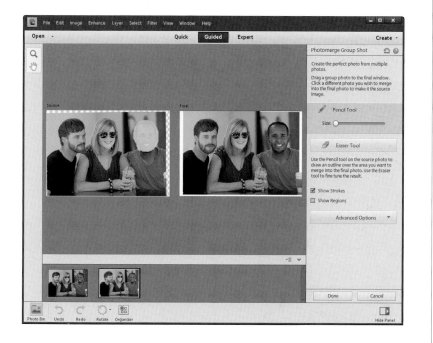

Step Six:

The rest is pretty easy: Click on the Pencil Tool button on the right-hand side. Then, paint on the area in the Source image that you want to appear in the Final image. In this example, I want the guy looking straight and his eyes to be open, so I painted over the Source image where his face is. Elements will think for a moment, and magically re-place the guy's face in the Final photo with the one from the Source photo.

TIP: Change Your Brush Size

Sometimes the default brush size is way too small and it takes you a while to paint in your source image. If that happens, then increase the Size setting in the Pencil Tool section to something larger.

(Continued)

Step Seven:

At this point, if things look good (and trust me, things don't always look good here, although it may work on the first try), then click the Done button at the bottom right of the window to return to Expert mode. Your merged photo is in a new document with two layers (the original on the bottom and new merged photo on the top) in the Layers palette (use the Crop tool **[C]** to crop away any excess canvas).

TIP: Use the Eraser Tool to Fix It

If the Group Shot merge doesn't work perfectly, you can finesse it by painting with the Eraser tool **(E)** on the top layer to reveal the layer below. You'll want to zoom in really close, but it's a good trick to fix any flaws that remain.

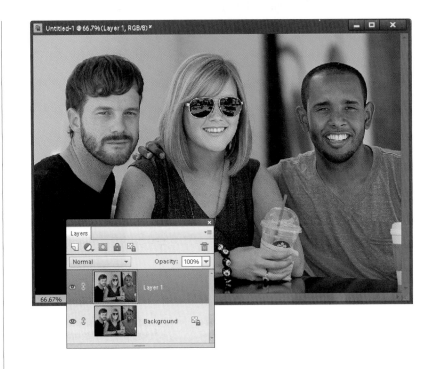

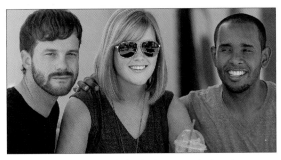

Before #1 (the guy on the left is looking straight, but the guy on the right is squinting and looking away)

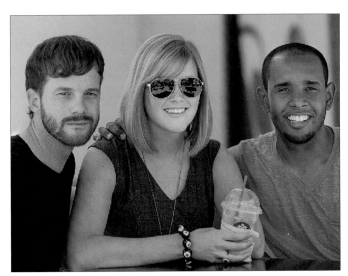

After (we've got the best of both worlds—the guy on the left is looking straight, and the guy on the right is also looking straight with his eye open)

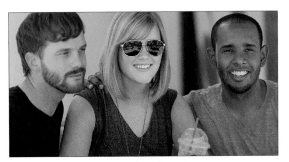

Before #2 (the guy on the right is now looking straight, but the guy on the left is now looking away)

As an outdoor photographer, one of the biggest battles you face is balancing the details in the highlights and shadows. Usually, you have to make a choice and set the camera's exposure to capture detail in the shadows (which produces bright, blown-out skies), or set the exposure for the brighter areas (which makes the darker areas almost black). With the Photomerge Exposure feature, we can do both. If you've heard of HDR (High Dynamic Range) photography and software, it's similar—we take multiple photos with differing exposures and combine them together in Elements automatically (without a bunch of selections and layers).

Blending Multiple Exposures (a.k.a. Pseudo-HDR Technique)

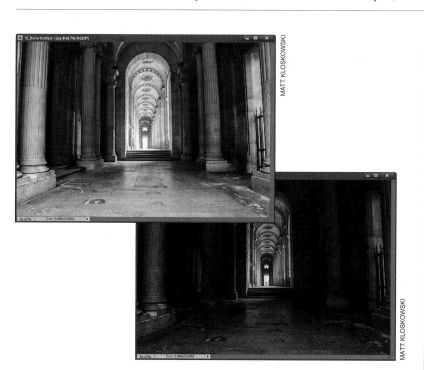

MATT KLOSKOWSKI

MATT KLOSKOWSKI

Step One:
Open the photos you're going to merge together. Here are a couple of photos of the same subject. To make these photos, I set my camera on a tripod and just changed exposure settings to capture one photo with lots of details in the shadows (even though it looks really bright) and one photo with lots of detail in the highlight areas, such as the archway (even though the other areas look too dark).

TIP: Try This with Portraits, Too
This doesn't just work on landscape or architectural photos. You can try this with people, too. The key here is to have them be as still as possible. Oh, and you don't always have to be on a tripod, but it sure helps you get a better result in the end.

Step Two:
Go to the Enhance menu, choose Photomerge®, and then choose **Photomerge® Exposure**. In the resulting dialog, click Open All.

(Continued)

Step Three:

This takes you into the Photomerge Exposure window. On the right side, you'll see two tabs: Automatic and Manual. Automatic has two modes in it: Simple Blending and Smart Blending. Manual mode has some settings, as well, but we'll check out Automatic first.

Step Four: Automatic Mode— Simple Blending

When you're in Automatic mode, Elements starts you out using the Smart Blending option. In this example (in the top capture), it looks pretty good, but try clicking on the Simple Blending option just to compare. It's not bad (the bottom capture). The columns and foreground look a little darker, and the archway has a little more detail in it than the original bright photo revealed. I do think the columns still look a little dark, though. Elements has essentially taken the best parts of each photo and automatically blended them together. If you're happy with it, then just click Done near the bottom right of the window to return to Expert mode (you may have to crop off some excess areas). The problem with this option, though, is that it has no settings at all (the sliders in the panel are not active). You get what you get and if you're not happy with it, well, you'll have to resort to another method. So, we'll go back and look at the Smart Blending option next.

TIP: Using More Photos

Even though I'm only using two photos here, you can use Photomerge Exposure with up to 10 photos of the same scene. Honestly, 10 is kinda overkill, but if you had a really contrasty scene with lots of bright highlights and dark shadows (say, inside of a house with lots of windows on a bright, sunny day), you may want to take three or four of the same scene with different exposures.

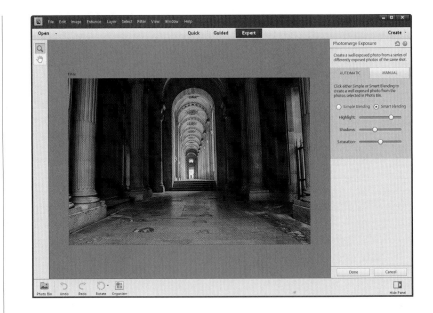

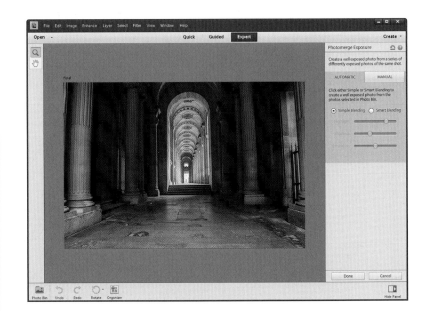

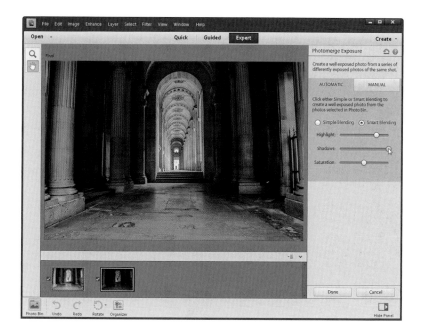

Step Five: Automatic Mode— Smart Blending

Okay, since the columns are just too dark using the Simple Blending option, let's switch back to Smart Blending by clicking on the Smart Blending radio button. Like we saw earlier, it does a pretty good job even though Elements is still trying to automatically blend the photos. However, in the Smart Blending mode, you'll see the three sliders are now available to help you get better results. The second one is Shadows. Move this slider if the shadows (or really dark parts of the photo) look too dark. In this example, I thought the columns were looking a little too dark, so I moved the Shadows slider to the right to lighten them a little.

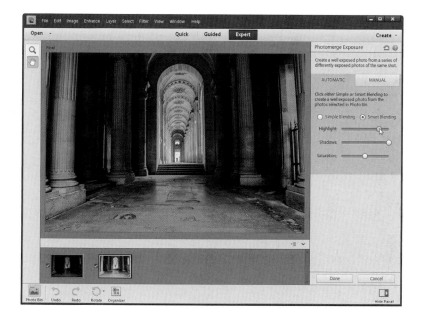

Step Six:

Now take a look at the highlight areas, of the blended photo. If they look too bright or too dark, then you can move the Highlight slider to help out. Let's move it to the right to darken the archway a little here, since it got brighter in Step Five. Be careful of big moves either way, though. If you make your highlight areas too dark, then you won't be able to see what's there. If they're too light, then things start to look fake. You won't immediately know what's wrong with the photo, but your mind just kinda knows something isn't right here, since it's not used to seeing a bright, sunlit background and well-lit foreground areas, as well.

(Continued)

Step Seven:

When you're merging different exposures together, you'll often lose some saturation in the photo, so Adobe included a Saturation slider, as well, in case you need to bump it up a little. Be careful here, though. I've never run into a photo that needed a Saturation setting of more than 30–35. If you start moving it too far, your photo will end up looking radioactive. If you're not happy with the results, you can always hit the Reset Panel icon (next to Photomerge Exposure at the top right) to get back to the default settings.

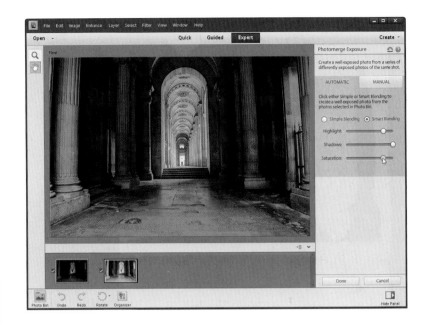

Step Eight: Manual Mode

So far, Elements has been doing most of the blending for us. Sure we had a few sliders to work with, but we really didn't have that much control. However, with Manual mode, you get a lot more control over exactly which parts of each photo you'd like to keep in your final image. So, click on the Reset Panel icon, and then click on the Manual tab at the top of the palette. First, click on the darker photo (where the archway looks okay, but the columns are too dark) in the Project Bin to put it into the Source window on the left. Then drag the photo where the columns look better (but the archway is too bright) to the Final window on the right.

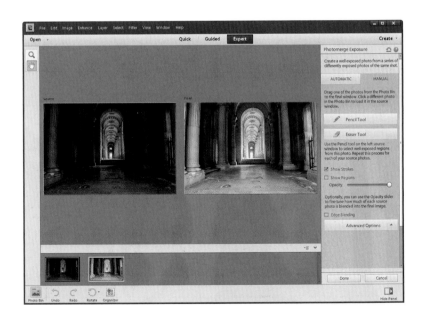

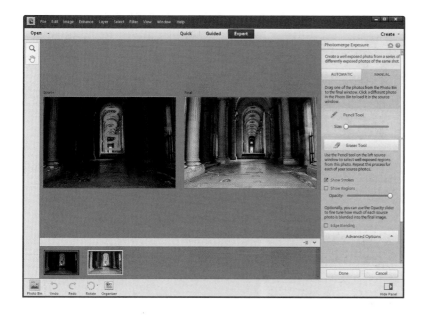

Step Nine:
Now, click on the Pencil Tool button in the middle of the Manual tab, choose a brush size using the Size slider, and draw over the archway on the darker photo (the one on the left) that you want to appear in the Final image (the one on the right). Just a few quick scribbles over it should do it here. If you happen to scribble too much, or Elements pulls too much over from the darker photo, then click on the Eraser Tool button and use it to erase some of the scribbles.

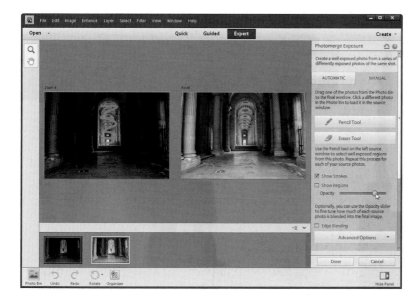

Step 10:
At this point, it probably looks really fake with the darker archway and brighter foreground. One way to combat this is to drag the Opacity slider (at the bottom of the Photomerge Exposure palette) to the left to increase the brightness of the Source image (the darker archway) in the Final image on the right. Give it a try here. I dragged mine to about 75 or so to brighten the archway a little.

(Continued)

Step 11:

If you see a fringe along the edge of your selected area (I could see some around the archway), then try turning the Edge Blending checkbox on (below the Opacity slider) to blend them together. I'll be the first to say that sometimes I wonder if this checkbox is even tied to anything because it doesn't always appear to work (or do anything for that matter). But sometimes you'll see an improvement, so it's worth a quick try.

Below are the two before photos. Neither one of them look that great, and both would have needed some pretty heavy editing to turn them into what I actually "saw" when I took the shot.

Pencil Tool

Size:

Eraser Tool

Use the Pencil tool on the left source window to select well exposed regions from this photo. Repeat this process for each of your source photos.

☑ Show Strokes
☐ Show Regions
Opacity:

Optionally, you can use the Opacity slider to fine tune how much of each source photo is blended into the final image.

☑ Edge Blending

Advanced Options ▲

Done   Cancel

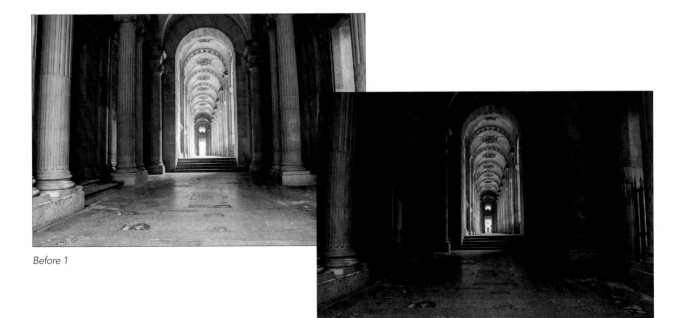

Before 1

Before 2

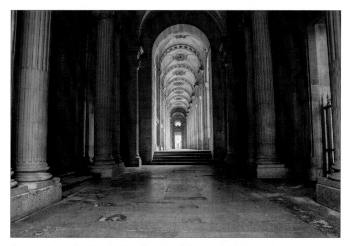

Automatic mode: Simple Blending (no sliders available)

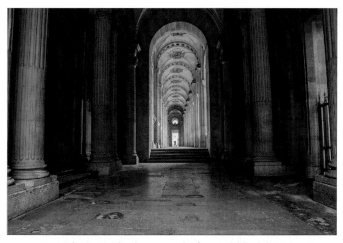

Automatic mode: Smart Blending (using the few available sliders)

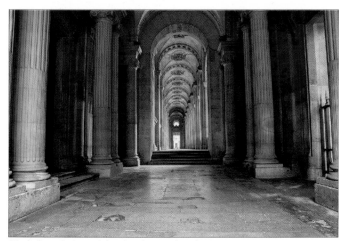

*Manual mode (a quick brush selection, but that's it.
No major selections or layering needed)*

Here are the end results (I've compared both Automatic modes and the Manual mode).

ONE LAST TIP: If You Don't Shoot on a Tripod

If you didn't shoot on a tripod, the Photomerge feature can cause some pretty funky results in the final image, because Elements doesn't know which parts of the photos should overlap. In other words, if you laid them on top of each other, where the subject is in the top photo may not exactly match where it is in the bottom one. But you can help out by using the Alignment tool (the little blue target-looking thing on the button at the bottom of the palette in Manual mode, under Advanced Options). Click on the button to select the tool, then place three targets in key areas (corners, logos on a shirt, eyes, etc.) on the Source photo. Move over to the Final photo and do the same thing. Click the Align Photos button beneath the tool and Elements will do its best to align the photos with each other, so your end results look better.

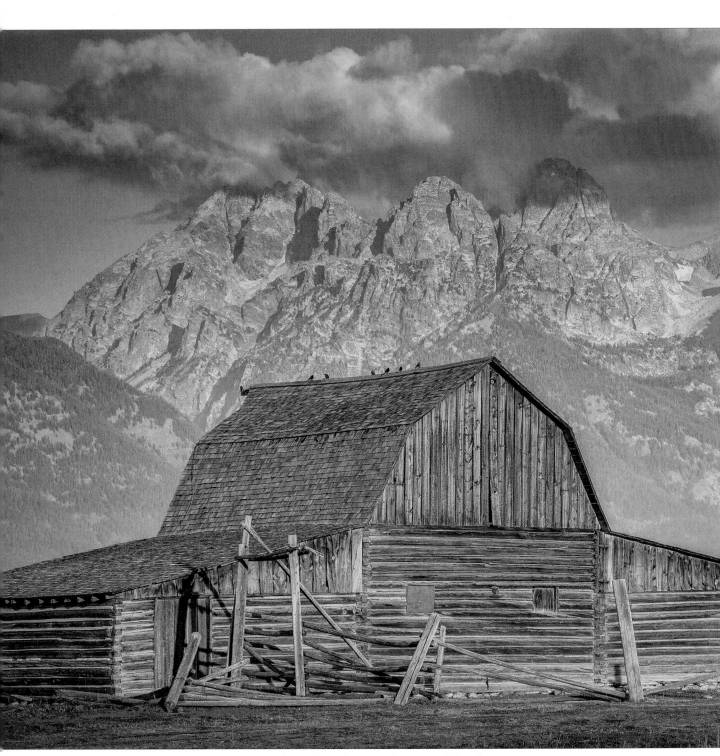

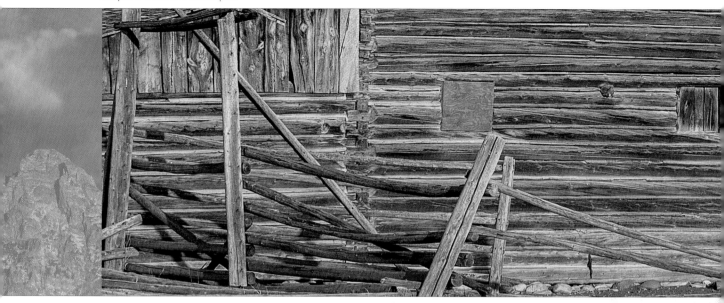

SELECT START
selection techniques

This chapter is actually named after the band Select Start, because the name of the song that came up when I searched on the iTunes Store for the word "Select" was their song, titled "She's Not a Hottie Hotty," but I thought that "She's Not a Hottie Hotty" would make a weird name for a chapter on how to make selections. I listened to "She's Not a Hottie Hotty" and it actually wasn't bad, but I really thought the song could use more references to making selections and fewer references to b-double-o-t-y. Okay, I have to be honest, I only listened to the free 90-second preview of the song, and I didn't actually hear the word "booty" per se, but seriously, what song that includes the word "hottie" doesn't have the word "booty" in there somewhere? I mean, how many words are there that rhyme with hottie that aren't used regularly by a toddler (made ya stop and think for a moment, didn't I?). Anyway, Select Start (the band's name) is really a pretty good name for the chapter, because we start with teaching you how to make simple selections, and then take you through Elements' most important selection techniques, because being able to easily select and adjust just one particular area of your photo is really important. Once you've mastered selections, the next logical step is to learn how to break down people's names rap-style, like Fergie (F to the E-R-G-I-E), but if you just wondered, "Why would the Duchess of York talk like that?" we have an entirely different problem.

Selecting Square, Rectangular, or Round Areas

Selections are an incredibly important feature in Elements. They're how you tell Elements to affect only specific areas of your photos. Whether it's moving part of one photo into another or simply trying to draw more attention to or enhance part of a photo, you'll have so much more control if you know how to select things better. For starters, Elements includes quick and easy ways to make basic selections (square, round, rectangle). These are probably the ones you'll use most, so let's start here.

Step One:
To make a rectangular selection, choose (big surprise) the Rectangular Marquee tool by pressing the **M key**. Adobe's word for selection is "marquee." (Why? Because calling it a marquee makes it more complicated than calling it what it really is—a selection tool—and giving tools complicated names is what Adobe does for fun.)

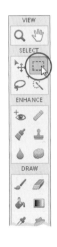

Step Two:
We're going to start by selecting a rectangle shape, so click your cursor in the upper left-hand corner of the window and drag down and to the right until your selection covers the trees and grass, then release the mouse button. That's it! You've got a selection, and anything you do now will affect only the area within that selected rectangle (in other words, it will only affect the trees and grass).

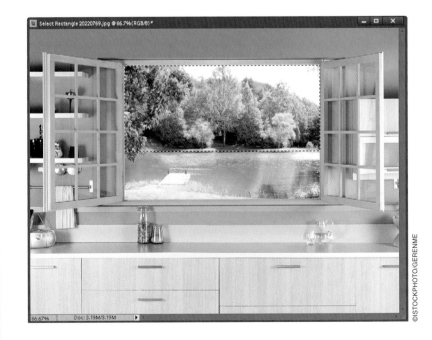

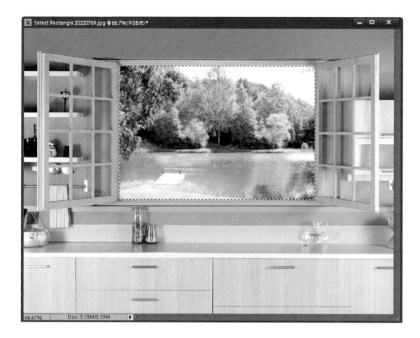

Step Three:
To add another area to your current selection, just press-and-hold the Shift key, and then draw another rectangular selection. In our example here, let's go ahead and select everything outside the window, so press-and-hold the Shift key, drag out a rectangle around the bottom half of the window, and release the mouse button. Now everything outside the window is selected.

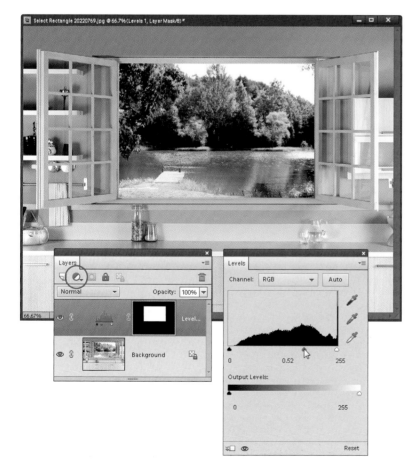

Step Four:
Now let's make an adjustment and you'll see that your adjustment will only affect your selected area. Click on the Create New Adjustment Layer icon at the top of the Layers palette, and choose **Levels** from the pop-up menu. In the Levels adjustments palette, drag the middle gray slider under the histogram to the right (or left), and you'll see the color of the trees and water change as you drag. More importantly, you'll see that nothing else changes—just that area. This is why selections are so important—they are how you tell Elements you only want to adjust a specific area. You can also drag the white and black sliders to get the lighting you want. You'll notice your selection goes away when you add the adjustment layer.

(Continued)

Step Five:

Okay, you've got rectangles, but what if you want to make a perfectly square selection? It's easy—the tool works the same way, but before you drag out your selection, you'll want to press-and-hold the Shift key. Let's try it: open another image, get the Rectangular Marquee tool, press-and-hold the Shift key, and then draw a perfectly square selection (around the white area inside of this fake Polaroid frame, in this case).

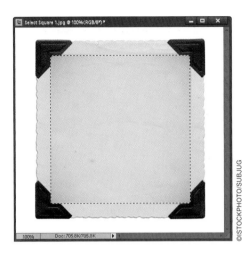

©ISTOCKPHOTO/SUBJUG

Step Six:

While your selection is still in place, open a photo that you'd like to appear inside your selected area and press **Ctrl-A (Mac: Command-A)**; this is the shortcut for Select All, which puts a selection around your entire photo at once. Then press **Ctrl-C (Mac: Command-C)** to copy that photo into Elements' memory.

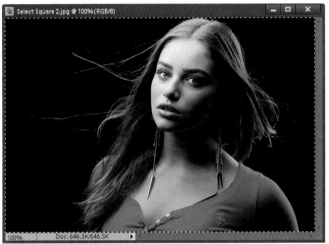

SCOTT KELBY

Step Seven:

Switch back to the Polaroid image, and you'll notice that your selection is still in place. Go under the Edit menu and choose **Paste Into Selection**. The image held in memory will appear pasted inside your square selection. If the photo is larger than the square you pasted it into, you can reposition the photo by just clicking-and-dragging it around inside your selected opening.

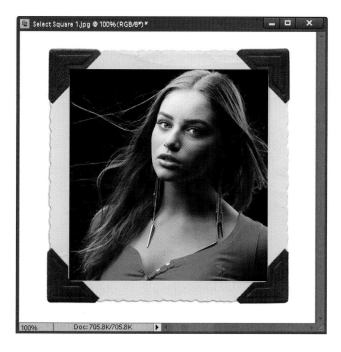

Step Eight:

You can also use Free Transform (press **Ctrl-T [Mac: Command-T]**) to scale the pasted photo in size. Just grab a corner point (press **Ctrl-0** [zero; **Mac: Command-0**] if you don't see them), press-and-hold the Shift key (or turn on the Constrain Proportions check-box in the Tool Options Bar), and drag inward or outward. When the size looks right, press the **Enter (Mac: Return) key** and you're done. (Well, sort of—you'll need to press **Ctrl-D [Mac: Command-D]** to Deselect, but only do this once you're satisfied with your image, because once you deselect, Elements flattens your new image into your Background layer, meaning there's no easy way to adjust this image.) Now, on to oval and circular selections…

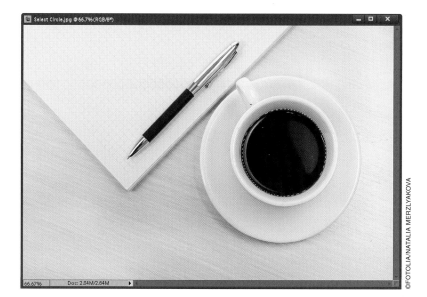

©FOTOLIA/NATALIA MERZLYAKOVA

Step Nine:

Open an image with a circle shape you want to select (a cup of coffee here), and then press **M** to switch to the Elliptical Marquee tool (pressing M toggles you between the Rectangular and Elliptical Marquee tools by default). Now, just click-and-drag a selection around your circle. Press-and-hold the Shift key as you drag to make your selection perfectly round. If your round selection doesn't fit exactly, you can reposition it by moving your cursor inside the border of your round selection and clicking-and-dragging to move it into position. You can also press-and-hold the Spacebar to move the selection as you're creating it. If you want to start over, just deselect, and then drag out a new selection. *Hint:* With circles, it helps if you start dragging before you reach the circle, so try starting about ¼" to the top left of the circle.

(Continued)

Step 10:

We'll change the lighting on the coffee to bring out the reflections, so click on the Create New Adjustment Layer icon and choose Levels. In the Levels adjustments palette, drag the white slider (beneath the right side of the histogram) to the left to bring out the reflections.

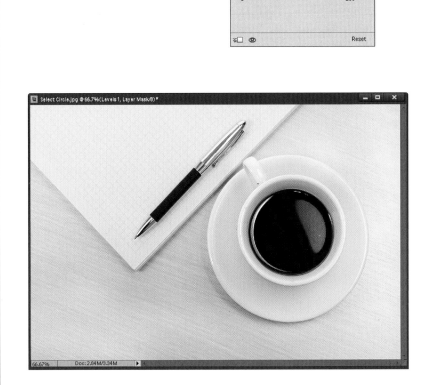

Step 11:

This isn't really a step, it's more of a recap: To make rectangles or ovals, you just grab the tool and start dragging. However, if you need to make a perfect square or a circle (rather than an oval), you press-and-hold the Shift key before you start dragging. You're starting to wish you'd paid attention in geometry class now, aren't you? No? Okay, me either.

Saving Your Selections

If you've spent 15 or 20 minutes (or even longer) putting together an intricate selection, once you deselect it, it's gone. (Well, you might be able to get it back by choosing Reselect from the Select menu, as long as you haven't made any other selections in the meantime, but don't count on it. Ever.) Here's how to save your finely-honed selections and bring them back into place anytime you need them.

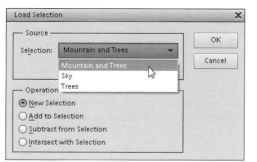

Step One:
Open an image and then put a selection around an object in your photo using the tool of your choice. Here I used the Quick Selection tool **(A)** to select the sky, then went under the Select menu and chose **Inverse** to select the mountains, trees, and lake. Then, I **Alt-clicked (Mac: Option-clicked)** on the sky's reflection to remove it from the selection. To save your selection once it's in place (so you can use it again later), go under the Select menu and choose **Save Selection**. This brings up the Save Selection dialog. Enter a name in the Name field and click OK to save your selection.

Step Two:
Now you can get that selection back (known as "reloading" by Elements wizards) at any time by going to the Select menu and choosing **Load Selection**. If you've saved more than one selection, they'll be listed in the Selection pop-up menu—just choose which one you want to "load" and click OK. The saved selection will appear in your image.

Softening Those Harsh Edges

When you make an adjustment to a selected area in a photo, your adjustment stays completely inside the selected area. That's great in many cases, but when you deselect, you'll see a hard edge around the area you adjusted, making the change look fairly obvious. However, softening those hard edges (thereby "hiding your tracks") is easy—here's how:

Step One:

Let's say you want to darken the area around the woman and girl, so it looks almost like you shined a soft spotlight on them. Start by drawing an oval selection around them using the Elliptical Marquee tool (press **M** until you have it). Make the selection big enough so the woman, girl, and the surrounding area appear inside your selection. Now we're going to darken the area around them, so go under the Select menu and choose **Inverse**. This inverses the selection so you'll have everything but the woman and girl selected (you'll use this trick often).

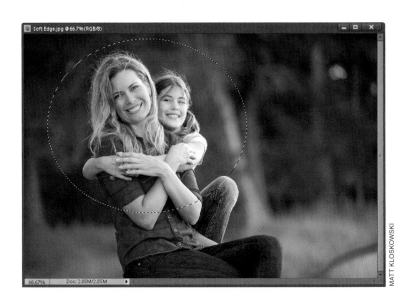

Step Two:

Click on the Create New Adjustment Layer icon at the top of the Layers palette, and choose **Levels**. In the Levels adjustments palette, drag the black (shadows) slider beneath the histogram to the right to about 66. You can see the harsh edges around the oval, and it looks nothing like a soft spotlight—it looks like a bright oval. That's why we need to soften the edges, so there's a smooth blend between the bright oval and the dark surroundings.

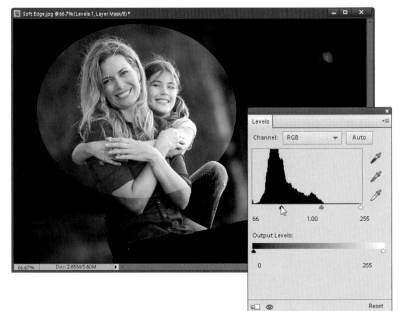

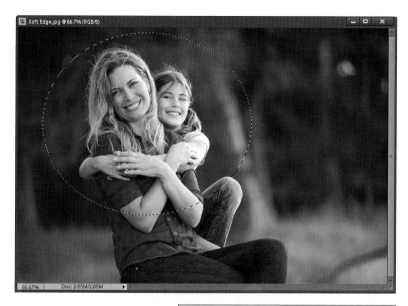

Feather Selection

Learn more about: Feather Selection

OK

Cancel

Feather Radius: 150 pixels

Step Three:

Press **Ctrl-Z (Mac: Command-Z)** three times so your photo looks like it did when you drew your selection in Step One (your selection should be in place—if not, drag out another oval). With your selection in place, go under the Select menu and choose **Feather**. When the Feather Selection dialog appears, enter 150 pixels (the higher the number, the more softening effect on the edges) and click OK. That's it—you've softened the edges. Now, let's see what a difference that makes.

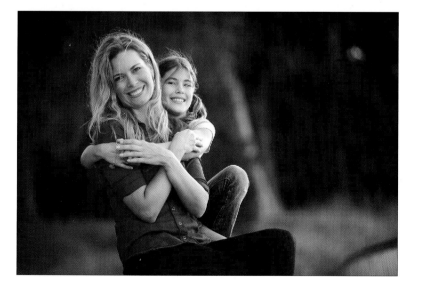

Step Four:

Go under the Select menu and choose Inverse again. Add a Levels adjustment layer again, drag the shadow Input Levels slider (that black slider under the histogram) to around 43, and you can see that the edges of the area you adjusted are soft and blending together smoothly, so it looks more like a spotlight. Now, this comes in really handy when you're doing things like adjusting somebody with a face that's too red. Without feathering the edges, you'd see a hard line around the person's face where you made your adjustments, and it would be a dead giveaway that the photo had been adjusted. But add a little bit of feather (with a face, it might only take a Feather Radius amount of 2 or 3 pixels), and it will blend right in, hiding the fact that you made an adjustment at all.

Easier Selections with the Quick Selection Tool

This is another one of those tools in Photoshop Elements that makes you think, "What kind of math must be going on behind the scenes?" because this is some pretty potent mojo for selecting an object (or objects) within your photo. What makes this even more amazing is that I was able to inject the word "mojo" into this introduction, and you didn't blink an eye. You're one of "us" now....

Step One:
Open the photo that has an object you want to select (in this example, we want to select the butterfly). Go to the Toolbox and choose the Quick Selection tool (or just press the **A**, for Awesome, **key**).

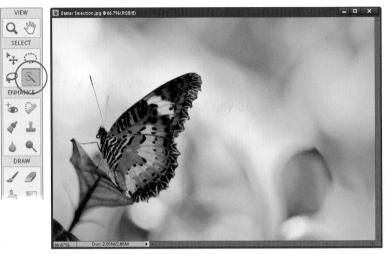

Step Two:
The Quick Selection tool has an Auto-Enhance checkbox down in the Tool Options Bar. By default, it's turned off. My line of thinking is this: when would I ever not want an enhanced (which in my book means better) selection from the Quick Selection tool? Seriously, would you ever make a selection and say, "Gosh, I wish this selection looked worse?" Probably not. So go ahead and turn on the Auto-Enhance checkbox, and leave it that way from now on.

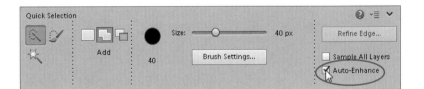

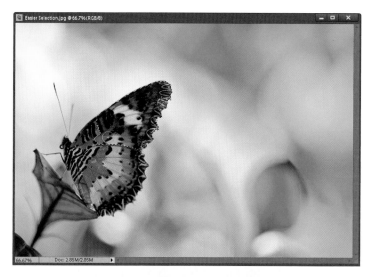

Step Three:
Take the Quick Selection tool and simply paint squiggly brush strokes inside of what you want to select. You don't have to be precise, and that is what's so great about this tool—it digs squiggles. It longs for the squiggles. It needs the squiggles. So squiggle.

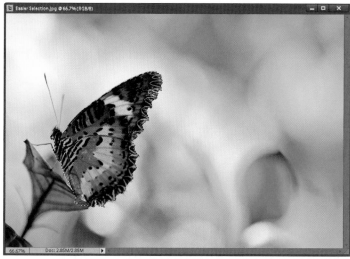

Step Four:
As you paint, the Quick Selection tool makes your selection for you, based on the area that you painted over. If the selection includes areas you don't want, such as a little bit of the leaf here, simply press-and-hold the **Alt (Mac: Option) key** and paint over the unwanted part. This removes it from your selection.

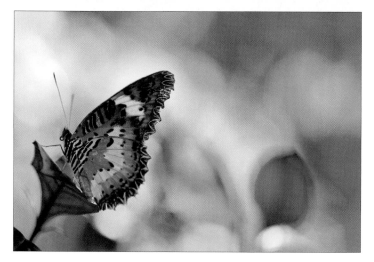

Step Five:
Now that we've got it selected, we might as well do something to it, eh? How about this: let's leave the butterfly in color, and make the background black and white. You start by going under the Select menu and choosing **Inverse** (which inverses your selection so you've got everything selected but the butterfly). Go under the Enhance menu, under Adjust Color, and choose **Remove Color**. That's it. Now you can deselect by pressing **Ctrl-D (Mac: Command-D)**.

Making Really Tricky Selections, Like Hair (and Some Cool Compositing Tricks, Too!)

Up until now, Elements hasn't had the best selection tools. You could get a decent selection using the Quick Selection tool, but if you wanted to make a really tricky or detailed selection (especially hair), you were outta luck. Well that has all changed in Elements 11. It now has what I think is one of the most powerful selection tools out there. In fact, the Quick Selection tool, coupled with what you're about to see here, can conquer nearly all of your selection needs in Elements (easy or difficult). This is, hands down, one of the most useful, and most powerful, tools in all of Photoshop Elements.

Step One:
Start by opening an image that has a challenging area to select (like our subject's hair here, which has all kinds of flyaways). Then, get the Quick Selection tool **(A)** from the Toolbox (as shown here).

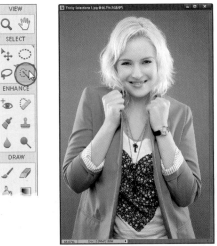

MATT KLOSKOWSKI

Step Two:
Here's how it works: you just take the tool and paint loosely over the areas you want to select, and it expands to select the area. One thing I've learned about this tool is it actually seems to work best when you use it quickly—really zoom over your subject with the tool and it does a pretty decent job. Here, I selected the subject, and while you can see some problems with the selection (the area of hair above her shoulder on the left), it's not that bad overall. If it selects too much, press-and-hold the **Alt (Mac: Option) key** and paint over that accidentally selected area to remove it from your selection. Don't worry—it's not going to look perfect at this point.

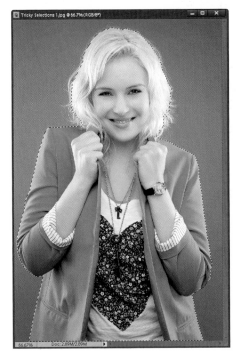

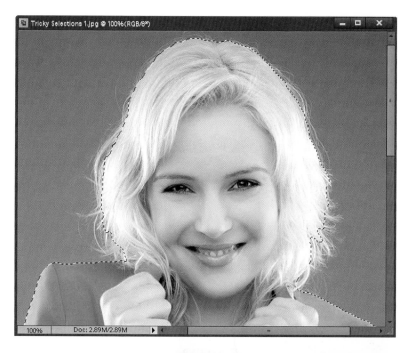

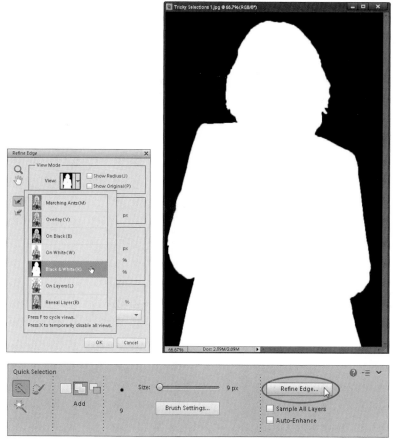

Step Three:

Okay, here comes a very important part of this stage of the process, and that is making sure that when you select her hair, you don't select any background area with it. In other words, try to make sure there's no hair selected with the gray background showing through. In fact, I basically follow the rule that I don't get too close to the outside edges of my subject's hair unless an area is pretty flat (in other words, no flyaway, tough-to-select hair in that area). You can see what I mean in the close-up here, where I avoided the thinner edges of her hair (we'll let Elements select those hard parts later—we'll just get close to the edge then stop). Also, you can see where I stopped before some areas where the hair is finer. Again, we'll let Elements grab those parts later, but for now we're most concerned with avoiding selecting areas where you can see gray background through her hair. If you accidentally select an area with gaps, then just press-and-hold the Alt key, and paint over those gap areas to deselect them.

Step Four:

Once your selection looks pretty decent, it's time to unlock the real selection power (the Quick Selection tool is just the warm-up act). Go down to the Tool Options Bar and click on the Refine Edge button (shown circled here). This is where the magic happens. In the Refine Edge dialog, you have a number of choices for how you can view your selected image (including just the standard old marching ants), but just for now, as part of our learning process, go ahead and choose **Black & White** from the View pop-up menu. This shows your selection as a standard layer mask. As you can see, the Quick Selection tool, by itself, isn't gettin' the job done (the edges are jaggy and harsh, and there's no wispy hair selected at all). That's okay, though, because we're just gettin' started.

(Continued)

Step Five:

Next, turn on the Smart Radius check-box (you won't see anything happen yet, but turn it on anyway). Smart Radius is the edge technology that knows the difference between a soft edge and a hard edge, so it can make a mask that includes both. This checkbox is so important that I leave it on all the time (if you want it always on, as well, just turn it on and then turn on the Remember Settings checkbox at the bottom of the dialog). Now, again, just for learning purposes, drag the Radius slider all the way over to the right (to 250), and all of her hair gets selected instantly (pretty amazing isn't it?). While it did a great job on her hair, there are parts of her (like her elbows and shoulders) that are being "overselected." Those areas will wind up being transparent, and you don't want that, so we always have to back it way down. But, I just wanted you to see the incredible math at work.

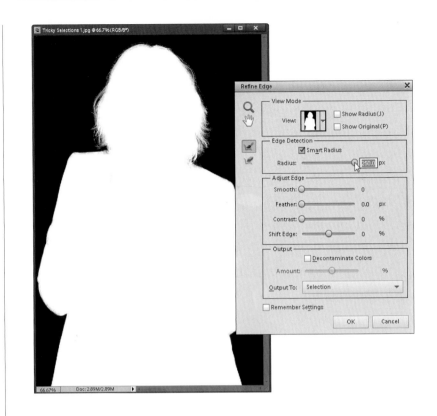

Step Six:

Okay, let's drag that Radius slider back down until her elbows and shoulders look more solid white. Here's how this works: We want our subject to be solid white and we want the background to be solid black. Anything that appears in gray will be semi-transparent. That's okay if this happens in her hair in wispy areas, but it's not good on her arms or clothes or anything that's supposed to have a well-defined hard edge. Otherwise, we'd leave the Radius up at 250 and be done with it. But, there's more to most portraits than just hair, so we have to keep those other areas pretty much intact, too. Here, I rolled back the Radius to 10, but you might be able to bring it up a bit more, maybe to somewhere in between 10 and 20. By the way, for simple selections, leave the Radius amount down low. When you have a tricky selection, like fine hair blowing in the wind, you'll have to increase it. So, just remember: trickier selections mean higher Radius amounts.

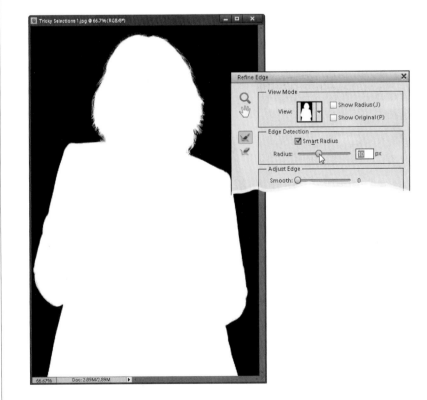

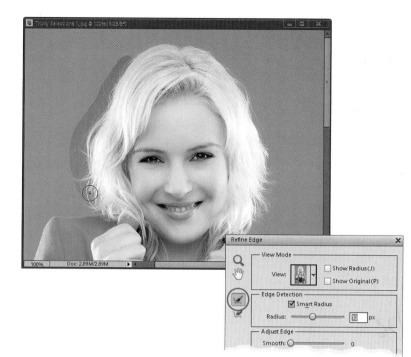

Step Seven:

Now, let's change the View to **Overlay** to see if there are any areas we missed. The parts that are selected appear in full color, and the parts that aren't appear in red. If you see the background color showing through (in our case, gray), you've got a problem (and we do here, on the left side). You need to tell Elements exactly where the problem areas are, so it can better define those areas. You do that with the Refine Radius tool (**E**; shown circled here). It's active by default, so just take your cursor and simply paint over the areas where you see the background peeking through (as shown here), and it redefines those areas. This is what picks up that fine hair detail.

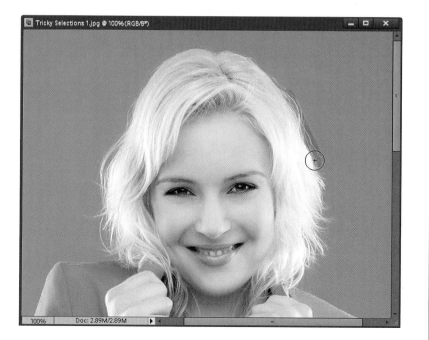

Step Eight:

As you look around her hair, if you see parts of it that are tinted red, those parts aren't selected. So, just paint a stroke or two over those areas (like I'm doing here), and they become full color (letting you know they're added to your selection) as Elements refines those edge areas where you're painting. It'll look like it's painting in white sometimes, but when you're done, it just redefines the area and tells Elements that this area needs some work, and it "redoes" its thing. Here, I've gone over some areas that were tinted red on the left side of her hair, and on the right side, too, and you can see those areas are now appearing in color. I also went over any areas where the background was poking through.

(Continued)

Step Nine:

I recommend avoiding the Adjust Edge section sliders in the center of the dialog altogether, because you'll spend too much time fussing with them, trying to make them work. (I figure you want me to tell you when to avoid stuff, too.) Down at the bottom of the dialog, there's a Decontaminate Colors checkbox, which basically desaturates the edge pixels a bit. So, when you place this image on a different background, the edge color doesn't give you away. I usually turn it on and move the setting to around 75%. Just below that, you get to choose what the result of all this will be: will your selected subject be sent over to a new blank document, or just a new layer in this document, or a new layer with a layer mask already attached, etc.? I always choose to make a new layer with a layer mask in the same document. That way, I can just grab the Brush tool and fix any areas that might have dropped out, which we're probably going to have to do next, so choose **New Layer with Layer Mask** and click OK.

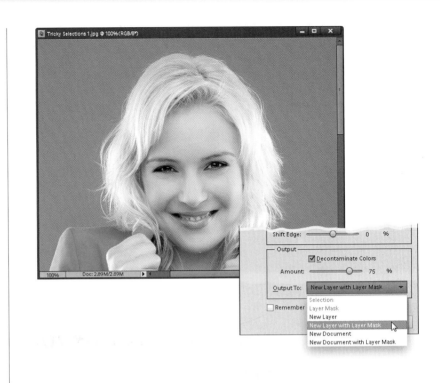

Step 10:

When you click OK, your image will now appear on a transparent layer (as seen here) and if you look in the Layers palette, you'll see a new layer with a layer mask attached (just what you asked for). You can also see it does a pretty amazing job. It won't get every little thin, wispy hair strand, but it gets most of the important ones. Now, let's do a quick check of that mask and fine-tune it just a bit before we put her over a different background (that's right, baby, we're doing some compositing!). Press-and-hold the Alt (Mac: Option) key and click directly on that layer mask thumbnail in the Layers palette to see just the mask (you can see it in the next step).

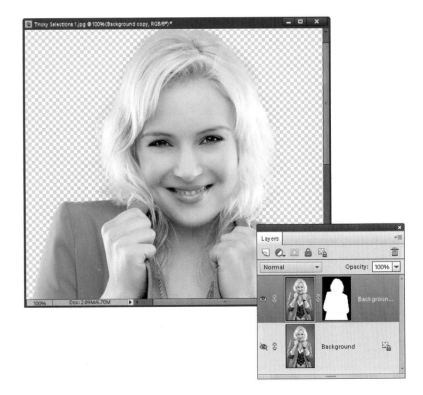

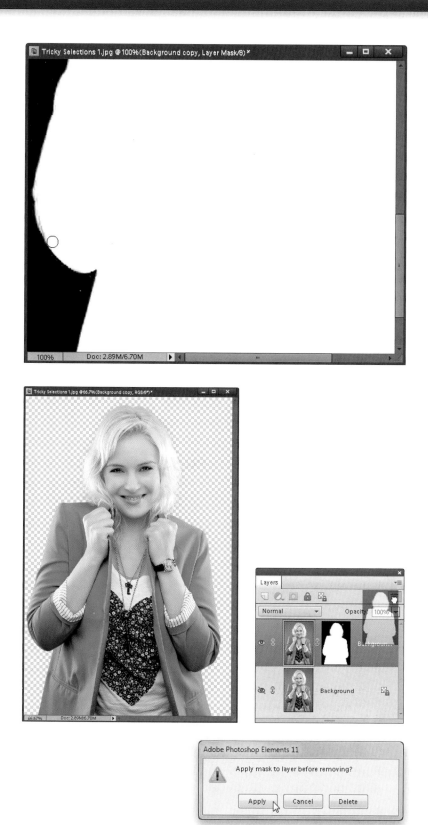

Step 11:

Now, zoom in tight near her elbow on the left, and you can see some areas that aren't solid white (which means these areas will be semi-transparent and that's not what you want). So, get the Brush tool (B) and, with your Foreground color set to white, choose a small, hard-edged brush from the Brush Picker in the Tool Options Bar (click on the Brush thumbnail to open it), and then paint along that edge, right over the grayish area, to make it solid white. For a little help cleaning up tricky areas, switch your Brush's blend Mode to **Overlay**. That way, when you're painting with white, it automatically avoids painting over the color black (and vice versa). Move around the edge of the selection and clean up any other areas that aren't solid white. If you see any areas of white that spilled outside the selection into the black area (like below and to the left of her elbow here), press **X** to switch your Foreground color to black and clean up those areas, as well.

Step 12:

At this point, we're done with our mask, so you can apply it permanently to your image by clicking directly on the layer mask thumbnail (in the Layers palette) and dragging it onto the Trash icon at the top of the palette (as shown here) to delete it. When you do this, a warning dialog pops up asking if you want to "Apply mask to layer before removing?" Click Apply, and the masking you did is now applied to the layer (and the layer mask thumbnail is deleted). This just makes things a little easier from here on out.

(Continued)

Step 13:

Next, open the background image you want to use in your composite. Get the Move tool **(V)**, then drag-and-drop your subject onto this background (as shown here) and it will appear on its own layer. (*Note:* If you're in tabbed viewing, click-and-drag the subject image onto the background image's tab and hover there for a moment, until it lets you drop the image onto the background, or just copy-and-paste it onto the background.) If your subject is larger than the background, press **Ctrl-T (Mac: Command-T)** to bring up Free Transform, make sure the Constrain Proportions checkbox is turned on in the Tool Options Bar, and then click-and-drag a corner handle inward to resize (press **Ctrl-0** [zero; **Mac: Command-0**] if you can't see the corner handles). Press **Enter (Mac: Return)** to lock in your transformation.

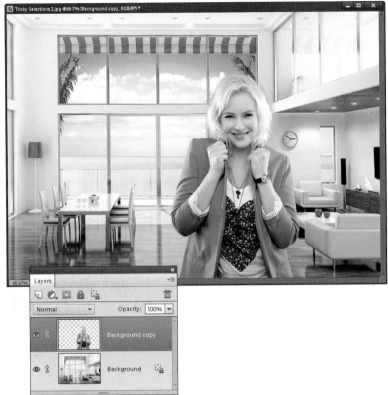

Step 14:

Now, you see our next challenge? She has a tiny dark fringe around her outside edge (clothes and hair), which is a dead giveaway that this was faked. Let's get rid of that fringe. To remove it, go under the Enhance menu, under Adjust Color, and choose **Defringe Layer**. Enter a Width setting of 1 pixel and click OK. Most of the time, you'll immediately see the fringe disappear. If it doesn't, press **Ctrl-Z (Mac: Command-Z)** to Undo and reapply Defringe Layer with a 2-pixel setting instead.

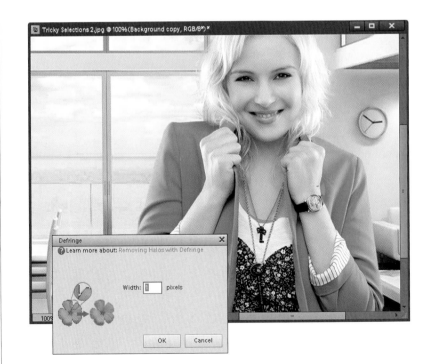

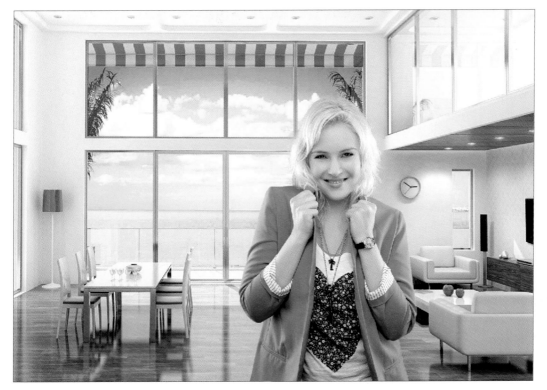

Final

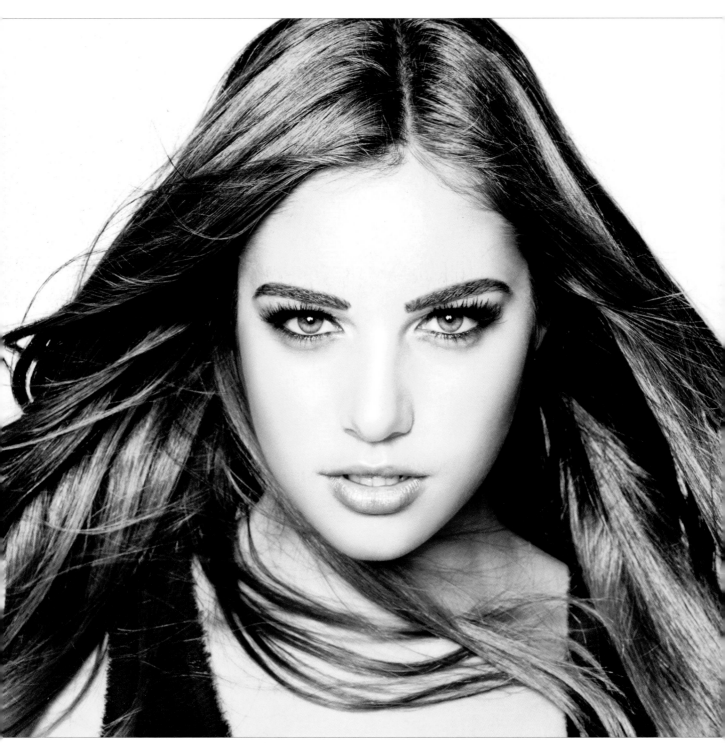

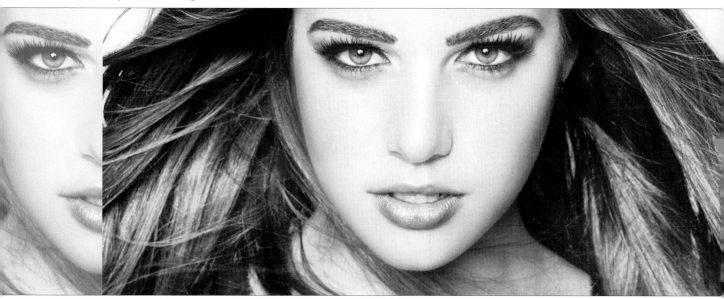

RETOUCH ME
retouching portraits

You gotta love it when you search the iTunes Store for the word "retouching" and a song called "Retouch Me" comes up. It's too perfect. Now, this chapter is about retouching, but it's not about making people look perfect—it's about making them look as good in a flat, two-dimensional photo as they do when you see them in person. There's something wonderful that happens when you see someone in person: your mind doesn't focus on their facial flaws, and wrinkles, and blemishes. Instead, your mind focuses on how big their nose is. It's a sad truth, that's been proven scientifically by a faux science group of unlicensed clinicians, that no matter how smooth and silky their skin may be, no matter how alluring their eyes are, and no matter how toothy their teeth are, if they have a giant honker, they might as well be Jabba the Hutt. And their only chance of finding an actual date would be to either (a) have a crew of bounty hunters enslave a princess (or prince) when they least expect it, or (b) talk you into taking the retouching techniques you're about to learn in this chapter to retouch their eHarmony.com photo, so they look less like Jabba and more like George Clooney (or in other words...more like me, because I've been told numerous times I look like his identical twin. Well, except for the nose).

Quick Skin Tone Fix

In photos of people, the most important thing is that the skin tone looks good. That's because it's really hard for someone looking at your photo to determine if the grass is exactly the right shade of green or if the sky is the right shade of blue; but if the skin tone is off, it sticks out like a sore thumb (which would be red if it were really sore). Here's a quick fix to get your skin tones patched up in a hurry:

Step One:

Open an image in which the skin looks like it has a specific color cast to it. In this example, because of the lighting and the time of day, the bride's skin has a very bluish color to it. We'll want to add more yellow, since yellow will counteract the blue color (they're opposites on a color wheel), and make it look more lifelike and warm.

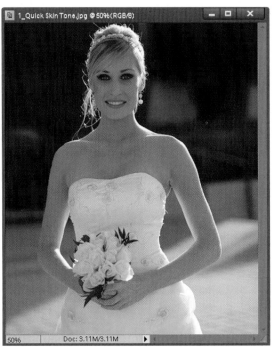

SCOTT KELBY

Step Two:

Go under the Enhance menu, under Adjust Color, and choose **Adjust Color for Skin Tone**.

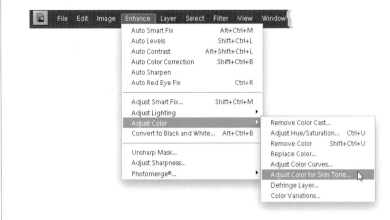

Step Three:
When the Adjust Color for Skin Tone dialog appears, move your cursor over an area of skin tone and click once to set the skin tone for the image. If you don't like your first results, click in a different area of skin tone until you find a skin-tone adjustment you're happy with.

Step Four:
You can also manually tweak the skin tone by using the Tan and Blush sliders, and you can control the overall tint of the light by dragging the Temperature slider to the left to make the skin tones cooler or to the right to make them warmer. *Note:* This skin-tone adjustment affects more than just skin—it usually affects the entire photo. If that creates a problem, use one of the selection tools (even the Lasso tool) to put a selection around the skin-tone areas first, add a 2-pixel Feather (under the Select menu), and then use the Adjust Color for Skin Tone command.

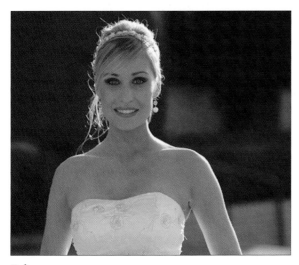

Before

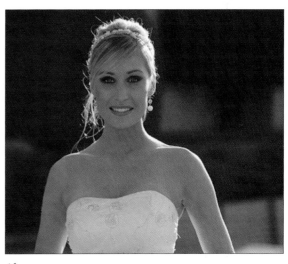

After

Removing Blemishes and Hot Spots

Over the years, we've learned lots of different ways to remove hot spots, blemishes, and other imperfections on the skin. I believe the technique you're about to see here is the easiest and best way, though. It not only removes the blemishes, but it's flexible enough so you can maintain the original skin texture, as well. That way the skin looks real and not like the fakey, smooth skin that's always a dead giveaway the photo has been retouched in Elements.

Step One:

Open a photo containing some skin imperfections you want to remove (in this example, we're going to remove a series of blemishes). Get the Zoom tool (**Z**) and zoom in, if needed, on the area you want to retouch, then get the Healing Brush tool (press **J** until you have it) from the Toolbox (as shown here). You might be tempted to use the Spot Healing Brush tool because it's so easy to use (and it's the default healing tool in the Toolbox), but don't fall for it. Although it does a pretty good job on its own, you can do better and work faster with the Healing Brush because you won't have to redo anything (and you generally will have several redos using the Spot Healing Brush). Besides, you only save one click using the Spot Healing Brush over the regular Healing Brush. (*Note:* We'll use the Healing Brush instead of the Spot Healing Brush again later in this chapter.)

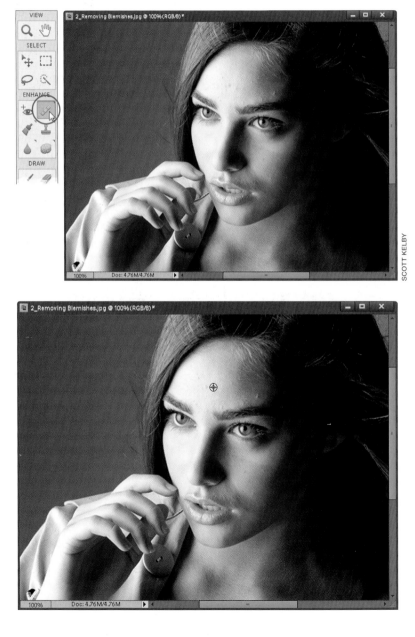

SCOTT KELBY

Step Two:

The key to using the Healing Brush correctly is to find an area of skin to sample that has a similar texture to the area you want to repair (this is different than the Clone Stamp tool, where you're looking for matching color and shading, as well). Move your cursor over this "clean" area of skin, press-and-hold the Alt (Mac: Option) key, and click once to sample that area. Your cursor will momentarily change to a target as you sample (as shown here).

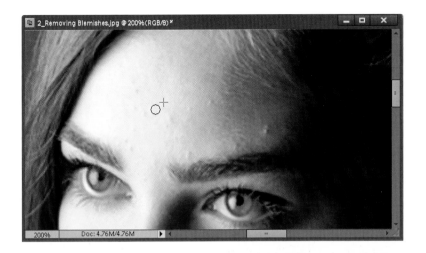

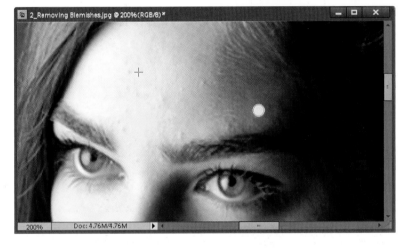

Step Three:
Now, just move the Healing Brush directly over the blemish or hot spot you want to remove and simply click. Don't paint—click. Once. That's it. That's the whole technique—BAM—the blemish is gone!

TIP: Resizing Your Brush
For the best results, use a brush size that is just a little bit larger than the blemish or hot spot you want to remove (use the **Left/Right Bracket keys** on your keyboard [they're to the right of the letter P] to change brush sizes). Also, you don't have to worry about sampling an area right near where the blemish or hot spot is—you can sample from another side of the face, even in the shadows—just choose a similar texture, that's the key.

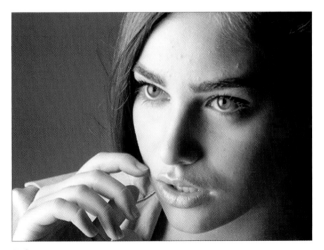

Before

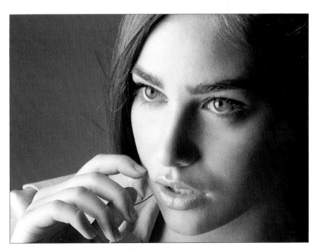

After

Lessening Freckles or Facial Acne

This technique is popular with senior class portrait photographers who need to lessen or remove large areas of acne, pockmarks, or freckles from their subjects. This is especially useful when you have a lot of photos to retouch and don't have the time to use the method shown previously, where you deal with each blemish individually.

Step One:
Open the photo that you need to retouch. Make a duplicate of the Background layer by going to the Layer menu, under New, and choosing **Layer via Copy** (or just pressing **Ctrl-J [Mac: Command-J]**). We'll perform our retouch on this duplicate of the Background layer, named "Layer 1."

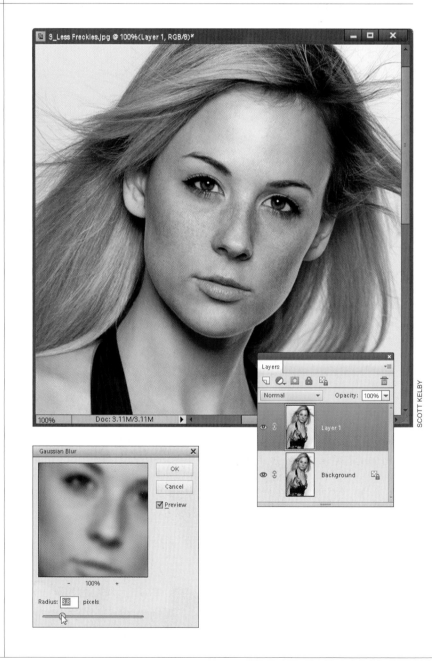

Step Two:
Go under the Filter menu, under Blur, and choose **Gaussian Blur**. When the Gaussian Blur dialog appears, drag the slider all the way to the left, then drag it slowly to the right until you see the freckles blurred away. The photo should look very blurry, but we'll fix that in just a minute, so don't let that throw you off—make sure it's blurry enough that the freckles are no longer visible. Click OK.

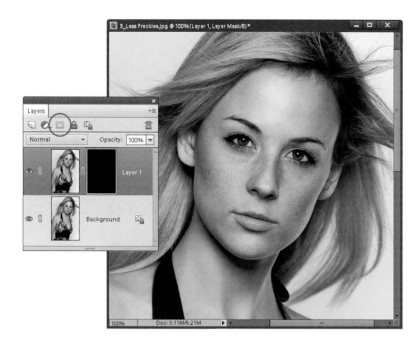

Step Three:
Press-and-hold the Alt (Mac: Option) key and click once on the Add Layer Mask icon at the top of the Layers palette. This adds a black layer mask to your current layer (the blurry Layer 1), hiding the blurriness from view (and that's exactly what we want to do at this point).

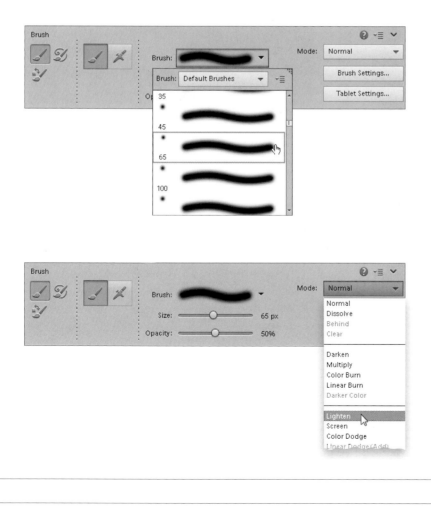

Step Four:
In the Layers palette, make sure the layer mask is active (you'll see a blue frame around its thumbnail), as you're going to paint on this layer mask. Press the letter **D** to set your Foreground color to white. Press the letter **B** to switch to the Brush tool, then click on the Brush thumbnail in the Tool Options Bar, and from the Brush Picker, choose a soft-edged brush.

Step Five:
Lower the Opacity setting of your brush in the Tool Options Bar to 50%, and change the Mode pop-up menu from Normal to **Lighten**. Now when you paint, it will affect only the pixels that are darker than the blurred state. Ahhh, do you see where this is going?

(Continued)

Step Six:

Now you can paint over the freckle areas, and as you paint, you'll see them diminish quite a bit. If they diminish too much, and the person looks "too clean," undo **(Ctrl-Z [Mac: Command-Z])**, then lower the Opacity of the brush to 25% and try again. If they don't diminish enough, paint over them again to build up the blurriness.

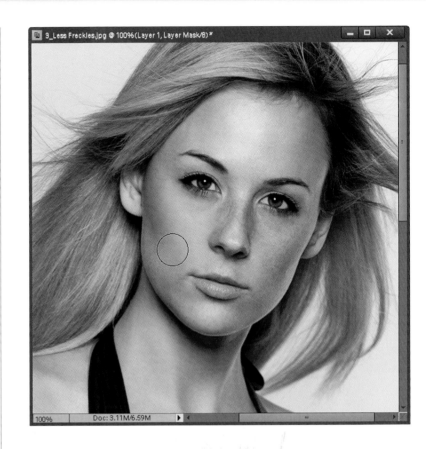

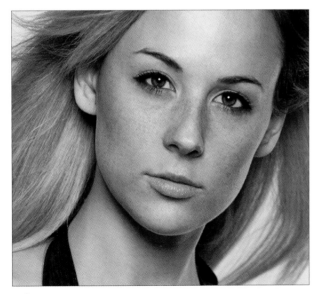

Before

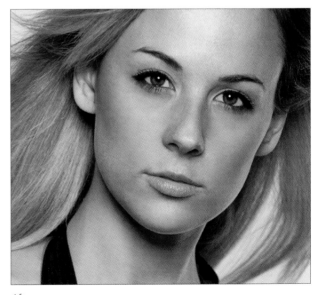

After

Here's a quick technique for removing or lessening dark circles under the eyes. It's one of those things that happen to a lot of people. It could be you've been working late (or, even better, partying late), or were just up late. Regardless of where they came from, there is a quick way to remove these dark circles.

Removing Dark Circles Under Eyes

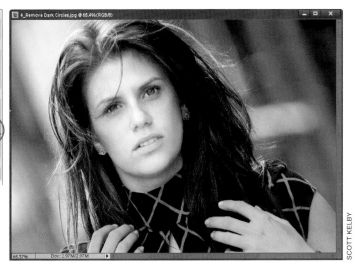

SCOTT KELBY

Step One:
Open the photo that has the dark circles you want to remove or lessen. Select the Clone Stamp tool in the Toolbox (or press the **S key**). Then, click on the Brush thumbnail in the Tool Options Bar to open the Brush Picker, and choose a soft-edged brush that's half as wide as the area you want to repair. *Note:* Press the letter **Z** to switch to the Zoom tool and zoom in if needed.

Step Two:
Also in the Tool Options Bar, lower the Opacity of the Clone Stamp tool to 50%. Then, change the Mode pop-up menu to **Lighten** (so you'll only affect areas that are darker than where you'll sample from).

(Continued)

Step Three:

Press-and-hold the Alt (Mac: Option) key and click once in an area near the eye that isn't affected by the dark circles. If the cheeks aren't too rosy, you can click there, but more likely you'll click on (sample) an area just below the dark circles under the eyes.

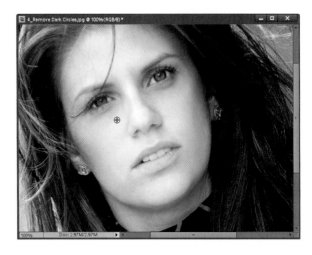

Step Four:

Now, take the Clone Stamp tool and paint over the dark circles to lessen or remove them. It may take two or more strokes for the dark circles to pretty much disappear, so don't be afraid to go back over the same spot if the first stroke didn't work. *Note:* If you want the dark circles to completely disappear, try using the Healing Brush tool **(J)** from the Toolbox. Simply Alt-click (Mac: Option-click) the Healing Brush in a light area under the dark circles, and then paint the circles away.

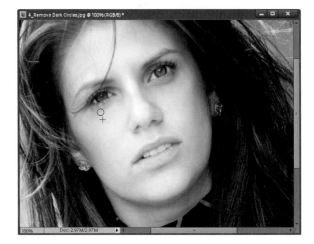

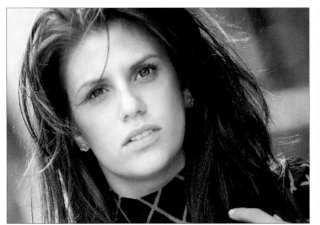

Before

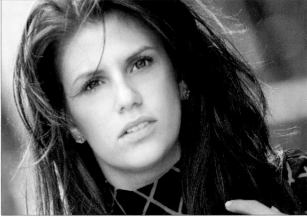

After

This is the first edition of this book to not include an "official" tutorial on the Healing Brush. If you've used Elements before, you've probably become good friends with this tool. But, when the Content Aware option was added to the Spot Healing Brush (covered in Chapter 9) back in Elements 10, it made it work better and faster. That said, when it comes to removing or lessening wrinkles, I still turn to the Healing Brush, mainly because when I'm removing (really, reducing) wrinkles, I want to be sure I don't pick up another wrinkle while trying to fix one. It lets me sample which area of skin I want to heal with, and I find it gives much better results for this.

Removing or Lessening Wrinkles (and Why You Still Need the Healing Brush)

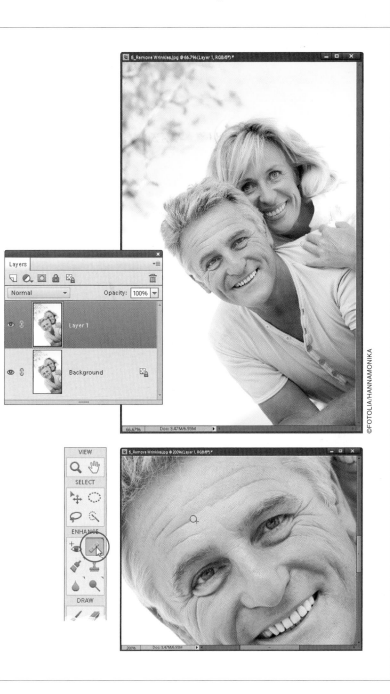

©FOTOLIA/HANNAMONIKA

Step One:
Open the photo that needs some wrinkles or crow's-feet lessened or removed. Start by duplicating the Background layer by going to the Layer menu, under New, and choosing **Layer via Copy** (or pressing **Ctrl-J [Mac: Command-J]**). You'll perform your "wrinkle removal" on this duplicate layer, named "Layer 1" in the Layers palette.

Step Two:
Get the Healing Brush tool from the Toolbox (or press **J** until you have it). Then, use the **Left ([)** and **Right Bracket (])** **keys** to make your brush close to the size of the wrinkles you want to remove. Find a clean area that's somewhere near the wrinkles (perhaps the upper cheek if you're removing crow's-feet, or if you're removing forehead wrinkles, perhaps just above or below the wrinkle). Press-and-hold the Alt (Mac: Option) key and click once to sample the skin texture from that area. Now, take the Healing Brush tool and paint over the wrinkles. As you paint, the wrinkles will disappear, yet the texture and detail of the skin remains intact, which is why this tool is still so amazing.

(Continued)

Step Three:

Now that the wrinkles are gone, it's time to bring just enough of them back to make it look realistic. Simply go to the Layers palette and reduce the Opacity of this layer to bring back some of the original wrinkles. This lets a small amount of the original photo (the Background layer, with all its wrinkles still intact) show through. Keep lowering the Opacity until you see the wrinkles, but not nearly as prominent as before.

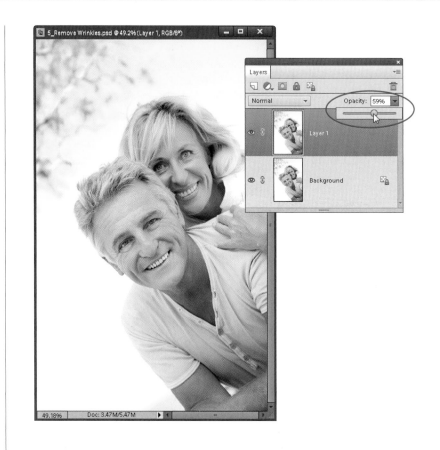

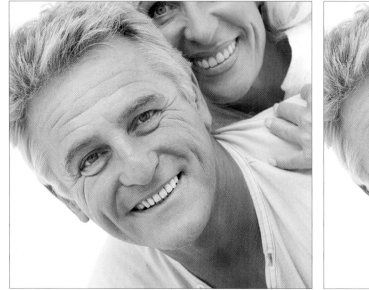

Before

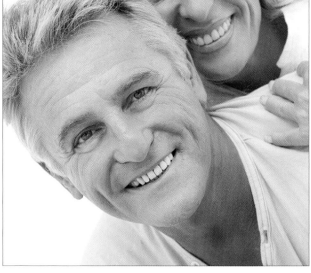

After

This is a retouch that I do to every single photo where the subject's eyes are open. It seems like no matter how much light you get into the eyes during the shoot, the whites of the eyes end up off-white at best, but usually a light gray. This is one of those retouches that you just have to do once or twice—even if you think the eyes look white enough—because once you see the difference, you'll do this every single time. It makes that big a difference.

Brightening the Whites of the Eyes

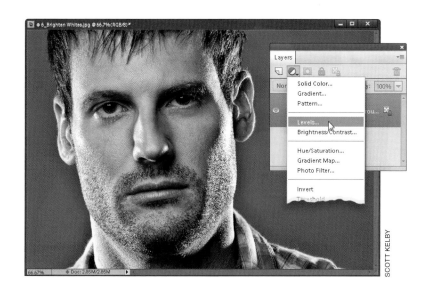

SCOTT KELBY

Step One:
In this example, the whites of his eyes look almost gray (or off-white at the very least). So, start by clicking on the Create New Adjustment Layer's icon at the top of the Layers palette and choosing **Levels** (as shown here). By the way, it doesn't really matter which adjustment you add at this point—we just need some adjustment layer, any adjustment layer, so we can change its blend mode. Why not just duplicate the Background layer? Because doing it this way doesn't add any size to your document, which keeps Elements running faster. Hey, it all adds up.

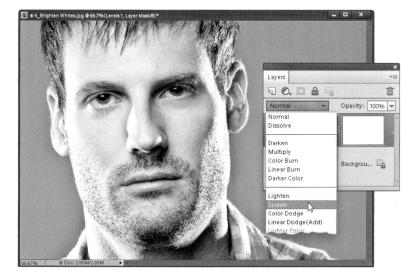

Step Two:
At the top of the Layers palette, change your blend mode for this adjustment layer from Normal to **Screen**. The Screen blend mode makes your image much brighter (compare the brighter image shown here with the one in Step One and you'll see what I mean).

(Continued)

Step Three:

The problem with our image at this point is we only want the whites of his eyes brighter (and maybe his irises), but not his skin or anything else. So, we'll have to do some simple masking. Start by pressing **Ctrl-I (Mac: Command-I)**, which inverts the layer mask, making it black and hiding the brightening brought on by changing the blend mode to Screen.

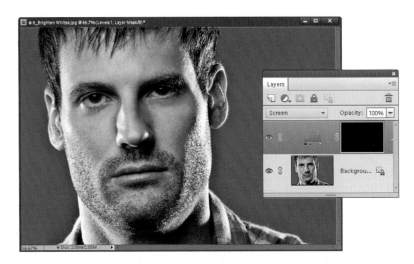

Step Four:

Zoom in on one of the eyes, press **D** to set your Foreground color to white, then press **B** to get the Brush tool. Click on the Brush thumbnail in the Tool Options Bar, choose a very small, soft-edged brush from the Brush Picker, and begin painting over the whites of the eyes (as shown here, where I'm painting over the left side of the eye on the left). As you paint, this area becomes much brighter, because you're revealing the Screen layer you applied earlier.

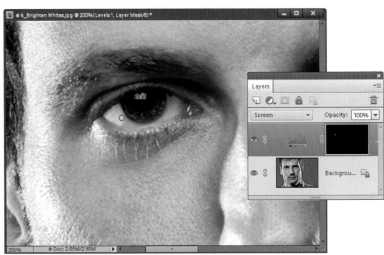

Step Five:

The tricky part of this technique comes when you try to paint that little bit of white that appears right below the iris. It's just so tiny that getting in there and doing it without spilling over onto the edge of the iris, or the bottom eyelid, is really a pain. So, what's the solution? Don't worry about it—just paint right over the whites, and if your brush extends over onto the iris or the bottom eyelid (like you see here), it's okay. The reason it's okay is I've found it's much easier to erase the spillover than it is to try to paint it just right with a super-small brush. After all, you've already got a layer mask applied; to clean this up will be a five-second fix (as you'll see in the next step).

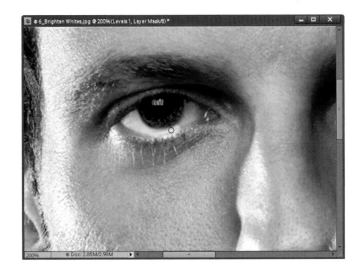

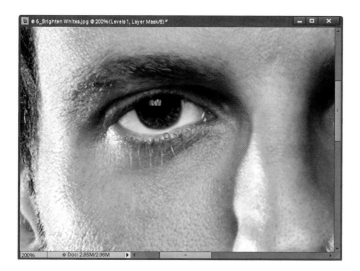

Step Six:
To get rid of the spillover (brightening of the iris or lower eyelid), just press the letter **X** to set your Foreground color to black, then paint over the spillover to remove it (as shown here). It couldn't be easier or faster. When you're done, just press X again to swap your Foreground and Background colors, making white your Foreground color again. Now, move over to the other eye and do the same thing.

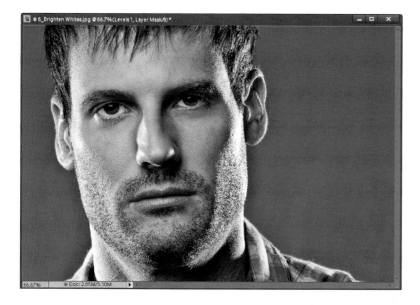

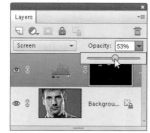

Step Seven:
When you're done painting over both eyes, they'll probably look too white (giving your subject a freaky, possessed look), so in most cases, leaving the Opacity of this layer at 100% is unlikely. The best way to judge how white the whites of the eyes should be is to zoom out (like you see here), then lower the Opacity of this layer to around 50% and see how that looks. If it's still too bright, lower it a little bit more. The Opacity slider becomes your "whiteness amount slider," so just adjust it to where it looks natural, but brighter than it was before. A before/after is shown on the next page (I painted over the irises a little bit, too. They looked a little dark).

(Continued)

TIP: Brightening the Entire Eye Socket
If you need to lighten the entire eye socket area (his are a little dark), you can use the Screen blend mode, but in a slightly different way. Press **Ctrl-J (Mac: Command-J)** to duplicate the Background layer, then change the blend mode to **Screen** to make the whole image brighter. Option-click (PC: Alt-click) on the Add Layer Mask icon in the Layers panel to hide this brighter version behind a black mask. With your Foreground color set to white, get the Brush tool **(B)**, and choose a medium-sized, soft-edged brush set to 100% Opacity. Now, paint over his eyes and the surrounding eye socket areas. I know he looks like he's been lying in the sun with sunglasses on, but we'll fix that by lowering the layer's Opacity until the brightening matches the rest of his face. If any edges look brighter, switch your Foreground color to black and paint right over them. Then, if the whites still need brightening, you can do the rest of this tutorial.

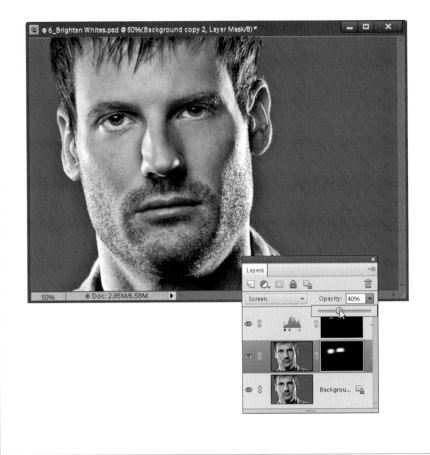

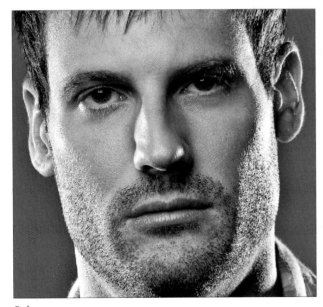

Before

After

Making Eyes That Sparkle

This is another one of those 30-second miracles for enhancing the eyes. This technique makes the eyes seem to sparkle by accentuating the catch lights, and generally draws attention to the eyes by making them look sharp and crisp (crisp in the "sharp and clean" sense, not crisp in the "I-burned-my-retina-while-looking-at-the-sun" sense).

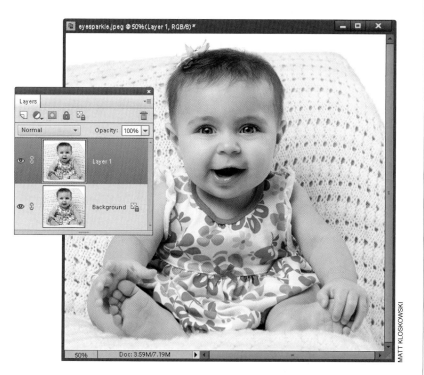

MATT KLOSKOWSKI

Step One:

Open the photo that you want to retouch. Make a duplicate of the Background layer by going under the Layer menu, under New, and choosing **Layer via Copy** (or pressing **Ctrl-J [Mac: Command-J]**), which creates a new layer named "Layer 1." *Note:* Press the **Z key** to switch to the Zoom tool and zoom in if needed.

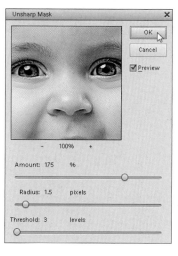

Step Two:

Go under the Enhance menu and choose **Unsharp Mask**. (It sounds like this filter would make things blurry, but it's actually for sharpening photos.) When the Unsharp Mask dialog appears, enter your settings. (If you need some settings, go to the first technique, named "Basic Sharpening," in Chapter 11.) Here, we seem to be able to get away with a lot of sharpening (and I mean a lot), so I'm going to use Amount: 175, Radius: 1.5, and Threshold: 3. Then click OK to sharpen the entire photo.

(Continued)

Step Three:

After you've applied the Unsharp Mask filter, apply it again using the same settings by pressing **Ctrl-F (Mac: Command-F)**. If you think it's still not enough, apply it one more time using the same keyboard shortcut (although I didn't do that here). The eyes will probably look nice and crisp at this point, but the rest of the person will be severely oversharpened, and you'll probably see lots of noise and other unpleasant artifacts.

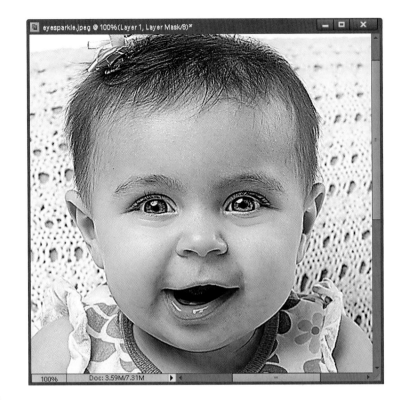

Step Four:

Press-and-hold the Alt (Mac: Option) key and click once on the Add Layer Mask icon at the top of the Layers palette. This adds a black layer mask to your sharpened layer, removing all the visible sharpness (at least for now). In the Layers palette, make sure the layer mask is active (you'll see a blue frame around its thumbnail).

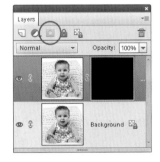

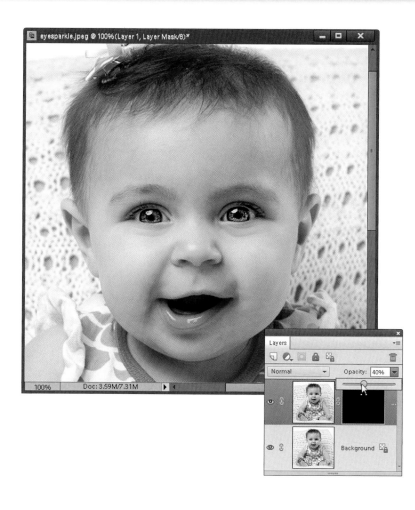

Step Five:

Press the letter **D** to set your Foreground color to white. Then, press **B** to switch to the Brush tool. Click on the Brush thumbnail in the Tool Options Bar to open the Brush Picker, and choose a soft-edged brush that's a little smaller than your subject's eyes. Now paint over just the irises and pupils of the eyes to reveal the sharpening, making the eyes really sparkle and completing the effect. If the effect seems too strong (it did here), just lower the Opacity of the layer with the layer mask.

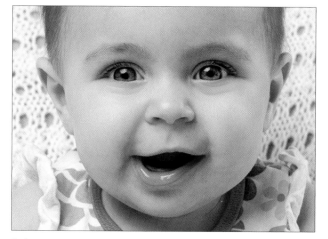

Before

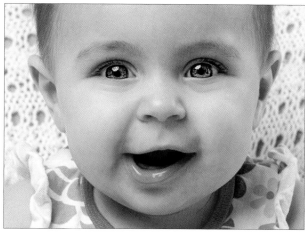

After

Whitening and Brightening Teeth

This really should be called "Removing Yellowing, Then Whitening Teeth" because almost everyone has some yellowing, so we remove that first before we move on to the whitening process. This is a simple technique, but the results have a big impact on the overall look of the portrait, and that's why I do this to every single portrait where the subject is smiling.

Step One:
Open the photo you need to retouch. Press **Z** to switch to the Zoom tool and zoom in if needed.

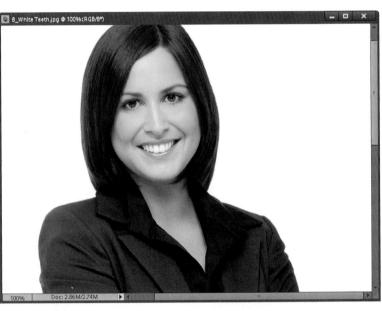

Step Two:
Press **L** to switch to the Lasso tool, and carefully draw a selection around the teeth, making sure you don't select any of the gums or lips. If you've missed a spot, press-and-hold the **Shift key** while using the Lasso tool to add to your selection, or press-and-hold the **Alt (Mac: Option) key** and drag the Lasso to remove parts of the selection. If you've grown fond of the Quick Selection tool, then give that one a try here, as it works great, too.

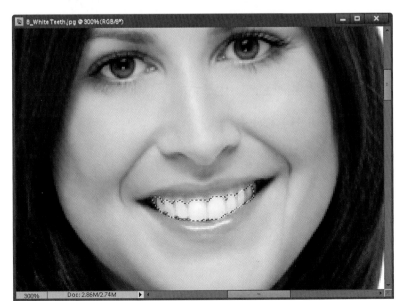

©ISTOCKPHOTO/CAP53

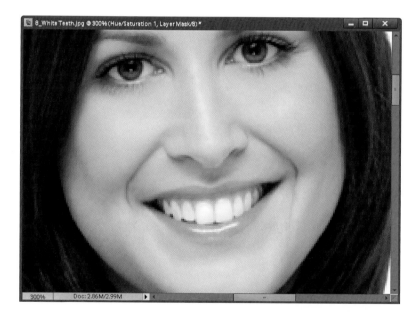

Step Three:

Go under the Select menu and choose **Feather**. When the Feather Selection dialog appears, enter 1 pixel and click OK to smooth the edges of your selection. That way, you won't see a hard edge along the area you selected once you've whitened the teeth.

Step Four:

Click on the Create New Adjustment Layer icon at the top of the Layers palette (it's the half-blue/half-white circle icon) and choose **Hue/Saturation**. When the Hue/Saturation controls appear in the adjustments palette, choose **Yellows** from the Channel pop-up menu at the top. Then, drag the Saturation slider to the left to remove the yellowing from the teeth.

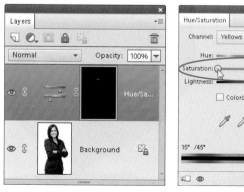

(Continued)

Step Five:

Now that the yellowing is removed, switch the Channel pop-up menu back to **Master**, and drag the Lightness slider to the right to whiten and brighten the teeth. Be careful not to drag it too far, or the retouch will be obvious. *Note:* The Smart Brush tool **(F)** has an effect (under the Portrait preset in the pop-up menu) called Pearly Whites, which does pretty much the same thing but in a little different way. And if that one doesn't do the trick for you, then there's another effect called Very Pearly Whites (you think I'm kidding, don't you?) that does, well, the same thing but more intense.

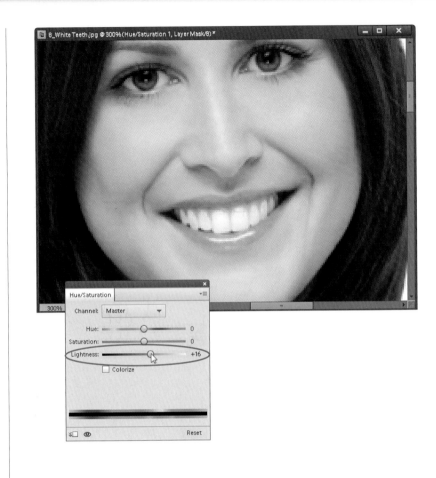

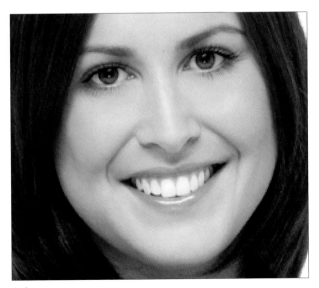

Before

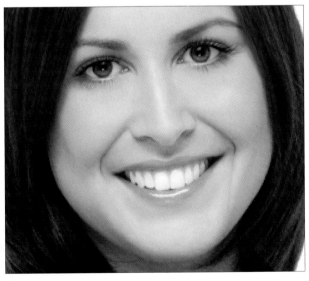

After

Depending on your subject, this can be just a minor tweak, or a major reconstruction. Luckily, in most cases, you'll be able to fix most problems with teeth using the Liquify filter.

Repairing Teeth

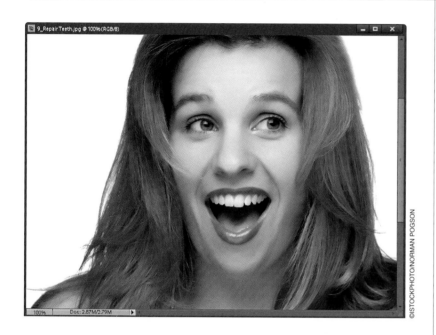

Step One:
Here's the image with teeth we want to retouch. First, let's evaluate what we need to do: the two front teeth look a little too long compared to the other teeth (they should only be a little longer than the surrounding teeth) and they're a bit uneven. So, that's one thing to fix. Then, I would remove the points from the canine teeth and repair the gaps.

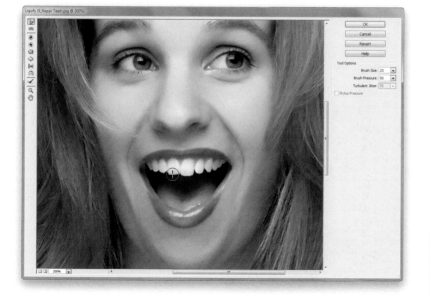

Step Two:
Go under the Filter menu, under Distort, and choose **Liquify**. When the Liquify dialog appears, zoom in tight (press **Ctrl-+ [Mac: Command-+]** a few times). Then, select the first tool at the top of the Toolbox (on the left side of the dialog; it's called the Warp tool, and lets you nudge things around like they were made of molasses). The key here is to make a number of very small moves—don't just get a big brush and push stuff around. Make your brush size (in the Brush Size field on the right) a little larger than what you're retouching (here, my brush is a little larger than one of the front teeth). Gently nudge the front tooth on the left upward a few times to shorten it.

(Continued)

Step Three:

Go ahead and do the same thing to the front tooth on the right. Gently nudge it upward a few times and then nudge once or twice between the two front teeth to make them even. While you're there, flatten out the bottoms of them, too—just choose a smaller brush and gently nudge upward. They're already looking better.

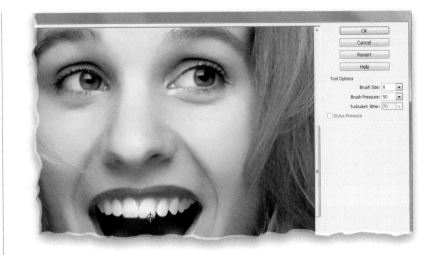

Step Four:

Let's now work on the teeth to the left of the front two—same tool, same technique, smaller brush (because these teeth are smaller in size). Gently nudge these teeth upward just a little to even them out.

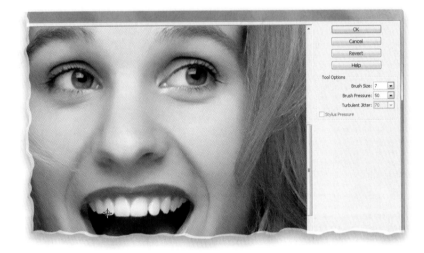

Step Five:

Next, let's work on the teeth on the right. Nudge upward to flatten out the bottom of the two teeth on the far right a little (one's kinda pointy). Then, move to the canine tooth to the left.

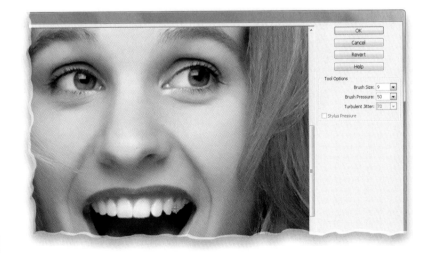

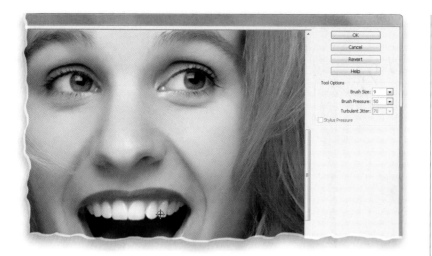

Step Six:
Notice how the point in the canine tooth leaves a small gap between the teeth, even after you flatten out the bottom? So, instead of pushing up on the bottom of the tooth, try putting your brush in the middle of the tooth and pushing it toward the left a little to fill in that space. Then, flatten it out, as needed.

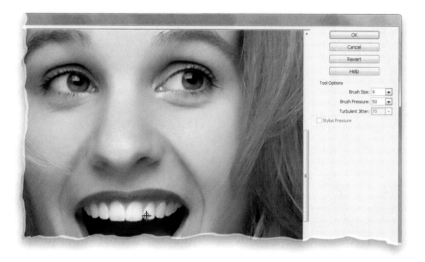

Step Seven:
Go ahead and do the same thing for the next tooth to the left (the one to the right of the right front tooth). Since its shape is a bit rounded, there's a small gap between it and the tooth next to it, as well. So, use a really small brush and nudge the center of the tooth to the left to fill in the gap. You may even want to try nudging part of the right front tooth to the right, so you're closing that small gap from both ends. Then, just even out the bottom.

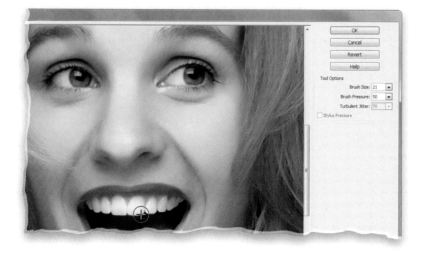

Step Eight:
As a last step, I'll usually take a larger brush and go along the bottom of all the teeth just to make sure they're mostly even. They don't have to be perfect, but doing a quick pass when you're all done fixing them is always a good idea to even them out a little. Then, just click OK to apply the Liquify filter changes.

(Continued)

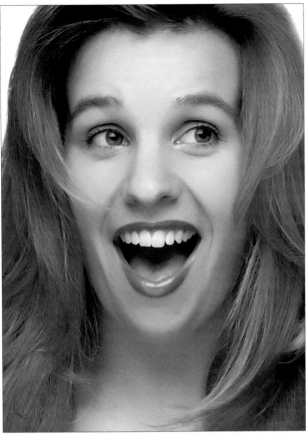

Before

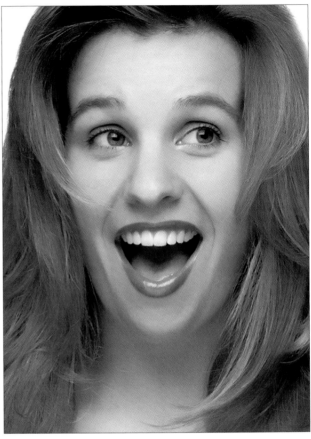

After

Digital Nose Jobs Made Easy

The tutorial you're about to read is perfect for (as Scott calls it) desnozilization, dehonkerizing, and unsnoutilation. The coolest part about it is that it uses a tool that you'd never think about using in your normal everyday Elements use. In fact, when you hear the name in Step Two you'll probably even laugh to yourself thinking we're going to play a joke on someone. Trust me, though—we're not. This tool has a ton of uses, and getting pro-quality retouching results is one of them.

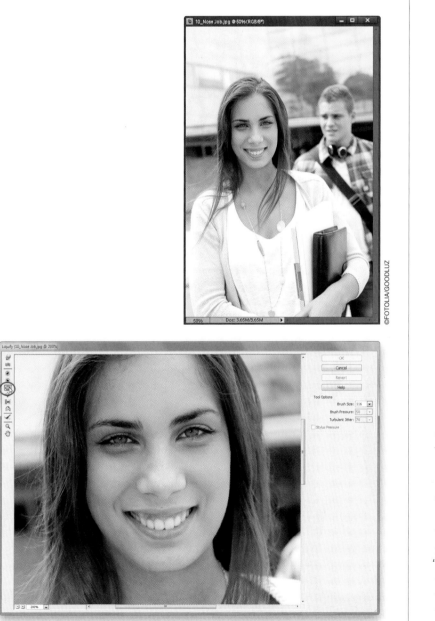

©FOTOLIA/GOODLUZ

Step One:
Open the photo that you want to retouch. By the way, did you notice how gentle I was in that opening phrase, and how I made no mention whatsoever of a somewhat minor facial retouch that might be considered in this instance? (Wait for it... wait for it...no! I'm not going to do it! Not this time. Not here. Not now.) Let's continue, shall we?

Step Two:
Go to the Filter menu and, under Distort, choose **Liquify**. When the Liquify dialog appears (as seen here), choose the fifth tool down from the top in the Liquify Toolbox (the Big Honker tool), shown circled here in red. Okay, I tried to slip one past you. Actually, the real name of this tool is the Bulbous Nasal Retractor, or BNR for short. (Aw, come on, that last one was pretty funny. Even I heard you giggling.) Okay, if you must know, the official "Adobe name" for the tool is the Pucker tool, and basically it "puckers in" the area where you click it. The more you click it, the more it puckers.

(Continued)

Step Three:

Take the tool and move it right over your subject's nose (as shown here), and make the brush size a little bigger than the entire nose itself. The quickest way to do that is to press-and-hold the **Shift key** and press the **Right Bracket (]) key** on your keyboard. Each time you press that, it will jump up 10 points in size. Once you have the size right, just click it a couple of times (don't paint—just click). Here, I clicked twice, for obvious reasons. (Sorry, I couldn't help myself.)

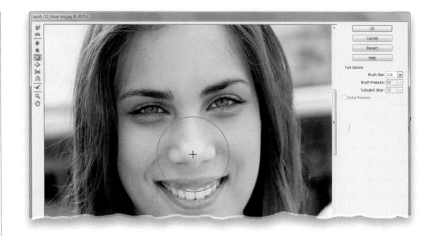

Step Four:

Move the center of the brush over her left nostril and click once or twice, then do the same to the right nostril. Move to the bridge of the nose and click once or twice there, and you're done. Here, the entire retouch took about eight clicks (12 seconds—I timed it). Also, if you make any mistakes, you have multiple Undos by pressing **Ctrl-Z (Mac: Command-Z)**. When it looks good, click OK.

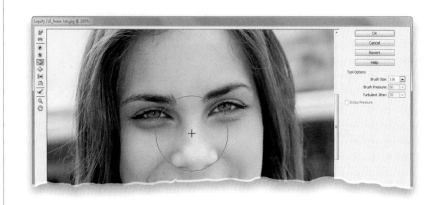

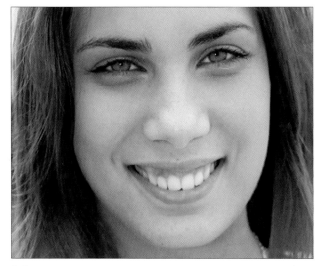

Before

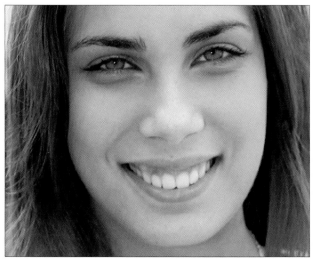

After

This is a pretty slick technique for taking a photo where the subject is frowning or grim and tweaking it just a bit to add a pleasant smile—which can often save a photo that otherwise would've been ignored.

Transforming a Frown into a Smile

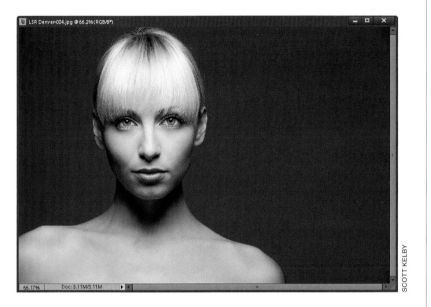

SCOTT KELBY

Step One:
Open the photo that you want to retouch.

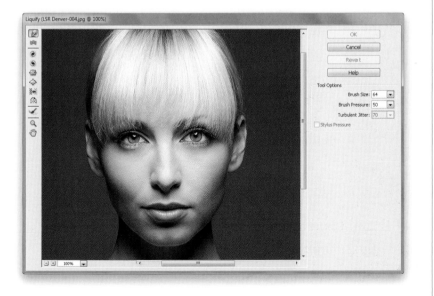

Step Two:
Go under the Filter menu, under Distort, and choose **Liquify**. When the Liquify dialog appears, choose the Zoom tool (it looks like a magnifying glass) from the Liquify Toolbox (found along the left edge of the dialog). Click it once or twice within the preview window to zoom in closer on your subject's face. Then, choose the Warp tool (it's the top tool in the Liquify Toolbox).

(Continued)

Step Three:

In the Tool Options on the right side of the dialog, choose a brush size that's roughly the size of the person's cheek. Place the brush at the base of a cheek and click-and-"tug" slightly up. This tugging of the cheek makes the corner of the mouth turn up, creating a smile.

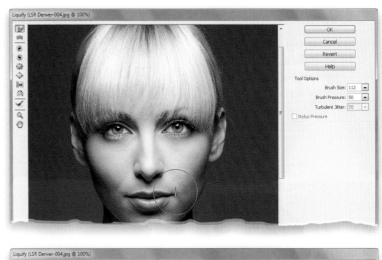

Step Four:

Repeat the "tug" on the opposite side of the mouth, using the already tugged side as a visual guide as to how far to tug. Be careful not to tug too far, or you'll turn your subject into the Joker from *Batman Returns*. Click OK in Liquify to apply the change, and the retouch is applied to your photo.

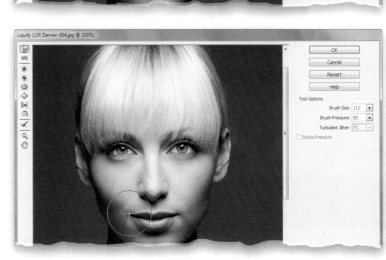

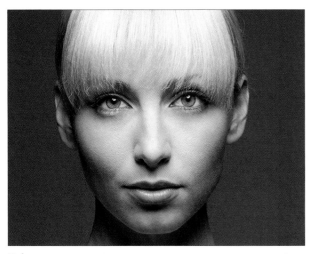

Before

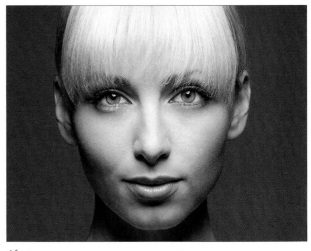

After

This is an incredibly popular technique because it consistently works so well, and because just about everyone would like to look about 10 to 15 pounds thinner. I've never applied this technique to a photo and (a) been caught, or (b) not had clients absolutely love the way they look. The most important part of this technique may be not telling the client you used it. In Elements 11, also check out the new Actions palette, which has two actions for this. They're handy if you have a bunch of photos you want to apply them to.

Slimming and Trimming

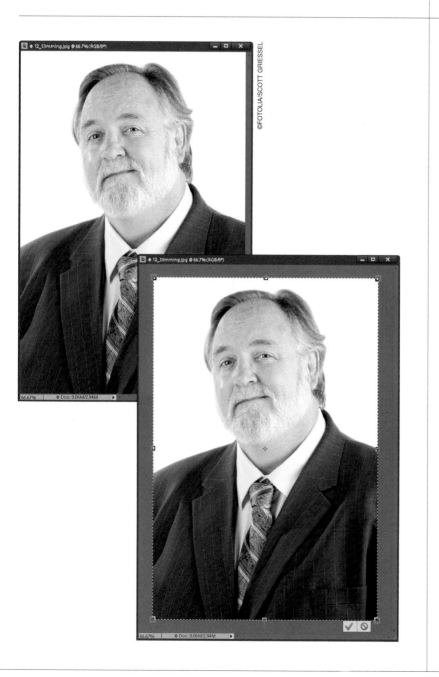

Step One:
Open the photo of the person that you want to put on a quick diet.

Step Two:
Click on the bottom-right corner of your image window and drag it out, so you see some gray background behind your image (if you're in tabbed viewing, zoom out of your image a little). Now, press **Ctrl-A (Mac: Command-A)** to put a selection around the entire photo. Then, press **Ctrl-T (Mac: Command-T)** to bring up the Free Transform command. The Free Transform handles will appear at the corners and sides of your photo.

(Continued)

Step Three:

Grab the right-center handle and drag it horizontally toward the left to slim the subject. The farther you drag, the slimmer the subject becomes.

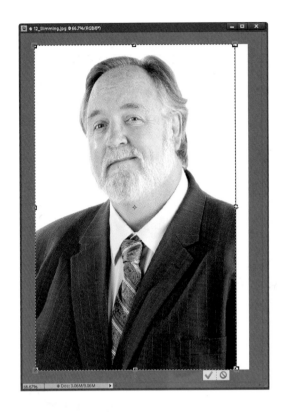

Step Four:

How far is too far (in other words, how far can you drag before people start looking like they've been retouched)? Use the Width field in the Tool Options Bar as a guide. You're pretty safe to drag inward to around 95%, although I've been known to go to 94% or even 93% once in a while (it depends on the photo). I settled on 94.1% for this photo.

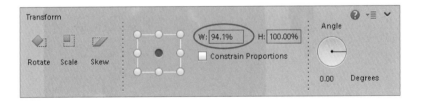

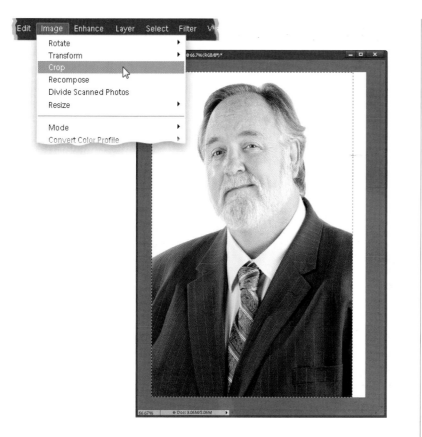

Step Five:

Press **Enter (Mac: Return)** to lock in your transformation. Then, before you deselect, go to the Image menu and choose **Crop**. That'll crop to the selection you had and remove the background area that is now visible on the right side of your photo (you could always use the Crop tool, too). Then, press **Ctrl-D (Mac: Command-D)** to Deselect. You can see how effective this simple little trick is at slimming and trimming your subject. Also, notice that because we didn't drag too far, the subject still looks very natural.

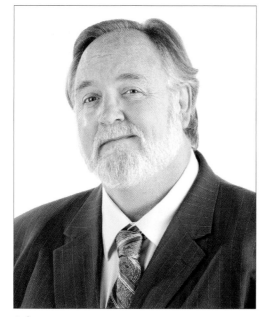

Before

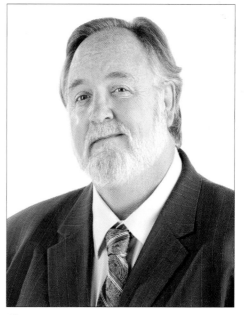

After

Advanced
Skin Softening

Although this technique has a number of steps, it's actually very simple to do and is worth every extra step. It breaks away from the overly soft, porcelain-skin look that is just "so 2006" to give you that pro skin-softening look, along with keeping some of the original skin texture, which makes it much more realistic. This "keeping some of the original skin texture" look is totally "in" right now, so it's worth spending an extra two minutes on. I also want to give credit to Ray 12, whose article on RetouchPro.com turned me on to the texture mask, which I now use daily.

Step One:

Start by pressing **Ctrl-J (Mac: Command-J)** to duplicate the Background layer, as shown here. (See? I told you these steps were going to be simple.)

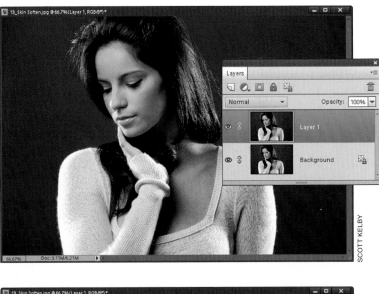

Step Two:

Go under the Filter menu, under Blur, and choose **Surface Blur**. There are big advantages to using this filter over Gaussian Blur, and one is that it does a better job of preserving edges (rather than Gaussian Blur, which just blurs everything equally). Set the Radius (which controls the amount of blur) to around 39, and make sure the Threshold slider (which controls the tonal values that get blurred) doesn't get higher than the Radius amount (here, I have set it to 31, and I usually have it between 5 and 10 lower than the Radius setting). This gives a blocky, almost posterized look to your subject's skin at this point. Go ahead and click OK to apply this filter to your image (it's doing a lot of math to make some parts blurry while the edges maintain detail, so don't be surprised if a progress bar appears onscreen, as this one usually takes a few extra seconds to apply).

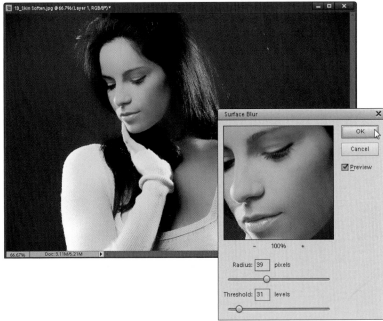

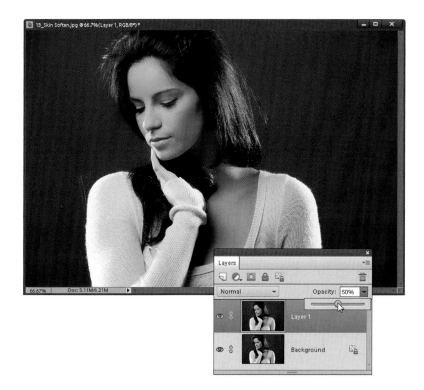

Step Three:
Now, go to the Layers palette and lower the Opacity of this Surface Blur layer to 50% (as shown here). Although it looks a lot better at this point (and the skin looks pretty decent), the rest of the image also has the effect applied. We just want it on her skin, so we're going to have to mask it.

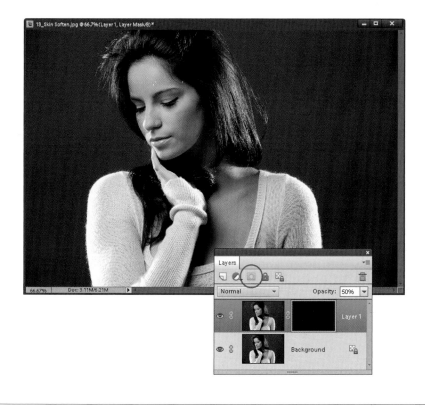

Step Four:
Press-and-hold the Alt (Mac: Option) key and click once on the Add Layer Mask icon at the top of the Layers palette. This adds a black layer mask to your current layer (the blurry Layer 1). Doing this re-moves all the blurriness from view (and that's exactly what we want to do at this point). The idea is to reveal the blurry layer just where you want it (on her skin), while avoiding all the detail areas (like the eyes, hair, clothing, eyebrows, nostrils, lips, jewelry, etc.). That's what we'll do next.

(Continued)

Step Five:

In the Layers palette, make sure the layer mask is active (you'll see a blue frame around its thumbnail), as you're going to paint on this layer mask. Press the letter **D** to set your Foreground color to white. Get the Zoom tool **(Z)** and zoom in on her face. Then get the Brush tool **(B)**, click on the Brush thumbnail down in the Tool Options Bar, choose a medium-sized, soft-edged brush from the Brush Picker, and begin painting over her skin (as shown here). You're not actually painting over the photo—you're painting in white on the layer mask, and as you paint, it reveals that part of the blurry layer that it's linked to. Remember the rule: don't paint over detail areas—avoid the eyes, hair, etc., as I mentioned earlier. In the example shown here, I have only painted over (softened) the left side of her face, so you can see the effect of the skin softening.

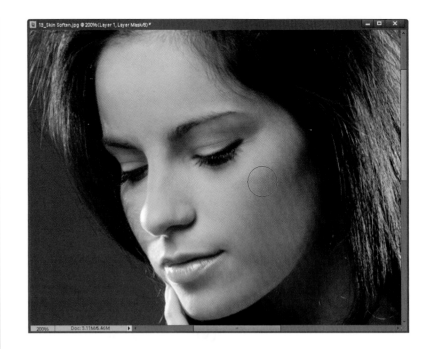

Step Six:

Continue painting on both sides of her face until you've carefully covered all the non-detail areas of her face. You'll have to vary the size of the brush to get under her nose, and paint carefully between the eyes and the eyebrows. Then, continue to paint over all the other areas that need softening, and I know I sound like a broken record but avoid those detail areas, like her hair, and her eyebrows, and her lips, etc.

TIP: Resizing Your Brush

You can use the Bracket keys on your keyboard to change brush sizes—the **Left Bracket key ([)** makes the brush size smaller; the **Right Bracket key (])** makes it larger. By the way, the Bracket keys are to the right of the letter P. Well, if you're using a U.S. English keyboard anyway.

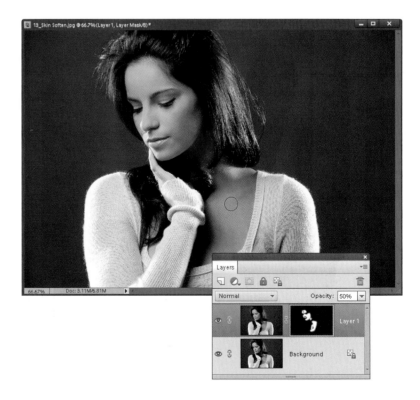

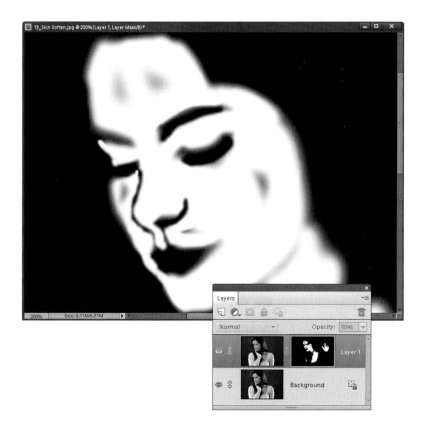

Step Seven:

Let's first make sure you haven't missed any areas, so press-and-hold the Alt (Mac: Option) key, and in the Layers palette, click directly on the layer mask thumbnail (as shown here). This displays just the layer mask itself, and you'll see instantly whether you missed any areas or not. In this case, you can see I missed areas on both her cheeks, as well as some on her upper lip and forehead.

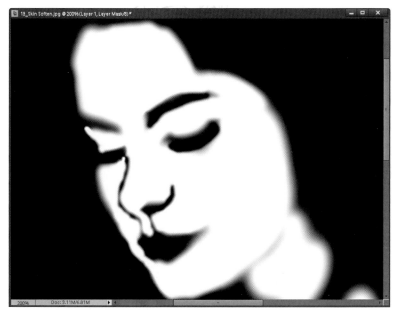

Step Eight:

These missed areas are really easy to fix—just take your Brush tool and paint right over them. Now, to get back to your regular view, Alt-click (Mac: Option-click) on the layer mask again and things will be back to normal, so you'll see your image again.

(Continued)

Step Nine:

Now that you can see your full-color image again, you're going to load your white brush strokes as a selection (it's easier than it sounds). Just press-and-hold the Ctrl (Mac: Command) key and click once directly on the layer mask thumbnail. This loads it as a selection, as seen here.

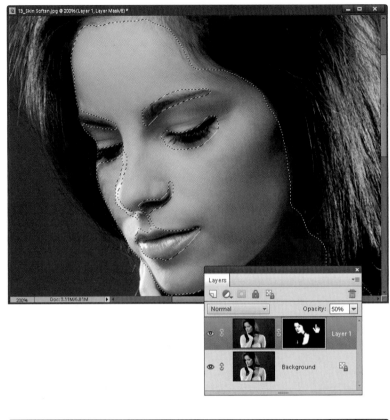

Step 10:

Next, click on the Background layer (your selection will still be in place), then press **Ctrl-J (Mac: Command-J)** to take those selected areas of your Background layer and put them up on their own separate layer, and then click-and-drag that "just the skin" layer up to the top of the layer stack (so it's the top layer, as seen here).

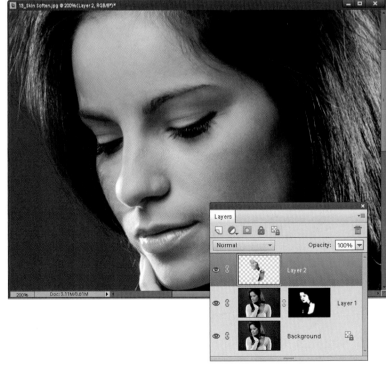

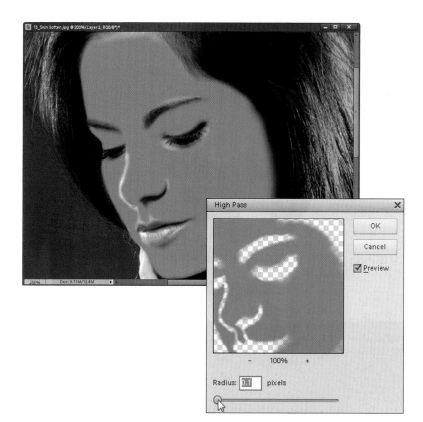

Step 11:

Now, to bring the texture, highlights, and shadows back into the skin, go under the Filter menu, under Other, and choose **High Pass** to bring up the High Pass filter dialog (seen here). Drag the Radius slider all the way to the left (as shown) to make the image pretty flat-looking. Don't click OK quite yet.

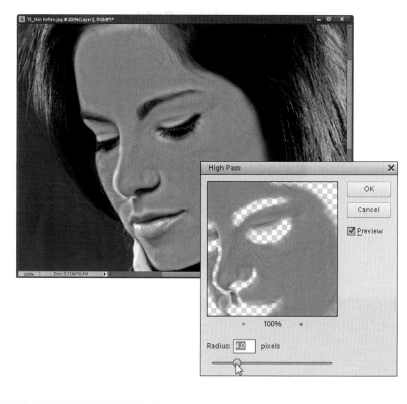

Step 12:

Drag the Radius slider to the right until some of the texture, highlights, and shadows start to return to the image (as shown here). Stop when you see a glow starting to develop (here, I was able to go to around 4. When I went too much higher, things started to glow). Click OK.

(Continued)

Step 13:

Now to bring her original skin texture and highlights back into our photo, you're going to change the layer blend mode of this top layer (the gray texture layer) from Normal to **Soft Light**, in the pop-up menu at the top left of the Layers palette (as shown here). When you first do this, it brings back the skin texture with a vengeance, which is not our goal. Okay, it's not as much as the original texture, because there is some softening on the layers below it, but it's too intense at this point.

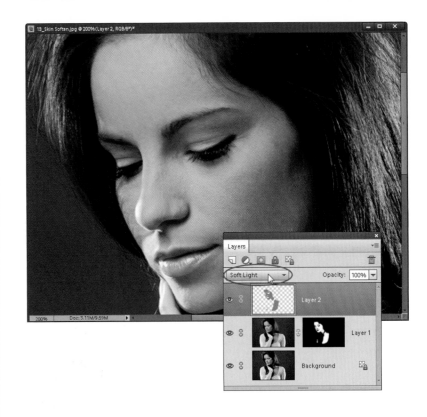

Step 14:

So (and here's where the cool part is), you're going to dial in the exact amount of original skin texture you'd like visible by lowering the Opacity setting of this texture layer. The lower you make the opacity, the less skin texture is visible. For this particular photo, lowering the Opacity to 30% looks like it gives about the right balance between softening and texture. Compare the before and after photos on the next page.

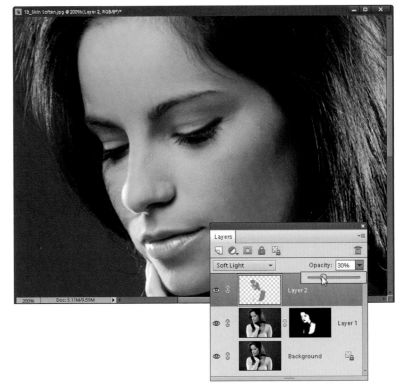

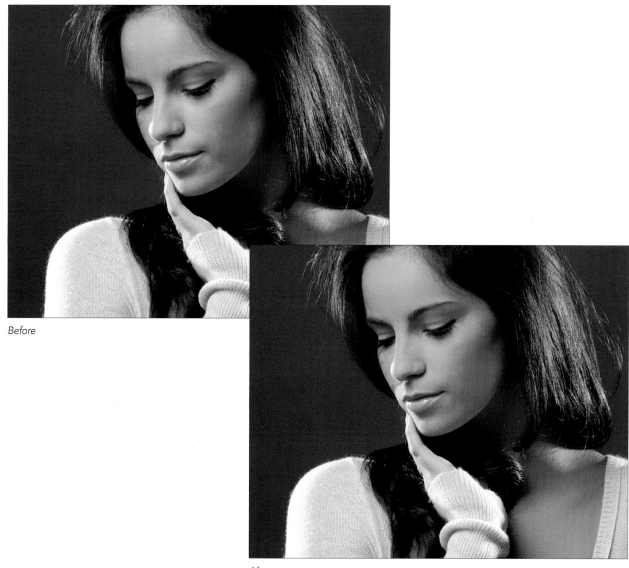

Before

After

Fixing Reflections in Glasses

I get more requests for how to fix this problem than probably all the rest combined. The reason is it's so darn hard to fix. If you're lucky, you get to spend an hour or more desperately cloning. In many cases, you're just stuck with it. However, if you're smart, you'll invest an extra 30 seconds while shooting to take one shot with the glasses off (or ideally, one "glasses off" shot for each new pose). Do that, and Elements will make this fix absolutely simple. If this sounds like a pain, then you've never spent an hour desperately cloning away a reflection.

Step One:
Before we get into this, make sure you read the short intro up top here first, or you're going to wonder what's going on in Step Two. Okay, here's a photo of our subject with her glasses on, and you can see the reflection in them (pretty bad on the left side, not quite as bad on the right, but it definitely needs fixing). The ideal situation is to tell your subject that after you take the first shot, they need to freeze for just a moment while you (or a friend, assistant, etc.) walk over and remove their glasses (that way they don't change their pose, which they absolutely will if they take their own glasses off), then take a second shot. That's the ideal situation.

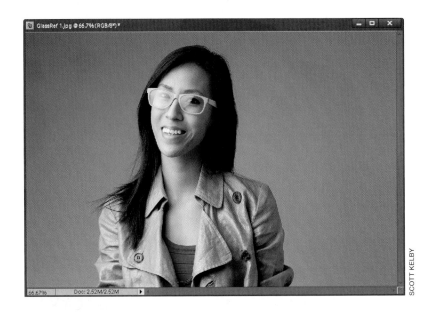

Step Two:
Unfortunately, that's not what happened for my second shot—our subject decided (maybe 10 minutes later) to remove her glasses. But, luckily, I had shots in the same shoot both with and without her glasses on (of course, that was luck—you should definitely plan to shoot some with them on, then some off, during the shoot). So, I had to look for one where her head position was somewhat similar. This shot isn't right on the money, so we'll have to tweak it a bit to make it work, but at least we have a shot to work with, so I'm not complaining.

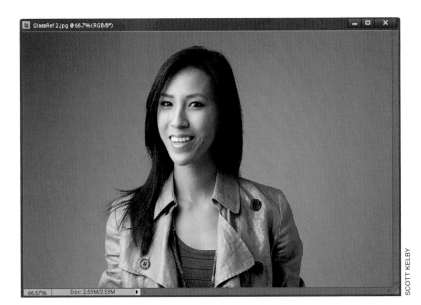

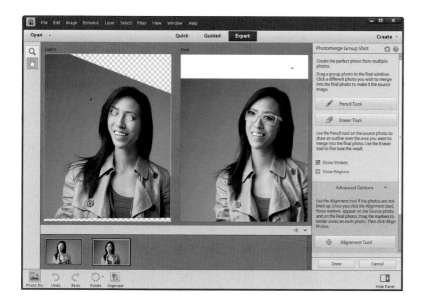

Step Three:
Now, if you planned ahead and took shots with and without the glasses (one right after the other), then you can try using Photomerge Group Shot. (From the Enhance menu, under Photomerge®, choose **Photomerge® Group Shot**). Click-and-drag the "glasses" photo to the Final side and the "no glasses" photo to the Source side. Then, just use the Pencil tool to paint over the eyes on the Source photo, which will replace the eyes on the Final side. Now, if you did all of this "the right way" in the studio, then you can jump to the second part of Step Six. However, since the shots we're using here were taken hand-held, about 10 minutes apart, we can't use Photomerge Group Shot (you can see here how it distorted things really badly), so we'll have to do it manually (another reason why setting this up the right way in the studio really pays off). *Note:* If the two shots are only a little off, then go under the Advanced Options in Photomerge Group Shot and try the Alignment tool.

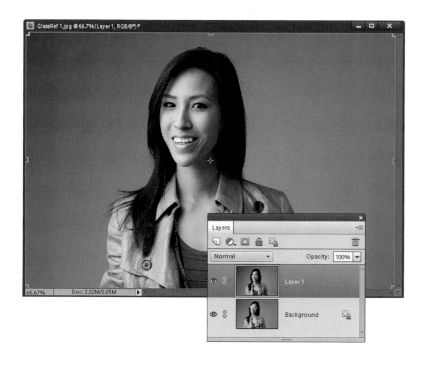

Step Four:
Click Cancel at the bottom right of Photomerge, and with both images open in the Editor, get the Move tool **(V)**, press-and-hold the Shift key, and then click-and-drag the "no glasses" photo on top of the "glasses" photo (as I did here). (*Note:* To see both images at the same time, make sure you have the Allow Floating Documents in Expert Mode checkbox turned on in the Elements General Preferences, and then go under the Window menu, under Images, and choose **Float All in Windows**.)

(Continued)

Step Five:

You need to be able to "see through" the top layer, so you can see her eyes on the bottom layer (that way, you can line them up). So, start by going to the Layers palette and lowering the Opacity of the top layer to around 50% or 60% (as shown here). Now, with the Move tool, position the eyes on the top layer as close as you can get to those on the bottom layer (it won't match exactly, of course, because her head is tilted differently. So, at this point, just get as close as you can, even though you'll still be quite a bit off, as seen here at bottom. We're a little closer, but still not there).

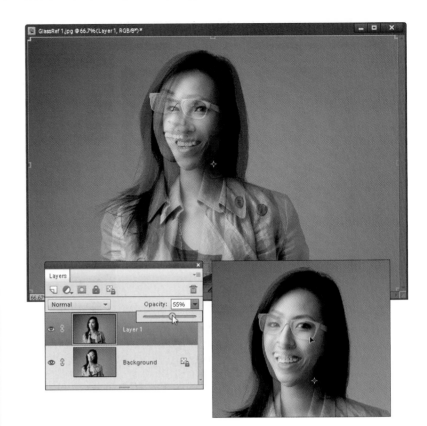

Step Six:

If you look at her shoulders back in Step Five, you can see that not only is her head tilted, but I either zoomed in or zoomed out just a little because she is a different size in each of the photos. So, press **Ctrl-T (Mac: Command-T)** to bring up Free Transform, make sure the Constrain Proportions checkbox is turned on in the Tool Options Bar, then click on a corner point and drag inward until her shoulders look about the same size in each of the photos. Now, we can rotate the top photo, so her eyes match up better. To rotate this top layer, use the Zoom tool **(Z)** to zoom out (to shrink the size of your image window), then pull out the corners of the image window, so you see some of the dark gray canvas area around your image (as seen here). Now, when you move your cursor outside the Free Transform bounding box, it will change into a two-headed rounded arrow, so you can click-and-drag in a circular motion to rotate the top layer. (*Note:* You may need to move your cursor inside the bounding box to reposition the top layer, as well.)

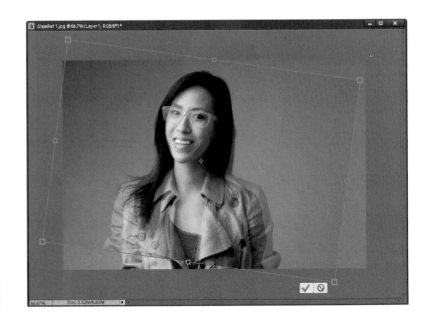

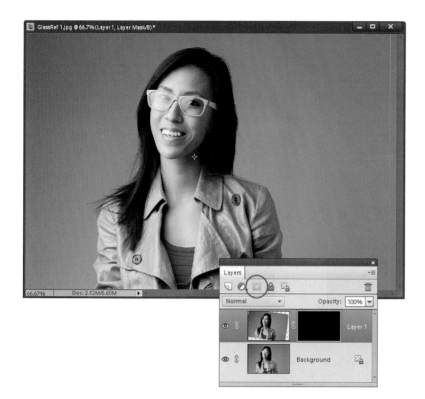

Step Seven:
Once it looks pretty well lined up, press **Enter (Mac: Return)** to lock in your resizing and rotation, then raise the Opacity of this top layer back to 100%. Now, all we really need from the image on the top layer is the area that appears inside her frames. So, press-and-hold the Alt (Mac: Option) key and click on the Add Layer Mask icon at the top of the Layers palette to hide this rotated layer behind a black layer mask (as shown here).

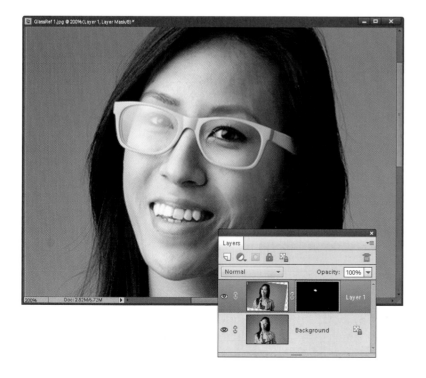

Step Eight:
Now, with your Foreground color set to white, get the Brush tool **(B)**, click on the Brush thumbnail down in the Tool Options Bar, and choose a small, soft-edged brush from the Brush Picker. Then, start painting over the lens on the right, and it reveals the version of her eye without the glasses on (as seen here). What you're doing is revealing the top layer, but just where you want it.

(Continued)

Step Nine:

Once the eye on the right is done, do the same thing for the eye on the left. Make sure you use a small brush and be careful not to accidentally paint over any part of the frames. If you do make a mistake, no biggie. Just press **X** to switch your Foreground color to black and paint the frames back in. Now, remember, this process would be made a whole lot easier (you could skip Steps Five and Six altogether) if you remember, once you get a look you like in the studio, to have your subject freeze, remove their glasses, and take another shot. Then, Photomerge Group Shot can do its thing and save you a lot of time and trouble (though, you may have to fix the frames once the images are opened in Expert mode, if they're removed along with the reflection. Just switch to the Difference blend mode and use the Eraser tool to erase over the frames outline you see on the top layer to get them back). A before and after are shown below.

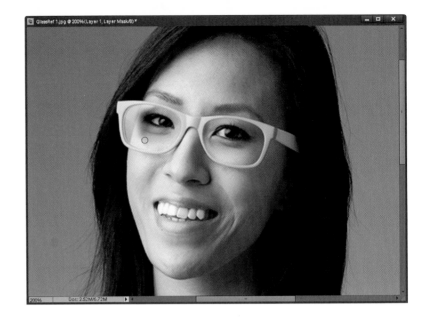

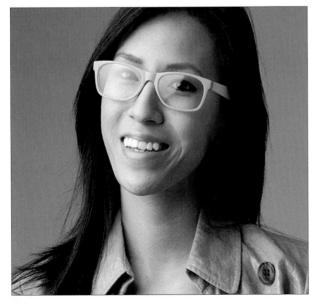

Before

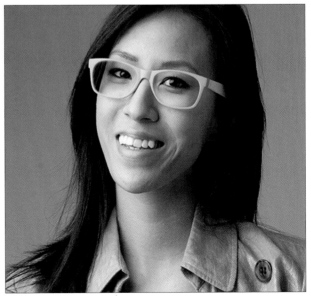

After

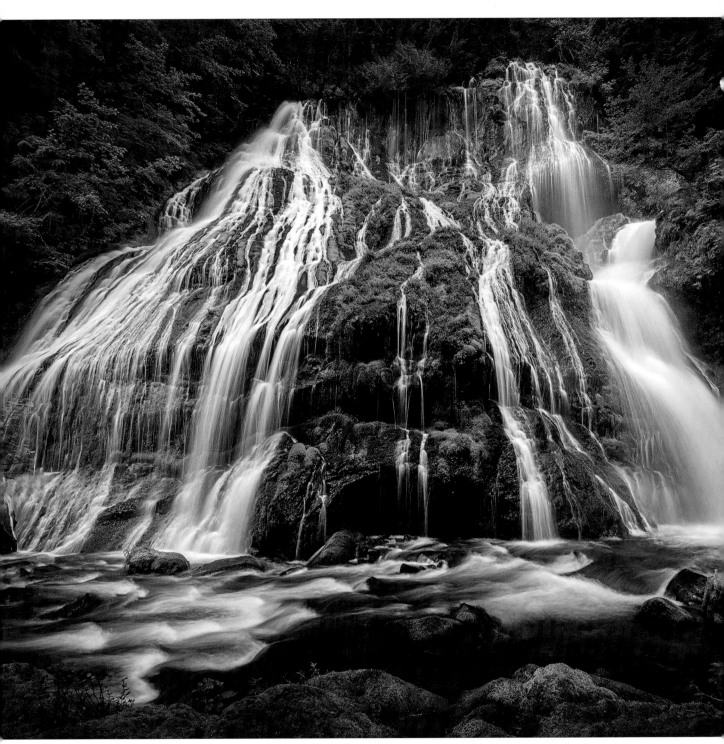

Photo by Matt Kloskowski | Exposure: 1 sec | Focal Length: 16 mm | Aperture Value: *f*/11

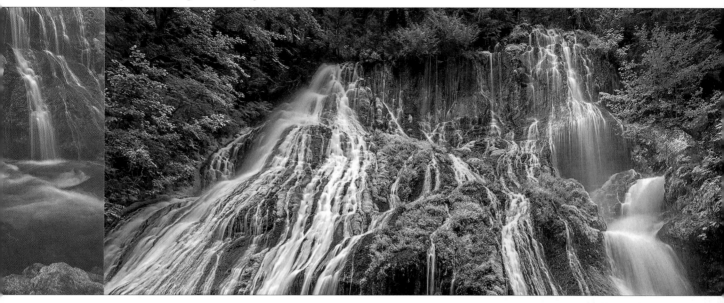

CLONE WARS
removing unwanted objects

Have you ever taken a photo of some majestic landscape and when you open the photo in Elements, only then do you notice a crushed beer can just off to the side of the image? Or you see some really ugly power lines you didn't see when you took the shot. Or, maybe it's a crushed beer can balanced on top of some really ugly power lines (okay, that last one was a stretch, but you get the idea). At this point, you have to make an ethical and moral decision. Now, this is an easy decision if you're a photojournalist—you have to maintain the total integrity of the image, so that beer can and those power lines stay. But what if you're not a photojournalist? You're an artist, which means your job is to create the most beautiful, pleasing image you can. In that case, as an artist, you have full license to remove those unwanted, distracting elements from the scene, and then clone in a stock photo of a Ferrari in the background that you downloaded from the web. Errr...I mean, perhaps you should consider using Elements' tools, like the Spot Healing Brush and the Clone Stamp tool, to remove those unwanted objects in order to return the scene to how it looked when you were actually there. Now, there is a third alternative: when you're taking the photo, pick up the crushed beer can and put it in the trash. However, this is actually frowned upon in the photo community because it breaks the sacred rule of all photographers, which is to expend as little physical energy as possible, so we're fully rested when called upon to gently press the shutter button on the top of our cameras. Hey, I'm sorry I had to be the one to tell you, but that's how we roll.

Cloning Away Distractions

The Clone Stamp tool has been the tool of choice for removing distracting or other unwanted objects in photos for years now. Although the Spot Healing Brush (with the Content Aware option) in many ways offers a better and more realistic alternative, there are certain situations where the Clone Stamp tool is still the best tool for the job. Here's an example of how this workhorse removes unwanted objects:

Step One:
Nothing ruins a nice shot like distracting objects or people. Here we have a nice photo of a beach with someone fishing from it. He's not really large enough to be a useful part of the photo, so he ends up distracting us a bit. So, we'll use the Clone Stamp tool to remove him, and while we're at it, we'll remove that green channel marker that appears above his head.

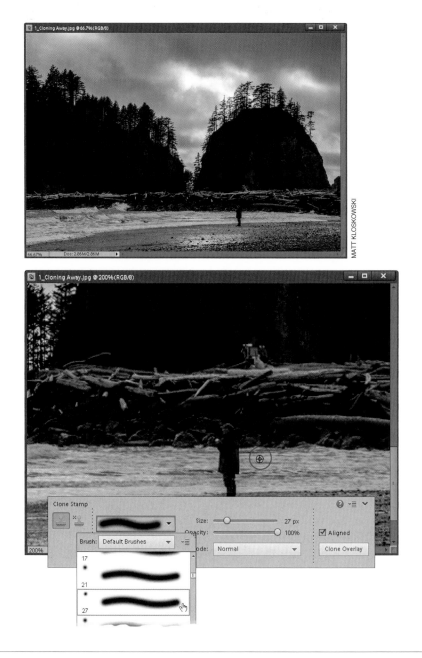

Step Two:
Use the Zoom tool **(Z)** to zoom in if you need to. Then, press **S** to get the Clone Stamp tool. In the Tool Options Bar, click on the brush thumbnail and choose a small, soft-edged brush in the Brush Picker. Now, press-and-hold the Alt (Mac: Option) key and click once in an area to the right of the man on the beach. This is called "sampling." You just sampled a clean area of water and, in the next step, you're going to clone that area over the person to completely cover him. (By the way, when you sample, a little "target" cursor appears, letting you know you're sampling, as you see here.)

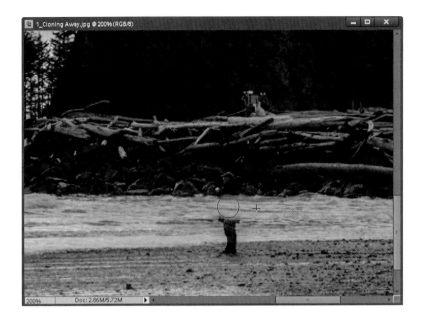

Step Three:
Move directly over the man and begin painting with the Clone Stamp tool. As you paint over him, the water you sampled is cloned right over him, so it looks like he has disappeared. But what if you're not able to clone the whole distraction in one brush stroke? Read on to the next page, and I'll show you a little trick.

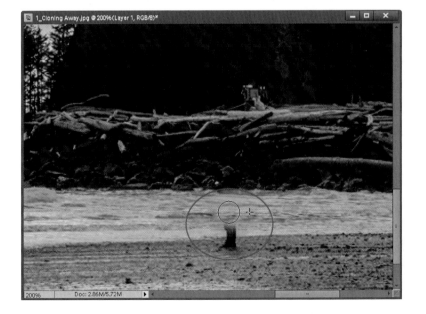

TIP: Sample a Similar Area
The key technique to remember is to sample in an area where the basic light and texture are the same (next to the man), then move straight over him. *Note:* The little plus-sign cursor (the area where you sampled) is immediately to the rght of the circular brush cursor (where you're painting now). By keeping them next to each other, you're making sure you don't pick up patterns or colors from other parts of the photo that would make your cloning look obvious (you'll want to Alt-click [Mac: Option-click] in different but nearby areas to sample the same overall brightness and texture).

(Continued)

Step Four:

Now, what happens if you can't clone all the way over the man in one brush stroke? This actually happens a lot. In my example here, if I continue to paint with one brush stroke over the man, my sample point starts going over the original of him and I wind up cloning him back in.

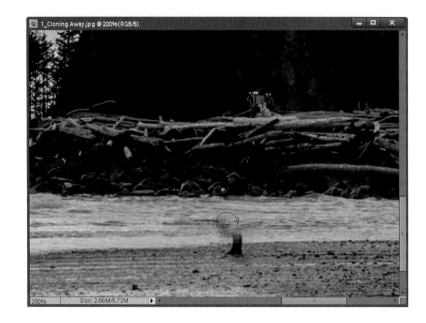

Step Five:

Here's the trick: You'll need to release your mouse button and click to paint again. Each time you release your mouse button, Elements resamples the area you're cloning from and basically resets it. This lets you paint a little more of the water over the man each time. Just keep an eye on that little crosshair as you're cloning. If it starts going over a part of the man where he once existed, then weird things are going to happen. So, release the mouse button often, let the source reset itself on the clean water, and paint smaller areas at a time, instead of one large area. Do the same thing down on the beach to remove his feet and up near the rocks to remove his head.

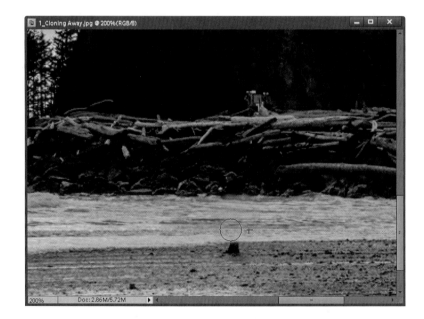

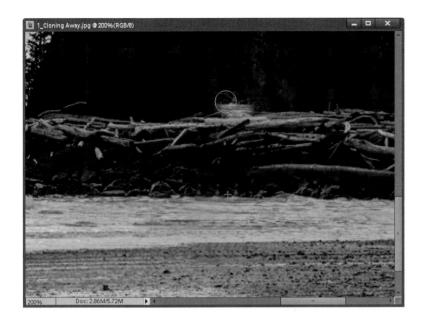

Step Six:

One more thing: You'll want to sample from an area similar to what you're removing. For example, try this: Alt-click (Mac: Option-click) in an area near that green marker, but closer to where the rocks meet the water. Then, go back and start cloning over the marker. See how it doesn't match up? That's why you usually have to sample very close to where you clone. If not, it's a dead giveaway. And you want to sample often, so you don't get a repeating pattern from using the same sample point each time you paint.

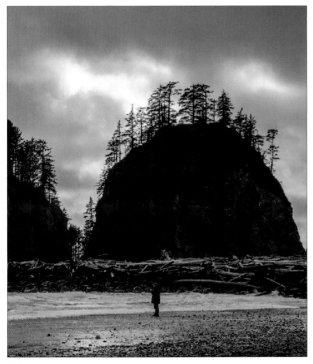

Before

After

Removing Spots and Other Artifacts

Elements has a tool, the Spot Healing Brush tool, which is just about perfect for getting rid of spots and other artifacts. (By the way, the term "artifacts" is a fancy "ten-dollar" word for spots and other junk that wind up in your photos.) Believe it or not, it's even faster and easier to use than the regular Healing Brush, because it's pretty much a one-trick pony.

Step One:
Open a photo that has spots (whether they're in the scene itself or are courtesy of specks or dust on either your lens or your camera's sensors). In the photo shown here, there are all sorts of distracting little spots in the sky.

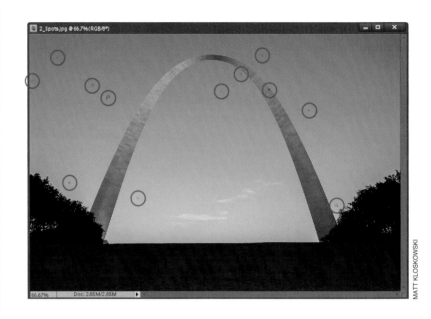

MATT KLOSKOWSKI

Step Two:
Press **Z** to get the Zoom tool and zoom in on an area with lots of spots (here, I zoomed in on the sky and Gateway Arch). Now get the Spot Healing Brush tool from the Toolbox (or just press the letter **J** until you have it).

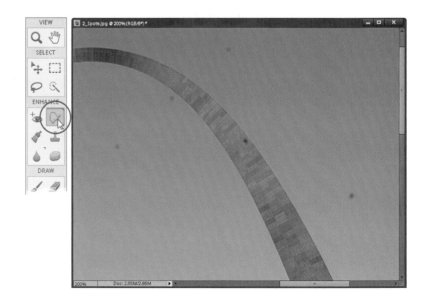

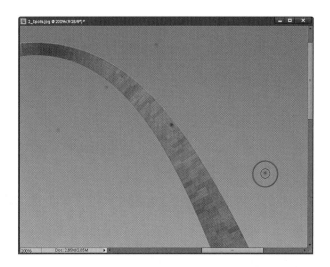

Step Three:
Position the Spot Healing Brush directly over the spot you want to remove and click once. That's it. You don't have to sample an area or Alt-click anywhere first—you just move it over the spot and click, and the spot is gone. (*Note:* If the fix doesn't look quite right, make sure Content Aware is chosen for Type in the Tool Options Bar.)

Step Four:
You remove other spots the same way—just position the Spot Healing Brush over them and click. I know it sounds too easy, but that's the way it works. So, just move around and start clicking away on the spots. Now you can "de-spot" any photo, getting a "spotless" version in about 30 seconds, thanks to the Spot Healing Brush.

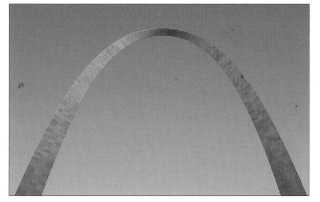

Before

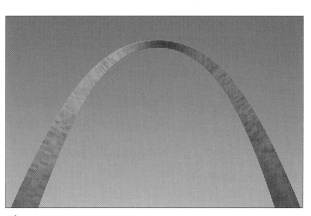

After

The Magic of Content Aware

Content Aware is probably one of the best-kept secrets of Photoshop Elements, and it's just incredibly amazing. It was a huge hit in the full version of Photoshop, but few people know that it exists in Elements, too. Anyway, as amazing as it is, it's also incredibly simple to use, so don't let the fact that it only took four pages here in the book to cover it throw you off. What makes the feature even more amazing is that you have to do so little—Elements does all the heavy lifting. Here's an example of how to use it to remove distracting things you wish weren't in the photo:

Step One:
Open a photo that has something distracting that you'd like to remove. In this case, we have a street light on the right side of the photo that's pretty distracting, so we'll remove it.

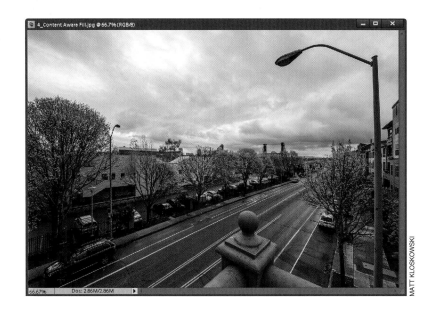

Step Two:
Normally, you'd think we'd have to spend some time cloning it, and even some extra time sampling, because part of the light is over the sky and part of it is over the building and tree. But with Content Aware, we just let the tool do all (well, most of) the work. So, get the Spot Healing Brush tool from the Toolbox (or just press **J**), and then click on the Content Aware radio button in the Tool Options Bar.

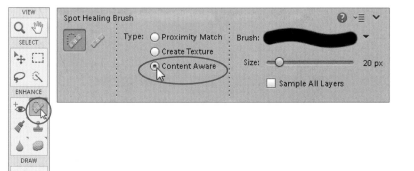

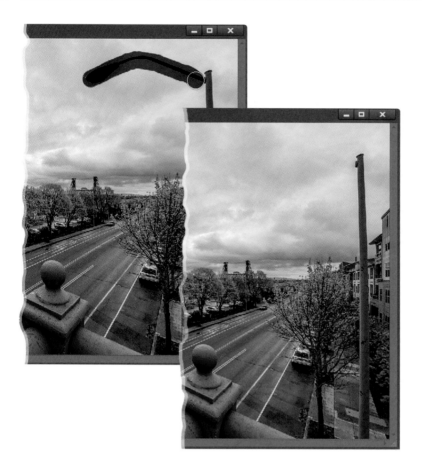

Step Three:
Press the **Right** or **Left Bracket key** to resize the brush, so it's about the size of the pole. Then, paint with the tool over the top-left portion of the light, all the way over to the top-right edge of it (as shown here). Yep, the whole thing. Just paint. When you release your mouse button, sit back, and prepare to be amazed. I know—it's freaky. Look at how it replaced the sky all in one brush stroke. The color looks spot on, and the texture is a perfect match. This is the essence of being "content aware" and being totally aware of what's around it.

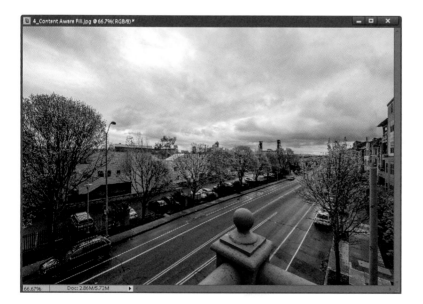

Step Four:
Go ahead and paint a few more brush strokes over the top of the light post. I usually help Content Aware out by picking regions that look similar—like painting from the sky down to the buildings and tree here.

(Continued)

Step Five:

Next, paint one more stroke from the buildings and tree down to the ground. The more I use Content Aware, the more it amazes me, but part of using this effectively is learning its weaknesses, and how to get around them when possible.

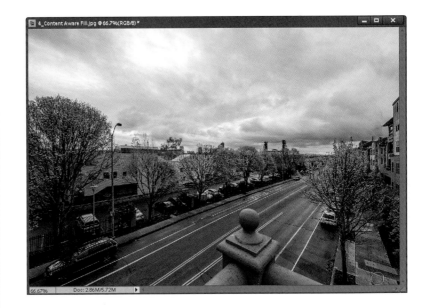

Step Six:

For example, while Content Aware removed the light almost flawlessly from this photo, there is one little spot that it didn't leave perfect—right near the top of the buildings, where they meet the sky. You can see it where I've zoomed in on it here.

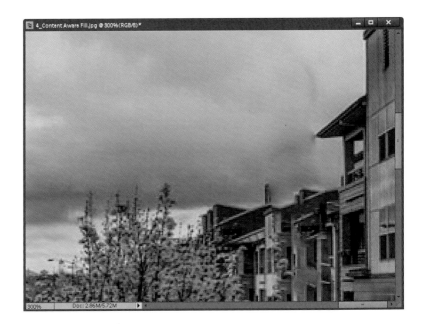

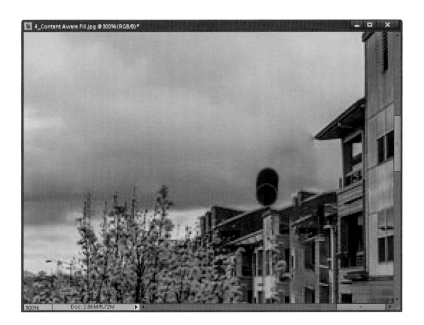

Step Seven:

If this ever happens, I try one of two things: First, I'll zoom in real close and try painting over it again with the Spot Healing Brush (again, with Content Aware turned on). Most of the time, that does the trick right away (but not in this example). If it picks up areas you don't want, just press **Ctrl-Z (Mac: Command-Z)** to Undo and try again. If that doesn't work, then I simply resort to the Clone Stamp tool to get a little more precise in that one spot. But, I'd still try Content Aware first. It may not take care of removing the distraction in one brush stroke, but it sure gets you about 90% of the way there in a fraction of the time that cloning and healing would.

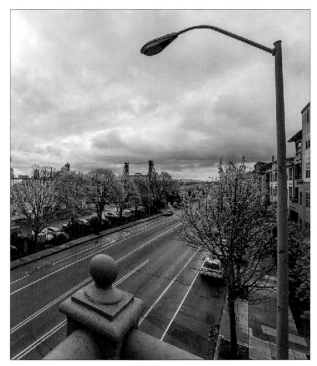

Before

After

Automatically Cleaning Up Your Scenes (a.k.a. The Tourist Remover)

If you've ever tried to photograph a popular landmark or national monument, you'll know that it's pretty unlikely you'll be there alone. Unless you're willing to get up really early in the morning (when most people are still sleeping), you're bound to get a tourist or two (or 20) in your photos. In this tutorial, you'll learn a few tricks to help clean up those scenes and remove the tourists with just a few brush strokes.

Step One:

The first step starts in the camera. You'll need to photograph at least two shots of the same scene (but you can use up to 10 if you'd like). So, if you're in one of those situations where you just can't get a photo with no people in it, then take a few photos in the hope that the people move around a little (even if they don't ever exit the area completely).

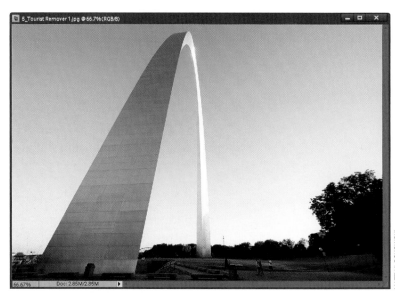

Step Two:

Here, I realized it was going to be really difficult for me to get a photo when someone wasn't walking under or around the Gateway Arch. But, I knew that I had a feature that could fix this available to me in Elements, so I decided to take another photo. As you can see, I wasn't able to capture a photo with no one walking by, but at least I had another one where they had moved.

TIP: Keep Your Camera Steady

I wasn't on a tripod when I shot this, but Elements does a great job of auto-aligning photos. If you can't shoot on a tripod, the key is to try to be as steady as possible, so the actual photo doesn't change too much.

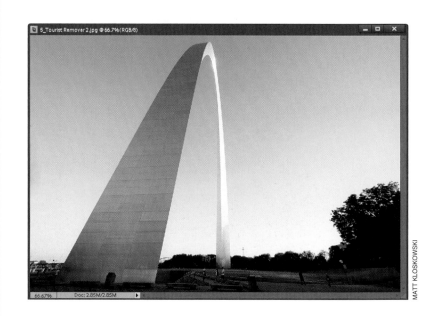

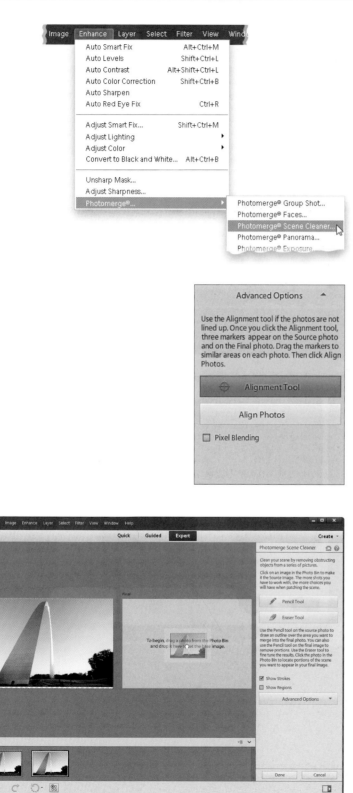

Step Three:

Go ahead and open the photos you've taken (remember, you'll need at least two but can use up to 10. In this example, I'm only using two) in the Elements Editor. Then select them down in the Project Bin by clicking on the first one and Shift-clicking on the last one. Now, go under the Enhance menu, under Photomerge®, and choose **Photomerge® Scene Cleaner**. This will take you into Photomerge.

ADVANCED TIP: Try the Advanced Options

Here's a follow-up to the previous tip. In fact, just file this tip away, because you may or may not need it. If you didn't shoot on a tripod, and you're not getting good results from Photomerge, then click on the Advanced Options button at the bottom of the Photomerge palette. Use the Alignment tool to place three markers in the Source window and three in the Final window, on similar places in the photos. Then click Align Photos, and Elements will do its best to align the photos based on those markers. This helps the Scene Cleaner give more predictable results. Again, give Step Three through Step Seven a try first and see how things work out. If everything looks good, then you don't need the Advanced Options.

Step Four:

The Source window on the left will automatically be populated with the first photo you chose. You'll need to create a Final photo though, so drag the other photo from the Project Bin into the Final window on the right.

(Continued)

Step Five:

Now look over at the Source window and find the clean areas from this photo that you'd like copied over to the Final photo. In this example, we'll start with the area to the left of the light post. You can use the Zoom tool (the one that looks like a magnifying glass in the Toolbox on the left) to zoom in to the area if you need to.

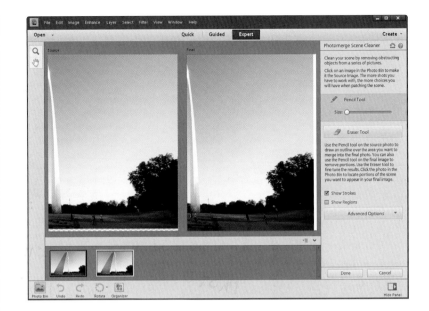

Step Six:

All right, let's get rid of these people. First, use the Pencil tool to paint on the Source image (on the left) in the area where the two people are to the left of the light post in the Final image to get rid of them there. It doesn't have to be perfect, so just paint a small area, and when you release your mouse button, you'll see the Scene Cleaner automatically remove them from the Final image on the right. If you don't get the results you're looking for, grab the Eraser tool (it's just below the Pencil tool on the right) and click to erase away some of the blue pencil marks in the Source image on the left. Get the Hand tool (H) from the Toolbox, move around the image, and do the same thing in the Source image to remove the other people from the Final image. When you're done cleaning up the image, click the Done button to return to the Editor.

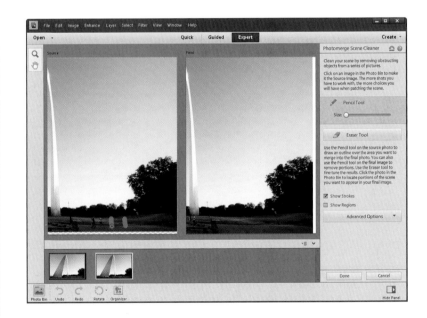

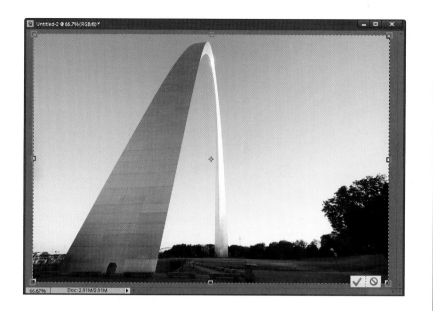

TIP: Getting Rid of the Pencil Marks
If you move your mouse over the Final image, you'll see the blue pencil marks on it, too. If you want to see your Final image without the blue pencil marks over it, just move your mouse away from it and they'll disappear. If you want to see the Source image without the blue marks, then turn off the Show Strokes checkbox in the Photomerge palette on the right.

Step Seven:
If Photomerge left some extra white canvas around your final image, first flatten your image by choosing **Flatten Image** from the Layers palette's flyout menu, then just use the Crop tool **(C)** to remove the extra white canvas.

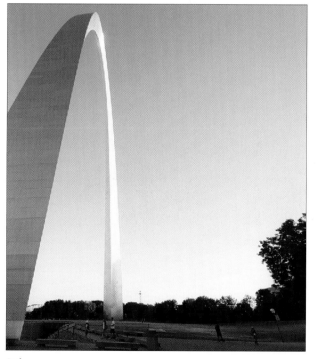

Before

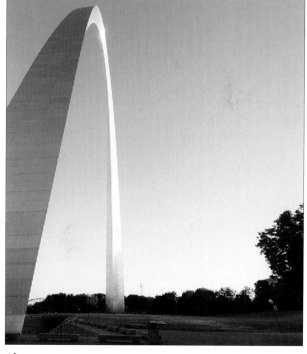

After

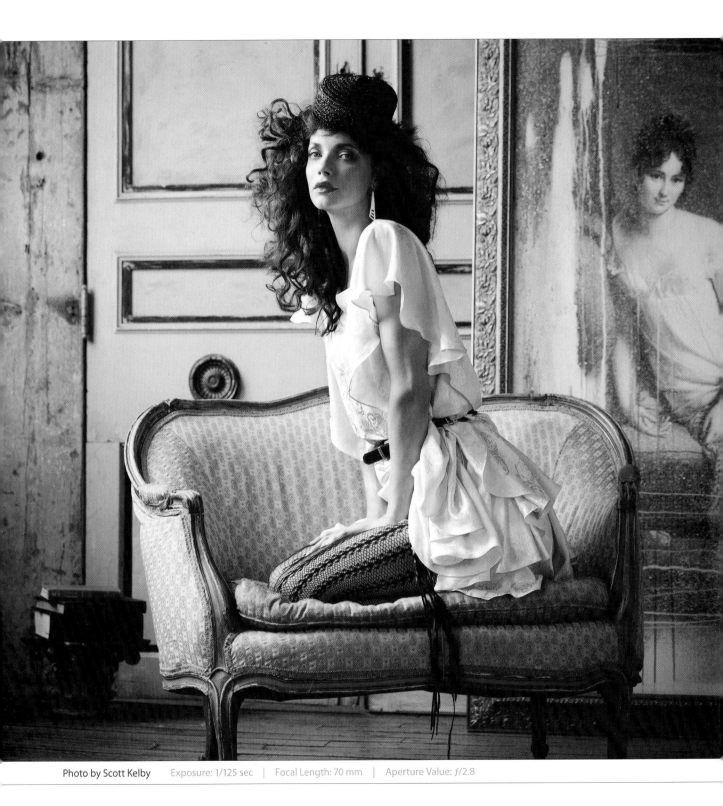

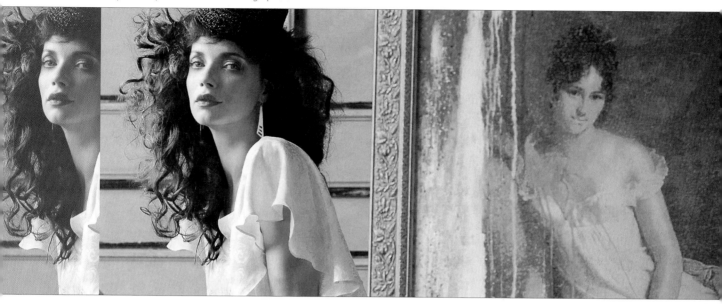

SIDE EFFECTS
special effects for photographers

The name of this chapter comes from the 2009 movie short *Side Effects* (it's less than 20 minutes long, which is probably why you can buy it for only $1.99 in the iTunes Store. It's either that, or it's so cheap because of its lack of zombies). Anyway, here's how they describe *Side Effects* (say this in your best movie voice-over guy voice): "An ordinary guy becomes a human guinea pig in an experimental drug test and meets the girl of his dreams…" Sounds like a pretty typical everyday story. At least the human guinea pig in an experimental drug test part. Anyway, I looked at the movie poster, and the guys in the poster all have this creepy-looking bluish/green color cast that makes them look kind of sickly, but then the female lead's photo looks fine, with regular-looking flesh tones, and that's when I realized why this guy thinks he's found the woman of his dreams. She doesn't have a creepy bluish/green color cast. I mean, think about it. If all the girls around you had a serious white balance problem, and then all of sudden you meet a girl carrying around her own 18% gray card, so she looks correctly color balanced in any lighting situation, wouldn't you fall in love with her, too? Exactly. I'll bet in the last 10 minutes of the movie, you find out that this guy actually starts an online business for people using dating sites like eHarmony, or Match.com, or HandsomeStalker.com, where he offers to remove bluish/green color casts from your profile photo for a price. Things are going pretty well for him for a while, but then in about the eighteenth minute, the experimental drug wears off, and he finds himself trapped in a dank, dimly-lit room, forced to write nonsensical chapter intros late into the night, until his wife comes in and says "Honey, come to bed," but right then, he notices she has a bluish/green color cast, and….

Creating a Picture Stack Effect

Picture Stack is one of my favorite Guided edits, because this one would seriously take a ton of time if you tried to do it manually. The idea is to take one photo and make it look like it was cut up into smaller photos with white borders stacked on top of each other. The effect looks pretty cool and is a fun way to show off your photos. Plus, it even goes so far as to add shadows under each photo, so it really looks like they're lying on top of each other.

Step One:

In the Editor, open the photo that you want to use for the Picture Stack effect. I usually find landscape and travel photos look good here. You can use photos of people, too, but sometimes Elements will cut the photo right in the middle of someone's face, so you have to watch out when using these. Click on Guided at the top of the window and then, on the right, under Photo Play, click on Picture Stack.

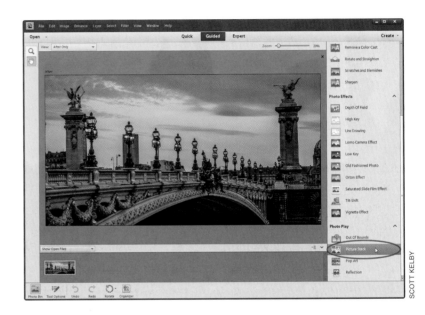

Step Two:

First, you'll choose how many pictures you want your photo to be chopped up into. My favorite is 8 Pictures. To me, 4 Pictures doesn't look like enough and 12 Pictures makes the photo look too busy. The good thing is that you don't really have to commit to too much at this point. So, click on the 8 Pictures button on the right and Elements will go to work. It takes a minute, but you'll eventually see your photo cut into smaller square/rectangular pieces.

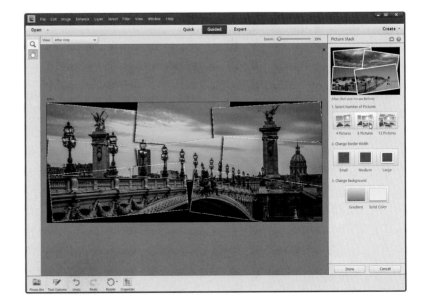

SCOTT KELBY

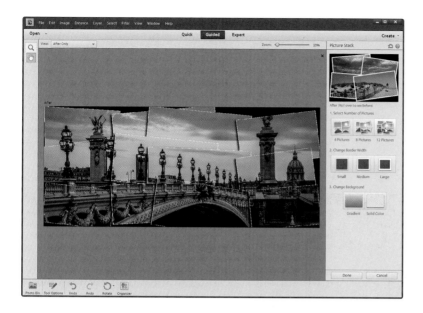

Step Three:

If you want to see what it looks like using four or 12 pictures, then just click on one of those buttons and Elements will redo the stack. It's pretty easy to figure out which one looks best for your photo by just trying out each option.

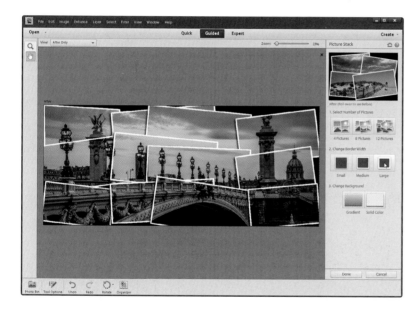

Step Four:

You'll notice that each photo has a white border around it and, in section 2, you can control the width of that border. I usually go with the Medium setting here—the Small setting is too thin, so I barely ever use it, but the Large setting isn't bad (sometimes it's a little over-powering, but sometimes it looks cool). Just like with selecting the number of pictures, this one is easy to experiment with, so click on the three border buttons to see which one you like better.

(Continued)

Step Five:

Lastly, you can change the background color and style (I switched back to eight photos with a medium border here). You have a choice between a gradient or just a simple solid-color background— I usually stick with a solid color. While the default black looks pretty cool, let's try a white background. Click on the Solid Color button and when the New Layer dialog appears, click OK. In the Color Picker, choose white and then click OK. I kinda like white, because it lets you see the shadows under the photos. It gives the image a little more depth, so each picture in the stack really looks like it's lying on the background.

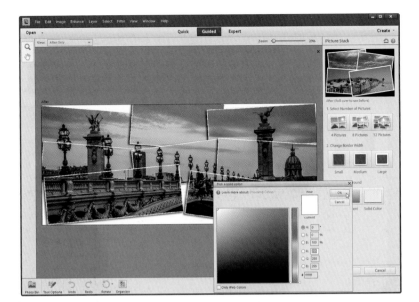

Step Six:

When you've settled on your background color, just click the Done button at the bottom of the Palette Bin.

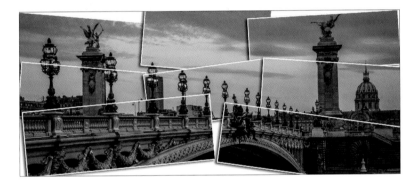

TIP: Edit the Layers

If you switch back to Expert mode and look in the Layers palette, you'll see the behind-the-scenes work that went on. Elements adds quite a few layers to your document. If you're brave enough, you can go into the separate layers and adjust them. The drop shadows, the outline around each photo—they each have their own layer, so if there's something you want to change, you can do so right on the layer.

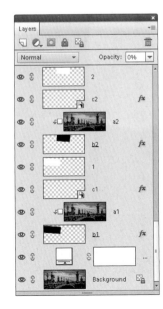

Another built-in special effect in Elements 11 is called the Orton Effect. The technique comes from traditional photography, where a photo was created by "sandwiching" two photos, one in focus and one out of focus, together. It adds a semi-soft focus, an almost dreamy style, to your photo, while still looking like the photo is sharp.

The Orton (Dreamy-Focus-Like) Effect

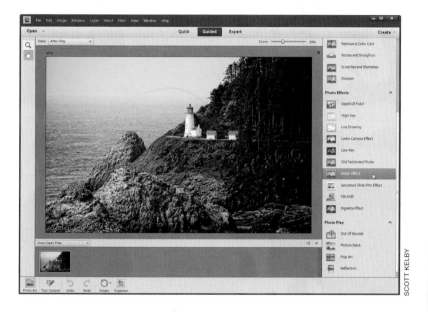

SCOTT KELBY

Step One:
Open a photo in the Editor to apply the effect to. You can use it on just about any photo, but I find photos that have a softer look to them work best. Portraits tend to get too blurry, but hey, you can always give it a try. In this photo, the misty, overcast day works really well. Click on Guided at the top of the window, scroll down to Photo Effects on the right, and click on Orton Effect.

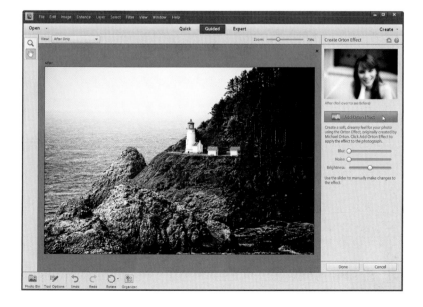

Step Two:
You'll see the Palette Bin on the right side of the window change to show all of the settings you have control over for the effect. The first thing you'll want to do is click the Add Orton Effect button. This adds an overall contrasty feel to your photo and it also makes the colors look a little more saturated.

(Continued)

Step Three:

Next, move the Blur slider to the right a little, and when I say "a little," I mean a little. Be careful when cranking this slider up, as things can get bad really quickly. Just drag it over slightly—somewhere between 5 and 10 should do it (you'll see the number appear in a white box above the slider knob when you click on it).

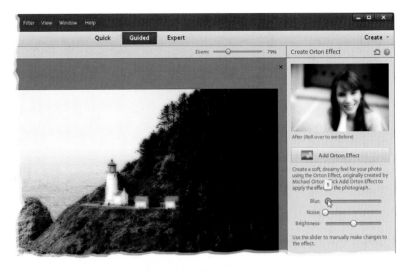

Step Four:

The Noise setting is totally optional here. It gives a slightly more nostalgic film grain look to the photo. I dragged to around 500 here. Unless you really zoom in on the photo, it's kinda hard to see, but you should be able to see a little texture.

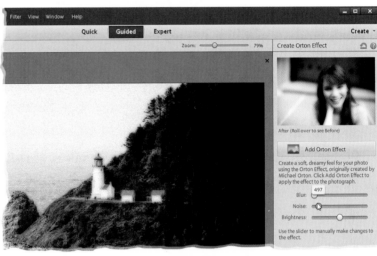

Step Five:

Another characteristic of the Orton effect is overexposure (the photos were deliberately overexposed before they were sandwiched together). This part is also optional, but you'll usually find that what we did in Step Two (clicking the Add Orton Effect button) darkened the photo, so I always increase the Brightness setting a little. Somewhere between 20 and 30 usually works well here. Here, the trees on the right were really dark, so I went a little further.

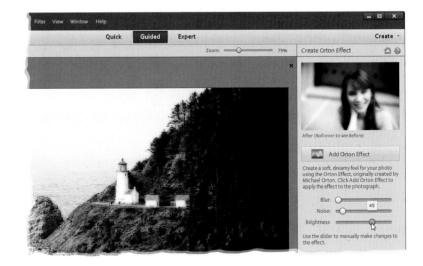

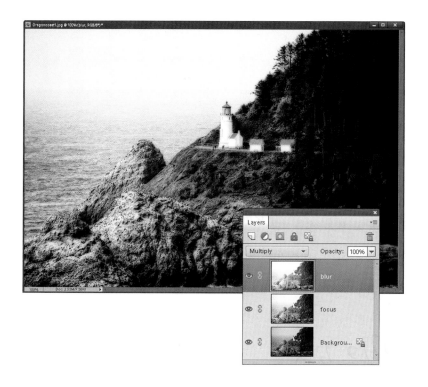

Step Six:
When you're ready, click the Done button at the bottom right. If you then click on Expert at the top of the window and look in the Layers palette, you'll see Elements has added some layers here: one layer adds the blur and the other works more with the overall focus and brightness of the image. Since the whole effect is layer based, you can always reduce the opacity of either of the layers to pull back the overall effect if you find it's too strong.

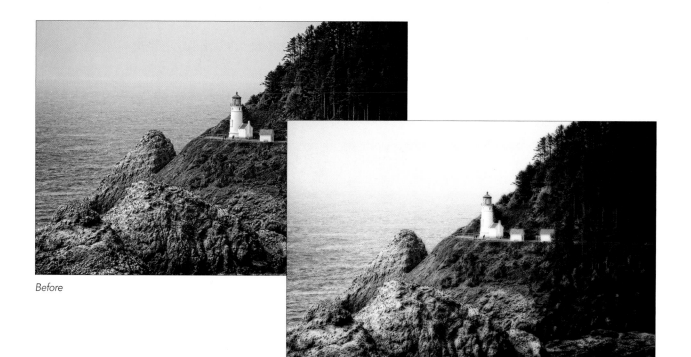

Before

After

Enhancing Depth of Field (or Faking That 85mm f/1.4 Look)

Depth of field is a great way to really make your subjects stand out from the background by blurring it. Sure, we can do a lot of this work in-camera with our lens and f-stop choice, but sometimes the creative idea doesn't strike until the photo hits the computer. The Depth Of Field lens effect in Elements 11 will help you fix that, though.

Step One:

In the Editor, open a photo that has a busier background than you'd care for, or just one where you'd like to draw attention to a specific part of the image. In this example, we'll keep the bride in focus and blur the background. Click on Guided at the top of the window, scroll down to Photo Effects on the right, and click on Depth Of Field.

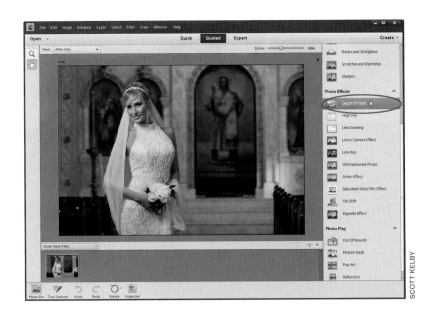

Step Two:

You'll see this effect has two modes: Simple and Custom. Let's start by clicking on the Simple button. Elements pretty much walks you through what to do in Simple mode. First, click the Add Blur button at the top to simply add some blur to the entire photo. At this point, you haven't defined the subject yet, so Elements will blur everything in the photo.

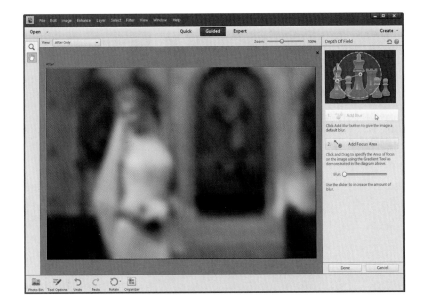

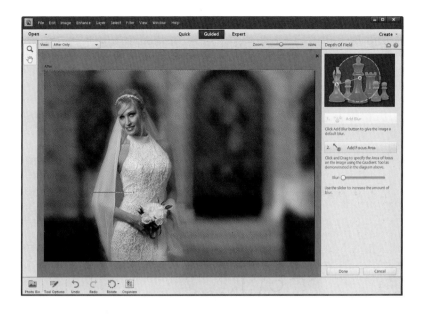

Step Three:
Next, you need to tell Elements what parts of the photo you want in focus. So, start by clicking on the Add Focus Area button in section 2, then click in the middle of whatever you want to be in focus and drag outward. The farther out from the center you drag, the smoother your sharp-to-blur transition will be. You can also click-and-drag more than once, as I did here, where I dragged once to get her head in focus, once to get her dress in focus, and once to get her arm more in focus on the left.

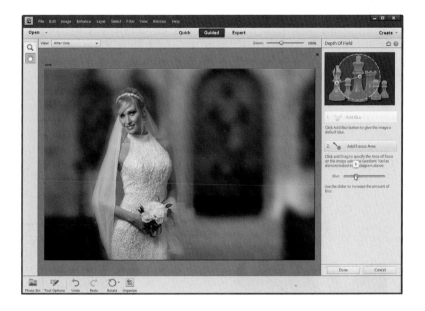

Step Four:
Once you've defined the part of the photo you want sharp, you can use the Blur slider to add more blur if you want. I dragged my slider to 6 to make the background even blurrier. Now, if you haven't realized yet, the simple method is, well, simple, but it's limited because of the way it fades the blur away. Like most things in Elements, however, this effect gives you a simple way and a more custom way to do things. We'll take a look at the custom method next.

(Continued)

Step Five:

I've got another photo open here in the Editor. In this example, the bride, bench, and background are all in focus, but I'd like to make it so the bride seems like the center of attention. So, once again, in the Guided options, go down to the Photo Effects, and click on Depth Of Field. This time, though, click on Custom.

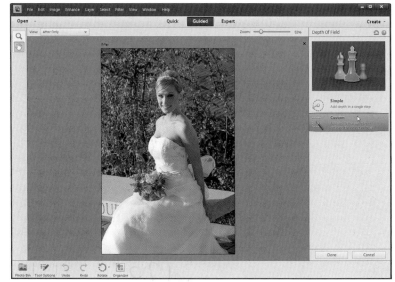

Step Six:

The first thing we'll do here is define our subject (the part of the photo that we don't want to blur). We did it before using a gradient tool, which didn't give us too much control, but in the Custom options, we get to make a selection. So, click on the Quick Selection Tool button (by the way, we covered this tool in greater detail back in Chapter 7), and then just start painting over the bride in the photo. Don't worry if you select part of the background, though, because we'll take care of that in the next step.

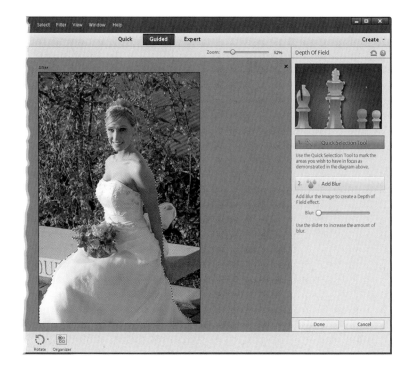

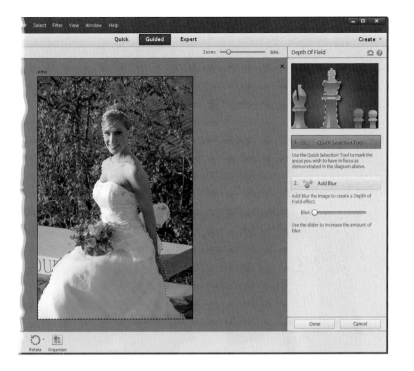

Step Seven:

Chances are that you've probably selected something you didn't want to during your first pass with the Quick Selection tool. No sweat. Just press-and-hold the **Alt (Mac: Option) key** to put the tool into Subtract mode and click on any areas you didn't want selected.

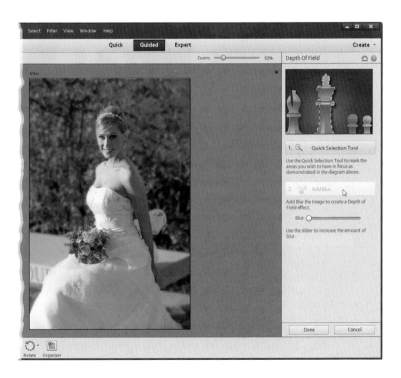

Step Eight:

The rest is a piece of cake. Just click on the Add Blur button in section 2 to blur everything that wasn't selected in the photo. Now the bride should really stand out from the background behind her. Just like before, if you want to add more blur to the background, just drag the Blur slider to the right some. If you find the blur is too intense (when using either the Simple or Custom method), click the Done button, then click Expert at the top of the window, and lower the blurred layer's opacity.

Automating Special Effects with Actions

Actions are a feature that has been around in the full version of Photoshop for a while. But, now we have them in Elements 11. If you've never heard of them before, then think of an action like a little tape recorder. It records the steps that you do in Photoshop, so you can replay them later without doing each one manually over and over again. Here's the catch: In Elements 11, you can only play actions; you can't record them. But, you'll see in this tutorial that there's a never-ending supply of actions available for you to try out. So, when it comes to special effects, I think you'll be able to find what you need.

Step One:
Open an image that you'd like to apply an action to. In this example, we'll use a portrait. Then, go under the Window menu and choose **Actions** to open the Actions palette.

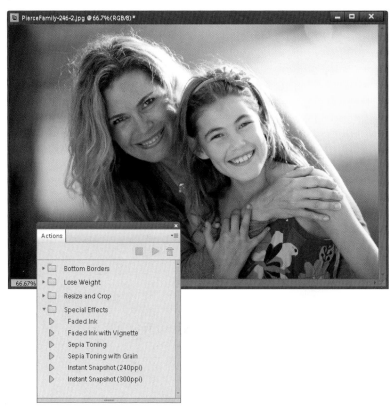

MATT KLOSKOWSKI

Step Two:
The actions in the Special Effects folder in the Actions palette are pretty cool, so we'll choose one of those. Faded Ink with Vignette is one of my favorites, so click on it to select it. You can even click on the little right-facing arrow to expand an action and see what steps are inside of it.

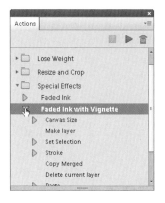

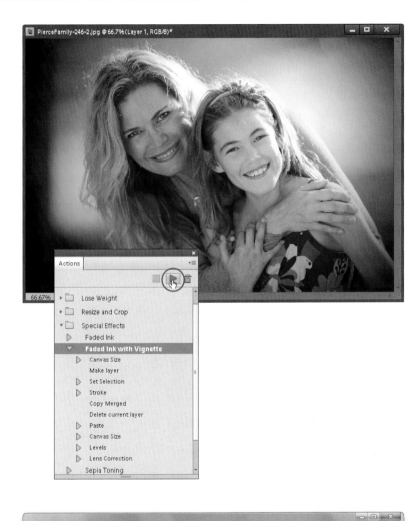

Step Three:
Once you select an action, just click on the Play Selection icon at the top right of the Actions palette. Elements will automatically run through the steps in the action and apply them to your photo. When it's done, you'll have something like the image you see here.

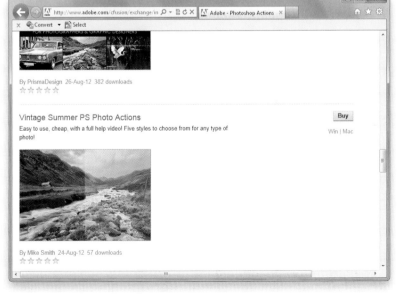

Step Four:
Okay, that's pretty cool, but (to me at least) the real power of actions comes in the fact that there are literally thousands of actions available on the Internet for you to use. Most of these actions were made for the full version of Photoshop, but a lot of them will work in Elements. My guess is that you'll see a lot more made for Elements now that it supports actions. A lot of them are free, too, but some you have to pay for. In this case, I downloaded a set called Vintage Summer Actions from the Adobe Marketplace & Exchange website for $4. To get there, go to www.adobe.com and type "Adobe Exchange" in the Search field in the top right, choose Adobe Exchange from the results list, and then under Exchanges by Product, click on Photoshop. Under Browse by Category on the right, click on Actions to only see actions and action sets.

(Continued)

Step Five:

Once you download (and usually unzip) the action, go back to the Actions palette in Elements. Click on the down-facing arrow with four lines in the top right to open the flyout menu, and choose **Load Actions**. Find the ATN file you just downloaded, select it, and click Open. This loads the action set into Elements, so you can use it there.

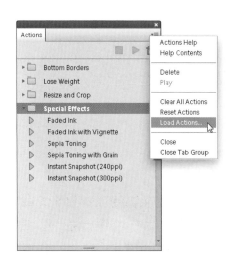
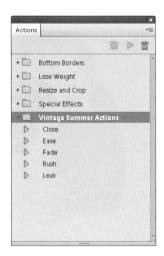

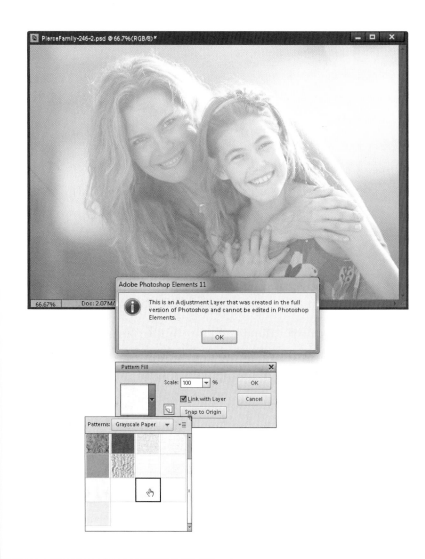

Step Six:

Now, it's just a matter of opening a photo, choosing an action (I chose Fade), and clicking the Play Selection icon. I found that some actions made for Photoshop would open the dialog you see here, but after clicking OK, they worked just fine. You may also get some settings dialogs, as I did with this one, where I could change the layer style settings and had to choose a pattern (I chose Pebbled in the Grayscale Paper patterns). When you're done, you've got a fast way to create some pretty cool effects. And, trust me, once you start searching, you'll find a ton of free actions out there worth trying.

This is just about the hottest Photoshop portrait technique out there right now, and you see it popping up everywhere, from covers of magazines to CD covers, from print ads to Hollywood movie posters, and from editorial images to billboards. It seems right now everybody wants this effect (and you're about to be able to deliver it in roughly 60 seconds flat using the simplified method shown here!).

Trendy Desaturated Skin Look

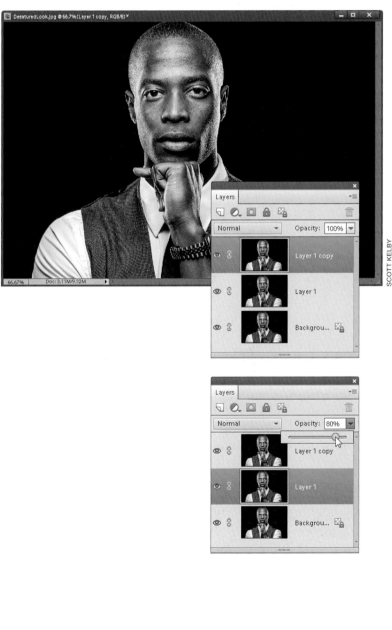

Step One:
Open the photo you want to apply this trendy desaturated skin look to. Duplicate the Background layer by pressing **Ctrl-J (Mac: Command-J)**. Then duplicate this layer using the same shortcut (so you have three layers in all, which all look the same, as shown here).

Step Two:
In the Layers palette, click on the middle layer (Layer 1) to make it the active layer, then press **Ctrl-Shift-U (Mac: Command-Shift-U)** to desaturate and remove all the color from that layer. Now, lower the Opacity of this layer to 80%, so just a little color shows through. Of course, there's still a color photo on the top of the layer stack, so you won't see anything change onscreen (you'll still see your color photo), but if you look in the Layers palette, you'll see the thumbnail for the center layer is in black and white (as seen here).

(Continued)

Step Three:

In the Layers palette, click on the top layer in the stack (Layer 1 copy), then switch its layer blend mode from Normal to **Soft Light** (as shown here), which brings the effect into play. Now, Soft Light brings a very nice, subtle version of the effect, but if you want something a bit edgier with even more contrast, try using Overlay mode instead. If the Overlay version is a bit too intense, try lowering the Opacity of the layer a bit until it looks good to you, but honestly, I usually just go with Soft Light myself.

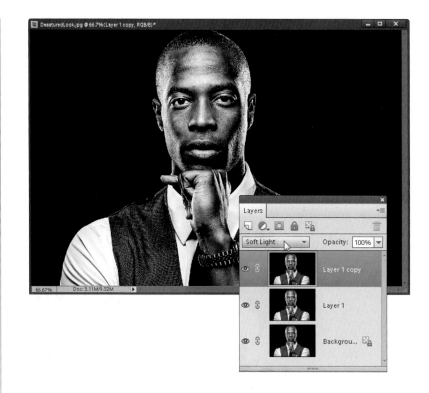

Step Four:

Our last step is to limit the effect to just our subject's skin (of course, you can leave it over the entire image if it looks good, but normally I just use this as a skin effect). So, if it looks good to you as is, you can skip this step). To limit it to just the skin, press **Ctrl-Alt-Shift-E (Mac: Command-Option-Shift-E)** to create a merged layer on top of the layer stack (a merged layer is a new layer that looks like you flattened the image). You don't need the two layers below it any longer, so you can hide them from view by clicking on the Eye icon to the left of each layer's thumbnail (like I did here), or you can just delete them altogether. Now, press-and-hold the Alt (Mac: Option) key and click on the Add Layer Mask icon at the top of the Layers palette to hide our desaturated layer behind a black mask. Press **D** to set your Foreground color to white, get the Brush tool **(B)**, choose a medium-sized, soft-edged brush from the Brush Picker in the Tool Options Bar, and just paint over his face and hand (or any visible skin) to complete the effect. If you think the effect is too intense, just lower the Opacity of this layer until it looks right to you. That's it!

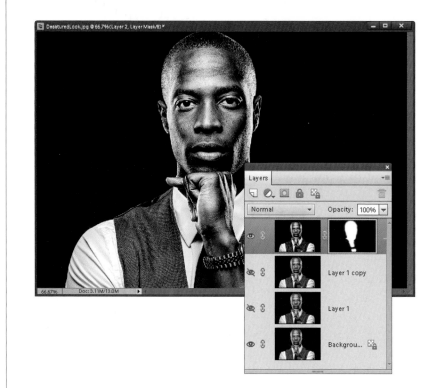

High-Contrast Portrait Look

The super-high-contrast look is incredibly popular right now, and while there are a number of plug-ins that can give you this look, along with a Camera Raw technique I'll show you next, I wanted to include this version, which I learned from German retoucher Calvin Hollywood, who shared this technique during a stint as my special guest blogger at my daily blog (www.scottkelby.com). The great thing about his version is you don't need to buy a third-party plug-in to get this look. My thanks to Calvin for sharing this technique with me, and now you.

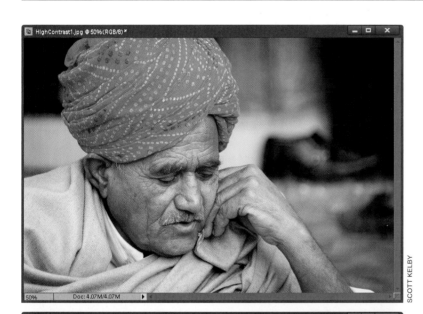

Step One:
Open the image you want to apply a high-contrast look to.

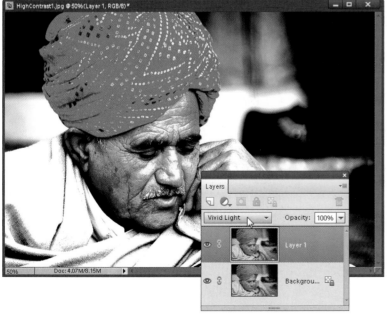

Step Two:
Make a copy of your Background layer by pressing **Ctrl-J (Mac: Command-J)**. Then, change the blend mode of this duplicate layer to **Vivid Light** (I know it doesn't look pretty now, but it'll get better in a few more moves).

(Continued)

Step Three:

Now press **Ctrl-I (Mac: Command-I)** to Invert the layer (it should look pretty gray at this point). Next, go under the Filter menu, under Blur, and choose **Surface Blur**. When the dialog appears, enter 40 for the Radius and 40 for the Threshold, and click OK (it takes a while for this particular filter to do its thing, so be patient. If you're running this on a 16-bit version of your photo, this wouldn't be a bad time to grab a cup of coffee. Maybe a sandwich, too).

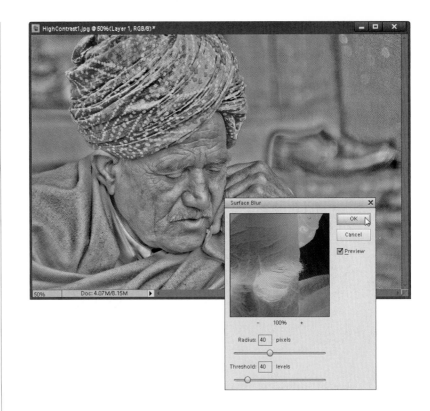

Step Four:

We need to change the layer's blend mode again, but we can't change this one from Vivid Light or it will mess up the effect, so instead we're going to create a new layer, on top of the stack, that looks like a flattened version of the image. That way, we can change its blend mode to get a different look. This is called "creating a merged layer," and you get this layer by pressing **Ctrl-Alt-Shift-E (Mac: Command-Option-Shift-E)**.

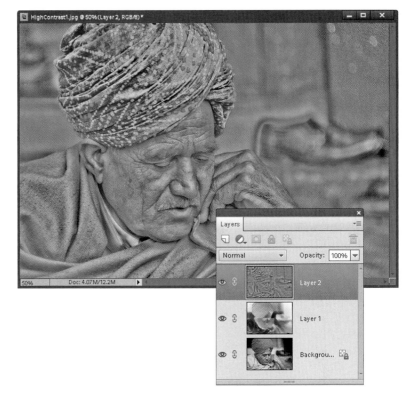

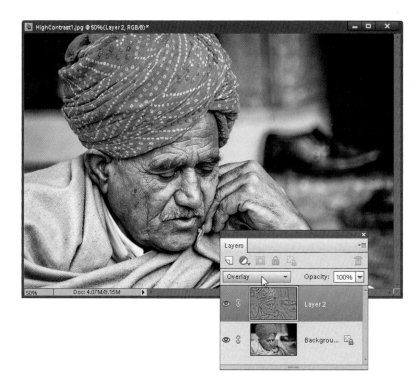

Step Five:

Now that you have this new merged layer, you need to delete the middle layer (the one you ran the Surface Blur upon), so drag it onto the Trash icon at the top of the Layers palette. Next, we have to deal with all the funky neon colors on this layer, and we do that by simply removing all the color. Click on your merged layer (Layer 2) to make it active again, then go under the Enhance menu, under Adjust Color, and choose **Remove Color**, so the layer only looks gray. Then, change the blend mode to **Overlay**, and now you can start to see the effect taking shape. You can stop right there (I usually do), but if you think you need an even stronger high-contrast effect (hey, it's possible. It just depends on the image, and how much texture and contrast you want it to have), you can continue on and crank your amp up to 11 (sorry for the lame *This Is Spinal Tap* movie reference).

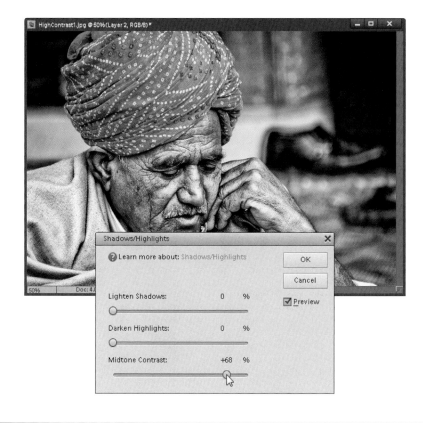

Step Six:

Go under the Enhance menu again, under Adjust Lighting, and choose **Shadows/Highlights**. When the dialog appears, drag the Lighten Shadows slider down to 0. Then, you're going to add what amounts to Camera Raw's Clarity by increasing the amount of Midtone Contrast on this Overlay layer. Go to the bottom of the dialog and drag the Midtone Contrast slider to the right, and watch how your image starts to get that crispy look (crispy, in a good way). Of course, the farther to the right you drag, the crispier it gets, so don't go too far, because you're still going to sharpen this image. Here, I dragged to +68%. Click OK. The next step is optional, so if you don't need it, go to the Layers palette's flyout menu and choose **Flatten Image**.

(Continued)

Step Seven:

Okay, this high-contrast look looks great on a lot of stuff, but one area where it doesn't look that good (and makes your image look obviously post-processed) is when you apply this to blurry, out-of-focus backgrounds, like the one you see here. So, I would only apply it to our subject and not the background. Here's how: Alt-click (Mac: Option-click) on the Add Layer Mask icon at the top of the Layers palette to hide the contrast layer behind a black mask (so the effect is hidden from view). With your Foreground color set to white, get the Brush tool **(B)**, choose a medium-sized, soft-edged brush from the Brush Picker in the Tool Options Bar, and paint over his face, hand, and arm to add the high-contrast effect there. Now, lower the brush's Opacity in the Tool Options Bar to 70% (so the effect isn't as intense), then paint over his turban and clothes. This way, you avoid adding the contrast to the blurry background altogether. Lastly, go to the Layers palette and lower the Opacity of this layer until it looks more natural, as shown here at 67%. Now, you can flatten the layers and sharpen it using Unsharp Mask (see Chapter 11. Here, I used Amount: 120, Radius: 1, Threshold: 3) to finish off the effect.

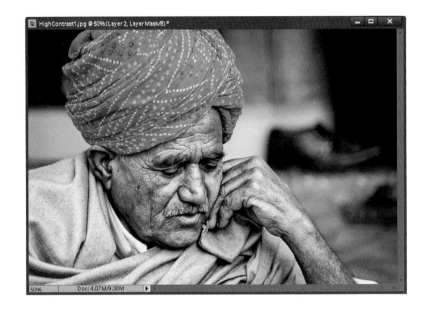

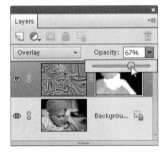

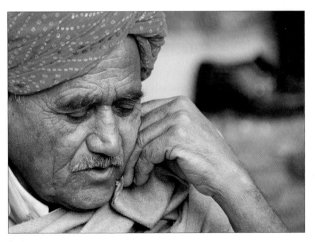

Before

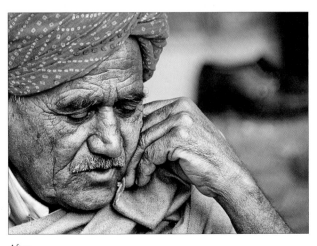

After

If you want that extreme contrast, grungy look, you can create it right within Camera Raw itself by just dragging a few sliders in the Basic panel. If you're going to leave Camera Raw and go to Elements at some point anyway, you should try poppin' some edge sharpening on this puppy. Shots with lots of texture or metal just love a little edge sharpening tossed on them, so give it a try. But let's not get ahead of ourselves—here's the grungy look made easy:

Getting the Grungy, High-Contrast Look Within Camera Raw

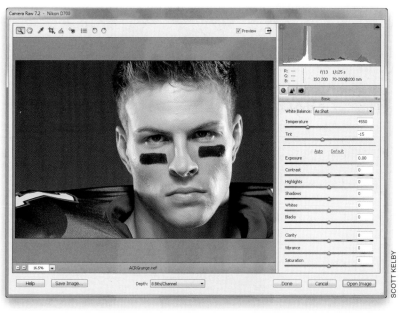

SCOTT KELBY

Step One:

Open a photo in Camera Raw. This is one of those effects that needs the right kind of image for it to look right. Photos with lots of detail, texture, along with anything metallic, and lots of contrast seem to work best (it also works great for sports portraits like this one, cars, and even some landscapes. In other words: I wouldn't apply this effect to a shot of a cute little fuzzy bunny). Here's the original RAW image open in Camera Raw. (*Note:* This effect actually seems to come out better when you run it on RAW images, rather than JPEGs, TIFFs, or PSDs, but it does work on all four.)

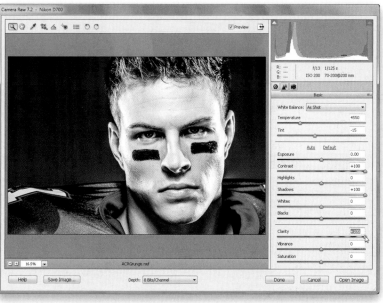

Step Two:

Set these three sliders all at 100: Contrast, Shadows, and Clarity (as shown here). Depending on the photo, this can make it look a little too bright or a little too washed out (his face looks a lot brighter and a bit washed out). So, you might have to tweak the Exposure slider a bit (most likely dragging it to the left to make the overall photo a little darker). I didn't do that here, but I wanted you to be aware, just in case it happens to you.

(Continued)

Step Three:

To keep the photo from looking too washed out in the deepest shadow areas, drag the Blacks slider to the left until the photo looks more balanced (like it does here, where I dragged it over to –54). Also, to "crush" back the highlights (it's part of the look of this high-contrast effect), you're going to drag the Highlights slider all the way to the left to –100. Okay, we're getting close.

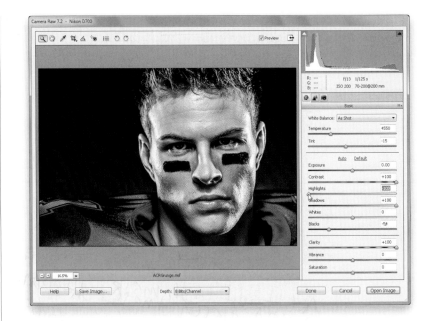

Step Four:

Dragging that Blacks slider over like you did in the previous step generally makes your colors really vivid and saturated, but part of this effect is to intentionally desaturate the image. So, lower the Vibrance amount until it looks desaturated quite a bit (remember, that's part of the look). Here, I lowered it to –64. Lastly, if the image looks a little too dark, you can bring out the brightest highlights by dragging the Whites slider over to the right (as I did here—just a bit—over to +25). You won't do this to every image, but when it needs that little kicker in the highlights, dragging the Whites slider to the right a bit will often do the trick. A before/after is shown on the next page. One more thing: is this image just screamin' for some edge sharpening, or what? (See the next chapter for how to add it.)

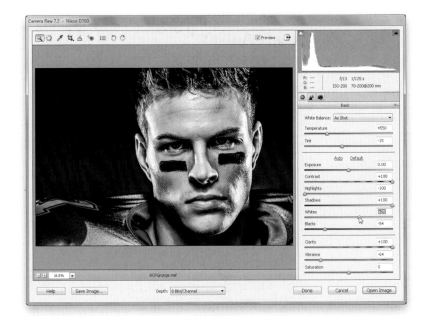

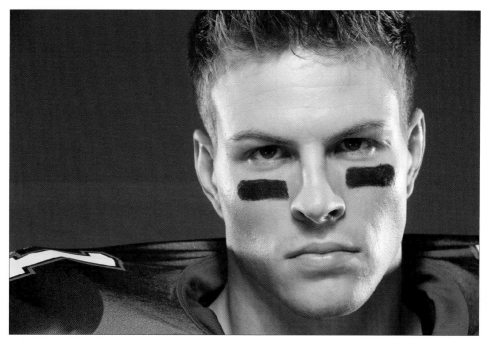

Before

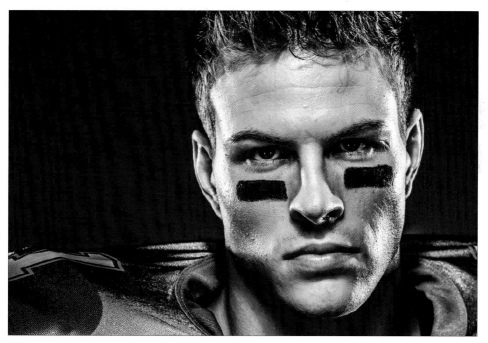

After

Converting to Black and White

There are a few different ways to convert to black and white in Elements. You could simply use the Remove Color enhancement, but that leaves you with kind of a blah result. That's because Elements simply removes the color from the photo and leaves a very bland looking black-and-white image. Plus, there are no settings, so you can't customize your black-and-white image in any way. Here are two great techniques that create a better looking black-and-white and give you plenty of control to really customize the way it looks:

Step One:
The first technique is simple—pretty much one or two clicks and that's it. So, open the color photo you want to convert to black and white (yes, you need to start with a color photo), and then go under the Enhance menu and choose **Convert to Black and White** (as shown here).

Step Two:
When you choose Convert to Black and White, a dialog appears and your photo (behind the dialog) is converted to black and white on the spot (in other words, you get a live preview of your changes). At the top of the dialog is a before and after, showing your color photo on the left, and your black-and-white conversion on the right. Your first step is to choose which style of photo you're converting from the list of styles on the lower-left side of the dialog. These styles are really just preset starting points that are fairly well-suited to each type of photo. The default setting is Scenic Landscape, which is a fairly non-exciting setting. Since I'm generally looking to create high-contrast, black-and-white photos with lots of depth, I recommend the Vivid Landscapes style, which is much punchier. Go ahead and choose that now, just so you can see the difference.

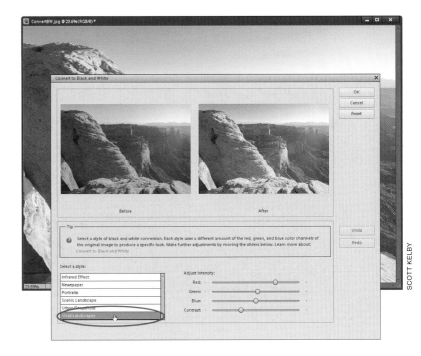

SCOTT KELBY

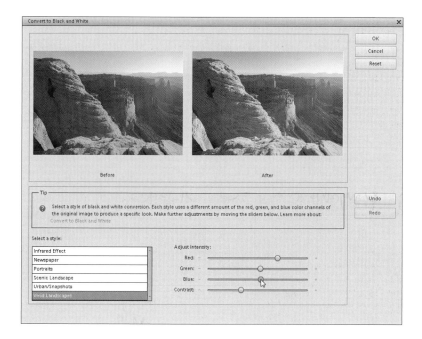

Step Three:

Whether you stay with the default Scenic Landscape, or try my suggested Vivid Landscapes (or any of the other styles to match the subject of your photo), these are just starting places—you'll need to tweak the settings to really match your photo, and that's done by dragging the four Adjust Intensity sliders that appear on the bottom-right side of the dialog. The top three (Red, Green, and Blue) let you tweak ranges of color in your photo. So, for example, if you'd like the rocks darker, you'd drag the Red slider to the left. If you want the sky brighter, which is mostly blue, you'd drag the Blue slider to the right, as shown here.

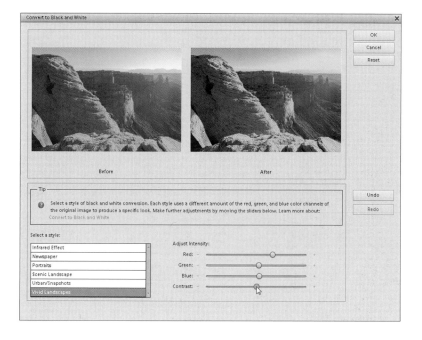

Step Four:

So, basically, you use those three sliders to come up with a mix that looks good to you. You don't have to use these sliders, but if you can't find one of the presets that looks good to you, find one that gets you close, and then use the Red, Green, and Blue sliders to tweak the settings. The fourth slider, Contrast, does just what you'd expect it would—if you drag to the right, it adds contrast (and to the left removes it). I'm very big on high-contrast black-and-white prints, so I wouldn't hesitate to drag this a little to the right just to create even more contrast (so, personally, I'm more likely to start with a preset, like Vivid Landscapes, and then use the Contrast slider, as shown here, than I am to spend much time fooling with the Red, Green, and Blue sliders. But hey, that's just me).

(Continued)

Step Five:

So, that technique isn't too bad and it's quick and easy. But, if you really want some control over creating a killer black-and-white, and have an extra minute or two, then give this second one a try: Start by opening the color photo you want to convert to black and white, then press **D** to set your Foreground and Background colors to their defaults of black and white.

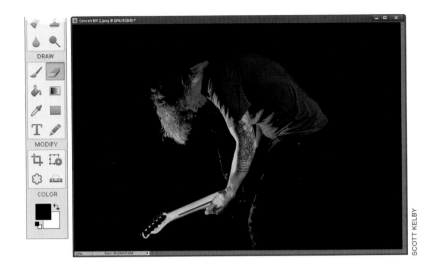

Step Six:

To really appreciate this technique, it wouldn't hurt if you went ahead and did a regular conversion to black and white, just so you can see how lame it is. So, go under the Image menu, under Mode, and choose **Grayscale**. When the Discard Color Information dialog appears, click OK, and behold the some-what lame conversion. Now that we agree it looks pretty bland, press **Ctrl-Z (Mac: Command-Z)** to undo the conversion, so you can try something better.

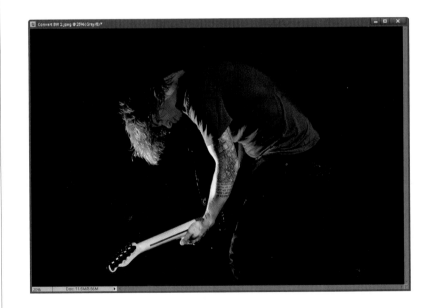

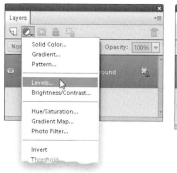

Step Seven:

Go to the top of the Layers palette and choose **Levels** from the Create New Adjustment Layer pop-up menu (it's the half-blue/half-white circle icon). The Levels options will appear in the Adjustments palette and a new layer will be added to your Layers palette named "Levels 1." Press **X** to set your Foreground color to black, then go back to the top of the Layers palette and choose **Gradient Map** from the Create New Adjustment Layer pop-up menu. This brings up the Gradient Map options in the Adjustments palette and adds another layer to the Layers palette (above your Levels 1 layer) named "Gradient Map 1."

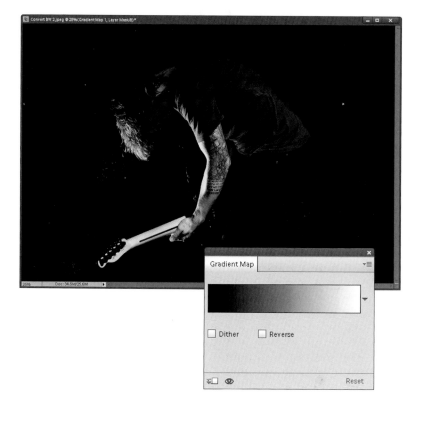

Step Eight:

Just choosing Gradient Map gives you a black-and-white image (and doing just this, this one little step alone, usually gives you a better black-and-white conversion than just choosing Grayscale from the Mode submenu. Freaky, I know). Now, if you don't get a black-to-white gradient, it's probably because your Foreground and Background colors were not set at their defaults of black and white. In that case, click-and-drag the Gradient Map and Levels adjustment layers onto the Trash icon at the top of the palette, press **D**, and then add both adjustment layers again.

(Continued)

Step Nine:

Now, in the Layers palette, click on the Levels 1 layer to bring up the Levels options again. From the Channel pop-up menu at the top of the palette, you can choose to edit individual color channels. So, choose the **Red** color channel.

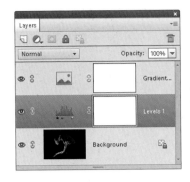

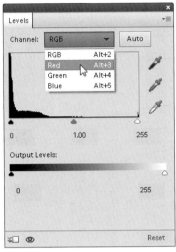

Step 10:

You can now adjust the Red channel, and you'll see the adjustments live on-screen as you tweak your black-and-white photo. (It appears as a black-and-white photo because of the Gradient Map adjustment layer above the Levels 1 layer. Pretty sneaky, eh?) You can drag the middle gray midtone Input Levels slider to the left to open the shadowy areas, especially in the skin, as shown here. You can also try dragging the white highlight Input Levels slider to the left a little, as I did here.

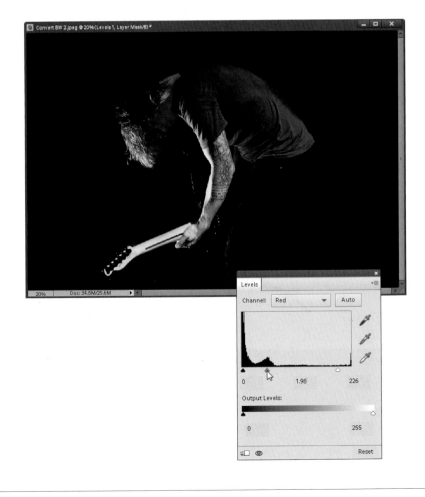

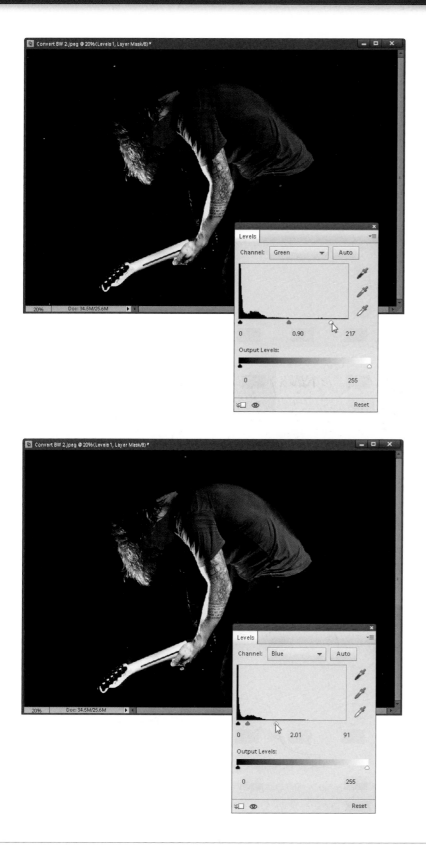

Step 11:

Now, switch to the **Green** channel in the Channel pop-up menu. You can make adjustments here, as well. Try increasing the highlights in the Green channel by dragging the same sliders to the left, as shown here.

Step 12:

Next, choose the **Blue** channel from the pop-up menu, and try increasing the highlights and midtones quite a bit by dragging the Input Levels sliders (the ones that we've been using below the histogram). These adjustments are not standards or suggested settings for every photo; I just experimented by dragging the sliders, and when the photo looked better, I stopped dragging. When the black-and-white photo looks good to you (good contrast, and good shadow and highlight details), just stop dragging.

(Continued)

Step 13:

To complete your conversion, go to the Layers palette, click on the flyout menu at the top right, then choose **Flatten Image** to flatten the adjustment layers into the Background layer. Although your photo looks like a black-and-white photo, technically, it's still in RGB mode, so if you want a grayscale file, go under the Image menu, under Mode, and choose **Grayscale**.

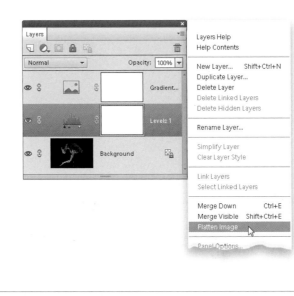

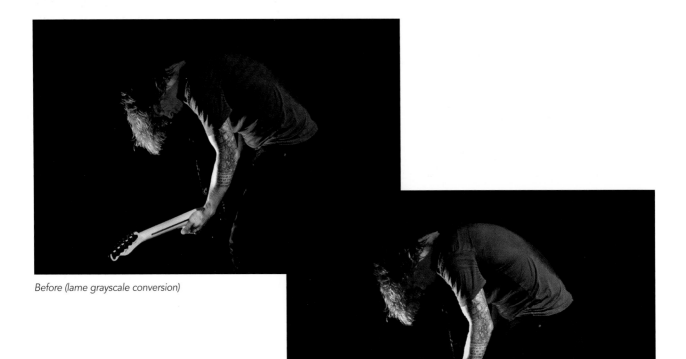

Before (lame grayscale conversion)

After (awesome adjustment layers conversion)

Elements has had a feature to help you stitch multiple photos into a single panoramic photo for years now. As long as you did everything right in the camera (shooting on a tripod with just about every auto feature turned off), Photomerge worked pretty well. However, Photomerge is now so vastly improved that you can pretty much hand-hold your camera without regard to the auto settings, and Photomerge will not only perfectly align the photos, but now it will also seamlessly blend the pieces together, even if the exposure or white balance isn't "on the money." This is very cool stuff.

Panoramas Made Crazy Easy

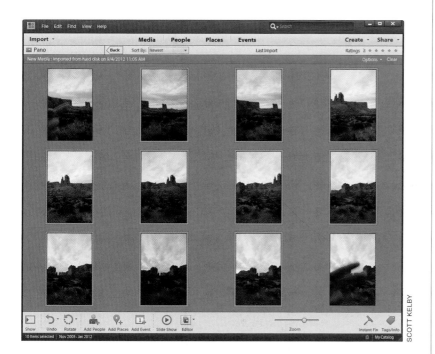

SCOTT KELBY

Step One:

This first thing isn't technically an Elements thing, but if you do it, it sure will make working with panos easier. When you're out shooting, and you're about to shoot a pano, before you shoot your first pano frame, hold your index finger up in front of your lens and take a photo. Then, go ahead and take your pano and right after you shoot your last frame, hold up two fingers in front of your lens and take another photo. Here's where this pays off: When you open all your photos from that day's shoot in the Organzier, you could easily have hundreds of photos (especially if these are vacation photos). As you scroll through, as soon as you see an index finger, you'll know these are your pano photos (by the way, if you have that whole self-loathing thing going on, or if you're a teen, you don't have to use your index finger). Plus, it not only tells you that you shot a pano, it tells you exactly where it starts and where it ends (as seen here). It sounds silly, but if you don't do this, you'll actually miss panos you took, and you'll just kind of wonder, "What was I thinking when I took those?" and you'll scroll right by them. It's happened to me, and so many of my friends, that we now all use this technique, and we never miss a pano. Okay, now press-and-hold the Ctrl (Mac: Command) key and click on each photo thumbnail between your two finger shots (as shown here).

(Continued)

Step Two:

Next, go under the Edit menu, under Photomerge®, and choose **Photo-merge® Panorama** (as shown here).

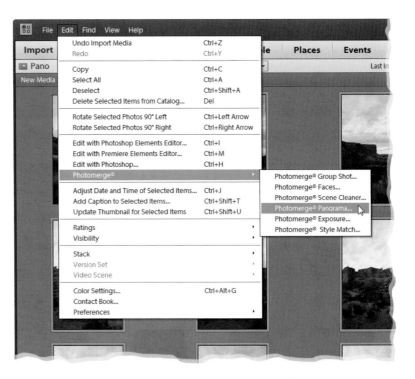

Step Three:

Before you go on and create your pano, here's something to consider: if you just jump over to the Editor and create your pano, when you see it next, it will be a regular 8-bit Photoshop image (in other words, it won't be a RAW image any longer). That's why I like to do some up-front image tweaking, while those images are still in RAW format, before we "bake it" and turn it into a regular PSD file. So, since these are RAW files, they open in Camera Raw when we choose Photomerge Panorama (as shown here). Press **Ctrl-A (Mac: Command-A)** to select all the images you just opened (that way, any changes you make to one image are automatically applied to the rest of the pano frames). Now, let's increase the Exposure (here, I went to +0.10) and Contrast (to +39), pull back the Highlights to –66 to bring back some detail and dimension in the sky, bump the Shadows up to +78, so we can see more detail in the shadow areas, and finally, let's crank the Clarity to +81 and the Vibrance to +24. When you're done, click the Open Images button.

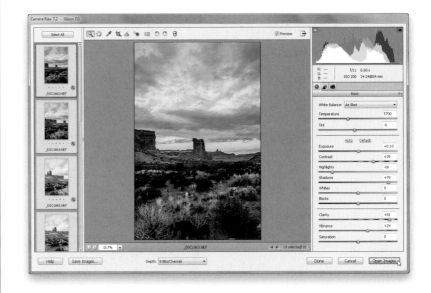

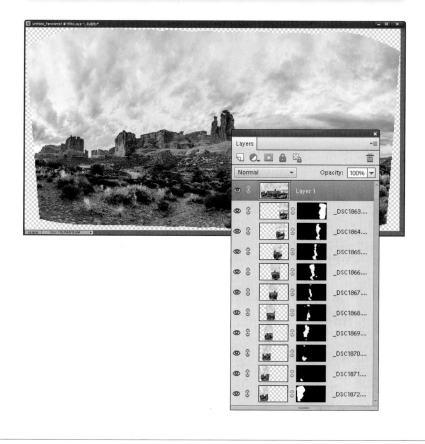

Step Four:

This opens your images in the Editor and brings up the dialog you see here. Since you opened your photos through Camara Raw, the center column will be empty, so click the Add Open Files button. (*Note:* If you opened images from the Organizer, without going through Camera Raw, you'll see them listed in the center column. If you opened your photos directly in the Editor, then go under the Enhance menu, under Photomerge®, and choose **Photomerge® Panorama**. Each will get you to the same place, but I prefer going directly from the RAW images.) Below that center column, leave the Blend Images Together checkbox turned on. There are two other options you may need: (1) If you have lens vignetting (the edges of your images appear darkened), turn on Vignette Removal (as I did here; it will take a little longer to render your pano, but will try to remove the vignetting during the process). (2) If you used a Nikon, Sigma, or Canon fisheye lens, turn on the Geometric Distortion Correction checkbox at the bottom to correct the fisheye distortion.

Step Five:

In the Layout section on the left, the default setting is Auto (as seen in Step Four), and I recommend leaving it set to Auto to get the standard wide pano we're looking for. The five Layout choices below Auto all give you…well…funky looking panos (that's the best description I can give you)—they don't give you that nice wide pano most of us are looking for. So, let's stick with Auto. Click OK, and within a few minutes (depending on how many photos you're using), your pano is seamlessly stitched together (as seen here). You'll see status bars that let you know Elements is aligning and blending your layers to make this mini-miracle happen, and in the Layers palette, you'll see all the masks it created.

(Continued)

Step Six:

To make your pano fit perfectly together, Photomerge has to move and rearrange things in a way that will cause you to have extra canvas around your final pano. That's why the Clean Edges dialog will pop up. With it, you can have Elements try to fill in the blank space based on the image—it does an amazingly good job, although you may have to use the Clone Stamp tool **(S)** to finish it off. Or, you can click No, get the Crop tool **(C)**, and drag out your cropping border (encompassing as much of the pano as possible without leaving any gaps).

Step Seven:

Now for some finishing moves. I would generally create a neutral density gradient filter effect here to darken the sky (we'll look at this in more detail later in this chapter), which is simple to do in Elements. First, choose **Flatten Image** from the Layers palette's flyout menu, then click on the Create New Adjustment Layer icon at the top of the Layers palette and choose **Gradient**. When the Gradient Fill dialog appears, click on the downward-facing arrow to the right of the Gradient thumbnail to bring up the Gradient Picker. Double-click on the second gradient, which is Foreground to Transparent, then turn on the Reverse checkbox (otherwise, it does the opposite of what you want—it darkens the foreground instead of the sky). Now, click on the Gradient thumbnail to bring up the Gradient Editor. To control how far down this gradient extends into your image, click-and-drag the transparent Opacity stop (shown circled here in red) to the left. The farther you drag, the shorter the gradient extends down into your image. I usually like it in the top ¼ of the sky. When you're done, click OK twice, then in the Layers palette, change the blend mode of this layer to **Overlay**.

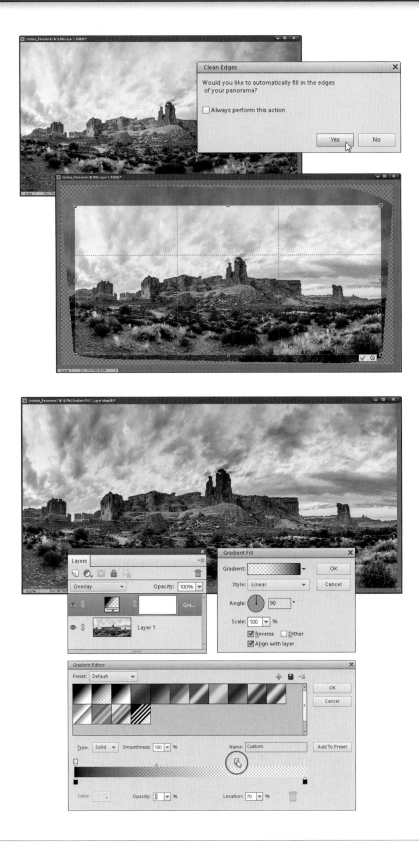

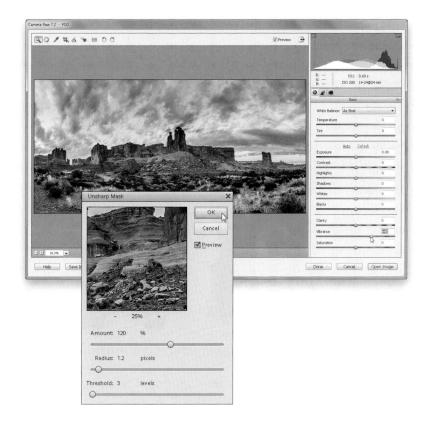

Step Eight:
At this point, to make the color more vibrant, flatten the image again, then save the file as a JPEG, TIFF, or PSD, reopen it in Camera Raw, and increase the Vibrance amount. Finally, you can sharpen it in the Editor by going under the Enhance menu, and choosing **Unsharp Mask**. Pick some nice strong settings (here, I chose Amount: 120, Radius: 1.2, Threshold: 3), and click OK to finish the image (seen below).

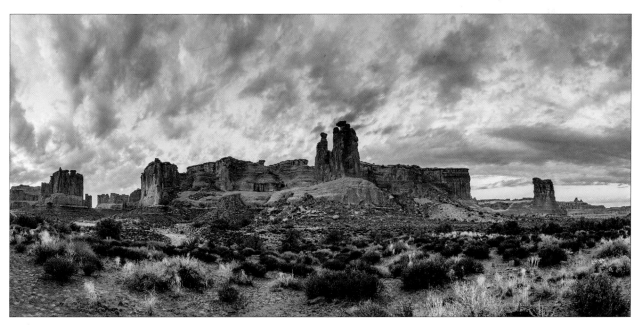

Final

Creating Drama with a Soft Spotlight

This is a great technique that lets you focus attention by using dramatic, soft lighting. The technique I'm showing you here, I learned from famous nature photographer Vincent Versace. I had been getting a similar look by filling a layer with black, making an oval selection, feathering the edges significantly, and then knocking a hole out of the layer, but Vincent's technique, using the Lighting Effects filter, is so much easier that it's just about all I use now.

Step One:
Open the RGB photo to which you want to apply a soft spotlight effect. In this example, I want to focus attention on the woman by darkening the area around her. Next, press **Ctrl-J (Mac: Command-J)** to duplicate the Background layer.

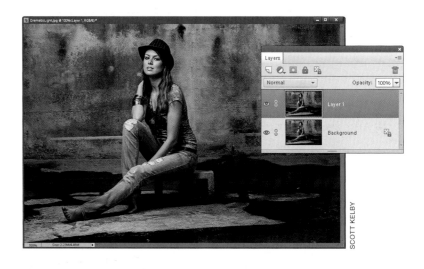

SCOTT KELBY

Step Two:
Go under the Filter menu, under Render, and choose **Lighting Effects**. I have to tell you, if you haven't used this filter before, it's probably because its interface (with all its sliders) looks so complex, but luckily there are built-in presets (Adobe calls them "Styles") that you can choose from, so you can pretty much ignore all those sliders. Once you ignore the sliders, the filter is much less intimidating, and you can really have some fun here. The small preview window on the left side of the dialog shows you the default setting, which is a large oval light coming from the bottom right-hand corner.

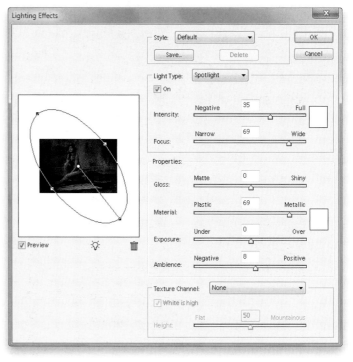

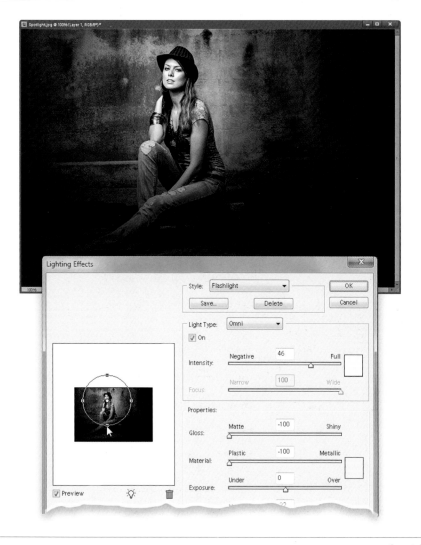

Step Three:
For this effect, we're going to use a very soft, narrow beam, so go under the Style pop-up menu at the top of the dialog (this is where the presets are) and choose **Flashlight**.

Step Four:
Once you choose Flashlight, look at the preview window and you'll see a small spotlight in the center of your image. Click on the center point (inside the circle) and drag the light into the position where you want it. If you want the circle of light a little bit larger, just click on one of the side points and drag outward. When you click OK, the filter applies the effect, darkening the surrounding area and creating the soft spotlight effect you see here.

(Continued)

Step Five:

If the Lighting Effects filter seems too intense, you can remedy it immediately after the fact by lowering the Opacity setting in the Layers palette to reduce the effect of the filter. The lower the setting, the less the intensity of the effect. Then, while in the Layers palette, change the blend mode of this layer to **Darken**, so the Flashlight effect doesn't make the colors seem too saturated.

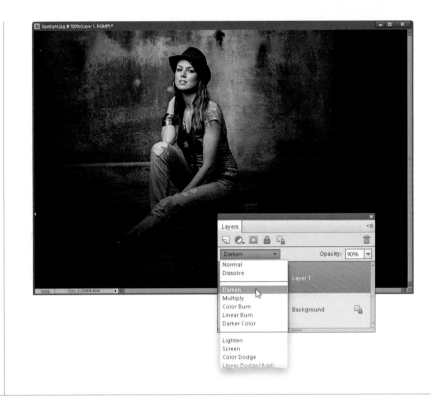

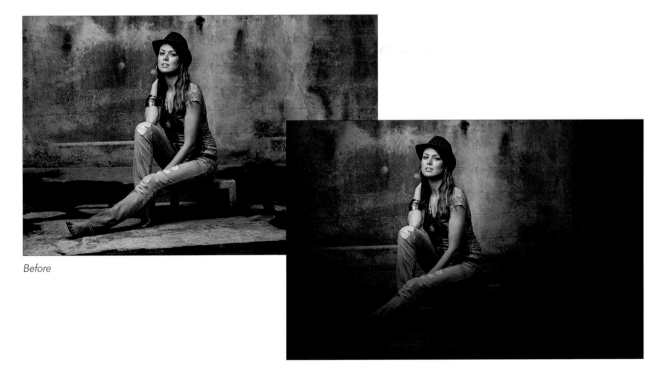

Before

After

If you want to focus attention on something within your image, applying a wide vignette that acts like a soft light is a great way to do this (which is really just an alternative to the previous tutorial or the Vignette Effect in Guided mode). What you're doing is creating a dark border that will burn in the edges of your image. Here's how to do just that:

Burned-In Edge Effect (Vignetting)

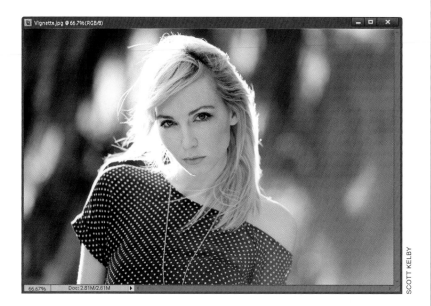

Step One:
Open the photo to which you want to apply a burned-in edge effect. Just so you know, what we're doing here is focusing attention through the use of light—we're burning in all the edges of the photo (not just the corners, like lens vignetting, which we learned how to fix in Chapter 6 and I usually try to avoid), leaving the visual focus in the center of the image.

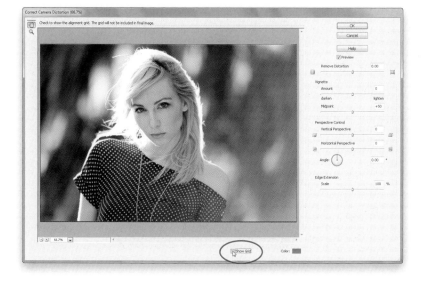

Step Two:
Go under the Filter menu, and choose **Correct Camera Distortion**. By default, when your image opens in the Correct Camera Distortion dialog, it has an annoying grid over it, so start by turning off the Show Grid checkbox beneath the bottom right of the preview area.

(Continued)

Step Three:

In the Vignette section near the top, you're going to drag the Amount slider to the left, and as you drag left, you'll start to see vignetting appear in the corners of your photo. But since it's just in the corners, it looks like the bad kind of vignetting, not the good kind. You'll need to make the vignetting look more like a soft spotlight falling on your subject.

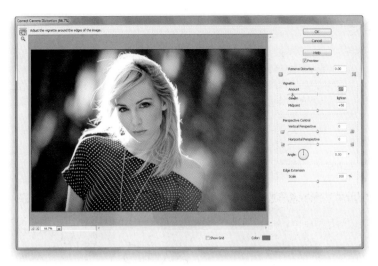

Step Four:

To do just that, drag the Midpoint slider quite a bit to the left, which increases the size of the vignetting and creates a soft, pleasing effect that is very popular in portraiture, or anywhere you want to draw attention to your subject. That's it!

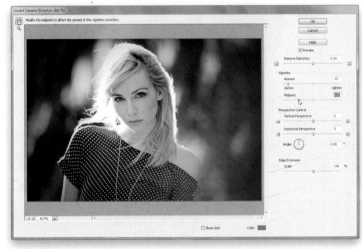

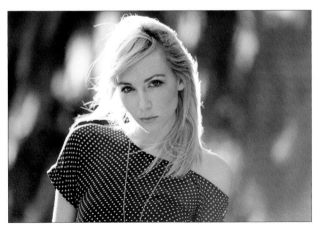

Before

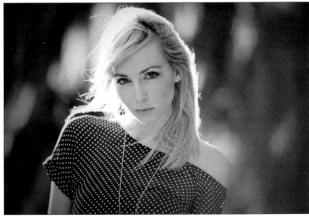

After

Using Color for Emphasis

This is a popular technique for focusing attention by the use of color (or really, it's more like the use of less color—if everything's in black and white, anything that's in color will immediately draw the viewer's eye). As popular as this technique is, it's absolutely a breeze to create. Here's how:

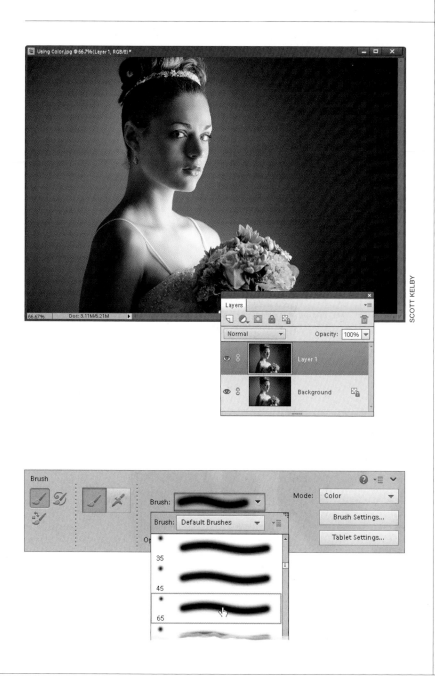

SCOTT KELBY

Step One:
Open a photo containing an object(s) you want to emphasize through the use of color. Go under the Layer menu, under New, and choose **Layer via Copy** (or just press **Ctrl-J [Mac: Command-J]**). This will duplicate the Background layer onto its own layer (Layer 1).

Step Two:
Press **B** to get the Brush tool from the Toolbox and choose a medium, soft-edged brush from the Brush Picker in the Tool Options Bar (just click on the Brush thumbnail to open the Picker). Also in the Tool Options Bar, change the Mode pop-up menu to **Color** for the Brush tool.

(Continued)

Step Three:
Set your Foreground color to black by pressing the letter **D** and begin painting on the photo. As you paint, the color in the photo will be removed. The goal is to paint away the color from all the areas *except* the areas you want emphasized with color.

TIP: Fixing Mistakes
If you make a mistake while painting away the color or later decide that there was something else that you really wanted to keep in color, just switch to the Eraser tool by pressing the **E key**, paint over the "mistake" area, and the original color will return as you paint. (What you're really doing here is erasing part of the top layer, which is now mostly black and white, and as you erase, it reveals the original layer, which is still in full color.)

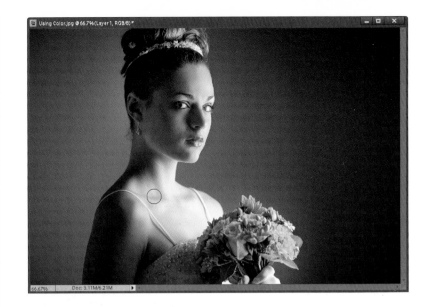

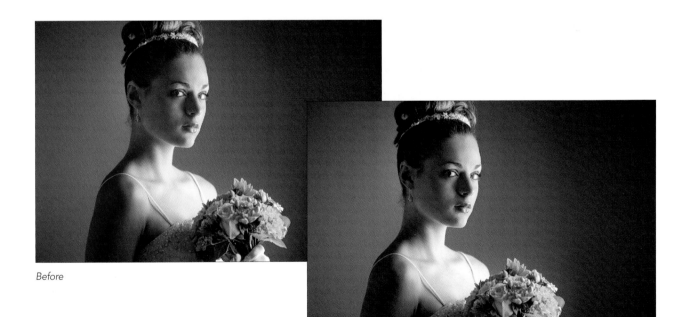

Before

After

Matching Photo Styles

Now that I've given you some special effects you can apply to your images, I'll show you a feature in Elements that lets you match the style of one photo to another. For example, let's say you see a photo that has a really cool color treatment. Well, you can use the Photomerge Style Match feature to take the "look" from that photo and apply it to your own. Here's how it works:

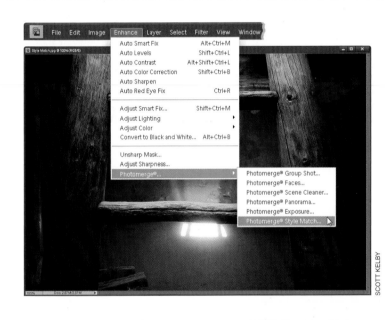

SCOTT KELBY

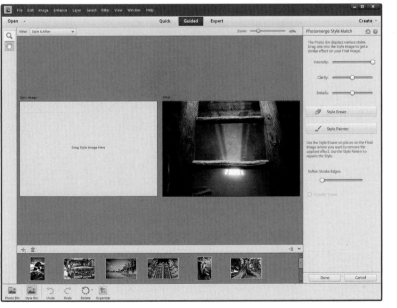

Step One:
Open the photo you'd like to add an effect to, then go under the Enhance menu, under Photomerge®, and choose **Photomerge® Style Match** to begin.

Step Two:
This screen is fairly consistent with the other Photomerge features in Elements—on the left you pick a source image, and on the right is your final image. In this case, we need to choose the image that we want to style our photo (the photo on the right) after. Elements comes with a few style images already, and you'll find them in the Style Bin at the bottom of the window.

(Continued)

Step Three:

You can also add your own style images. Let's say you have a cool sepia-tinted photo that you'd like to use. Just click on the small green plus icon at the top left of the Style Bin. Then, choose where you'd like to import the photo from (it could be the Organizer, or any place on your hard drive). Once you've imported the photo, it shows up at the end of the Style Bin images.

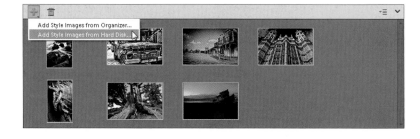

Step Four:

After you've decided which photo you want to style your photo after, drag it from the Style Bin to the left side of the window under Style Image (I used one of the black-and-white included photos in my example). You'll see the image on the right change to include some style elements from this photo. *Note:* If you want to see your After photo larger, just click on the View pop-up menu at the top left of the preview area, and choose **After Only**, then zoom in with the Zoom tool or by using the Zoom slider at the top right of the preview area.

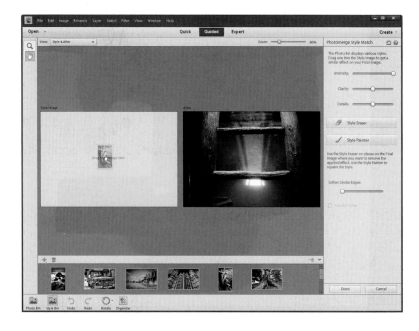

Step Five:

Now, you may be totally happy with the way your photo looks. If so, just click Done. But if you want to experiment a little, Elements has some settings on the right side that'll let you change the look and feel of your photo. For starters, the first thing I always do is turn on the Transfer Tones checkbox at the bottom. I know it's at the bottom, and you typically don't think to start there, but it's one of the key settings for me whenever I'm using this feature (especially if my style image is black and white or sepia).

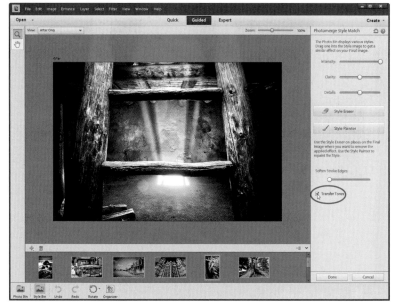

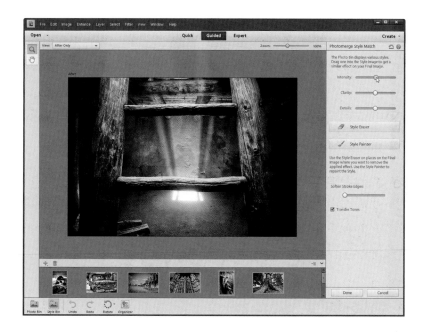

Step Six:

Next, we'll move to the top to the Intensity slider. This one is like an opacity slider. In our black-and-white example, reducing the intensity leaves us with a semi-saturated photo. As you move it all the way to the left, the style image eventually has no effect on the final.

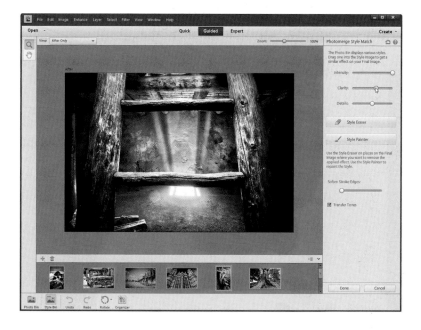

Step Seven:

The next slider, Clarity, works like a contrast slider. The further you move it toward the right the more contrasty the photo becomes. If you move it too far to the left, then the photo becomes kinda flat and loses a lot of the snap that it had before (which is why I rarely move it to the left).

(Continued)

Step Eight:

Details is like an ultra-contrast/sharpening slider. It takes whatever was dark and pushes it toward black. Then it takes whatever was lighter, and pushes it toward white. Be careful with this one, though. It tends to have some really strong effects, even if you just move it in small amounts (as seen here).

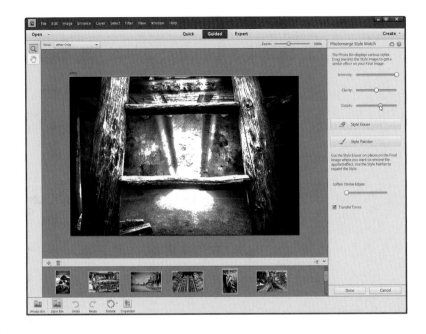

Step Nine:

Below the sliders are two buttons: Style Eraser and Style Painter. Click on Style Eraser if you want to erase the style from a specific area of the photo, then click on Style Painter if you wanted to paint it back in. These are brushes, similar to what you have in Expert mode, so you can change the Size and Opacity of each one. When you're done, just click the Done button at the bottom and then click Expert at the top of the window to return to Expert mode. At that point, your photo is on a layer just like any other photo and you're free to edit and retouch like usual.

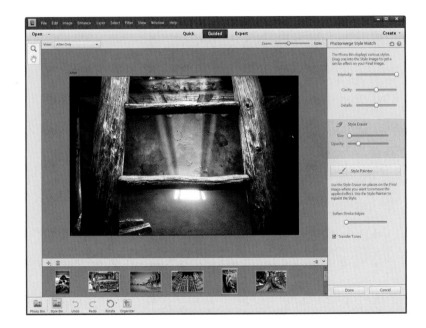

One of the most popular lens filters for outdoor photographers is the neutral density gradient filter, because often (especially when shooting scenery, like sunsets) you wind up with a bright sky and a dark foreground. A neutral density gradient lens filter reduces the exposure in the sky by a stop or two, while leaving the ground unchanged (the top of the filter is gray, and it graduates down to transparent at the bottom). Well, if you forgot to use your ND gradient filter when you took the shot, you can create your own ND gradient effect in Photoshop Elements.

Neutral Density Gradient Filter

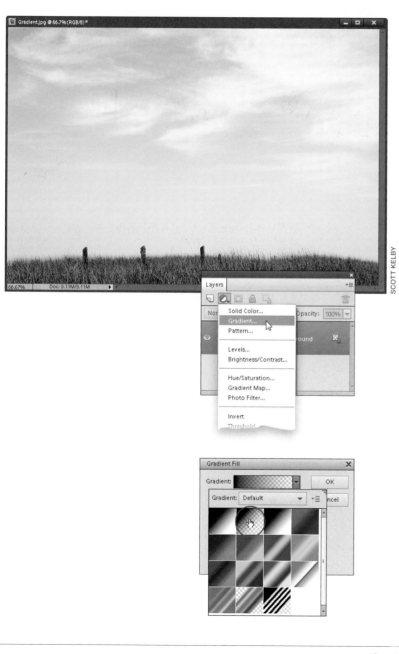

SCOTT KELBY

Step One:
Open the photo (preferably a landscape) where you exposed for the ground, which left the sky too light. Press the letter **D** to set your Foreground color to black. Then, go to the Layers palette and choose **Gradient** from the Create New Adjustment Layer pop-up menu (it's the half-white/half-blue circle icon) at the top of the palette.

Step Two:
When the Gradient Fill dialog appears, click on the little, black, downward-facing arrow to the right of the Gradient thumbnail to bring up the Gradient Picker. Double-click on the second gradient in the list, which is the gradient that goes from Foreground to Transparent. Don't click OK yet.

(Continued)

Step Three:

By default, this puts a dark area on the ground (rather than the sky), so turn on the Reverse checkbox to reverse the gradient, putting the dark area of your gradient over the sky and the transparent part over the land. Your image will look pretty awful at this point, but you'll fix that in the next step, so just click OK.

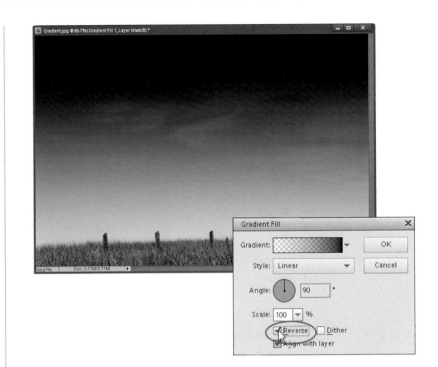

Step Four:

To make this gradient blend in with your photo, go to the Layers palette and change the blend mode of this adjustment layer from Normal to **Overlay**. This darkens the sky, but it gradually lightens until it reaches land, and then it slowly disappears. So, how does it know where the ground is? It doesn't. It puts a gradient across your entire photo, so in the next step, you'll basically show it where the ground is.

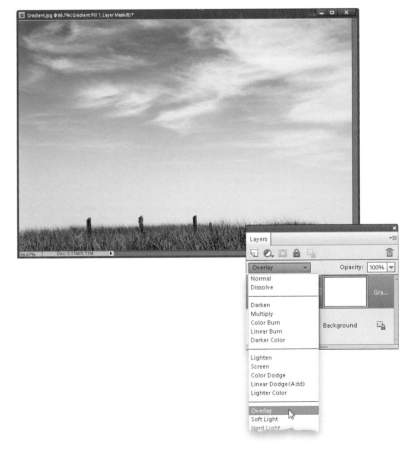

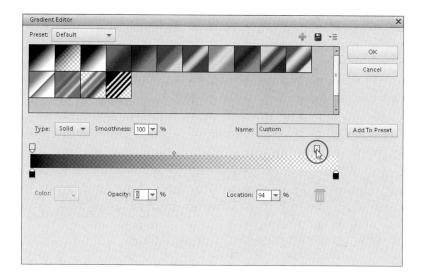

Step Five:

In the Layers palette, double-click on the thumbnail for the Gradient adjustment layer to bring up the Gradient Fill dialog again. To control how far down the darkening will extend from the top of your photo, just click once on the Gradient thumbnail at the top of the dialog. This brings up the Gradient Editor. Grab the top-right transparent Opacity stop above the gradient ramp near the center of the dialog and drag it to the left. The darkening will "roll up" from the bottom of your photo, so keep dragging to the left until only the sky is affected, and then click OK in the Gradient Editor.

Step Six:

By default, the gradient you choose fills the entire image area, smoothly transitioning from a dark gray at the top center to transparent at the very bottom. It's a smooth, "soft-step" gradient. However, if you want a quicker change from black to transparent (a hard step between the two), you can lower the Scale amount in the Gradient Fill dialog.

(Continued)

Step Seven:

Also, if the photo you're working on doesn't have a perfectly straight horizon line, you might have to use the Angle control by clicking on the line in the center of the Angle circle and dragging slowly in the direction that your horizon is tilted. This literally rotates your gradient, which enables you to have it easily match the angle of your horizon. When it looks good to you, click OK to complete the effect.

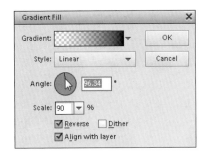

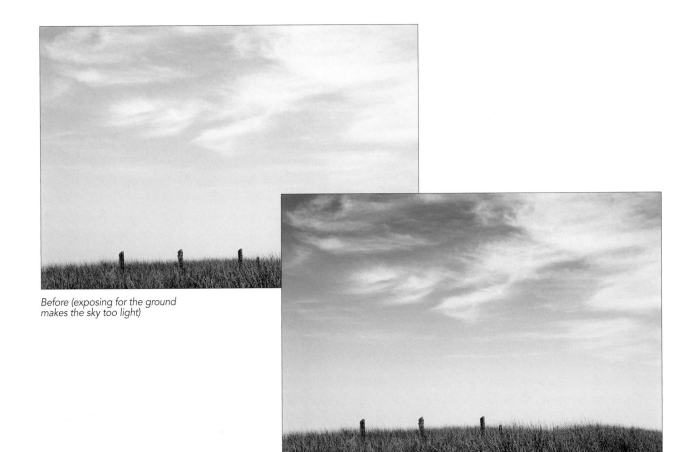

Before (exposing for the ground makes the sky too light)

After (the ground is the same, but the sky is now bluer and more intense)

Here's a quick and easy way to get the wildly popular Instagram app look. Of course, there isn't just one "look," because Instagram has like 15 different ones, but this will at least take you in the right direction. One more thing: I know you're thinking, "Do people really want to learn how to do phone app looks in Elements?" Yup. It's one of the most-requested effects people ask to learn (don't get me started). Luckily, it's easy, and the looks are actually based on classic darkroom effects, so that can't be a bad thing.

Getting the Instagram Look

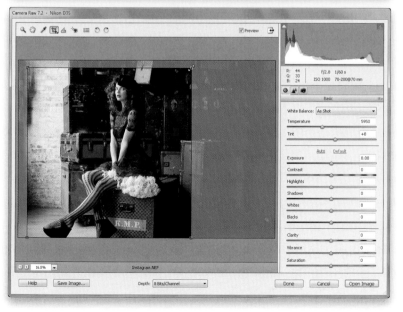

SCOTT KELBY

Step One:

Start by opening an image in Camera Raw. One of the trademark looks of the Instagram app is its square cropping ratio, so let's start there. Click-and-hold on the Crop tool in the toolbar at the top and a list of cropping ratios appears. Choose the 1 to 1 ratio (as shown here), which gives you a square crop.

Step Two:

Drag your cropping border out over the part of the image you want to have the effect (in this case, it's pretty obvious which part of the image we should keep). Once the crop is where you want it, just press the **Enter (Mac: Return) key** to lock in your square crop. From here on out, it's pretty darn easy—I'll give you some sliders to set, a couple of minor little moves, and you're there. Let's do it.

(Continued)

Special Effects for Photographers | Chapter 10 | 363 ◀

Step Three:

Another trademark part of the Instagram look is that the images have very flat contrast (after all, these are imitating some vintage camera looks), so start by dragging the Contrast slider all the way to the left to –100. Then, go ahead and crank up the Vibrance a bunch to +100. Now, we'll add a little contrast back in by dragging the Whites to the right to increase the very brightest highlights (here, I dragged over to +55), and bring some color back to the darkest shadow areas by dragging the Blacks slider to the left (here, I dragged it over to –70). At this point, the photo looks kind of yellowish. Not for long, though. Click Open Image to open the image in the Editor.

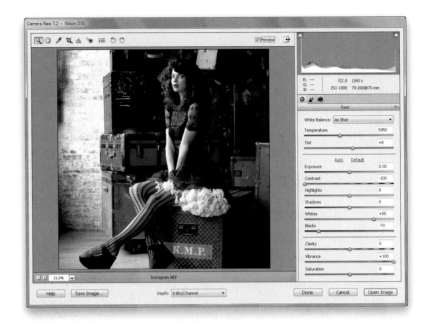

Step Four:

Next, go under the Enhance menu, under Adjust Lighting, and choose **Levels**. We're going to use some different settings in Levels than you may be used to. Under the Channel pop-up menu, you'll see you have the choice of adjusting the Red, Green, or Blue channels. Don't worry, though, even if you've never used Levels this way before, you'll absolutely be able to do this, since we pretty much use the same settings all the time. So, first, from the Channel pop-up menu, choose **Green**. Then, grab the gray Input Levels slider beneath the histogram and drag it to the left to 1.51 (as shown here) to bump up the greens. See, that was easy, eh?

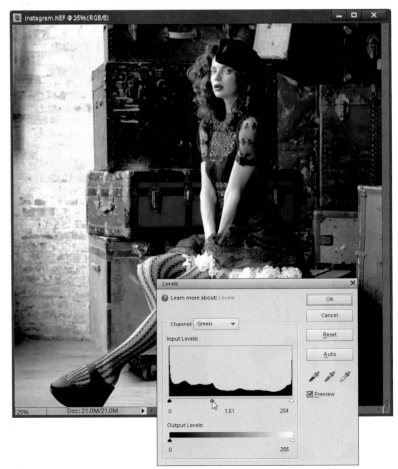

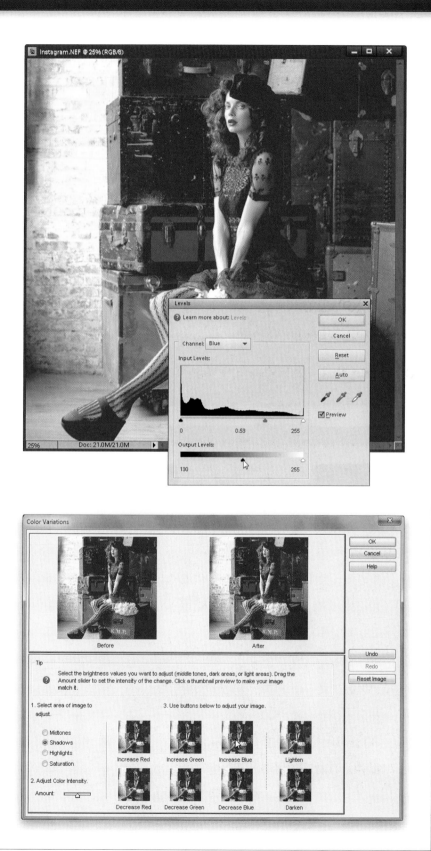

Step Five:

Now that you've got the hang of adjusting the Levels this way, choose **Blue** from the Channel pop-up menu. Grab the same gray middle slider, but this time drag it to the right to 0.53. Then, go to the bottom of the dialog and drag the black Output Levels slider on the left to the right to around 130 (as shown here). This gives the image more of a teal-and-yellowish feel. When you're done, click OK to close the Levels dialog.

TIP: Add Grain for a Film-Like Look

One of the trademarks of the Instagram effect is a grainy look, and you can always hop into Guided mode and apply the Old Fashioned Photo effect to the image. But, instead of using all of the settings, just click on the Add Texture button.

Step Six:

Next, go under the Enhance menu again, under Adjust Color, and choose **Color Variations**. This opens a cool dialog that just lets you click on a few versions of the photo we like. But, you can pretty much follow a recipe for the Instagram effect here. First, we want to add some yellow to the brightest parts of the photo (high-lights), so click on the Highlights radio button at the bottom left, and then click on the Decrease Blue image thumbnail twice. Then, we want to add some blue into the shadows, so click on the Shad-ows radio button, and then click on the Increase Blue image thumbnail twice (as shown here). Click OK to close the dialog and apply the effect.

(Continued)

Step Seven:

Now, we're going to add a fake border. Press **Ctrl-A (Mac: Command-A)** to select the entire photo, then go under the Select menu, under Modify, and choose **Border**. For a low-resolution photo, enter a Width setting of 10 pixels in the Border Selection dialog, or enter around 40 pixels for a higher resolution photo like this one, and click OK. This creates a selected border around the edge of your image. Now, we just need to fill it with a color. Instagram gives you the choice between black or white. I usually like black, so just press the letter **D** to set your Foreground color to black, then press **Alt-Backspace (Mac: Option-Delete)** to fill the selected area with black. Continue pressing Alt-Backspace and the border will get darker and thicker (I pressed it four times here). When you're done, press **Ctrl-D (Mac: Command-D)** to Deselect.

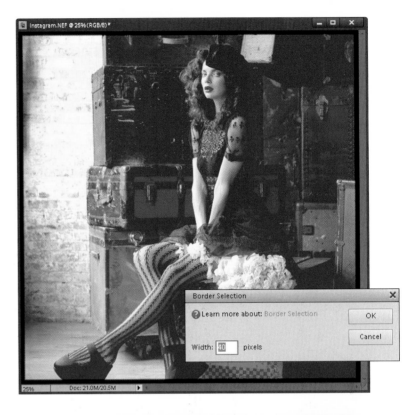

Step Eight:

That's it. If you want a variation on the look we've created, in Step Four, after choosing the Green channel, try dragging the gray Input Levels slider to the right instead of to the left to add a red tint to the photo instead. Then, in Step Five, after choosing the Blue channel, drag only the black Output Levels slider to around 65 (as seen here) and you'll have a whole different style, but one that still has that old look to it.

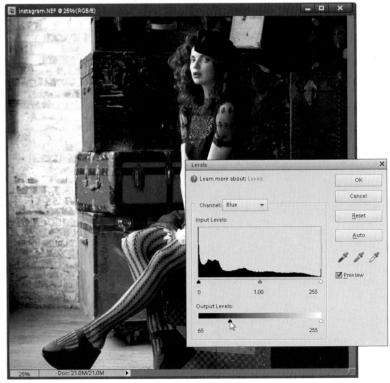

The duotone tinting look is all the rage right now, but creating a real two-color duotone that will separate in just two colors on press is a bit of a chore. However, if you're outputting to an inkjet printer, or to a printing press as a full-color job, then you don't need all that complicated stuff—you can create a fake duotone that looks at least as good (if not better).

Fake Duotone

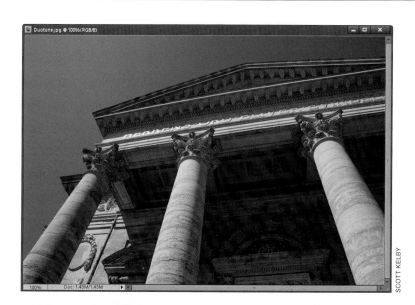

SCOTT KELBY

©ISTOCKPHOTO/SHERWIN MCGEHEE

Step One:

Open the color RGB photo that you want to convert into a duotone (again, I'm calling it a duotone, but we're going to stay in RGB mode the whole time). Now, the hard part of this is choosing which color to make your duotone. I always see other people's duotones, and think, "Yeah, that's the color I want!" but when I click on the Foreground color swatch and try to create a similar color in the Color Picker, it's always hit or miss (usually miss). That's why you'll want to know this next trick.

Step Two:

If you can find another duotone photo that has a color you like, you're set. So, I usually go to a stock photo website (like iStockphoto.com) and search for "duo-tones." When I find one I like, I return to Elements, press I to get the Color Picker tool, click-and-hold anywhere within my image area, and then (while keeping the mouse button held down) I drag my cursor outside Elements and onto the photo in my web browser to sample the color I want. Now, mind you, I did not and would not take a single pixel from someone else's photo—I'm just sampling a color.

(Continued)

Step Three:

Return to your image in Elements. Go to the Layers palette and click on the Create a New Layer icon at the top of the palette. Then, press **Alt-Backspace (Mac: Option-Delete)** to fill this new blank layer with your sampled color. The color will fill your image area, hiding your photo, but we'll fix that.

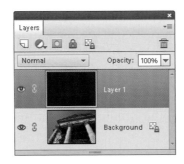

Step Four:

While still in the Layers palette, change the blend mode of this sampled color layer to **Color**.

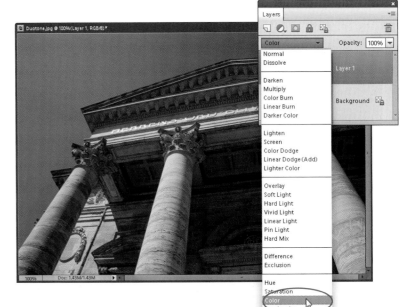

Step Five:

If your duotone seems too dark, you can lessen the effect by clicking on the Background layer, and then going under the Enhance menu, under Adjust Color, and choosing **Remove Color**. This removes the color from your RGB photo without changing its color mode, while lightening the overall image. Pretty sneaky, eh?

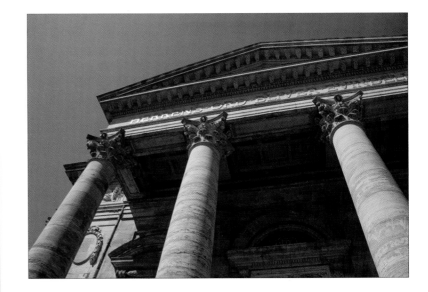

There's a big difference between digital noise and film grain. Digital noise (those red, green, and blue dots that appear when shooting at high ISOs) is what we want to avoid (or, at least, make less noticeable), because it ruins the image. However, simulating the look of traditional film grain (which doesn't have colored dots) is really popular. There are third-party plug-ins you can buy that specialize in recreating it, but I still do it myself, right in Elements (but I don't use the lame Film Grain filter, which to me never actually looks like film grain, or the Add Texture button in the Old Fashioned Photo effect in Guided mode, which adds those colored dots). Here's what I do:

Simulating Film Grain

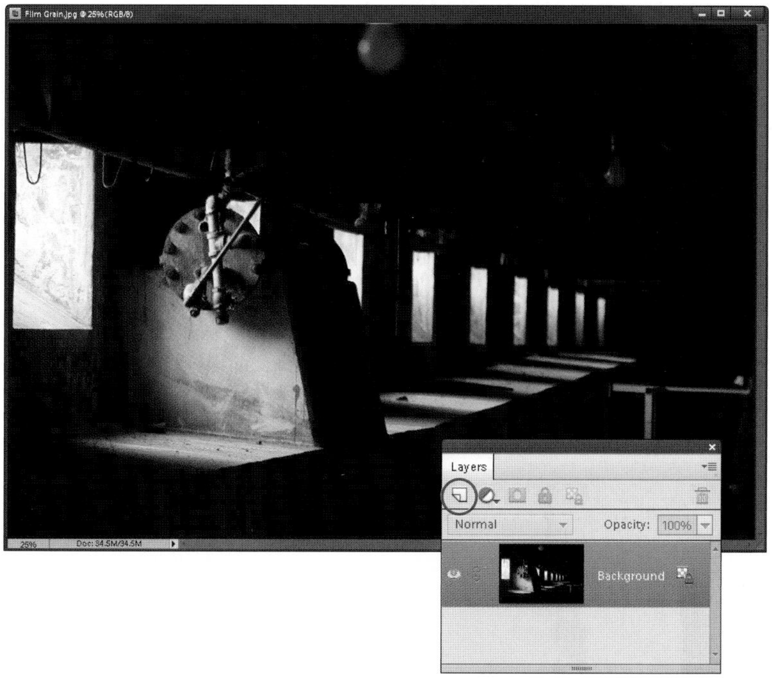

SCOTT KELBY

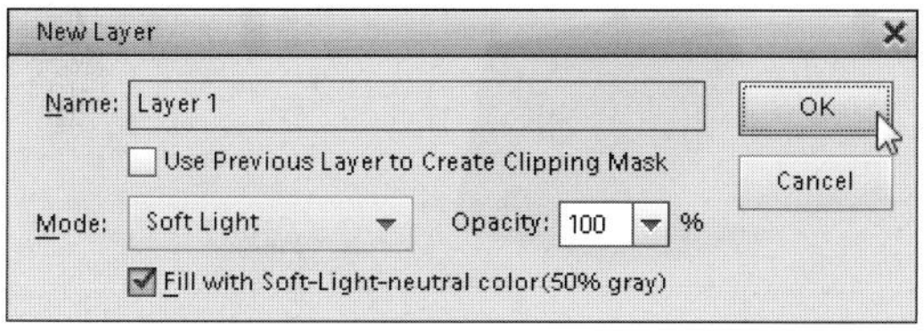

Step One:
Open the photo that you want to add a film grain look to. Go to the Layers palette and Alt-click (Mac: Option-click) on the Create a New Layer icon at the top of the palette to access the New Layer dialog. When the dialog appears, choose **Soft Light** from the Mode pop-up menu. When you choose Soft Light, you'll see the Fill with Soft-Light-Neutral Color (50% Gray) option (right under the Mode pop-up menu) is now available. Turn on its checkbox and click OK.

(Continued)

Step Two:

This creates a new blank layer filled with gray, but because you set the Mode to Soft Light first, this layer will be see-through. So, if it's see-through, why did we need it in the first place? Well, it's because some filters in Elements won't run on an empty, transparent layer (you'd get a "there's nothing there" warning). So, this way, it fools the filter into working, and then we can not only apply the filter to a transparent layer, we can control it after the fact. Sneaky. I know.

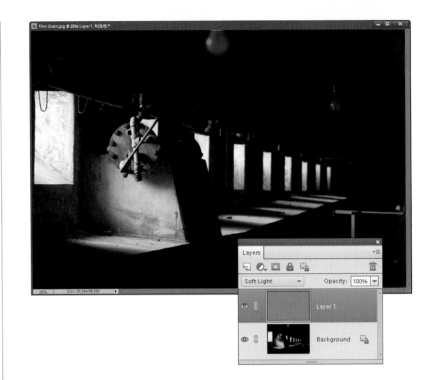

Step Three:

Now, go under the Filter menu, under Noise, and choose **Add Noise**. When the Add Noise filter dialog appears, we want to make sure that the noise we add doesn't have little red, green, and blue dots, so first choose Gaussian as your Distribution method, then turn on the Monochromatic checkbox at the bottom. Now, lower your Amount to around 4% (or 5% for 12-megapixel images), then click OK. This applies a noise pattern to your gray layer, and since this layer is transparent, you now see this film-grain-like look on your photo (if you don't see it right away—zoom in to 50% or 100%).

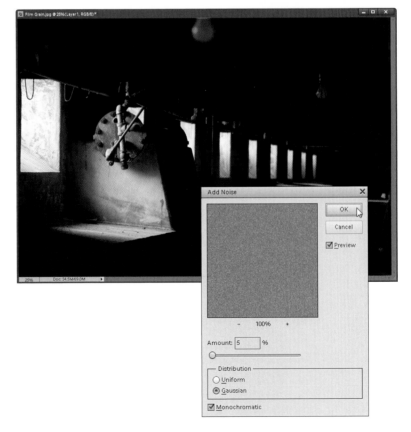

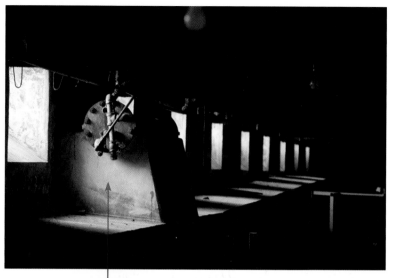

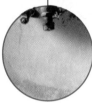

Step Four:
If the simulated film grain effect looks a bit too heavy, you can lower the Opacity of this noise layer in the Layers palette, until it blends in nicely (you are supposed to actually see the noise). Also, if you're going to be making a print of this image, let the grain be a little heavier onscreen, because when you print it, much of that grain will be hidden in the printing process. So, if I know I'm going to be printing, I go a little heavier with the Opacity amount, or even go back and redo it with a higher Amount setting (like 5% or 6%, which I did for this example) in the Add Noise filter. If you really want to make the noise more apparent (for effect), in the Layers palette, change the layer blend mode of this layer to Overlay (also done here), and it will become much more pronounced (again, don't forget you can control it afterward using the Opacity slider on that layer). By the way, Overlay mode supports the whole "gray is transparent" trick, too! That's it—simulated film grain made easy.

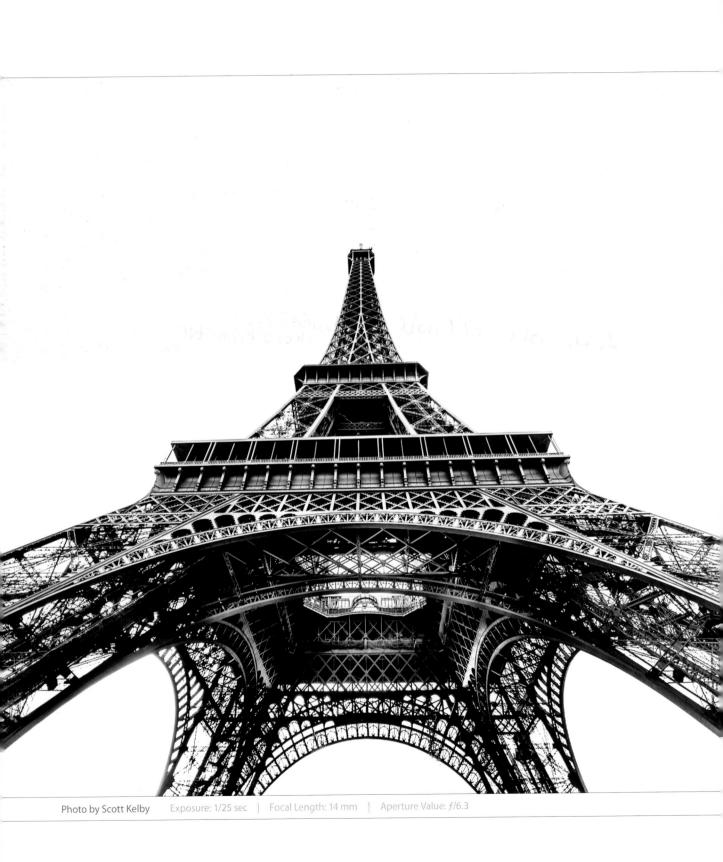

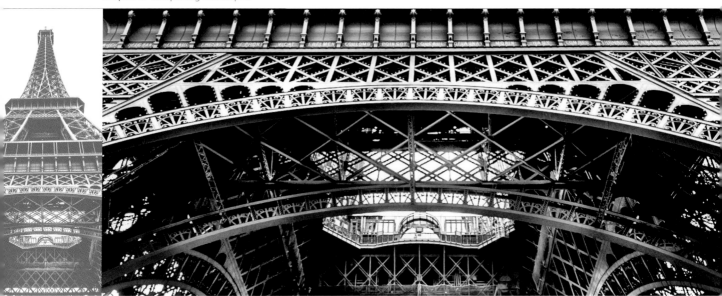

SHARPEN YOUR TEETH
sharpening techniques

I had two really good song titles to choose from for this chapter: "Sharpen Your Teeth" by Ugly Casanova or "Sharpen Your Sticks" by The Bags. Is it just me, or at this point in time, have they totally run out of cool band names? Back when I was a kid (just a few years ago, mind you), band names made sense. There were The Beatles, and The Turtles, and The Animals, and The Monkees, and The Flesh Eating Mutant Zombies, and The Carnivorous Flesh Eating Vegetarians, and The Bulimic Fresh Salad Bar Restockers, and names that really made sense. But, "The Bags?" Unless this is a group whose members are made up of elderly women from Yonkers, I think it's totally misnamed. You see, when I was a kid, when a band was named The Turtles, its members looked and acted like turtles. That's what made it great (remember their hit single "Peeking Out of My Shell," or who could forget "Slowly Crossing a Busy Highway" or my favorite "I Got Hit Crossing a Busy Highway"?). But today, you don't have to look ugly to be in a band named Ugly Casanova, and I think that's just wrong. It's a classic bait-and-switch. If I were in a band (and I am), I would name it something that reflects the real makeup of the group, and how we act. An ideal name for our band would be The Devastatingly Handsome Super Hunky Guys with Six-Pack Abs (though our fans would probably just call us TDHSHGWSPA for short). I could picture us playing at large 24-hour health clubs and Gold's Gyms, and other places where beautiful people (like ourselves) gather to high-five one another on being beautiful. Then, as we grew in popularity, we'd have to hire a manager. Before long, he would sit us down and tell us that we're living a lie, and that TDHSHGWSPA is not really the right name for our band, and he'd propose something along the lines of Muscle Bound Studs Who Are Loose With Money, or more likely, The Bags.

Basic Sharpening

After you've color corrected your photos and right before you save your files, you'll definitely want to sharpen them. I sharpen every digital camera photo I take, either to help bring back some of the original crispness that gets lost during the correction process, or to help fix a photo that's slightly out of focus. Either way, I haven't met a digital camera (or scanned) photo that didn't need a little sharpening. Here's a basic technique for sharpening the entire photo:

Step One:

Open the photo that you want to sharpen. Because Elements displays your photo in different ways at different magnifications, choosing the right magnification (also called the zoom amount) for sharpening is critical. Because today's digital cameras produce such large-sized files, it's now pretty much generally accepted that the proper magnification to view your photos during sharpening is 50%. If you look up in your image window's title bar, or down in the bottom-left corner of the window, it displays the current percentage of zoom (shown circled here in red). The quickest way to get to a 50% magnification is to press **Ctrl-+** (plus sign; **Mac: Command-+**) or **Ctrl--** (minus sign; **Mac: Command--**) to zoom the magnification in or out.

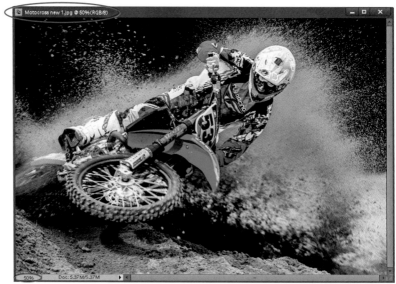

Step Two:

Once you're viewing your photo at 50% size, go under the Enhance menu and choose **Unsharp Mask.** (If you're familiar with traditional darkroom techniques, you probably recognize the term "unsharp mask" from when you would make a blurred copy of the original photo and an "unsharp" version to use as a mask to create a new photo whose edges appeared sharper.)

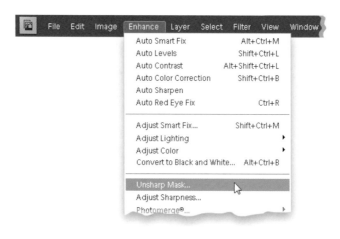

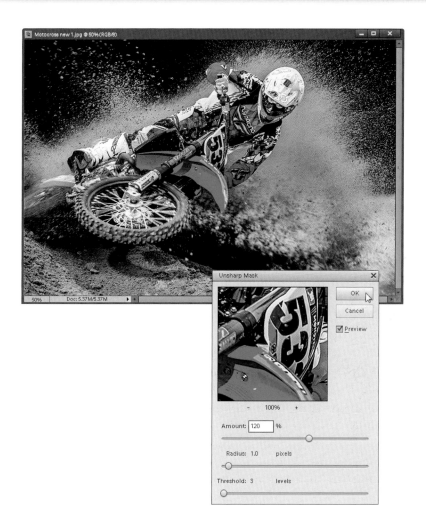

Step Three:

When the Unsharp Mask dialog appears, you'll see three sliders. The Amount slider determines the amount of sharpening applied to the photo; the Radius slider determines how many pixels out from the edge that the sharpening will affect; and the Threshold slider determines how different a pixel must be from the surrounding area before it's considered an edge pixel and sharpened by the filter. Threshold works the opposite of what you might think—the lower the number, the more intense the sharpening effect. So, what numbers do you enter? I'll give you some great starting points on the following pages, but for now, we'll just use these settings: Amount: 120%, Radius: 1, and Threshold: 3. Click OK and the sharpening is applied to the photo.

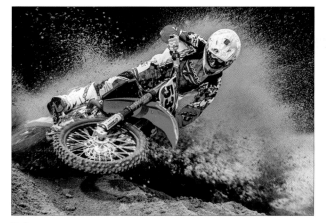

Before

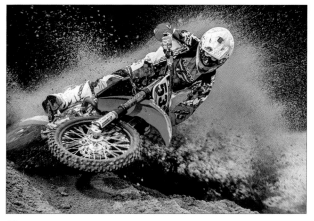

After

(Continued)

Sharpening Soft Subjects:

Here are the Unsharp Mask settings—
Amount: 120%, Radius: 1, Threshold: 10—
that work well for images where the subject is of a softer nature (e.g., flowers,
puppies, people, rainbows, etc.). It's a
subtle application of sharpening that is
very well suited to these types of subjects.

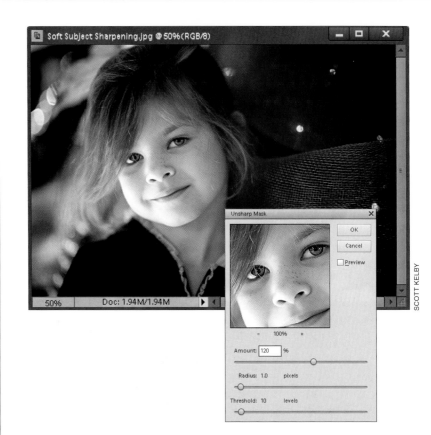

Sharpening Portraits:

If you're sharpening a close-up portrait
(head-and-shoulders type of thing),
try these settings—Amount: 75%,
Radius: 2, Threshold: 3—which applies
another form of subtle sharpening, but
with enough punch to make eyes sparkle a little bit, and bring out highlights
in your subject's hair.

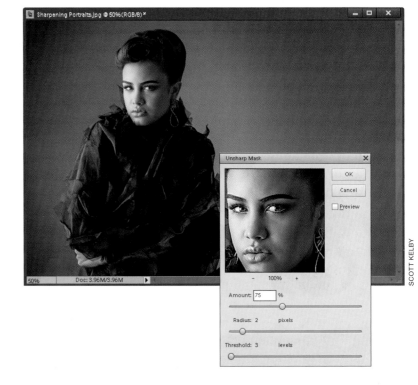

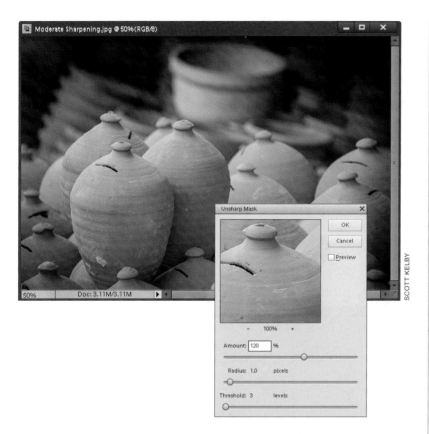

Moderate Sharpening:

This is a moderate amount of sharpening that works nicely on everything from product shots, to photos of home interiors and exteriors, to landscapes (and in this case, some clay pots). If you're shooting along these lines, try applying these settings—Amount: 120%, Radius: 1, Threshold: 3—and see how you like it (my guess is you will). Take a look at how it added snap and detail to the rings around the pots and the slits in the tops.

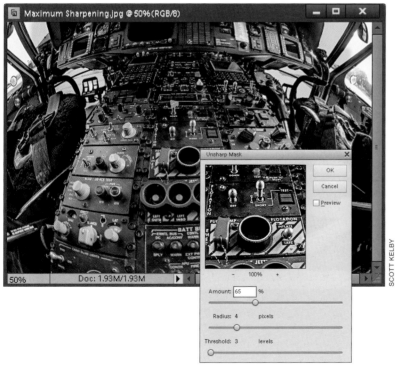

Maximum Sharpening:

I use these settings—Amount: 65%, Radius: 4, Threshold: 3—in only two situations: (1) The photo is visibly out of focus and it needs a heavy application of sharpening to try to bring it back into focus; or (2) the photo contains lots of well-defined edges (e.g., buildings, coins, cars, machinery, etc.). In this photo, the heavy amount of sharpening really brings out the detail in this cockpit control panel.

(Continued)

All-Purpose Sharpening:

These are probably my all-around favorite sharpening settings—Amount: 85%, Radius: 1, Threshold: 4—and I use these most of the time. It's not a "knock-you-over the-head" type of sharpening—maybe that's why I like it. It's subtle enough that you can apply it twice if your photo doesn't seem sharp enough after the first application (just press **Ctrl-F [Mac: Command-F]**), but once will usually do the trick.

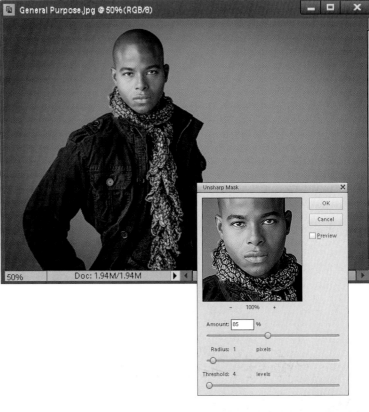

Web Sharpening:

I use these settings—Amount: 200%, Radius: 0.3, Threshold: 0—for web graphics that look blurry. (When you drop the resolution from a high-res, 300-ppi photo down to 72 ppi for the web, the photo often gets a bit blurry and soft.) If the sharpening doesn't seem sharp enough, try increasing the Amount to 400%. I also use this same setting (Amount: 400%) on out-of-focus photos. It adds some noise, but I've seen it rescue photos that I would have otherwise thrown away.

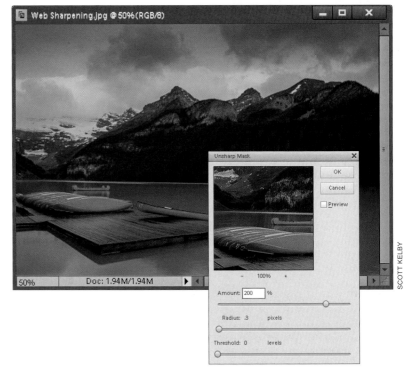

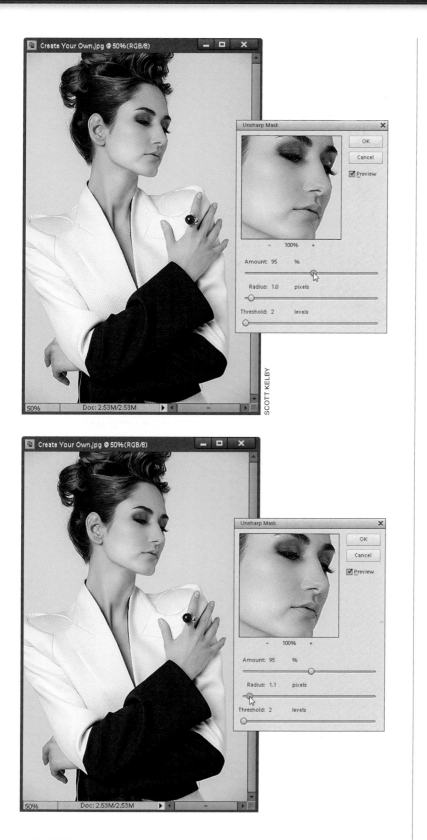

SCOTT KELBY

Coming Up with Your Own Settings:
If you want to experiment and come up with your own custom blend of sharpening settings, I'll give you some typical ranges for each adjustment so you can find your own sharpening "sweet spot."

Amount
Typical ranges go anywhere from 50% to 150%. This isn't a rule that can't be broken. It's just a typical range for adjusting the Amount, where going below 50% won't have enough effect, and going above 150% might get you into sharpening trouble (depending on how you set the Radius and Threshold). You're fairly safe staying under 150%. (In the example here, I reset my Radius and Threshold to 1 and 2, respectively.)

Radius
Most of the time, you'll use just 1 pixel, but you can go as high as (get ready)—2. I gave you one setting earlier for extreme situations, where you can take the Radius as high as 4, but I wouldn't recommend it very often. I once heard a tale of a man in Cincinnati who used 5, but I'm not sure I believe it. (Incidentally, Adobe allows you to raise the Radius amount to [get this] 250! If you ask me, anyone caught using 250 as their Radius setting should be incarcerated for a period not to exceed one year and a penalty not to exceed $2,500.)

(Continued)

Threshold

A pretty safe range for the Threshold setting is anywhere from 3 to around 20 (3 being the most intense, 20 being much more subtle. I know, shouldn't 3 be more subtle and 20 more intense? Don't get me started). If you really need to increase the intensity of your sharpening, you can lower the Threshold to 0, but keep a good eye on what you're doing (watch for noise appearing in your photo).

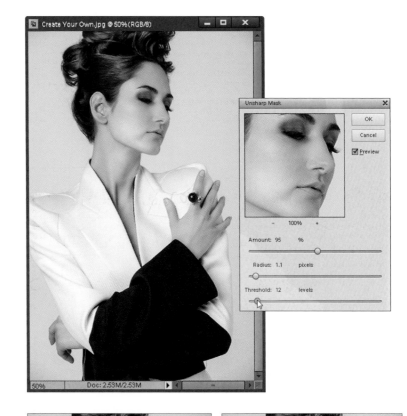

The Final Image

For the final sharpened image you see here, I used the Portrait sharpening settings I gave earlier, and then I dragged the Amount slider to the right (increasing the amount of sharpening), until it looked right to me (I wound up at around 95%), and I increased the Threshold to 12. If you're uncomfortable with creating your own custom Unsharp Mask settings, then start with this: pick a starting point (one of the set of settings I gave on the previous pages), and then just move the Amount slider and nothing else (so, don't touch the Radius and Threshold sliders). Try that for a while, and it won't be long before you'll find a situation where you ask yourself, "I wonder if lowering the Threshold would help?" and by then, you'll be perfectly comfortable with it.

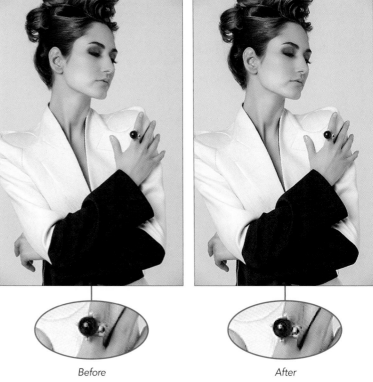

Before   *After*

Creating Extraordinary Sharpening

One of the problems we face when trying to make things really sharp is that things tend to look oversharpened, or worse yet, our photos get halos (tiny glowing lines around edges in our images). So, how do we get our images to appear really sharp without damaging them? With a trick, of course. Here's the one I use to make my photos look extraordinarily sharp without damaging the image:

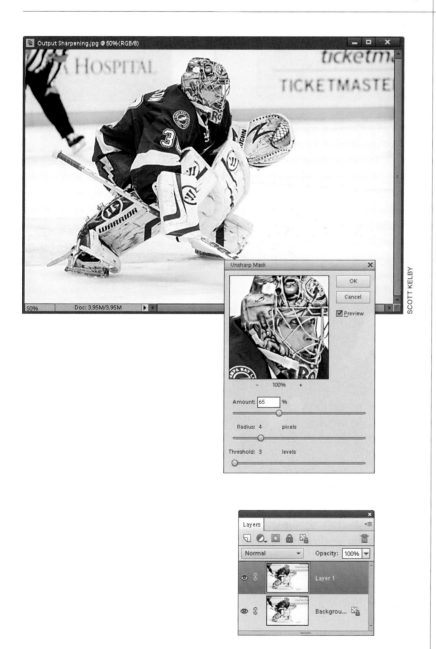

SCOTT KELBY

Step One:

Open your image, and then apply the Unsharp Mask filter (found under the Enhance menu) to your image, just as we've been doing all along. For this example, let's try these settings—Amount: 65%, Radius: 4, and Threshold: 3—which will provide a nice, solid amount of sharpening.

Step Two:

Press **Ctrl-J (Mac: Command-J)** to duplicate the Background layer. Because we're duplicating the Background layer, the layer will be already sharpened, but we're going to sharpen this duplicate layer even more in the next step.

(Continued)

Step Three:

Now apply the Unsharp Mask filter again, using the same settings, by pressing **Ctrl-F (Mac: Command-F)**. If you're really lucky, the second application of the filter will still look okay, but it's doubtful. Chances are that this second application of the filter will make your photo appear too sharp—you'll start to see halos or noise, or the photo will start looking artificial in a lot of areas. So, what we're going to do is hide this oversharpened layer, then selectively reveal this über-sharpening only in areas that can handle the extra sharpening (this will make sense in just a minute).

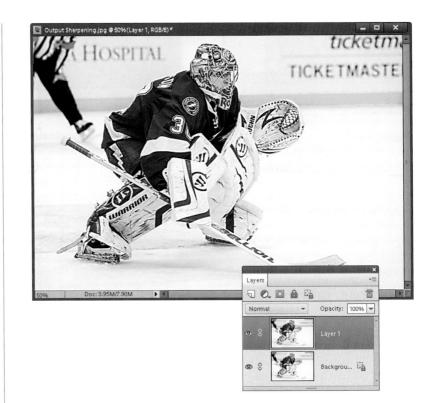

Step Four:

Go to the Layers palette, press-and-hold the Alt (Mac: Option) key, and click on the Add Layer Mask icon at the top of the palette (shown circled here in red). This hides your oversharpened layer behind a black layer mask (as seen here). *Note:* To learn more about layer masks, see Chapter 5.

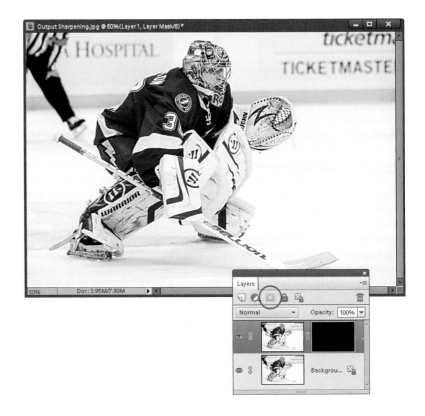

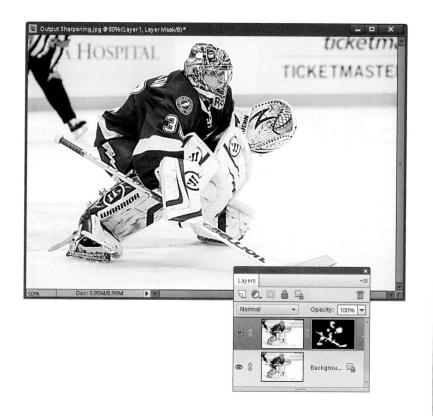

Step Five:
Here's the fun part—the trick is to paint over just a few key areas, which fool the eye into thinking the entire photo is sharper than it is. Here's how: Press **B** to get the Brush tool, and in the Tool Options Bar, click on the Brush thumbnail to open the Brush Picker and choose a soft-edged brush. With your Foreground color set to white, and with the layer mask active in the Layers palette (you'll see a little blue frame around it), start painting on your image to reveal your sharpening. (*Note:* If you make a mistake, press **X** to switch your Foreground color to black and paint over the mistake.) In this example, I painted over his helmet, glove, stick, logos, and the bottom of his skates. Revealing these few sharper areas, which immediately draw the eye, makes the whole photo look sharper.

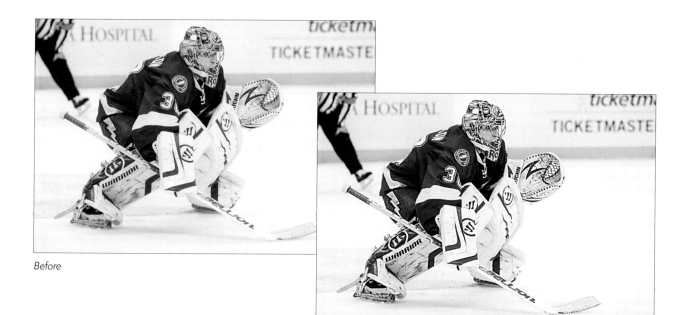

Before

After

Luminosity Sharpening

Okay, you've already learned that sharpening totally rocks, but the more you use it, the more discerning you'll become about it (you basically become a sharpening snob), and at some point, you'll apply some heavy sharpening to an image and notice little color halos. You'll grow to hate these halos, and you'll go out of your way to avoid them. In fact, you'll go so far as to use this next sharpening technique, which is fairly popular with pros shooting digital (at least with the sharpening-snob crowd).

Step One:
Open a photo that needs some moderate to serious sharpening.

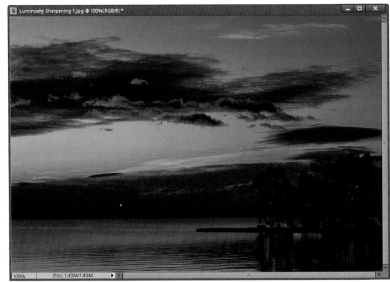

Step Two:
Duplicate the Background layer by going under the Layer menu, under New, and choosing **Layer via Copy** (or pressing **Ctrl-J [Mac: Command-J]**). This will duplicate the Background layer onto a new layer (Layer 1).

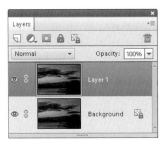

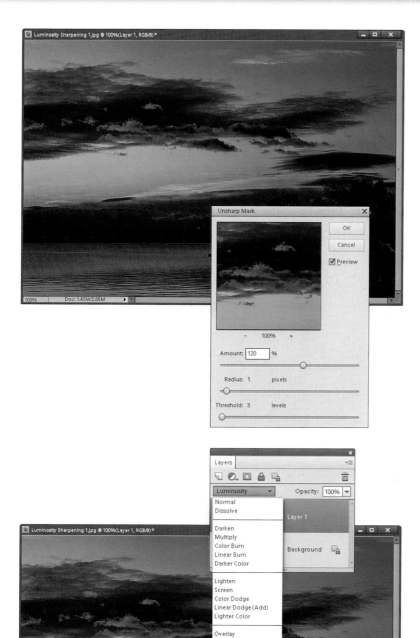

Step Three:
Go under the Enhance menu and choose **Unsharp Mask**. (*Note:* If you're looking for some sample settings for different sharpening situations, look at the "Basic Sharpening" tutorial at the beginning of this chapter.) After you've input your Unsharp Mask settings, click OK to apply the sharpening to the duplicate layer.

Step Four:
Go to the Layers palette and change the layer blend mode of this sharpened layer from Normal to **Luminosity**. By doing this, it applies the sharpening to just the luminosity (lightness details) of the image, and not the color. This enables you to apply a higher amount of sharpening without getting unwanted halos. You can now choose **Flatten Image** from the Layers palette's flyout menu to complete your Luminosity sharpening.

(Continued)

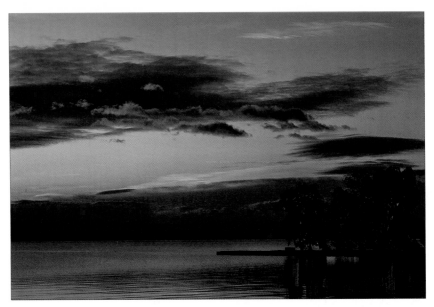

Before

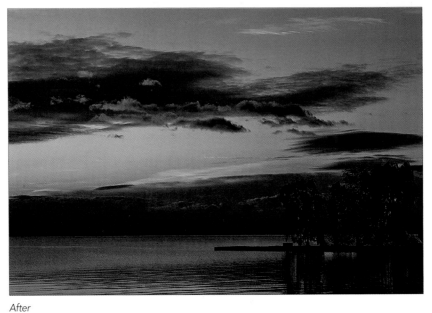

After

This is a sharpening technique that doesn't use the Unsharp Mask filter, but still leaves you with a lot of control over the sharpening, even after it's applied. It's ideal to use when you have an image that can really hold a lot of sharpening (a photo with a lot of edges) or one that really needs a lot of sharpening.

Edge Sharpening Technique

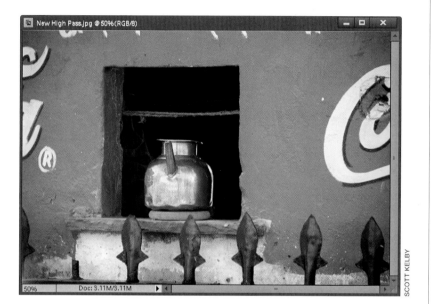

SCOTT KELBY

Step One:
Open a photo that needs edge sharpening.

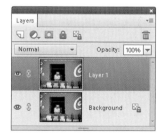

Step Two:
Duplicate the Background layer by going under the Layer menu, under New, and choosing **Layer via Copy** (or pressing **Ctrl-J [Mac: Command-J]**). This will duplicate the Background layer onto a new layer (Layer 1).

(Continued)

Step Three:

Go under the Filter menu, under Stylize, and choose **Emboss**. You're going to use the Emboss filter to accentuate the edges in the photo. You can leave the Angle and Amount settings at their defaults (135° and 100%), but if you want more intense sharpening, raise the Height amount from its default setting of 3 pixels to 5 or more pixels (in the example here, I left it at 3). Click OK to apply the filter, and your photo will turn gray, with neon-colored highlights along the edges.

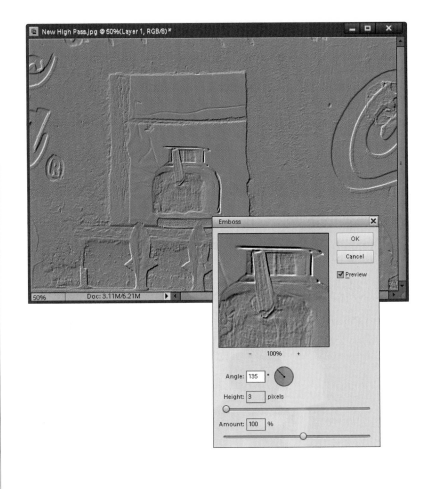

Step Four:

In the Layers palette, change the layer blend mode of this layer from Normal to **Hard Light**. This removes the gray color from the layer, but leaves the edges accentuated, making the entire photo appear much sharper.

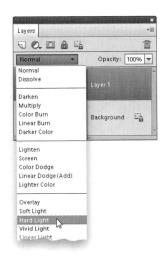

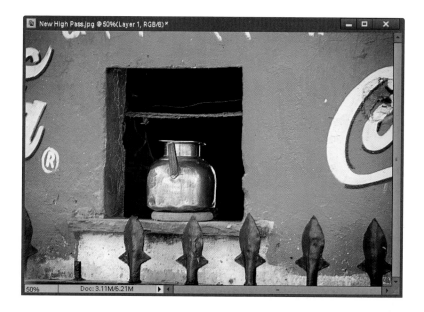

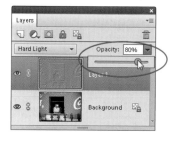

Step Five:
If the sharpening seems too intense, you can control the amount of the effect by simply lowering the Opacity of this top layer in the Layers palette.

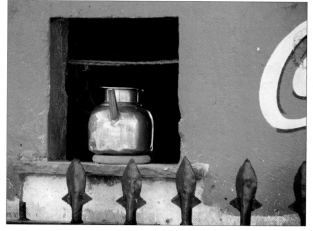

Before

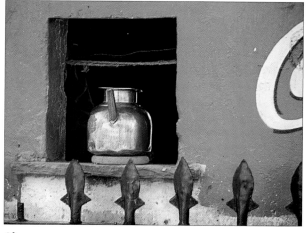

After

The Most Advanced Sharpening in Elements

We never used to use the Sharpen tool, until Adobe rewrote its underlying logic, taking it from its previous role as a "noise generator/pixel destroyer" to what Adobe Product Manager Bryan O'Neil Hughes has called "...the most advanced sharpening in any of our products." Here's how it works:

Step One:

Start by applying your regular sharpening to the overall image using Unsharp Mask or Smart Sharpen (more on this coming up next)—your choice. In this case, since this is a portrait of a woman, I'd use the portrait sharpening settings I gave you earlier in this chapter. Now, get the Sharpen tool (**R**; it's found nested beneath the Blur tool). Once you've got the tool, go to the Tool Options Bar and make sure the Protect Detail checkbox (shown circled here in red) is turned on (this is the checkbox that makes all the difference, as it turns on the advanced sharpening algorithm for this tool).

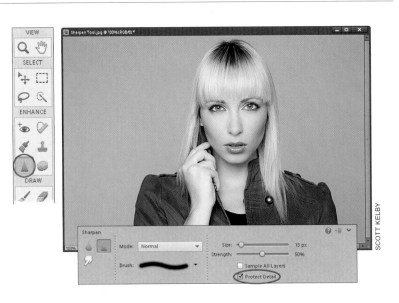

Step Two:

I recommend duplicating the Background layer at this point (by pressing **Ctrl-J [Mac: Command-J]**) and applying this extra level of sharpening to the duplicate layer. That way, if you think the sharpening looks too intense, you can just lower the amount of it by lowering the opacity of this layer. I also usually zoom in (by pressing **Ctrl-+** [plus sign; **Mac: Command-+**]) on a detail area (like her eyes), so I can really see the effects of the sharpening clearly (another benefit of applying the sharpening to a duplicate layer is that you can quickly see a before/after of all the sharpening by showing/hiding the layer).

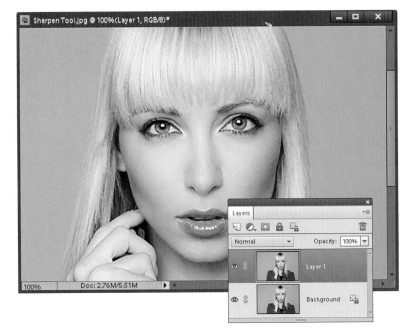

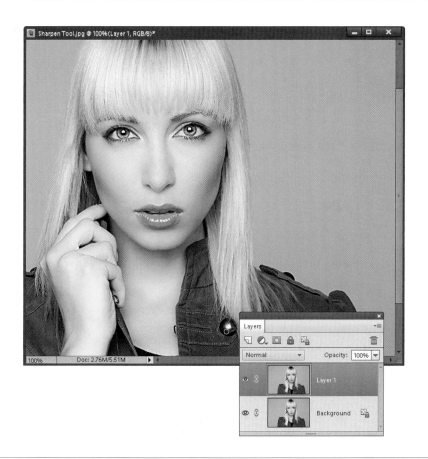

Step Three:
Now, click on the Brush thumbnail in the Tool Options Bar, choose a medium-sized, soft-edged brush from the Brush Picker, and then simply take the Sharpen tool and paint over just the areas you want to appear sharp (this is really handy for portraits like this, because you can avoid areas you want to remain soft, like skin, but then super-sharpen areas you want to be really nice and crisp, like her irises and the buttons on her jacket, like I'm doing here). Below is a before/after, after painting over other areas that you'd normally sharpen, like her eyes, eyebrows, eyelashes, and lips, while avoiding all areas of flesh tone. One more thing: This technique is definitely not just for portraits. The Sharpen tool does a great job on anything metal or chrome, and it's wonderful on jewelry, or anything that needs that extra level of sharpening.

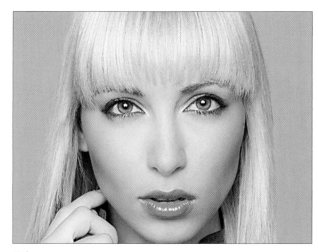

Before

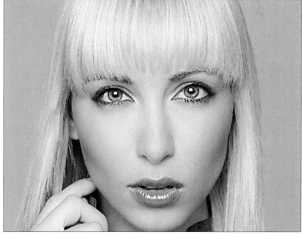

After

Advanced Sharpening Using Adjust Sharpness

Sometimes, I'll turn to the Adjust Sharpness control, instead of the Unsharp Mask filter, to sharpen my photos. Here's why: (1) it does a better job of avoiding those nasty color halos, so you can apply more sharpening without damaging your photo; (2) it lets you choose different styles of sharpening; (3) it has a much larger preview window, so you can see your sharpening more accurately; (4) it has a More Refined feature that applies multiple iterations of sharpening; and (5) it's just flat out easier to use.

Step One:

Open the photo you want to sharpen using the Adjust Sharpness control. (By the way, although most of this chapter focuses on using the Unsharp Mask filter, I only do that because it's the current industry standard. If you find you prefer the Adjust Sharpness control, from here on out, when I say to apply the Unsharp Mask filter, you can substitute the Adjust Sharpness control instead. Don't worry, I won't tell anybody.)

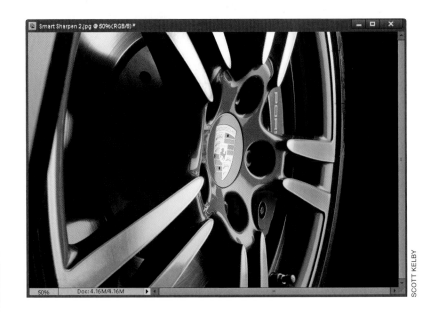

SCOTT KELBY

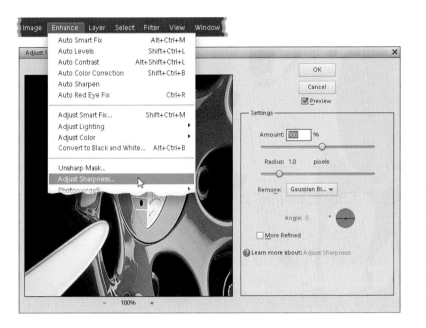

Step Two:

Go under the Enhance menu and choose **Adjust Sharpness**. When the dialog opens, you'll notice there are only two sliders: Amount (which controls the amount of sharpening—sorry, my editors made me say that) and Radius (which determines how many pixels the sharpening will affect). I generally leave the Radius setting at 1 pixel, but if a photo is visibly blurry, I'll pump it up to 2. (Very rarely do I ever try to rescue an image that's so blurry that I have to use a 3- or 4-pixel setting.)

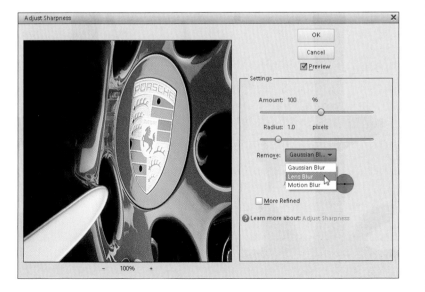

Step Three:

Below the Radius slider is the Remove pop-up menu, which lists the three types of blurs you can reduce using Adjust Sharpness. Gaussian Blur (the default) applies a brand of sharpening that's pretty much like what you get using the regular Unsharp Mask filter (it uses a similar algorithm). Another Remove menu choice is Motion Blur, but unless you can determine the angle of blur that appears in your image, it's tough to get really good results with this one. So, which one do I recommend? The other choice—Lens Blur. It's better at detecting edges, so it creates fewer color halos than you'd get with the other choices, and overall I think it just gives you better sharpening for most images. The downside? Choosing Lens Blur causes the filter to take a little longer to "do its thing." A small price to pay for better-quality sharpening.

(Continued)

Step Four:

Near the bottom of the dialog, there's a checkbox labeled More Refined. It gives you (according to Adobe) more accurate sharpening by applying multiple iterations of the sharpening. I leave More Refined turned on nearly all the time. (After all, who wants "less refined" sharpening?) *Note:* If you're working on a large file, the More Refined option can cause the filter to process slower, so it's up to you if it's worth the wait. I've also found that with the Adjust Sharpness control, I use a lower Amount setting than I would with the Unsharp Mask filter to get a similar amount of sharpening, so I usually find myself lowering the Amount to around 60% in most instances. But, for this image, I set it to 70% and set the Radius to 2.

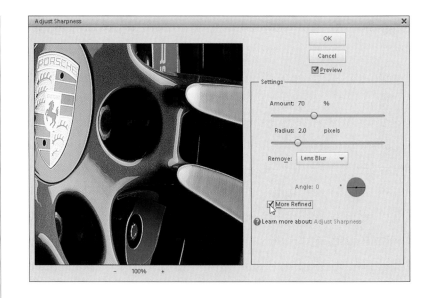

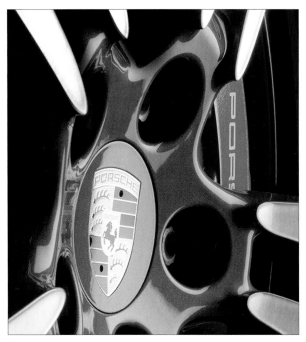

Before

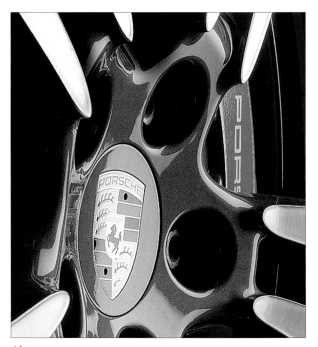

After

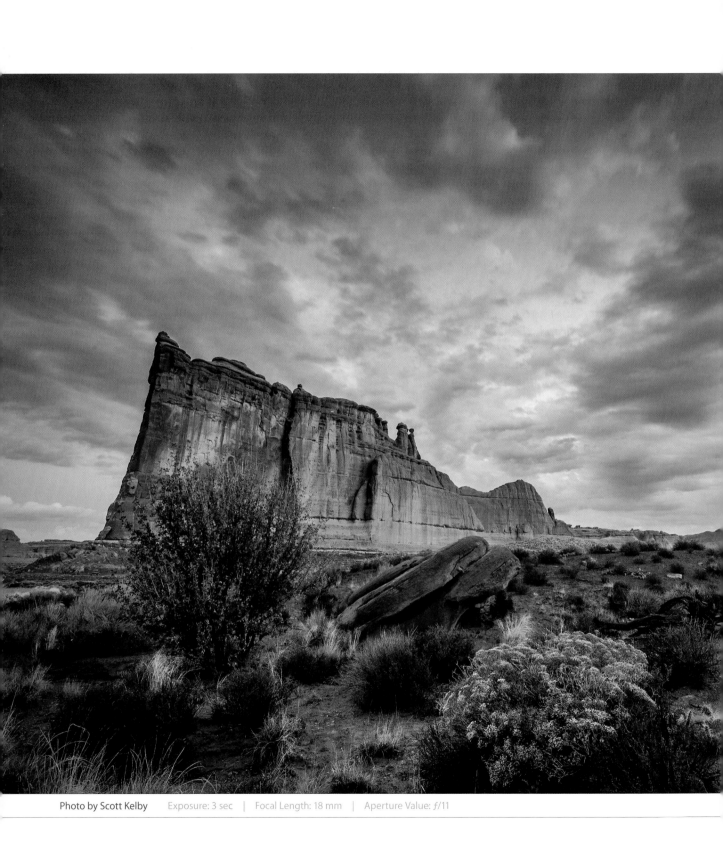

Photo by Scott Kelby   Exposure: 3 sec | Focal Length: 18 mm | Aperture Value: ƒ/11

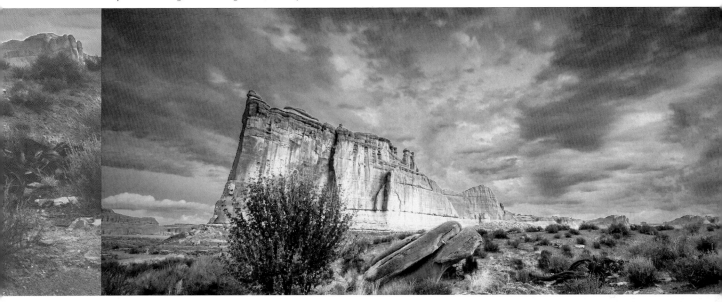

FINE PRINT
printing, color management, and my Elements 11 workflow

There is nothing like a photographic print. It's the moment when your digitally captured image, edited on a computer, moves from a bunch of 1s and 0s (computer code) into something real you can hold in your hand. If you've never made a print (and sadly, in this digital age, I meet people every day who have never made a single print—everything just stays on their computer, or on Facebook, or someplace else where you can "look, but don't touch"), today, all that changes, because you're going to learn, step by step, how to make your own prints. Now, if you don't already own a printer, this chapter becomes something else. Expensive. Actually, in all fairness, it's not the printer, it's the paper and ink, which is precisely why the printers aren't too expensive. But once you've bought a printer—they've got you. You'll be buying paper and ink for the rest of your natural life, and it seems like you go through ink cartridges faster than a gallon of milk.

This is precisely why I've come up with a workflow that literally pays for itself: I use my color inkjet printer to print out counterfeit U.S. bills. Now, I'm not stupid about it—I did some research and found that new ink cartridges for my particular printer run about $13.92 each, so I just make $15 bills (so it also covers the sales tax). Now—again, not stupid here—I don't go around using these $15 bills to buy groceries or lunch at Chili's, I only use them for ink cartridges, and so far, it has worked pretty well. I must admit, I had a couple of close calls, though, mainly because I put Dave Cross's face on all the bills, which seemed like a good idea at the time, until a sales clerk looked closely at the bill and said, "Isn't Dave Canadian?" (By the way, this chapter title comes from the song "Fine Print" by Nadia Ali. According to her website, she was born in the Mediterranean, which is precisely why you don't see her on my newly minted $18.60 bills.)

Setting Up Your Color Management

Most of the color management decisions in Elements come in the printing process (well, if you actually print your photos), but even if you're not printing, there is one color management decision you need to make now. Luckily, it's a really easy one.

Step One:
In the Elements Editor, go under the Edit menu and choose **Color Settings** (or just press **Ctrl-Shift-K [Mac: Command-Shift-K]**).

Step Two:
This brings up the Color Settings dialog. By default, Elements is set to Always Optimize Colors for Computer Screens, which uses the sRGB color space. However, if you're going to be printing to your own color inkjet printer (like an Epson, HP, Canon, etc.), you'll want to choose Always Optimize for Printing, which sets your color space to the Adobe RGB color space (the most popular color space for photographers), and gives you the best printed results. Now just click OK, and you've done it—you've configured Elements' color space for the best results for printing. *Note:* You only want to make this change if your final prints will be output to your own color inkjet printer. If you're sending your images out to an outside lab for prints (or your final images will only be viewed onscreen), you should probably stay in sRGB, because most labs are set up to handle sRGB files. Your best bet: ask your lab which color space they prefer.

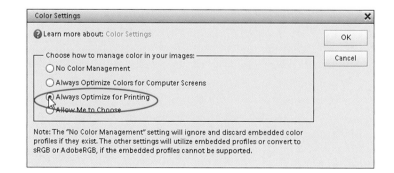

To get what comes out of your color inkjet printer to match what you see onscreen, you have to calibrate your monitor in one of two ways: (1) buy a hardware calibration sensor that calibrates your monitor precisely; or (2) use free software calibration, which is better than nothing, but not by much since you're just "eyeing" it. Hardware calibration is definitely the preferred method of monitor calibration (in fact, I don't know of a single pro using freebie software). With hardware calibration, it's measuring your actual monitor and building an accurate profile for the exact monitor you're using, and yes—it makes that big a difference.

You Have to Calibrate Your Monitor Before You Go Any Further

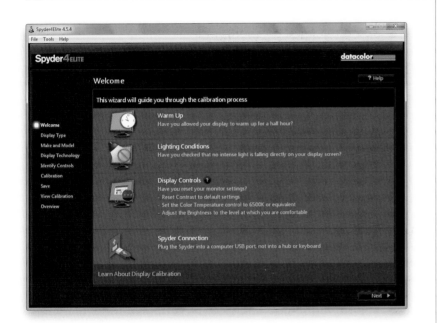

Step One:
To find the free software that comes with Windows 7, in the Control Panel, click on Appearance and Personalization, then click on Display, and click on Calibrate Color on the left. In Mac OS X, in the System Preferences dialog, click on Displays, then click on the Color tab to find it. You can also just search the web for "download Gamma" to find other free programs. I use Datacolor's Spyder4ELITE hardware color calibrator (around $249 street price), because it's simple, affordable, and a lot of the pros I know have moved over to it. So, I'm going to use it as an example here, but it's not necessary to get this same one, because they all work fairly similarly. You start by installing the software that comes with the Spyder4ELITE. Then, plug the Spyder4ELITE sensor into your computer's USB port and launch the software, which brings up the main window (seen here). You follow the "wizard," which asks you a couple of simple questions (stuff like, "Is this the first time you've calibrated your monitor using Spyder4ELITE?" Or, maybe, "What's the capital of Nebraska?"), and then it does the rest.

(Continued)

Step Two:

Start by clicking the Next button in the bottom right, and the window you see here will appear. Simply choose what type of display you are calibrating (once you've calibrated your monitor, these first few screens will be different, because it no longer needs that information—it already has it). If you have two monitors, choose which monitor to calibrate from the pop-up menu on the right. Then, click the Next button again.

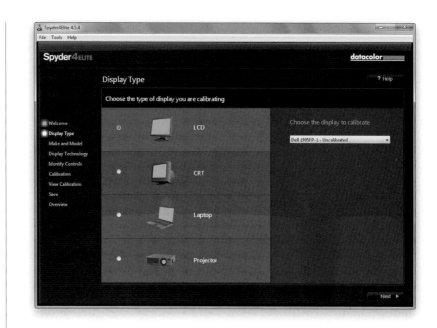

Step Three:

The next screen asks you to choose which controls you have on your monitor: Contrast, Brightness, and/or Kelvin Presets. It will automatically select the ones it detects, but press the settings button on the front of your monitor to check. When you're done, click the Next button.

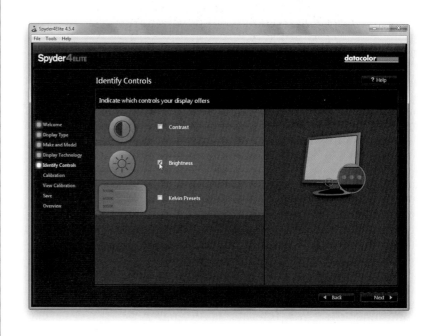

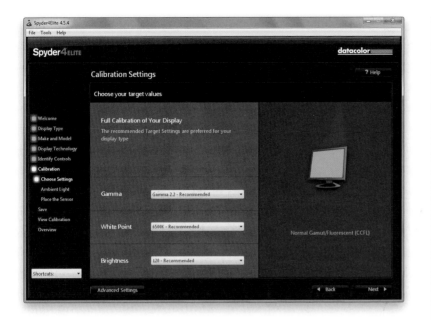

Step Four:
This brings up the Calibration Settings screen, which asks you to choose your target values. Choose your values from the pop-up menus, or leave them at the recommended values that show by default. If you want to have it calibrate for the ambient light around your monitor (if the lighting is always the same), then click on the Advanced Settings button at the bottom left of the screen and turn Ambient Light on. Then, just click the Next button.

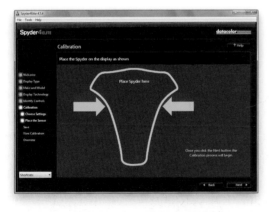

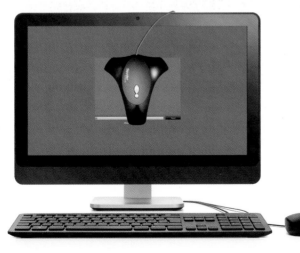

Step Five:
The next screen asks you to put the Spyder unit on your monitor, which means you drape the sensor over your monitor so it sits flat against it and the cord hangs over the back. It shows you exactly where to place it (the two blue arrows you see beside its outline actually flash on/off, so you can't possibly miss where it goes). The sensor comes with a counterweight you can attach to the cord, so you can position the sensor approximately in the center of your screen without it slipping down. Once the sensor is in position over your screen, click the Next button, sit back, and relax. You'll see the software conduct a series of onscreen tests, using gray, white, and various color swatches, as shown here.

(Continued)

Step Six:

This testing only goes on for a few minutes (at least, that's all it took for my monitor), and then it's done. It asks you to name your profile (it puts a default name in place for you), so enter a name, and then click the Save button. Below that is a pop-up menu where you can choose when you want an automatic reminder to recalibrate your monitor to pop up on your screen. The default choice is 2 Weeks (so please don't tell anyone that I actually set mine to 1 Month). Make your choice and then click the Next button.

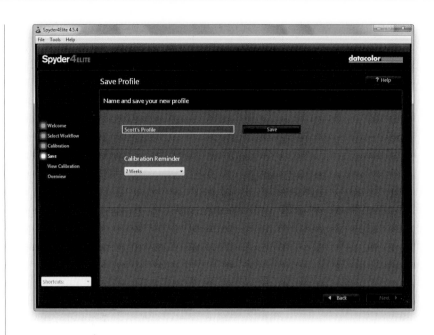

Step Seven:

Now you get to see the usually shocking before/after. Click on the Switch button at the bottom right and you can switch back and forth between your now fully calibrated monitor and your uncalibrated monitor. It's at that moment you say, "Ohhhhhh…that's why my prints never match my screen." Well, it's certainly one part of the puzzle, but without this one critical piece in place, you don't have a chance with the rest, so you did the right thing. Click Next one last time, and then click the Quit button in the Profile Overview screen.

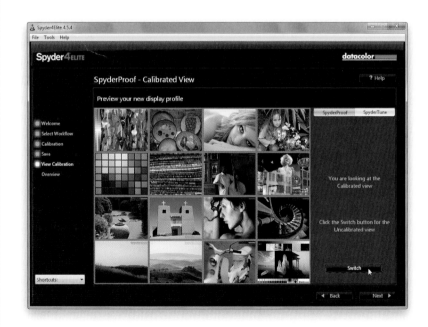

When you buy a color inkjet printer and install the printer driver that comes with it, it basically lets Elements know what kind of printer is being used, and that's about it. But to get pro-quality results, you need a profile for your printer based on the exact type of paper you'll be printing on. Most inkjet paper manufacturers now create custom profiles for their papers, and you can usually download them free from their websites. Does this really make that big a difference? Ask any pro. Here's how to find and install your custom profiles:

Getting Pro-Quality Prints That Match Your Screen

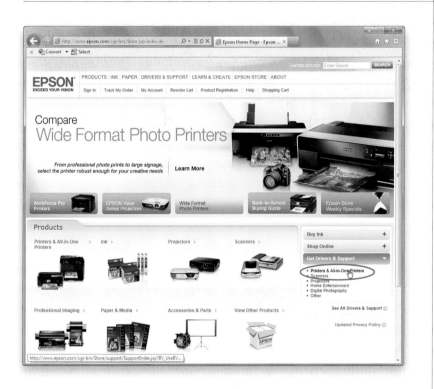

Step One:
Your first step is to go to the website of the company that makes the paper you're going to be printing on and search for their downloadable color profiles for your printer. I use the term "search" because they're usually not in a really obvious place. I use two Epson printers—a Stylus Photo R2880 and a Stylus Pro 3880—and I generally print on Epson paper. When I installed the 3880's printer driver, I was tickled to find that it also installed custom color profiles for all Epson papers (this is rare), but my R2880 (like most printers) doesn't. So, the first stop would be Epson's web-site, where you'd click on the Printers & All-in-One Printers link under Get Drivers & Support (as shown here). *Note:* Even if you're not an Epson user, still follow along (you'll see why).

(Continued)

Step Two:

Once you get to the Support page, choose your printer type, then find your particular printer in the list. Click on that link, and on the next page, click on Drivers & Downloads (choose Windows or Macintosh). On that page is a link to the printer's Premium ICC Profiles page. So, click on that Premium ICC Profiles link.

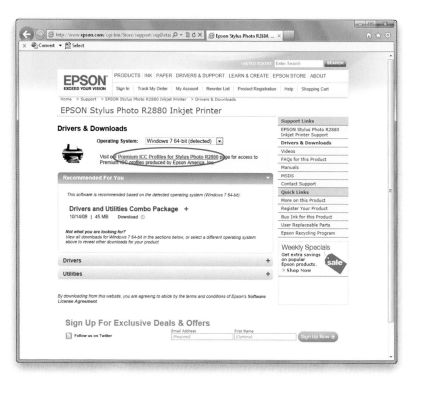

Step Three:

When you click that link, a page appears with a list of ICC profiles for Epson's papers and printers. I primarily print on two papers: (1) Epson's Ultra Premium Photo Paper Luster, and (2) Epson's Velvet Fine Art paper. So, I'd download their ICC profiles under Glossy Papers (as shown here) and Fine Art Papers (in the middle of the list). They download onto your computer, then you just double-click on the installer for each one, and they're added to your list of profiles in Elements (I'll show how to choose them in the Print dialog a little later). That's it—you download them, double-click to install, and they'll be waiting for you in Elements' print dialog. Easy enough. But what if you're not using Epson paper? Or if you have a different printer, like a Canon or an HP?

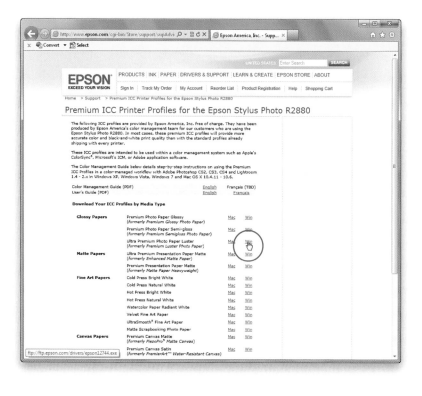

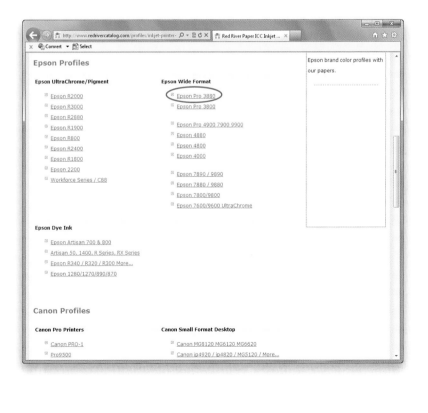

Step Four:

We'll tackle the different paper issue first (because they're tied together). I mentioned earlier that I usually print on Epson papers. I say usually because sometimes I want a final print that fits in a 16x20" standard pre-made frame, without having to cut or trim the photo. In those cases, I use Red River Paper's 16x20" UltraPro Satin instead. So, even though you're printing on an Epson printer, now you'd go to Red River Paper's site (www.redriverpaper.com) to find their color profiles for my other printer, the Epson 3880. (Remember, profiles come from the company that makes the paper.) On the Red River Paper homepage, click on the Click Here link for Premium Photographic Inkjet Papers. Then, click on the Color Profiles link under Helpful Info on the left side of the page.

Step Five:

Under the section named Epson Wide Format, there's a direct link to the ICC profiles for the Epson Pro 3880 (as shown here), but did you also notice that there are ICC Color profiles for Canon printers? The process is the same for other printers, but although HP and Canon now both make pro-quality photo printers, Epson had the pro market to itself for a while, so while Epson profiles are created by most major paper manufacturers, you may not always find paper profiles for HP and Canon printers. At Red River, they widely support Epson, and have a bunch of Canon profiles, but there are only a few for HP. That doesn't mean this won't change, but as of the writing of this book, that's the reality.

(Continued)

Step Six:

Although profiles from Epson's website come with an installer, with Red River (and many other paper manufacturers), you just get the profile (shown here) and instructions, so you install it yourself (it's easy). On a PC, just Right-click on the profile and choose **Install Profile**. On a Mac, go to your hard disk, in your Library folder, and in your Color-Sync folder, to the Profiles folder. Just drag the file in there and you're set. You don't even have to restart Elements—it automatically updates.

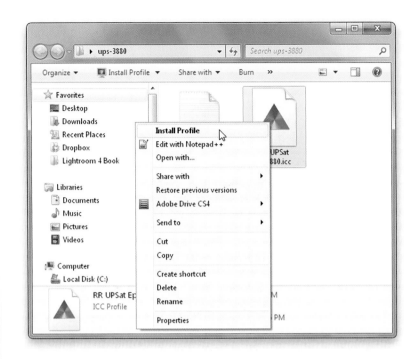

Step Seven:

You'll access your profile by choosing **Print** from Elements' File menu. In the Print dialog, click on the More Options button in the bottom left, then click on Color Management on the left of the dialog. Change the Color Handling pop-up menu to **Photoshop Elements Manages Color**, then click on the Printer Profile pop-up menu, and your new color profile(s) will appear. Here, I'm printing to an Epson 3880 using Red River's Ultra-Pro Satin paper, so that's what I'm choosing as my printer profile (it's named RR UPSat Ep3880.icc). That's it, but there's more on using these color profiles next in this chapter.

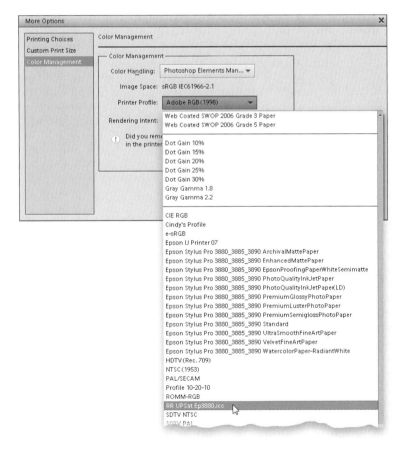

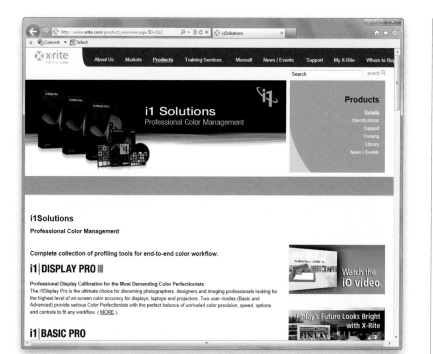

TIP: Custom Profiles for Your Printer
You can also pay an outside service to create a custom profile for your printer. You print a provided test sheet, overnight it to them, and they'll use an expensive colorimeter to measure your test print and create a custom profile, but it's only good for that printer, on that paper, with that ink. If anything changes, your profile is worthless. You could do your own personal printer profiling (using something like one of X-Rite's Eye-One Pro packages), so you can re-profile each time you change paper or inks. It's really just up to you.

Sharpening for Printing

When we apply sharpening, we apply it so it looks good on our computer screen, right? But when you actually make a print, a lot of that sharpening that looks fine on a 72- or 96-dpi computer screen gets lost on a high-resolution print at 240 ppi. Because the sharpening gets reduced when we make a print, we have to sharpen so our photo looks a bit too sharp onscreen, but then looks perfect when it prints. Here's how I apply sharpening for images I'm going to print:

Step One:

Start by doing a trick my buddy Shelly Katz shared with me: duplicate the Background layer (by pressing **Ctrl-J [Mac: Command-J]**) and do your print sharpening on this duplicate layer (that way, you don't mess with the already sharpened original image on the Background layer). Double-click on the new layer's name and rename it "Sharpened for Print," then go under the Enhance menu, and choose **Unsharp Mask**. For most 240 ppi images, I apply these settings: Amount 120; Radius 1; Threshold 3. Click OK.

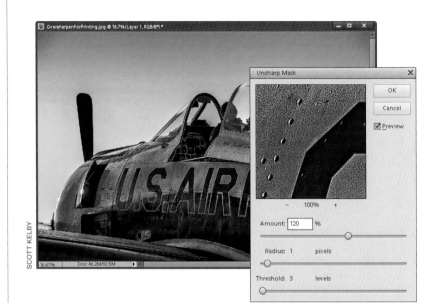

SCOTT KELBY

Step Two:

Next, reapply the Unsharp Mask filter with the same settings by pressing **Ctrl-F (Mac: Command-F)**. Then, at the top of the Layers palette, change the layer blend mode to **Luminosity** (so the sharpening is only applied to the detail of the photo, and not the color), and use the Opacity slider to control how much sharpening is applied. Start at 50% and see if it looks a little bit oversharpened. If it looks like a little bit too much, stop—you want it to look a little oversharpened. If you think it's way too much, lower the opacity to around 35% and re-evaluate. When it looks right (a little too sharp), make a test print. My guess is that you'll want to raise the opacity up a little higher, because it won't be as sharp as you thought.

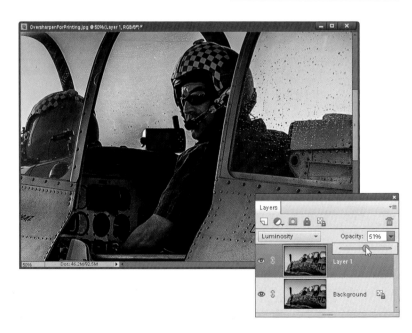

Okay, you've hardware calibrated your monitor (or at the very least—you "eyed it") and you've set up Elements' Color Management to use Adobe RGB (1998). You've even downloaded a printer profile for the exact printer model and style of paper you're printing on. In short, you're there. Luckily, you only have to do all that stuff once—now we can just sit back and print. Well, pretty much.

Making the Print

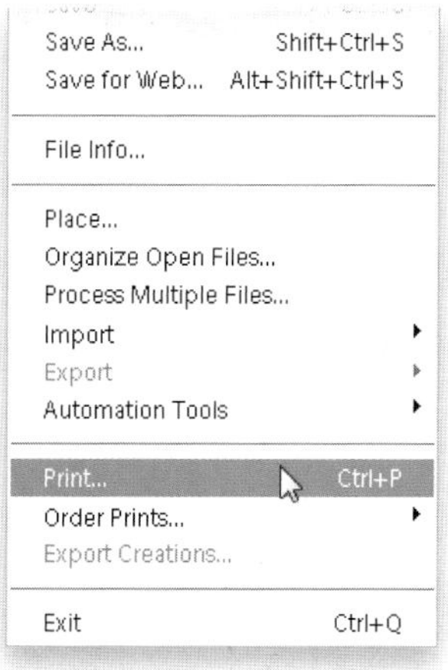

Step One:
Once you have an image all ready to go, just go under the Editor's File menu and choose **Print** (as shown here), or just press **Ctrl-P (Mac: Command-P)**.

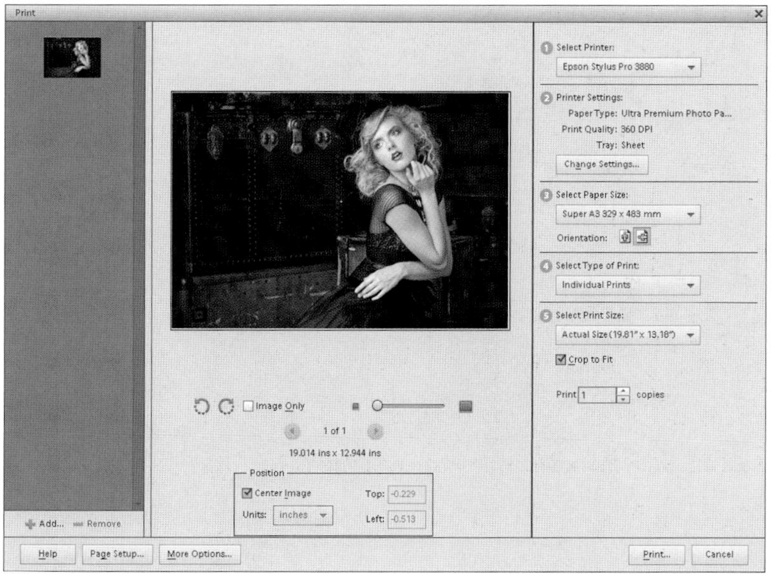

Step Two:
When the Print dialog appears, let's choose your printer and paper size first. At the top right of the dialog, choose the exact printer you want to print to from the Select Printer pop-up menu (I'm printing to an Epson Stylus Pro 3880). Next, choose your paper size from the Select Paper Size pop-up menu (in this case, a 13x19" sheet), choose your page orientation beneath that menu, and then from the Select Print Size pop-up menu (on the bottom right), be sure that Actual Size is selected. In the middle of the Print dialog, you'll see a preview of how your photo will fit on the printed page, and at the bottom of the column on the right, there's an option for how many copies you want to print. If you want to print more than one photo, just click the Add button below the filmstrip on the left side of the dialog. This brings up the Add Photos dialog (similar to the one you get when using the Create Slide Show feature), where you can choose from your photos in the Organizer. Select the one(s) you want and click the Add Selected Photos button. To remove a photo from the filmstrip, click on it, then click the Remove button.

(Continued)

Step Three:

Click on the More Options button (at the bottom left) and then click on Custom Print Size on the left. Here you can choose how large the photo will appear on the page (if it's a photo that's too large to fit on the paper, just turn on the Scale to Fit Media checkbox, as I did here, and it will do the math for you, and scale the image down to fit).

Step Four:

Now click on Printing Choices at the top left of the More Options dialog. Here you can choose if you want to have your photo's filename appear on the page, or change the background color of the paper, or add a border, or have crop marks print, or other stuff like that—you have but only to turn the checkboxes on (you like that "you have but only to" phrase? I never use that in normal conversation, but somehow it sounded good here. Ya know, come to think of it—maybe not). Anyway, I don't use these Printing Choices at all, ever, but don't let that stop you—feel free to add distracting junk to your heart's content. Now, on to the meat of this process.

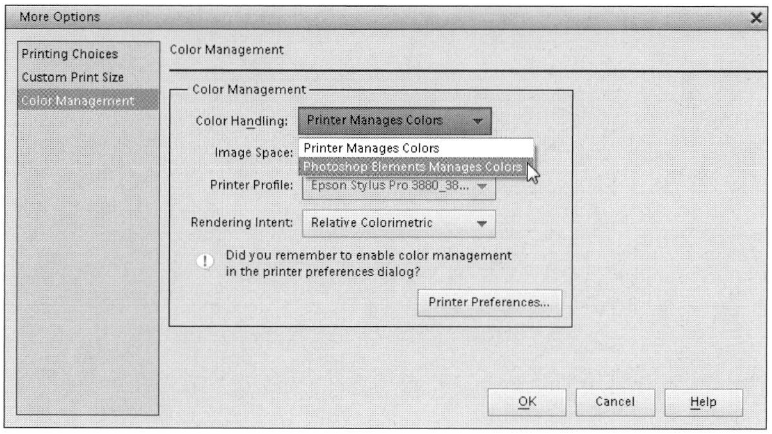

Step Five:

Click on Color Management on the left to get the all-important Color Management options. Here's the thing: by default, the Color Handling is set up to have your printer manage colors. You really only want to choose this if you weren't able to download the printer/paper profile for your printer. So, basically, this is your backup plan. It's not your first choice, but today's printers have gotten to the point that if you have to go with this, it still does a decent job. However, if you were able to download your printer/paper profile and you want pro-quality prints (and I imagine you do), then do this instead: choose **Photoshop Elements Manages Colors** from the Color Handling pop-up menu (as shown here), so you can make use of the color profile, which will give you the best possible color match.

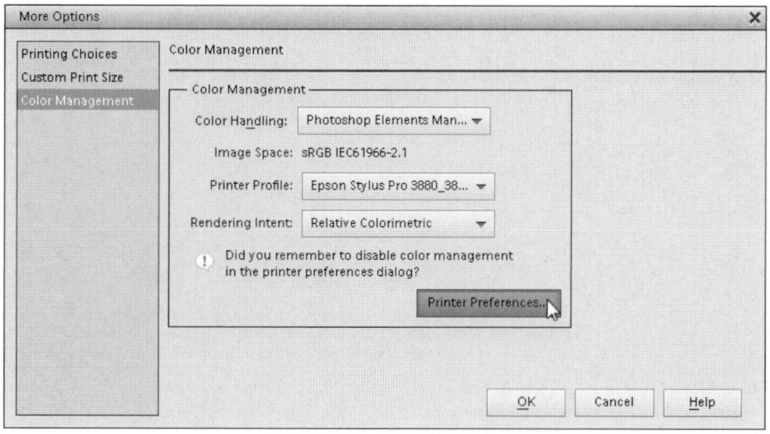

Step Six:

Below Rendering Intent, you'll see a warning asking if you remembered to disable your printer's color management. You haven't, so let's do that now. Click the Printer Preferences button that appears right below the warning (as shown here). (*Note:* On a Mac, once you click the Print button in the Elements Print dialog, the Mac OS X Print dialog will appear, where you can go under Printer Color Management and set it to Off [No Color Adjustment].)

(Continued)

Step Seven:

In your printer's Properties dialog (which may be different depending on your printer), you will turn off your printer's color management, but you have other stuff to do here, as well (on a Mac, you will do this in the OS X Print dialog, as mentioned in the previous step). First, choose the type of paper you'll be printing to (I'm printing to Epson Ultra Premium Photo Paper Luster). For the Print Quality setting, choose **Quality Options**, then in the resulting Quality Options dialog, drag the slider at the top to 5 and click OK. Now, be sure that the Custom radio button is chosen and **Off (No Color Adjustment)** appears in the Mode pop-up menu. Click OK to save your changes and return to the More Options dialog.

Step Eight:

After you've turned off your printer's color management (and chosen photo quality paper), you'll need to choose your color profile. Again, I'm going to be printing to an Epson Stylus Pro 3880 printer, using Epson's Premium Luster paper, so I'd choose that profile from the Printer Profile pop-up menu in the Color Management section. Doing this optimizes the color to give the best possible color print on that particular printer using that particular paper.

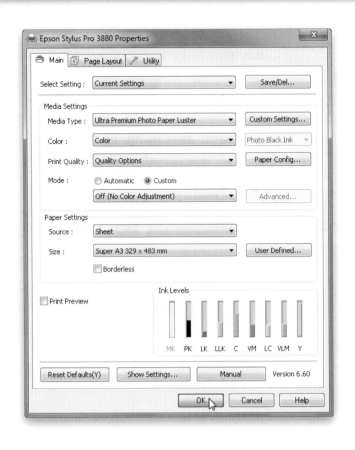

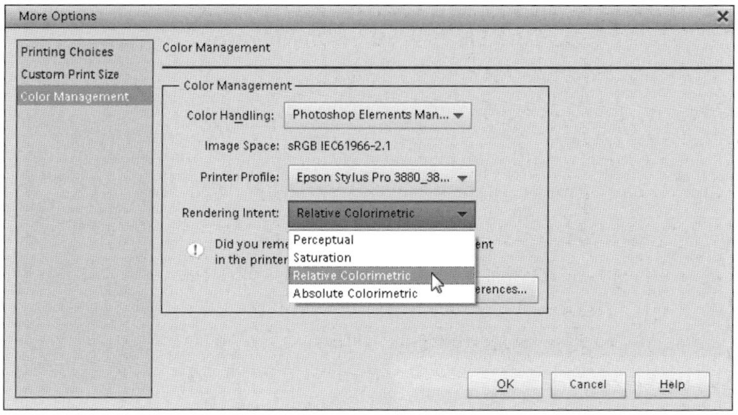

Step Nine:

Lastly, you'll need to choose the Rendering Intent. There are four choices here, but only two that I recommend—either Relative Colorimetric (which is the default setting) or Perceptual. Here's the thing: I've had printers where I got the best looking prints with my Rendering Intent set to Perceptual, but currently, on my Epson Stylus Pro 3880, I get better results when it's set to Relative Colorimetric. So, which one gives the best results for your printer? I recommend printing a photo once using Perceptual, then printing the same photo using Relative Colorimetric, and when you compare the two, you'll know. Just remember to add some text below the photo that tells you which one is which or you'll get the two confused. I learned this the hard way.

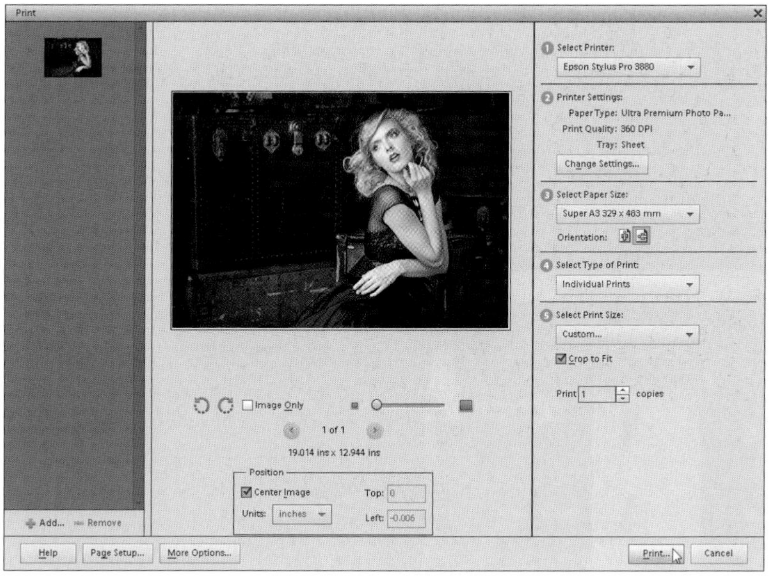

Step 10:

Now click the OK button, then click the Print button at the bottom of the Print dialog (this is where, on a Mac, you'll choose the options we talked about in Step Six and Step Seven).

What to Do If the Print Still Doesn't Match Your Screen

Okay, what do you do if you followed all these steps—you've hardware calibrated your monitor, you've got the right paper profiles, and color profiles, and profiles of profiles, and so on, and you've carefully turned on every checkbox, chosen all the right color profiles, and you've done everything right—but the print still doesn't match what you see onscreen? You know what we do? We fix it in Elements. That's right—we make some simple tweaks that get the image looking right fast.

Your Print Is Too Dark

This is one of the most common problems, and it's mostly because today's monitors are so much brighter (either that, or you're literally viewing your images in a room that's too dark). Luckily, this is an easy fix and here's what I do: Press **Ctrl-J (Mac: Command-J)** to duplicate the Background layer, then at the top of the Layers palette, change the layer blend mode to **Screen** to make everything much brighter. Now, lower the Opacity of this layer to 25% and (this is key here) make a test print. Next, look at the print, and see if it's a perfect match, or if it's still too dark. If it's still too dark, set the Opacity to 35% and make another test print. It'll probably take a few test prints to nail it, but once you do, your problem is solved.

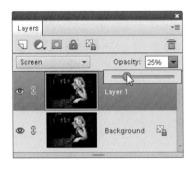

Your Print Is Too Light

This is less likely, but just as easy to fix. Duplicate the Background layer, then change the layer blend mode to **Multiply** to make everything darker. Now, lower the Opacity of this layer to 20% and make a test print. Again, you may have to make a few test prints to get the right amount, but once you've got it, you've got it.

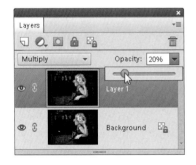

Your Print Is Too Red (Blue, etc.)

This is one you might run into if your print has some sort of color cast. First, before you mess with the image, press the **Tab key** on your keyboard to hide the Toolbox, palettes, and Tool Options Bar, and put a solid gray background behind your photo. Then, just look to see if the image onscreen actually has too much red. If it does, then click on the Create New Adjustment Layer icon (the half-white/half-blue circle) at the top of the palette, and choose **Hue/Saturation**. In the Hue/Saturation adjustments palette, from the Channel pop-up menu, choose **Reds**, then lower the Saturation amount to –20%, and then (you knew this was coming, right?) make a test print. You'll then know if 20% was too much, too little, or just right. You may have to make a few test prints before you nail it.

Your Print Has Visible Banding

The more you've tweaked an image, the more likely you'll run into this (where the colors have visible bands, rather than just smoothly graduating from color to color. It's most often seen in blue skies). Here's how to deal with this: Go under the Filter menu, under Noise, and choose **Add Noise**. In the dialog, set the Amount to 4%, click on the Gaussian radio button, and turn on the Monochromatic checkbox. You'll see the noise onscreen, but it disappears when you print the image (and usually, the banding disappears right along with it).

My Elements 11 Workflow from Start to Finish

One of the questions I get asked the most is "What is your suggested digital workflow?" (Which actually means, "What order are you supposed to do all this in?" That's all "digital workflow" means.) We wrote this book in kind of a digital workflow order, starting with importing and organizing your photos, correcting them, sharpening them, and then at the end, printing. But I thought that seeing it all laid out in one place (well, in these 10 pages), might be really helpful, so here ya go.

Step One:

You start your workflow by importing your photos into the Organizer (we learned this in Chapter 1). While you're in the Photo Downloader (shown here), I recommend adding your metadata (your name and copyright info) during this import process. Also, while you're in the Photo Downloader, go ahead and rename your photos now, so if you ever have to search for them, you have a hope of finding them (searching for photos from your trip to Hawaii is pretty tough if you leave the files named the way your camera named them, which is something along the lines of "DSC_1751.JPG"). So give them a descriptive name while you import them. You'll thank me later.

Step Two:

Once your photos appear in the Organizer, first take a quick look through them and go ahead and delete any photos that are hopelessly out of focus, were taken accidentally (like shots taken with the lens cap still on), or you can see with a quick glance are so messed up they're beyond repair. Get rid of these now, because there's no sense wasting time (tagging, sorting, etc.) and disk space on photos that you're going to wind up deleting later anyway, so make your job easier—do it now.

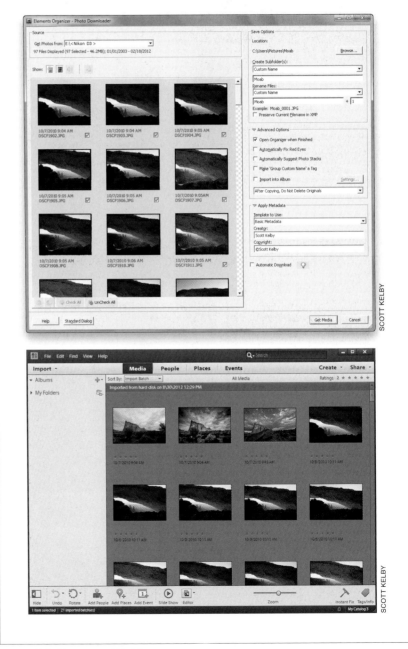

SCOTT KELBY

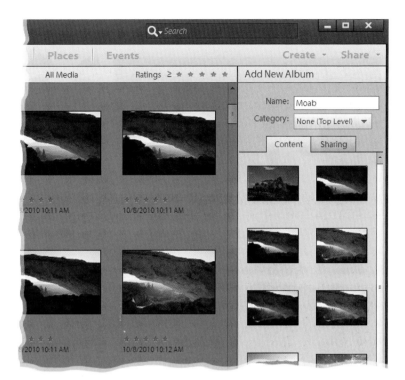

Step Three:

Once you've deleted the obviously bad ones, here's what I would do next: go through the photos one more time and then create an album of just your best images (see Chapter 1 for how to create an album). That way, you're now just one click away from the best photos from your shoot.

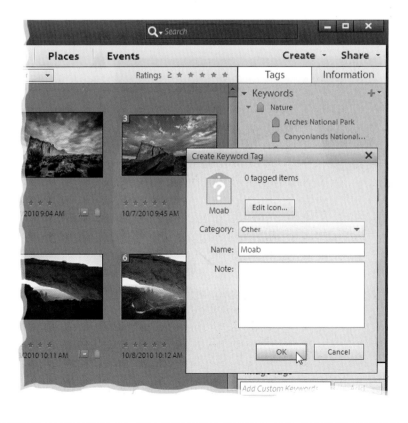

Step Four:

There's another big advantage to separating out your best images into their own separate album: now you're only going to tag and worry about color correcting and editing these photos—the best of your shoot. You're not going to waste time and energy on photos no one's going to see. So, click on the album, then go ahead and assign your keyword tags now (if you forgot how to tag, it's back in Chapter 1). If you take a few minutes to tag the images in your album now, it will save you literally hours down the road. This is a very important step in your workflow (even though it's not a fun step), so don't skip it—tag those images now!

(Continued)

Step Five:

Now it's time to start editing those photos. Most of my workflow takes place in Camera Raw, which I honestly believe is the fastest and easiest way to get your images looking the way you want them (even if you didn't shoot in RAW format; see Chapter 2 for how to open JPEGs, TIFFs, and PSDs in Camera Raw). We're going to edit one of the photos I shot during a workshop I taught in Moab, Utah. It's not a great shot, but it has enough problems to deal with that I thought it would give you a good insight into how I deal with them. The first thing I do at this point is figure out what's wrong with the photo, and the question I ask myself is simple: "What do I wish were different?" Here, I wish the sky was darker and there was more definition in the clouds. I wish the whole photo had a lot more contrast and detail and was more vibrant overall. Of course, I wish everything was sharper, but I always sharpen every photo.

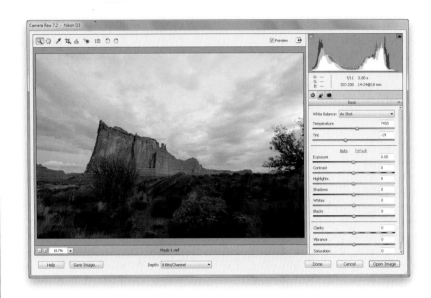

Step Six:

Normally, I start by adjusting the white balance (see page 56), but in this case, I'm okay with the overall color temperature (don't get me wrong, I'm going to pump up the color in just a moment, but as far as it being too warm or too cool, or just totally wrong, I'm okay with that part). We're going to start with the thing that bugs me the most (which is what I usually do), and in this case, it's the sky. It's just too stark and bland (take a look at the image in Step Five for a reference). Here's the recipe for darkening the sky: (1) Lower the Highlights slider a lot (here, I dragged it down to –43). Then, (2) lower the Exposure a bit (I lowered it to –0.65), which affects the sky big time (since it controls the midtones). Then, (3) increase the Contrast a lot (to +71 here) to give it some "oomph," and you can see that helped a lot (again, compare it to Step Five). If you need a refresher on the Basic panel sliders, go back to Chapter 2.

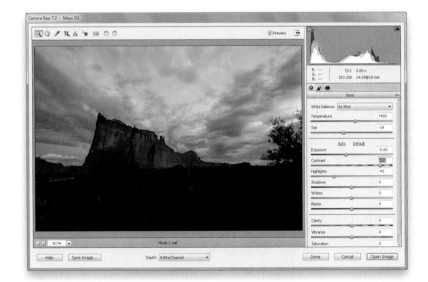

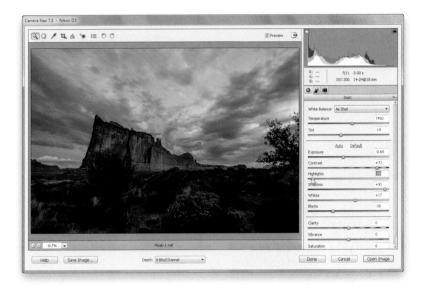

Step Seven:

Now, we stop and see what it needs next. Back in Step Six, the ground in front and the rock formation look way too dark, so we'll have to open up those dark shadow areas by dragging the Shadows slider way over to the right (here I went to +91). When you increase the Shadows a lot, like we did here, it can make the blacks look washed out, so I generally drag the Blacks slider to the left to balance it out (here, I dragged to –38). To bring out some highlights, I increased the Whites to +17 (I couldn't increase the Highlights—they were busy keeping the sky dark). The sky started getting a little bright from all that, so I lowered the Highlights even more (down to –89).

Step Eight:

A landscape photo like this, with lots of well-defined edges and texture, is just screaming out for Clarity! (You can hear it, can't you?) So, I cranked it up here quite a bit, to +53. This tends to give the image a little tiny bit of an HDR feel, so if you're an anti-HDRite (and you know who you are), then don't drag it as far as I did (you might want to stop at +20 or +25). I also increased the Vibrance to +17 to punch up the colors a little more. As I go through this process, at certain times the overall image may look a little too dark or too bright, and if either is the case, I just drag the Exposure slider a little to the right if I need it brighter, or left if it's too bright. It was looking a little dark, so I increased the Exposure from –0.65 up to –0.50.

(Continued)

Step Nine:

Okay, to me that sky is starting to look too light again, and I can't lower the Exposure any more, or the whole photo will be underexposed, so we're going to add a neutral density gradient filter effect (out in the field, I'd do this by putting a filter in front of my lens that graduates from a dark gray down to transparent. That way, it darkens the sky, but leaves the foreground alone, which helps balance landscape photos where your foreground exposure looks right, so your sky isn't way too bright). However, if you didn't have that filter with you, you can replicate it here in Elements, like we did back in Chapter 10 (see page 359). So, click the Open Image button to open it in the Editor, then set your Foreground to black and add a Gradient adjustment layer to your image (see Chapter 5 for more on adjustment layers).

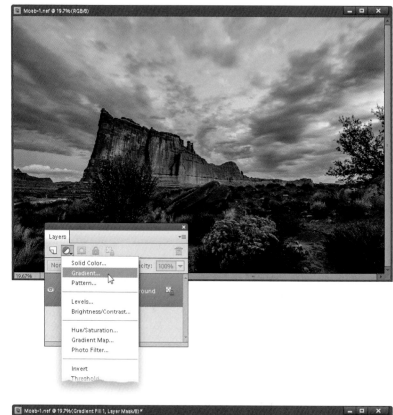

Step 10:

In the Gradient Fill dialog, choose the Foreground to Transparent gradient, turn on the Reverse checkbox, and click OK. Now, change the layer's blend mode to **Overlay**.

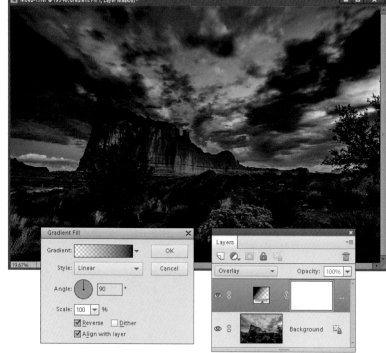

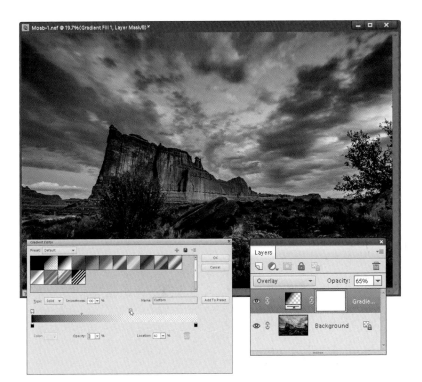

Step 11:

Then, double-click on the Gradient adjustment layer to open the Gradient Fill dialog again, and click on the Gradient thumbnail to open the Gradient Editor. Grab the top-right transparent Opacity stop above the gradient ramp and drag it to the left until the gradient rolls up to the horizon line, then click OK twice. If it looks a little dark (I thought it did here), then just lower the Opacity of the adjustment layer until it looks good (I lowered it to 65%).

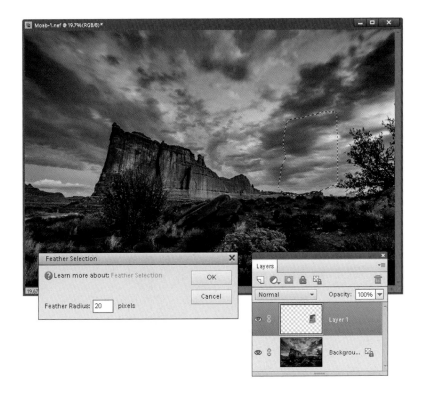

Step 12:

Now that the sky has been fixed, the next most annoying thing has got to be that ugly tree creeping into the frame from the right side. A "creeping edge tree" has killed more landscape photos than I can count, but it's not going to kill this one. First, press **Ctrl-E (Mac: Command-E)** to merge your Gradient adjustment layer into your Background layer. Then, get the Lasso tool **(L)**, and draw a selection around the offending tree. Go under the Select menu and choose **Feather**. For a high-res RAW file like this one, type in 20, and click OK. Now, move your cursor inside the selection (it will become an arrow), and click-and-drag your selection to the left until it is entirely off the tree (as shown here). **Press Ctrl-J (Mac: Command-J)** to duplicate your selection, which is now of the sky instead of the tree, and put it on its own layer (as seen in the Layers palette here).

(Continued)

Step 13:

Switch to the Move tool **(V)**, click on the duplicate selection, and drag it to the right until it covers the tree. If the duplicate sky covers the rocks on the very right edge of the image, just grab the Eraser tool **(E)** and erase the sky from the rocks (as shown here).

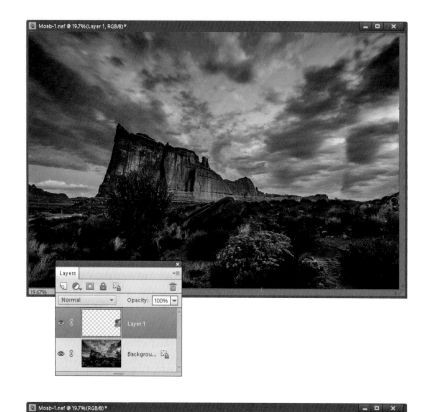

Step 14:

Go ahead and merge your duplicated sky layer into the Background layer. Now, it looks a little obvious that we duplicated part of the sky. To hide that obvious left edge of our duplicate sky, and to make it look a little different from the area we duplicated, we'll use the Spot Healing Brush **(J)**. Get it from the Toolbox and make sure the Type is set to Content Aware in the Tool Options Bar. Just paint horizontally across that obvious left edge, and paint a few strokes elsewhere in those duplicated clouds until it looks more natural.

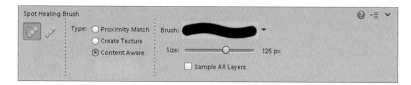

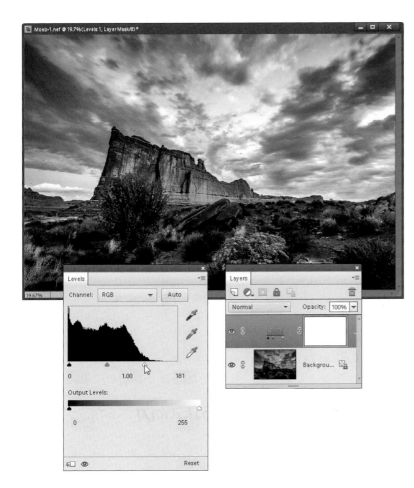

Step 15:
It's starting to look a little dark, so let's add a Levels adjustment layer to brighten it up a little. In the Levels options in the Adjustments palette, click on the white (highlights) slider on the far right below the histogram, and drag it to the left a bit, until the photo looks light enough.

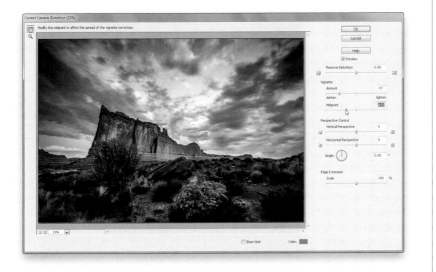

Step 16:
I try to keep the viewer's attention off the outside edges of my image and "focused on the subject instead. One trick to do that (well, my favorite any-way) is to darken the edges all the way around with an edge vignette. I used the Correct Camera Distortion filter here, which we learned how to do back on page 351 (in Chapter 10). Make sure you merge your layers again, first. You can see how this focuses your attention, through the use of light (your eye is auto-matically drawn to the brightest thing in the photo), on the rock formation.

(Continued)

Step 17:

At this point, it's time to sharpen (I usually save this until last), so press **Ctrl-J (Mac: Command-J)** to duplicate your layer. Then, go under the Enhance menu and choose **Unsharp Mask**. Enter 90% for Amount, set the Radius to 1.3, and set the Threshold to 3 (more on sharpening, starting back on page 374). This is some really punchy sharpening (note the Radius being increased past 1), but an image like this (and most landscape images), can really take a lot of sharpening and they look great. Go ahead and click OK.

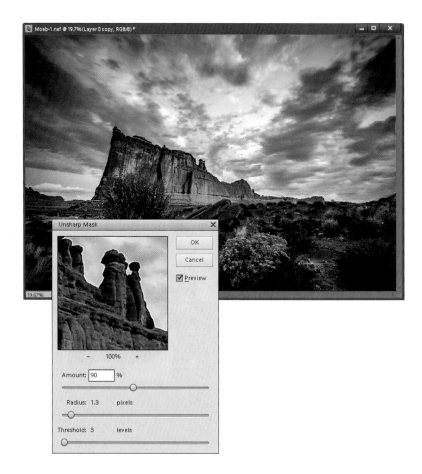

Step 18:

After I run the Unsharp Mask filter, I try to limit any halos or other color nasties that might appear by immediately changing the layer's blend mode to **Luminosity** (as seen here), which applies my sharpening to just the detail areas of the image, and not the color areas, which helps me avoid lots of sharpening hazards. I also lowered the layer's Opacity to 90%. A before/after is shown on the next page. Now that you have a complete and final image, you can turn it into a creation (photo collage, on-line album, slide show, etc. [see the "How to Show Your Work" video on the book's companion website]), or just simply print your finished image on your color inkjet printer (see the "Making the Print" tutorial earlier in this chapter for a refresher on that). Well, there you have it, a Photoshop Elements 11 workflow from import to output, done in the same order I do it myself. Remember, it all starts with asking "What do I wish were different?" Once you know that, go back and find the techniques in this book that will get you there.

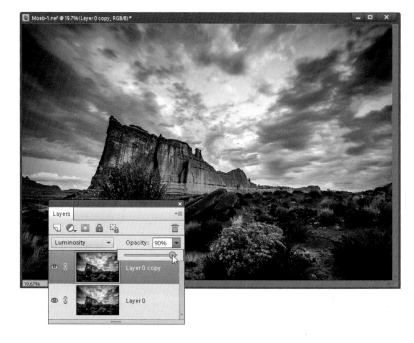

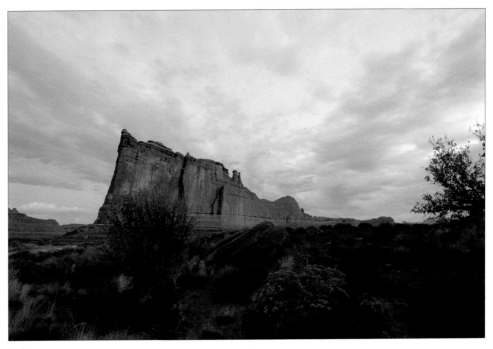

Before

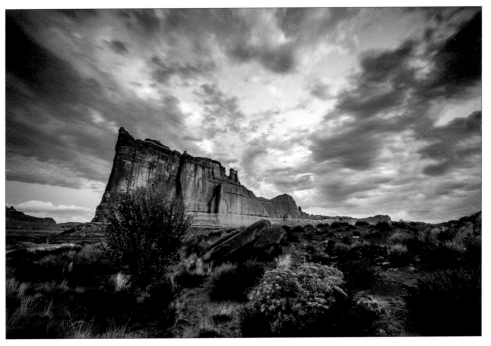

After

Index

(Bracket keys), 253, 276, 284
/ (Forward Slash key), 99
3D Pixelate transition, 39
18% gray card, 59
50% Gray option, 198, 369
50% magnification setting, 374
100% size view, 66, 78, 82

A

about this book, xiii–xvii
acne removal, 254–256
actions, 324–326
  automating effects with, 324–326
  cropping photos with, 103
  downloading from the Internet, 325
  loading into Elements, 326
  selecting and playing, 324–325
Actions palette, 103, 279, 324–326
Add Layer Mask icon, 89, 175
Add Noise filter, 370, 371, 415
Add Photos dialog, 409
Add Places dialog, 46
Adjust Color for Skin Tone dialog,
  251
Adjust Intensity sliders, 337
Adjust Sharpness control, 392–394
adjustment layers
  B&W conversions and, 339–342
  flesh tone fixes and, 182
  portrait retouching and, 261, 269
  selections and, 231, 234, 236
  Smart Brush tool and, 190
adjustment marker, 191
Adobe Camera Raw. *See* **Camera**
  Raw
Adobe Marketplace & Exchange,
  325
Adobe Revel, 2
Adobe RGB color space, 398
Advanced Dialog button, 5
albums, 27
  creating, 27, 46, 417
  deleting, 29
aligning layers, 163

Alignment tool, 227, 309
all-purpose sharpening, 378
ambient light calibration, 401
Amount slider
  Adjust Sharpness control, 393, 394
  Camera Raw Sharpening section, 79
  Correct Camera Distortion filter,
    216, 352
  Unsharp Mask dialog, 375, 379
Angle controls
  Emboss filter, 388
  Gradient Fill dialog, 362
Arrow keys, 105
artifact removal, 302–303
As Shot white balance, 56, 58, 59
Auto corrections, Camera Raw, 65, 93
Auto Tone adjustments, 65
Auto White Balance setting, 56
Auto-Analyzer, 19–20
Auto-Enhance checkbox, 238
automated processing, 121–122
Automatic Download checkbox, 4
automatic red-eye removal, 209–210

B

Background Color setting, 110
Background layer, 159
backgrounds
  blurring, 320–323
  cropping to remove, 114
  masking from effects, 328, 332
  Picture Stack effect, 316
  textured, 158, 159–160
backing up photos, 6–7
backlit photos, 63
Backup Catalog option, 6
Balance palette, 136
banding in prints, 415
basic sharpening, 374–380
Before & After previews, 134
Black & White selection view, 241
black-and-white conversions
  in Camera Raw, 93–95
  in Photoshop Elements, 336–342
Blacks slider, 64, 94, 334, 364, 419
blemish removal, 252–253

blend modes, 169–173
  Color, 186, 353, 368
  Color Burn, 187
  Darken, 350
  Difference, 294
  Hard Light, 388
  Lighten, 255, 257
  Luminosity, 385, 408, 424
  Multiply, 171–172, 414
  Overlay, 173, 187, 198, 245, 331, 360
  Screen, 169, 261, 264, 414
  Soft Light, 187, 200, 288, 328, 369
  Vivid Light, 329
blending
  layers, 155–156, 169–173
  multiple exposures, 221–227
Blue color channel, 341, 365
Blue Skies effect, 189, 192
blur
  background, 320–323
  Depth Of Field effect, 320–323
  Gaussian Blur filter, 254
  options for removing, 393
  Orton effect, 318
  Reduce Noise filter, 196
  Surface Blur filter, 282, 330
  Tilt-Shift effect, 140
Blur slider, 318, 321
Blush slider, 251
Border Selection dialog, 366
borders, Instagram, 366
Bracket keys ([ ]), 253, 276, 284
bright areas, 204–205
Brush Picker
  Brush tool and, 90, 255
  Clone Stamp tool and, 257, 298
  Eraser tool and, 155
Brush tool
  dodging/burning and, 198–200
  double processing and, 90–91
  drawing on layers with, 150
  emphasizing color using, 353–354
  eyeglass reflections and, 293–294
  fill flash technique and, 207–208
  layer masks and, 177–178, 293–294
  portrait retouching and, 255–256,
    262, 264, 267, 284–285

Getting more serious about digital photography?

Perfect your photography from shoot to finish

Adobe® Photoshop® Lightroom® 4 software provides a comprehensive set of digital photography tools, from powerfully simple one-click adjustments to cutting-edge advanced controls. Create images that inspire, inform, and delight.

Get your FREE 30-day trial at **www.adobe.com/go/lr_books**